Reviving the English Revolution

Reviving the English Revolution

Reflections and Elaborations on the Work of
Christopher Hill

————◆————

Edited by
GEOFF ELEY
and
WILLIAM HUNT

VERSO

London · New York

This edition published by Verso 1988

Verso
UK: 6 Meard Street, London W1V 3HR
USA: 29 West 35th Street, New York, NY 10001-2291

Verso is the imprint of New Left Books

British Library Cataloguing in Publication Data
Reviving the English revolution: reflections
    and elaborations on the work of Christopher
    Hill.
    1. English Civil War. Historiography. Hill,
    Christopher, 1912-
    I. Eley, Geoff, *1949*   II. Hunt, William,
    1944-
    942.06′2′0072024

ISBN 0-86091-194-2

US Library of Congress Cataloging in Publication Data
Reviving the English Revolution : reflections and elaborations on the
    work of Christopher Hill / edited by Geoff Eley and William Hunt.
        p.   cm.
    Includes bibliographies and index.
    ISBN 0-86091-194-2 : £24.95 ($42.00 : U.S. : est.)
    1. Great Britain—History—Stuarts, 1603-1714—Historiography.
2. Great Britain—History—Puritan Revolution, 1642-1660—
Historiography.   3. Hill, Christopher, 1912-
4. Historiography—Great Britain.   I. Eley, Geoff, 1949-
II. Hunt, William, 1944-
DA375.R48 1988
941.06—dc19

Typeset by Leaper & Gard Ltd, Bristol, England
Printed in Great Britain by Bookcraft (Bath) Ltd, Midsomer Norton, Avon.

Contents

Preface and Acknowledgements

Our thanks go first to our contributors, who stuck with us over an unexpectedly long haul. We are also grateful to the word processing center at St Lawrence University in Canton, New York: their swift and efficient service, on very short notice, prevented the haul from being longer still.

Our greatest debt, recorded in the dedication, is to Christopher Hill, with whose influence all of us have had to grapple. E.P. Thompson once described Hill as 'master of more than an old English college'. This volume testifies that he has been a master to us all.

We wish to thank those concerned for giving permission to reprint the following essays:

'Talking with Christopher Hill' first appeared in *University History: A Forum for Student Historians*, no. 1 (1980), pp. 5–15.

'On the Rant' by Edward Thompson was first published in *London Review of Books*, vol. 9, no. 13 (9 July 1987).

'All the Atlantic Mountains Shook' by Peter Linebaugh is reprinted from *Labour/Le Travailleur*, no. 10 (1982), pp. 87–121, with permission of the author and the editor. © Committee on Canadian Labour History.

'Good Hands, Stout Heart and Fast Feet' by Marcus Rediker is reprinted from *Labour/Le Travailleur*, no. 10 (1982), pp. 123–44, with permission of the author and the editor. © Committee on Canadian Labour History.

'The Bourgeois Revolution of Seventeenth-Century England Revisited' by Lawrence Stone is reprinted with the permission of the Past and Present Society and the author from *Past and Present*, no. 109 (November 1985), pp. 44–54. World Copyright: The Past and Present Society, 175 Banbury Road, Oxford, England.

viii

'The Counties and the Country: Some Thoughts on Seventeenth-Century Historiography' by Cynthia Herrup is reprinted from *Social History*, vol. 1, no. 2 (1983), pp. 169–81.

Introduction

Geoff Eley

To an outsider, the historiography of seventeenth-century Britain has
presented a perplexing picture. The dramatic events of the middle of the
century, combining civil war, regicide, religious radicalism and unprecedented political mobilization, make it a natural focus of interest and
research. Moreover, in the 1950s and 1960s they also attracted a high
level of general interpretative discussion. For a while it became usual to
treat the 1640s and 1650s as a coherent period, whose contents were
pivotal for the course of England's social and political development.
Seen as the English Revolution, the events of these years delivered an
agenda of questions which could only be tackled by breaching the
conventional divisions between different kinds of history. Political and
constitutional conflicts, the expression and organization of religious
belief, changes in the social structure and the growth of the economy,
shifts in the general intellectual climate and the structure of popular
belief – all were to be considered in their interrelations rather than in
isolation. This basic realization unlocked some interesting potential for a
totalizing history, or for a concept of historical change which stressed the
interconnections among different areas of a society's structure and
activity. More than any other individual, of course, Christopher Hill was
responsible for instating this approach to seventeenth-century studies.
Since that time the quantity of empirical research on the Civil War
period has been prodigious. In that obvious sense, we 'know' far more
than ever before about the circumstances of the English Revolution. But
this has become the knowledge of highly particularized investigations,
which are frequently indifferent, if not directly hostile, to the sort of
general debates mentioned above. We now have very fine historians of
seventeenth-century politics, religion, economics, demography, social
structure, science and popular culture, but not very many who try to

combine these fields into a coherent vision of the whole society and its global contradictions. In fact, the older interpretations of the 1950s and 1960s – for which Lawrence Stone's *The Causes of the English Revolution 1529–1642* (London, 1972) now reads like an epitaph – have been gradually disintegrated by the aggregate effect of the intervening local, regional and sectoral scholarship. As well as the political narratives, biographies, studies of institutions and professions, and dissections of particular events, the 'county study' became the main form of this empirical scholarship, although the detailed analysis of the Westminster parliamentary process also enjoyed a resurgence of popularity.

Such work has been characterized by a general retreat from the grand interpretative debates that stamped the seventeenth-century field a quarter of a century ago – the nature of the English Revolution, the rise of the gentry, the general crisis of the seventeenth century, the intellectual revolution, the relationship of science and religion, the ideology of possessive individualism and so on. The theses advanced in those debates were naturally full of problems; that was precisely the source of their importance. Their discussion imparted an excitement and vitality to seventeenth-century historiography that made it one of the most interesting periods of British history, to specialist and layperson alike. By contrast, more recent work steadfastly repudiated earlier generalizations, but without apparently putting anything in their place, beyond a general assertion of complexity. Some 'revisionists' (as they became known) proposed simply abstaining from large-scale questions while another mountain of empirical research accumulated, in the naive expectation (as John Morrill put it) that 'in scholarship, as in everything else, if we look after the pennies, the pounds will look after themselves'.[1] This has often gone so far as to question the legitimacy of any general interpretation, on the grounds that this substitutes 'theory' or 'making a case' for 'history', prejudges the outcome of empirical research, or simply violates the irreducible complexity of historical process and events.

There is a further factor contributing to the recession of generalizing debate, which has less to do with any specific hostility to the older generalizations as such, perhaps, than with a more general shift of interest in the profession. Much of the creative energy in seventeenth-century work – in common with most other periods – has gone into certain kinds of social history. In particular, we might mention two major fields of activity: the repertoire of demographic analysis associated with the Cambridge Population Group, including population *per se*, household and family, literacy and migration; and secondly, the study of crime and the law. Without questioning either the autonomous validity or wider potential usefulness of this work (quite the contrary, in fact), it is clear that it has rarely had much to say about the overall context of seventeenth-century society and its political development. By contrast with the eighteenth to twentieth centuries, where the older problematic of labour history has continued to harness much social-history discussion to certain grand themes of British historical development, social history in the sixteenth and seventeenth centuries has seen a pulling-away from the latter. To the revisionist trend already mentioned (empiricist scepticism about the possibility of generalizing, laced with philosophical hostility to the purposes of explicit theory), therefore, we must add an unfortunate fragmenting of the historian's enterprise, so that it becomes harder and harder to convene the proliferating special-isms of the profession (each with a highly technical and internalized discourse) on a common ground of general analysis. Despite the growth in our understanding of seventeenth-century society, we have come little closer to an understanding of the mid-century political crisis and its relationship to longer-run change.[2]

Finally, among this catalogue of historiographical factors, the work and influence (the mission, one might say) of Geoffrey Elton has also had its bearing on the construction of the seventeenth-century field. The Regius Professor has occasionally been known to participate directly in the discussion of Christopher Hill's own work, but is recognized chiefly, of course, as the leading historian of the mid-sixteenth-century Tudor polity. However, the expenditure of such an enormous career-long effort on establishing the founding importance of a Tudor 'revolution in government' for the course of British history – an effort which began, it should be remembered, when the various seventeenth-century controversies mentioned above were still at their invigorating height in the late 1950s and early 1960s – derives much of its point from an implicit hostility to the Marxist-cum-sociological conception of the English Revolution. It is not too fanciful to regard Hill and Stone (and the ghost of Tawney) as the hidden addressees of Elton's history: hard-headed administrative consolidation become the foundation stone of modern British history, and *not* the political and ideological conse-quences of condensed social change, the clash of organized social forces and the struggle to constitute a new moral order; the shrewd and improvised innovations required by the 1530s become the crucial locus of change, and not the political convulsions of the 1640s; and Thomas rather than Oliver becomes the heroic architect of England's future. Elton's influence on the early modern period (which, after all, in British history has always formed a 'Tudor–Stuart' unity) has been enormous, both in shaping the methodological and interpretative agenda and in encouraging a certain type of historiographical culture, not least through his training of several generations of graduate students. This, too, has obliquely constrained the further development of the seventeenth-century debates.

In this process of revision and fragmentation the work and reputation of Christopher Hill has a special place, and reactions to his view of the English Revolution have mirrored the broader historiographical shifts referred to above. Internationally, Hill is thought to be one of Britain's major contemporary historians. Measured by some criteria (for example, reputation outside immediate field, or influence on a wider public, through the adoption of his more general books in the universities and schools), he enjoys a similar standing in Britain, too. Yet, paradoxically, his influence among seventeenth-century historians themselves seemed during the 1970s to become rather low. To illustrate this, we might contrast Hill's centrality to R.C. Richardson's *The Debate on the English Revolution* (London, 1977), with his total absence from John Morrill's *The Revolt of the Provinces* (London, 1976; 2nd edn, 1980), which asserted claims to a new 'revisionist' perspective on the English Civil War and in some ways stands as a textbook of 'revisionist' work. Now, it can be argued that Hill's own work has never been centrally concerned with the political process as such, and that consequently one wouldn't expect him prominently cited in a book like Morrill's, with its explicit focus on the course of the political conflict in the 1630s and 1640s. In a limited sense, this is true. But there is a way in which the basic agenda of acceptable questions has been narrowed over recent years, so that the connections which Hill explores among the social, the political and the ideological have been placed beyond the boundaries of most present discussion. In this sense, it is not Hill's absence from a work of specifically 'political' history that is significant (in fact, there is one citation of an essay of Hill's tucked away in Morrill's footnotes), but the reduction of the mid-century crisis to a narrowly circum-scribed process of political manoeuvre, from which Hill's distinctive concerns – the social, cultural and ideological determinations of political conflict, in all their multiform complexity – have been systematically left out.

We would argue that this re-drawing of the agenda has become characteristic of the seventeenth-century discussion in general. More-over, it is no secret that Christopher Hill's work has come in for a good deal of hostile criticism in recent years, some of it of an extremely polemical nature. In part, this has taken the form of a personal attack on his credentials as a scholar: J.H. Hexter's 'The Burden of Proof' (*The Times Literary Supplement*, 24 October 1975) was the nadir of this traducement.[3] But it has also been directed at the general intellectual positions associated with Hill's work – not just Marxism, it should be said, but by extension at any materialist or sociological approach to the salient problems of seventeenth-century history, and in the worst cases at any attempt to deal with the large interpretative or conceptual issues. As Hill says, the connecting theme of his work over virtually half a century has been the attempt 'to understand the place of the English Revolution in history, and to document the mental transformations which accompanied and facilitated the rise of capitalism'.[4] More specifically, of course, he has been interested in Puritanism and its relationship both to the rise of capitalism and to the political upheavals of the Civil War, as a source of intellectual and political radicalism, and as a code of social practice. It is no exaggeration to say that a large part of recent research has defined itself negatively against these ambitious commitments.

The discounting of Hill's contribution to seventeenth-century studies (if that is not too strong an expression) has consequences beyond any injustice to the importance of his own work, though that is regrettable enough. As we have already suggested, the agenda of legitimate or acceptable questions has been crucially redrawn over the last two decades, with definite effects on how the seventeenth century and its problems tend to be viewed, particularly for graduate students and others entering the field. It has become increasingly difficult to pose certain kinds of questions, not because the latter are consciously suppressed, but because the conventional discourse is structured against them. This makes Hill's own perspectives all the more interesting. His salient emphases – on religion and society, on the seventeenth-century intellectual revolution, and on radicalism and popular culture – can be made to deliver a range of questions whose potential has perhaps never been fully grasped by British historiography in this period. In a sense, Hill's interests have been mainly focused on the history of *mentalités*, a project which is firmly (perhaps too firmly) established in French historical practice in the early modern period, but which has only ever caught fire in the work of a few individuals in the British field. Keith Thomas's work on religion and the decline of magic, and in a different way J.G.A. Pocock's on political ideas, augured well for this kind of departure. But despite the remarkable popularity of the *Annales* school, and with certain individual exceptions (like Bernard Capp's study of popular almanacs), there has been no general trend in this direction.[5] On the whole, most social history has been channelled into the discrete sub-disciplinary areas of concern referred to above – demography, family, crime, migration, poverty and so on – without engaging very directly with the problems of popular consciousness and popular culture. Arguably, a critical reaffirming of Hill's intellectual priorities in this region (most completely displayed in *Society and Puritanism in Pre-Revolutionary England* (London, 1964), and *The World Turned Upside*

Down (London, 1972) might fruitfully open up some of these possibilities.

The aim of this book is to address the above problems: to reaffirm the interest and importance of Christopher Hill's own body of work; to revivify discussion of the English Revolution, or at least to re-establish the legitimacy of that concept as a way of regarding the period of the Civil War; and to rejoin the fragmented discussions of social, economic, political and intellectual historians on a common ground of significant problems. Arguably, now is a good time to undertake such a project. Some serious critical assessment of Hill's place in post-war historiography is long overdue. There are also signs that the 'revisionist' wave may be breaking, and that discussion is beginning to escape from the excessive narrowness characteristic of the 1970s. Recent essays in *Past and Present* (by Theodore K. Rabb and Derek Hirst, with an ironic survey by Hill himself) give some evidence of this nascent shift and, as Hill notes, 1980 saw the publication of three similar essays, by Clive Holmes (in the *Journal of British Studies*), Derek Hirst (in the *Historical Journal*), and Austin Woolrych (in *History*).[6] Most significantly of all, perhaps, two of the best of the new social historians of this period have published a book which rebuilds some of the bridges between social history, the study of Puritanism, and the potentiality for social, political and ideological conflict in mid-seventeenth-century English society, namely, Keith Wrightson's and David Levine's *Poverty and Piety in an English Parish: Terling, 1525–1700* (New York, 1979). Moreover, it is now possible to point to a small cluster of significant monographs that are firmly nudging discussion in this direction: William Hunt's cognate study of the coming of the English Revolution in Essex; Buchanan Sharp's study of popular disorders in the west of England; Paul Seaver's exploration of the world of Nehemiah Wallington; Ann Hughes's much-awaited study of Warwickshire; Cynthia Herrup's analysis of legal process; and David Underdown's investigation of the 'clash of cultures'.[7]

In the meantime, several comments may be made on current work which is arguably widening the space for 'counter-revisionist' explorations. First, the 'one-damn-event-after-another' approach to the causes of the Civil War has surely run its course. It has reached its apotheosis in Anthony Fletcher's *The Outbreak of the English Civil War* (London, 1981). After this, it is unclear what the narrative mode of political analysis any longer has to offer, both because Fletcher's account of the years 1640–42 is so exhaustive and because he so resolutely avoids the deeper questions of causality, not least over the question of religious commitment, to whose mobilizing power he implicitly assigns such importance. Moreover, there are signs that two of the most forthright revisionists have become more willing to concede the importance of principle and partisanship in dividing the political nation during the first half of the seventeenth century: Conrad Russell seems to have acknowledged the dialectic of religious and constitutional dissidence in releasing the potential for political radicalism in the 1620s and 1630s; while Mark Kishlansky's new work on the electorate has nicely complemented the earlier contribution of Derek Hirst.[8]

Secondly, there has been further progress towards making the connections between the view from the counties and events at the centre, either on the social–historical ground marked out by Wrightson and Levine, or by exploring the social and cultural bases of popular activity during the Civil War, or by examining the intersection of the national with the local political arena. Significantly, perhaps, it is in carefully specified local settings – or, at least, in a far more concrete and richly textured social history, as opposed to the intermediate political level of an artfully constructed county community – that this work is tending to be done. Similarly, we need a far better understanding of the processes of social communication, including not just the impact and circulation of news and information, but the bases of cohesion in English society and the forms and mechanisms of collective identification, which bound Parliament, county and locality into a single polity, and allowed different understandings of national community to take shape.[9]

Thirdly, there has been much more explicit concern with matters of popular culture in the neo-anthropological sense doubly established during the last two decades by early modern French historians and the influence of Edward Thompson. So far, most of the interest in Britain has focused on the work of other countries (as in the work of Peter Burke, or that of R.W. Scribner on Reformation Germany) or on a later period of the British past (such as the eighteenth-century studies inspired by Thompson's work on crime, the moral economy and customary popular culture). But there are signs that this is slowly changing. Stuart Clark's programmatic, if somewhat opaque, discussion of problems arising from the French discussion should be mentioned in this respect, as should Michael MacDonald's continuing investigations of the early modern English mind, Barry Reay's accumulating publications on popular religion and the work of Martin Ingram.[10]

Fourthly, a major anti-revisionist counter-blast has come from in some ways a surprising quarter. J.H. Hexter, Hill's most ungenerous critic, has challenged the revisionist trivialization of the constitutional struggles of the early Stuart period by reasserting the pivotal importance of these struggles in the survival of Parliament and the history of liberty in Britain, and, by extension, the Western world. Whatever the merits of Hexter's own intellectual project, he thereby endorses a fundamental premise of Hill's career-long work: namely, the decisive nature of the century of revolution, and the contribution of ideals and convictions to the defeat of absolutism. More than this, Hexter's 'thesis' resounds with the words of S.R. Gardiner a hundred years before. But it is Hill, and not Hexter, who goes beyond Gardiner by locating these ideals and convictions – whose power he has always eloquently evoked – within their social setting, and by consistently asking, when the word 'liberty' is invoked, 'liberty for whom to do what?' Hexter's blinkered hostility to Hill's work (and to the tradition from which it comes) has prevented him from posing this question to begin with. Hexter's 'modern liberty' floats in ethereal abstraction, without material roots in the material worlds of conflict and domination, uncoupled from property, innocent of class connotation. Marxist accounts at least have the merit of anchoring abstract ideals in a determinate social setting. Hexter's 'thesis' is pre-Marxist in this sense, rather than post- or even anti-marxist. As vulgar idealism, it is no advance on vulgar Marxism. Hill's mature work transcends both, we would argue, and points the way to a genuinely complex historiography.[11]

Finally, each of the above (the dynamics of radicalization during the Long Parliament, the intersection of local and national analysis, the study of popular culture and the rediscovery of the constitutional conflict of the 1620s) re-emphasizes the importance of religion as the realm of activity and belief into which all the other social, political and cultural antagonisms of the mid seventeenth century were condensed, and which lent the generalized political confrontation of the 1640s its distinctive character. Of course, this is the grand theme of Christopher Hill's *Oeuvre*, from the early materialist analysis of the post-Henrician Church, through the studies of Puritanism, to the celebration of radical religion, and the studies of Milton and his fellow radicals in defeat. Likewise, this holistic conception of religion and its place in seventeenth-century life has always attracted the most polemical and destructive of Hill's critics. It thus becomes something of a surprise to find two of the most inveterate of the revisionists – John Morrill and Blair Worden – rediscovering the centrality of religion in their current writings. While clinging to the revisionist shibboleths (the Civil War was not a clash of social groups, it was caused by the incompetence of the King), and schematically separating the 'localist', 'legal-constitutionalist', and 'religious' sources of opposition to the Crown, Morrill defines the Civil War as a struggle between 'different concepts of the moral order', in which the 'Puritan vanguard' sought to realize the ideal of 'a godly and ordered commonwealth'. The failure of this goal, he argues, produced 'the modern secular state' (that is, the post-Restoration political-religious-constitutional settlement), and, it is strongly implied, laid the foundations for Britain's distinctive path of constitutional development between the Glorious Revolution and the Reform Act of 1832. There are intimations of a social content to this historic compromise (in the accommodation of the state to the social 'hegemony' of the gentry), although Morrill has nothing to say directly about the possible implications of this for capitalist development. But at all events, these conclusions have a suspiciously 'Hillian' or even a 'Whiggish' ring.[12]

Some revisionists, it seems, have grown bored with their revisionism, and the irony of the return to religion is worth savouring.[13] This renewed stress on the Puritan dimension of the mid-century conflict (it is not clear whether Morrill wants to call it a revolution) is an interesting vindication of Hill's most central works from an unexpected quarter; and unless 'religion' is to be separated unrealistically from 'society', any further discussion will have to enter precisely the terrain which Hill has so conscientiously and imaginatively mapped, namely, the broader-gauged social analysis where politics, religion and economics intersect. However, if our understanding is to be really deepened, that analysis will also have to leave the circles of religious activists, where Hill's own work has largely kept it, and enter the far less penetrable domain of popular culture, by drawing on the historiographical resources alluded to above. In this respect, David Underdown's work may prove especially fruitful, with its stress on the cultural bases of the Civil War conflict. His framework is continuous with Hill's *Society and Puritanism*, while pushing the latter into the kind of social history in which Hill himself has never engaged:

> In the end, the revolution was a conflict over the moral basis of English society. Behind the clash of cultures we can detect two social ideals, even two societies, in conflict: one stressing custom, tradition, and the cooperative, 'vertical' community; the other moral reformation, individualism, the ethic of work and responsibility. The middling sort's campaign to impose theirs as the national culture failed because deep-rooted social forces were too strong for them.[14]

Finally, a word should be said about Christopher Hill's place in this volume. It should be made clear that this collection is not offered as a Festschrift. For one thing, there is one already – Donald Pennington and Keith Thomas, eds., *Puritans and Revolutionaries* (Oxford, 1978) – and our aim is not to set ourselves up as a competitor. Our purpose is really quite different. We are less interested in merely celebrating Hill's achievements (though there is, indeed, plenty of reason for that), than in making a start at their critical evaluation, a task which has previously been hampered by the extreme nature of the attacks on his reputation.

In the past, those sympathetic to Hill's historical project have been placed in the position of rallying to his defence, so that the genuine problems arising from his work – theoretically, interpretatively, method-ologically – have tended to be kept off the agenda. Consequently, there are really two priorities at work: to reaffirm the value and legitimacy of the big questions, which to his credit Hill has kept on asking; but at the same time to begin the serious discussion of Hill's particular answers, which (as he has always cautioned his readers) are often far from the last word on the subject. Hitherto, the empirical criticism of Hill's work has tended to obliterate the larger questions he has tried to raise. But more than anything else, his work transcends the artificial segregation of experience into sub-disciplinary categories and aims for a coherent sense of the whole society. Whatever the durability of his substantive argu-ments, it is this general enterprise that deserves to be advanced.

We hope that this volume might contribute in some fashion to this task, and by that means make a substantial contribution to seventeenth-century and related discussions. While engaging critically with Christo-pher Hill's work at his own level of constructive generality, it might help reclaim the seventeenth century for a stimulating, generalizing historio-graphy. It seeks to reopen some of the large interpretative questions concerning the English Civil War and its place in British, European and Atlantic history.[15]

Notes

1. John Morrill, 'Proceeding Moderately', in *The Times Literary Supplement*, 24 October 1980.

2. The crowning achievement of the Cambridge Group's labours, E.A. Wrigley and Roger Schofield, *The Population History of England, 1541–1871: A Reconstruction* (Cambridge, Mass., 1981), has no explicit relationship to the earlier efforts at linking social-structural analysis with political history in the gentry controversy and other debates of the 1950s and 1960s, unless it is obliquely through the ancestry of Peter Laslett's *The World We Have Lost* (London, 1965), which of course was very much a part of the original turning-away from the English Revolution problematic. Similarly, seventeenth-century work on crime contrasts somewhat with that on the succeeding century, where the inter-vention of Edward Thompson and his collaborators forced discussion on to the ground of general history. Finally, the major representative of social-structural history to re-engage with grand questions, Alan Macfarlane, has done so by perversely shifting the locus of concern to a much earlier period, while maintaining the separation of social history from questions of political development and crisis. See *The Origins of English Individualism* (Oxford, 1978).

3. For a similar, equally mean-spirited attack, see Blair Worden's review of *Milton and the English Revolution* (London, 1977), in *The Times Literary Supplement*, 2 December 1977.

4. See Hill's rejoinder to Hexter's 'Burden of Proof', *The Times Literary Supplement*, 7 November 1975.

5. See Bernard Capp, *Astrology and the Popular Press: English Almanacs, 1500– 1800* (London, 1979).

6. Rabb, 'The Role of the Commons', and Hirst, 'The Place of Principle', in 'Revisionism Revised: Two Perspectives on Early Stuart Parliamentary History', *Past and Present*, no. 92 (August 1981), pp. 55–99; Hill, 'Parliament and People in Seventeenth-century England', ibid., pp. 100–124; Holmes, 'The "County Community" in Stuart Historiography', *Journal of British Studies*, vol. 19 (1980), pp. 54–73; Hirst, 'Parliament, Law and War in the 1620s', *Historical Journal*, vol. 23 (1980), pp. 455–61; Woolrych, 'Court, Country and City Revisited', *History*, vol. 65 (1980), pp. 236–45. See also Mary Fulbrook, 'The English Revolution and the Revisionist Revolt', *Social History*, vol. 7 (1982), pp. 249–64.

7. William A. Hunt, *The Puritan Moment: The Coming of the Revolution in an English County* (Cambridge, Mass., 1983); Buchanan Sharp, *In Contempt of All Authority: Rural Artisans and Riot in the West of England, 1586–1660* (Berkeley, 1980); Paul R. Seaver, *Wallington's World: A Puritan Artisan in Seventeenth-Century London* (Stanford, 1985); Ann Hughes, *Politics, Society and Civil War in Warwickshire, 1620–1660* (Cambridge, 1987); Cynthia B. Herrup, *The Common Peace: Participation and the Criminal Law in Seventeenth-Century England* (Cambridge, 1987); David Underdown, *Revel, Riot, and Rebellion: Popular Politics and Culture in England, 1603–1660* (Oxford, 1985).

8. See Russell's remarks in 'Christendom', *London Review of Books*, 7 November 1985. See also Derek Hirst, *The Representative of the People? Voters and Voting in England under the Early Stuarts* (Cambridge, 1975); Mark A. Kishlansky, *Parliamentary Selection: Social and Political Choice in Early Modern England* (Cambridge, 1986). Despite Kishlansky's taste for sterile personal polemics, in principle his findings may be fruitfully integrated with those of Hirst, rather than supplanting them.

9. See Richard Cust's suggestive discussion in 'News and Politics in Early Seventeenth-century England', *Past and Present*, no. 112 (August 1986), pp. 60–90. Aside from the works by Hunt, Hughes, Herrup and Underdown mentioned in note 7 above, see also the following: David Underdown, 'The Chalk and the Cheese: Contrasts among the English Clubmen', *Past and Present*, no. 85 (November 1979), pp. 25–48; David Harris Sacks, 'Bristol's "little businesses", 1623–41', *Past and Present*, no. 110 (February 1986), pp. 69–105; Sacks, 'The Demise of the Martyrs: The Feasts of St. Clement and St. Katherine in Bristol, 1400–1600', *Social History*, vol. 11 (1986), pp. 141–70; Sacks, *Trade, Society, and Politics in Bristol, 1500–1640* (New York, 1985).

10. Stuart Clark, 'French Historians and Early Modern Popular Culture', *Past and Present*, no. 100 (August 1983), pp. 62–99; Clark, 'Inversion, Misrule, and the Meaning of Witchcraft', *Past and Present*, no. 87 (May 1980), pp. 98–127; Michael MacDonald, *Mystical Bedlam: Madness, Anxiety, and Healing in Seventeenth-Century England* (Cambridge, 1981); MacDonald, 'The Secularization of Suicide in England 1660–1800', *Past and Present*, no. 111 (May 1986), pp. 50–97; Barry Reay, *The Quakers and the English Revolution* (New York, 1985); Reay, ed., *Popular Culture in Seventeenth-Century England* (New York, 1985); Reay and J.F. McGregor, eds., *Radical Religion in the English Revolution* (Oxford, 1984); Christopher Hill, Barry Reay and William Lamont, *The World of the Muggletonians* (London, 1983); Martin Ingram, 'Ridings, Rough Music and the "Reform of Popular Culture" in Early Modern England', *Past and Present*, no. 105 (November 1984), pp. 79–113.

11. See William H. Dray, 'J.H. Hexter, Neo-Whiggism and Early Stuart Historiography', *History and Theory*, vol. 26 (1987), pp. 133–49.

12. The phrases are taken from John Morrill's contribution to a symposium on 'What Was the English Revolution?', *History Today*, vol. 34 (March 1984), p. 16. See also his 'The Religious Context of the English Civil War', *Transactions of the Royal Historical Society*, 5th series, vol. 34 (1984), pp. 155–78.

13. See also Blair Worden, 'Providence and Politics in Cromwellian England', *Past and Present*, no. 109 (November 1985), pp. 55–99. It is hard to see how this would differ in principle from a text by Hill, both methodologically and in its implied conception of the significance of ideas.

14. The quotation comes from Underdown's contribution to the *History Today* symposium cited in note 12 above, p. 25. See also his discussion of Hill's work in 'Radicals

in Defeat', *New York Review of Books*, 28 March 1985, p. 41.

15. Two additional discussions have appeared since the completion of this intro-duction, from radically contrasting parts of the intellectual spectrum, whose arguments will have to be dealt with by those interested in conceptualizing the problem of the English Revolution. Mark Gould, *Revolution in the Development of Capitalism* (Berkeley, 1987), will almost certainly be ignored by most seventeenth-century specialist historians: a *tour de force* of sustained historical sociology, it seeks to build an original argument about the social structural determination of revolution by synthesizing the monographic research within a carefully elaborated theoretical scheme. On the other hand, J.C.D. Clark, *Revolu-tion and Rebellion: State and Society in England in the Seventeenth and Eighteenth Centuries* (Cambridge, 1986), and the same author's earlier *English Society, 1688-1832: Ideology, Social Structure and Political Practice During the Ancien Régime* (Cambridge, 1985), may be expected to exercise specialists endlessly. Yet Clark, the aspirant high priest of an extremely peculiar new right history, manages to get through an entire book on the subject of 'revolution and rebellion' without ever discussing the immediate effects of the Civil War on 'state and society' at all (for example, Cromwell, Commonwealth and Protectorate are completely absent from the account). See Joanna Innes, 'Jonathan Clark, Social History, and England's "Ancien Régime"', *Past and Present*, no. 115 (May 1987), pp. 165-200. Finally, despite its own excessive caution, there is a useful survey of current approaches in Barry Coward, 'Was There an English Revolution in the Middle of the Seventeenth Century?', in Colin Jones, Malyn Newitt, Stephen Roberts, eds., *Politics and People in Revolutionary England. Essays in Honour of Ivan Roots* (Oxford, 1986), pp. 9-39. Coward's nominalist answer is: Yes, but we can't define what kind of revolution it was, as all general models of revolution are – by definition – suspect.

PART I

Christopher Hill: The Work in Its Context

Modesty, judgement, imagination, a sensitivity to connexions: these are what all historians need over and above the special techniques of their particular sub-disciplines, need in order to keep these techniques in their proper place. The attempt to see connexions is hazardous and may lead to mistakes. But these can be corrected. Failure to look for connexions leads to barrenness, myopia, blinkers.

Christopher Hill, *The Times Literary Supplement*, 24 November 1972, p. 1431

Christopher Hill: A Profile

C.H. George

Christopher Hill's retirement as Master of Balliol some few years ago concluded (in one dreary sense) the most successful academic career ever achieved by a Marxist historian in the English-speaking world. The more oppressive truth is that there are few successors in sight – at Balliol or in the wider world of historical writing.[1] This volume may in its efforts to survey and evaluate the work of the most important twentieth-century historian of the world's first bourgeois revolution be justified by the hope that the challenge of what Hill has done, done badly, and left undone, will be seized upon by young scholars who have not yet made themselves known.

John Edward Christopher Hill was born two years before the first of this century's world wars in the beautiful city of York, his father a solicitor, his education given over to the ancient St Peter's School of that city. Both parents were strong-minded Methodists whose convictions, Hill believes, predisposed him to the political apostasy which dominated his life in the 1930s and 1940s.

Contributing to that apostasy was the unprecedented era of world-wide depression, wars across the planet, Fascism and communist-led revolutions. Hill's intellectual responses to this imposing world were conditioned by two Oxford dons (Hill matriculated at Balliol College in 1931) and one extraordinary non-academic woman. The dons were Vivian Galbraith, distinguished historian of Domesday and other medieval matters, and Kennith Bell, whose interests ranged from Shakespeare to Puritanism. The woman was Dona Torr, the brilliant communist editor and translator of Marx, Engels, and Russian literature whose influence on Hill was perhaps greater than that of anyone in his life.

15

On the academic side of Hill's development in his twenties, the most important paths led him to explorations of an early enthusiasm for English literature and along trails first blazed by Karl Marx and (curiously if one is simplistic about the intellectual pedigrees of Marxists) by Sir Lewis Namier. The influence of Marx was enveloping and permanent (Hill read Marx – the historian rather than the economist – as an undergraduate in the years 1932–4); the Namier he knew as an undergraduate also enormously impressed him (this in a period of only six weeks Namier spent at Oxford) with his powers of what Hill calls 'historical imagination'.

From Vivian Galbraith Hill got a solid dose of old-fashioned Rankean 'how it really was' history. Galbraith's uncompromising view that 'History is a science' was less imposing than Marx's definition of history as the *only* true science,[2] but Hill grew up in a hard school of no-nonsense disciplinary pride. Galbraith in his BBC lecture on 'The Historian at Work', resolutely compared 'the science of man in time' (Bloch's words) to the disciplines of mathematics and physics with no individuous implications for history.[3] He also (unlike Marx) thought 'Truth and rhetoric ... bad bedfellows'; 'Clio,' he told us, 'once a Muse, is now more commonly seen with a reader's ticket verifying her references at the Public Record Office.'[4] Nor had Hill's favourite teacher any patience with the view that personal prejudice was an insuperable obstacle to objective research in history any more than in the other sciences. Furthermore, Hill was taught that history was a recently revolutionized and incremental discipline like all the sciences: Galbraith believed that Gibbon and Macaulay were good reading but bad history.[5]

Following this regimen of undergraduate reading and tutorial discipline, Hill's experience was given new dimensions by a very intensely dedicated ten months in Moscow (1935–6), months he now regards as crucial to his intellectual development. After Moscow came two satisfying years (1936–8) as assistant lecturer at University College in Cardiff, Wales, and then fatefully ('it could only happen in the thirties'), the young communist was returned to Balliol as fellow and tutor in modern history.

Meanwhile the Marxist and socialist forces in Hill's life were continuing and deepening and challenging those academic values drawn from Oxford teachers, from his own teaching and from the Bodleian. Beside the unwavering stimulation of Dona Torr's Marxist expertise (and after managing to survive distinguished service during the war[6]), Hill got himself involved in the Historians' Group of the Communist Party from 1946 to 1956. He still regards these years with Communist Party intellectuals 'the greatest single influence' on his subsequent work.[7]

In 1940, the year he was commissioned in the Oxford and Bucks

Light Infantry, Hill published his first book. In the late 1930s he had written articles and reviews, mostly concerned with introducing to the English-speaking world Soviet historiography relevant to the English Revolution. He also wrote during the late 1930s and the war years under two pseudonyms in an effort to protect his job. A reasonably complete (to 1977) bibliography of Hill's work, incidentally, is available in the Festschrift which Oxford University Press has published.[8]

The book which appeared in 1940 was slight in volume but I still remember its impact on me – and the contempt with which it was greeted in the Eastern academic quarters I inhabited for a time. *The English Revolution, 1640,* contained a general interpretive essay by Hill as well as contributions by Margaret James and Edgell Rickword. It remains a minor classic (in the sense of a book that educated people actually read) in socialist and Marxist oriented countries; it has been translated into Russian, Polish, German, Czech, Japanese and probably a number of other languages I don't know about. Still, even in the 1949 edition which is the first I saw, the bibliography of 'reliable' Marxist titles was depressingly brief; indeed, the only fundamental work was that of Maurice Dobb and Margaret James. That little book emphasizes the fact that Hill almost single-handedly began the serious Marxist study of England's greatest century.

Except for a brief detour in 1947, Hill was devoted (and continues to devote) his life to making the English as aware of their revolutionary origins as the French are of theirs. And really there is no question that the remarkable recent – if incredibly belated – monographic investigation of the English Revolution owes more to Hill than to anyone of whatever philosophical persuasion. Why the intensely French-like concentration on events that almost all but Marxists had thought of as an unimportant interruption in the smooth and magical flow of English historical exceptionalism? There are a number of answers, including the obvious Marxist ones and the equally obvious 'why climb Mt Everest?' ones.

In an interview given some years ago, Hill specifically attributed his scholarship to the political imperative imposed by the twentieth-century crisis in British capitalism.[9] Forty years ago, he reminds us, even the phrase 'English Revolution' was exclusively Marxist. The period 1640–60 was that of the 'Puritan Revolution' – a religious and literary curiosity, dead, gone, un-English. To Hill and a very few others in the 1930s and 1940s it began to seem that the crucial decisions in the making of their contemporary problems were first visible for description and analysis in the 1600s: the decisions for capitalism, for empire, and for all consequent cultural and social advances, inequities and barbarities, though rooted in late medieval and Tudor England, as Marx had argued, seemed to have become discernable historical realities in the course of seventeenth-century developments.

In the brilliant essay which grew out of his participation in the Historians' Group of the Communist Party, published in *The Modern Quarterly*'s celebration of the tercentenary of the English Revolution, Hill began: 'If there is any point in studying history at all, its object must be to help us by understanding the past to control the present. Bad history will lead to bad politics.'[10] He continued with a brief agenda for himself and his students and whatever colleagues might turn up: 'The orthodox theory which stresses the continuity of English history is false just because it emphasizes constitutional forms and ignores their social content.'[11] Although Hill concluded that 'the English revolution ended in a sordid compromise' (a view recently revived by Perry Anderson),[12] that Nonconformity after 1660 produced the 'narrowness and provincialism of lower middle-class thought in England', that the precocious and incomplete revolution left England less democratic in the twentieth century than the more completely bourgeois revolutionized United States and France,[13] his real achievement was in seeing that the English needed to revisit their revolutionary origins. No more 'hiatus-history' foisted off on those great Cromwellian and Miltonic years in the interest of Churchillian 'continuity'.

Hill's next published contribution to reinterpreting the Interregnum as the English Revolution (in collaboration with Edmund Dell, a minister in the last Labour government) was a characteristic response to his early enthusiasm for discussion group learning and the needs of university students. *The Good Old Cause*, first published by Lawrence and Wishart in 1949 and later reprinted by both Cass and Kelley, was, as it still is, the only general 'source book' for the revolutionary years.[14] In organization and analytical commentary it is Marxist, but it also is typical Hill in the incredible latitude and sweep of data that challenges the reader. He was already suggesting the possibility of a comprehensive Marxist history of the English Revolution. At present, the only comprehensive interpretative alternative to Samuel Rawlinson Gardiner remains the collective work of Soviet scholarship edited by E.A. Kosminsky, published in Russian in 1954 under the title *The English Bourgeois Revolution of the Seventeenth Century*. The English Revolution has yet to find its Lefebvre.

Hill had thus by the mid-1950s done important pioneering work in pressing on the academic world the relevance of a Marxist reinterpretation of the so-called Puritan Revolution, and in outlining and giving evidence for that reinterpretation. He also was one of a small group of Marxists who took the lead in establishing a major new journal open to Marxist scholars; *Past and Present* has subsequently become possibly the best journal of general history published anywhere.[15] But what was most urgently needed, of course, was a lengthening shelf of major monographs exploring the great economic, social and cultural unknowns before a general political history could be definitively written.

Just at this critical juncture in the fortunes of the English Revolution Hill's personal life was radically changed. The most important and completely positive change was that he got out of an unhappy marriage relationship and into a splendid new one with Bridget Sutton that has opened rusted gates to a flow of energy that surprises everyone but her. The other major change was his decision in 1957 to leave the Communist Party. The issue was a compound of restlessness with the undemocratic procedures of a Leninist party, and a feeling that the party truckled too much to the USSR. Hill's break was clean, honest, and without any of the hideous scar tissue common to such political traumas. I know he does not credit the opinion (inevitably popularized by the gossipy and, of course, anti-communist scholarly community) that his departing the party is the explanation of his increased productivity.

In any case, free of and prior to this personal and political maelstrom, Hill completed his first book-length monograph, *Economic Problems of the Church*, published by Oxford in 1956. It established Hill's reputation for the first time with historians of the academic establishments; it was reviewed with surprised acclaim. I know some (I suspect they represented many) who were stunned by the image of a communist scholar soberly, patiently dissecting the institutional heart of Elizabethan and Stuart society.

I think *Economic Problems* is in fact an indispensable monograph for the student not only of the English Revolution but as well of the more important set of events which constitute the process by which England moved from feudal to bourgeois forms of social life. Hill decided that of the interlocked conflicts dividing England before 1640, those connected with religion were the way to open up the whole package for re-examination, and that the religious complex was least understood – both by contemporaries and modern students – on its institutional side.

So the otherwise tedious realities of Church livings, Church courts, and Church properties in the emerging capitalist environment were taken as a key to the locked and interlocked mystery of the making of the bourgeois revolution. A new and soon to be vintage brew of Hill historiography was thus introduced. To begin with, quite literally, there is Hill's way with epigraphs which reveal a mastery of sources that allows him to illuminate and epitomize abstruse subjects with contemporary language and concepts. But chiefly he revealed his richly textured way with massed data from marvellously varied sources: traditional institutional documents, pamphlets of all sorts, first-person accounts, and an incredible file of locally published information.

The value of the *Economic Problems* book is different for different scholars. Let me explain its value to me. First, Hill elucidates in great detail the complex economic aspects which are either basic to or part of every schism affecting the public exercise of religion in pre-revolutionary England. He puts together the scattered evidence from the late medieval condition of the Catholic establishment through the Henrician and Elizabethan settlements to demonstrate conclusively that the clergy from the parish up to the once mighty bishops were victims of an extraordinary long-range expropriation of Church properties and incomes which left them by the end of the sixteenth century economically and legally the minions of the laity and their law.

Thus was precipitated the major crisis in the feudal order of things: the Church had become a dependent creature of common law property ownership. The immediate political fall-out of that crisis was the Puritan movement under Elizabeth. For the new Protestant Church had greater and more expensive ambitions for the parish, essentially the demand for an incumbent, preaching and therefore educated ministry. But the inherited institutional structure simply could not meet that demand. The result was the movement of Protestant lay impropriators to bring fervour to the lukewarm hearts that beat in the vast majority of Christian breasts in 'this other Eden'. In turn, that movement, in a sense economically determined, was a principal ingredient in the constitutional and political revolution of the House of Commons within Parliament and of Parliament's subsequent confrontation with the monarchy.

Finally, not only did the bishops become the chief visible enemy of the new social orders I call bourgeois; their weakness, institutionally and socially (the dramatic declination in the social origins of the bishops was the direct result of the emptiness of Iscariot's purse), marked the decisive failure of the feudal monarchy. The Church had made the monarchy, staffed and served it in crucial ways as late as the reign of Henry VII. The Stuart Church came to symbolize the highly visible moral failure of the old regime primarily because it suffered from the largely invisible economic impotence which Hill had expressed fully for the first time.

In the same year that the *Economic Problems* appeared, Hill published an essay on 'Recent Interpretations of the Civil War' (reprinted in *Puritanism and Revolution*)[16] in which he set for himself (and any others with sympathetic imagination and suitable energy) a research task in cultural history that would occupy the rest of his formidably productive life. It was his 'what needs to be done' judgement that in addition to various continuations of the economic research of Nef, more on early imperialism, city oligarchies, the yeomanry and gentry and even, God help us, 'the people', as well as Hugh Trevor-Roper's and Gerrald Aylmer's state government, there was a massively compelling challenge to take not only religious history from the theologians but also legal history from the lawyers and to reconstruct for both kinds of information the historically accurate social environment. Thus it was that Hill began a series of investigations set less directly by his older Marxist orientation than by the Weber–Troeltsch–Tawney conceptualization of the relation of Protestantism to capitalism.

Most imperative from Hill's personal angle of vision was the nagging, historiographically mountainous problem of Puritanism. He even welcomed my first brash, largely mistaken published effort to present a 'social interpretation' of Puritanism. (Very incidentally in light of the recent Lilliputian assault on Hill by Jack Hexter, I might note that Hexter was the editor given my article by the *Journal of Modern History*; his only editorial contribution was to insist I could not use the concepts 'bourgeois' and 'bourgeoisie' because he had recently proved they did not conform to any historical reality before 1832. For my careless addiction to Marx, Hexter kindly sent me an antidote in the form of his then unpublished 'Myth of the Middle Class'. Somehow I stupidly persisted in my addiction and remain an uncured and unrepentant if not very successful practitioner of the black art of Marxism.)

Before his next two major monographs addressing the Puritan problems appeared, Hill published a collection of his essays which has enjoyed a continuing success and is filled with good ideas for research to be done, with questions that need answers and with some solid discoveries of his own. That collection, under the title *Puritanism and Revolution*, contains one of the best Marxist essays on literature that I know, 'Clarissa Harlowe and Her Times'. There are hints there of the deep love for the great English writers which recently has given us Hill's passionate version of Milton.

The first massive scholarly effort which Hill launched to get right the terrible but vital confusion of historic Puritanism in its pre-revolutionary guises, appeared in 1964 under the title *Society and Puritanism in Pre-Revolutionary England*.[17] This is an imposing work, which, typically, he once described to me as just something he did with the notes left over from the *Economic Problems* book. His intention was to discover all the 'non-theological' reasons for being a Puritan or for supporting Puritans. That intention led him to write what is unquestionably the most detailed social history of the whole body of English Puritans before the Revolution. Scores of stories, biographical vignettes, contemporary comments, court records, government reports at all levels, fragments of first-person accounts – all the resources possible are enlisted by Hill to attempt the identification of that historiographical monster, the English Puritan.

I am one of the few who thinks Hill still failed to identify the species. His results seem to me indecisive: there are too many definitions, never an analytical fix for any moment of time. That is, though there were certainly lots of Puritans alive during Hill's decades of investigation, his research convinces me that they were not a party nor quite a movement (just as my conceit is that I've proved they did not share a 'mind'). But not only does this study establish that (to me) important analytical fact (or, to most, the equally important opposite fact of the social nexus of Puritanism) – it also is a most valuable and totally reliable guide to the households, religious practices, social attitudes and moral concerns of a variety of the lesser bourgeoisie. It is as good as social history can be without any considerable quantity of first-person accounts. I read it, however, more as the social history of a section of the bourgeoisie than as a differentiation of the godly from the other Protestant bourgeois.

Hill's next – almost simultaneous – publication was by title even more ambitious than *Society and Puritanism*. These were the Ford Lectures in which Hill boldly attempted what, incredibly in a sense, had never before been tried: that is, to do for the English Revolution something comparable to Daniel Mornet's account of the intellectual origins of the French Revolution.

Intellectual Origins of the English Revolution[18] (without the article) was the result. Hill was by this time more interested in achieving a broad scholarly consensus than in further enlightening fellow Marxists and socialists. His growing fame and wide acceptance in unlooked-for quarters gave him extraordinary opportunities which he seized with considerable success.

The printed lectures have done what Hill intended – stirred up basic questions about the cultural nature of pre-revolutionary England. They do not of course supply answers. Of all Hill's publications, this book stimulates me most to a debating mood. If I didn't enjoy his company too much to waste our infrequent hours together, this is the book I'd use to focus our many differences in reading seventeenth-century intellectual history from a Marxist perspective.

On the specific subjects of Bacon and Baconianism, Raleigh and the new history, Sir Edward Coke as myth-maker, the struggles within the universities, Hill is typically full of interesting suggestions and recondite information and it would be ungrateful to quarrel with most of the revolutionary pattern he sees developing out of the cultural conflicts provoked by these men and related institutions.

But the interpretive pattern which emerges overall is another matter. Hill develops, to begin with, quite an original and strongly articulated view of the relation of science to the Revolution. The most common-place criticism centres upon his definition of science to include the 'mechanic arts' flourishing in seventeenth-century London. I have no problem with that thesis and think it a valuable corrective to the usual kind of guild obsession with mathematical sciences. But I do agree with even such otherwise flawed attacks as that of Hugh Kearney in targeting Hill's Puritan context as the stimulant to English science.[19]

In my view there are three problems with Hill's argument that Puritanism is the great catalyst to English scientific advance. First, he often stretches the facts beyond my credulity in identifying scientists as Puritan. Secondly, he gets so carried away with the argument for a Puritan science that he forgets the obvious comparative refutation of the equal or greater scientific advances in some of the most Catholic and backward social environments in Europe. Finally, I think his analytical drive to see scientific thought – however defined – as revolutionary in the social or political sense in early seventeenth-century England is seriously mistaken. He does so, I am convinced, because he sees the scientists as Puritan and thus Hill's science becomes a revolutionary force through its Puritan connections.

The other interpretive emphasis throughout the Ford Lectures with which I have problems is one which in a way characterizes all of Hill's work and arises, I suspect, from his philosophically radical democratic sentiments. However explained, the fact is that for him virtually all bourgeois progress in social discipline, economics, law, politics and culture is the work of the 'industrious sort of people', of Richard Baxter's prototype godly; he admits very little creativity to the upper bourgeoisie or aristocracy. His bourgeois revolution is not terribly dialectical in its play of contradictions; he tends to leave out the rich and powerful, just as in cultural terms he tends to ignore the bourgeois contributions of Anglicans and secularists. For Hill Greshamites and Puritans are the only forces pressing toward bourgeois modernizing and democratic development.

Those whom Hill leaves out of the revolutionary origins of modern Britain are the secular-minded likes of Sir Dudley and Roger North, Lords Shaftesbury and Bolingbroke and Sir Robert Walpole. He also pays much too little attention to the exploitive genius of such Northamptonshire worthies as the Ishams, Treshams and Spencers, or Yorkshire notables like Sir Thomas Osborne, Wentworth and the Saviles – because, I suspect, they were royalist or Catholic or just not very religious. But farmers like Henry Best or Robert Loder (to be sure probably not legion), London merchants like William Hewett and his rapacious colleagues among the aldermen, financial wizards like Charles Montagu or even Charles Duncombe, that hard crew of Sword Blade graduates to the directorate of the South Sea Company whom Defoe anatomized in *Exchange Alley*, and the community of Merchant Adventurers and their competing coteries of interloping entrepreneurs in the Levant and East India trade were the very heartbeat of the bourgeois revolution – Puritan though they certainly were not.

Another difficulty with Hill's wryly persistent return to the theme of Puritanism as the critical matrix of oppositional ideas (other than its limited applicability to the exploration of the bourgeois character of the revolution), is that it necessarily distracts from the investigation of those secularizing elements which from Marx's observations to such recent studies as those of W.S. Holdsworth, Louis Wright, Wilbur Jordan, Edwin Miller, Arthur Ferguson, H.S. Bennett, Joan Simon and Brough Macpherson have impressed Marxists and non-Marxists alike as the original and distinguishing culture of the seventeenth-century English. Certainly England had no secular 'Enlightenment' comparable to that in France before 1789, but changes in law, education, the whole 'Gutenberg galaxy' of effects, as well as the better understood changes in science, literature, drama and music, add up to something much deeper and more durable than Puritanism as the cultural soil from which the Great Rebellion sprang.

Hill knows this argument, of course. In his Curti lecture at the University of Wisconsin, he considered the heritage of the radicals to the world after 1660, and although retaining his interest in the pervasively construed Puritan ethos, Hill has typically shrewd and witty suggestions about the genesis of the world of secular bourgeois thought. Indeed, he included a quite splendid brief essay on the theme that 'the main long-term significance of the English Revolution was neither constitutional nor political nor religious but economic'.[20] But his chosen path, the one he sees leading to the destruction of the old regime in England, was blazed by Puritans and Puritanism. I regret that the brief, exhilarating excursions he took along the high road to a truly revolutionized culture in essays published in the late 1940s and early 1950s on Clarendon, Hobbes, Harrington and Richardson, and more recently in a piece on 'reason' and 'reasonableness' as a social concept[21] and in the 1969 Riddell Memorial Lectures,[22] were not continued into the great analytical journeys they might well have become. I might add here that as a textbook writer – which is one of Hill's skills I have ignored in this essay – he has done very well by secular culture within the severe limits of the form.[23]

In the decade of the 1970s when the left in the English-speaking world did rather less than distinguish itself, Hill kept on his stubborn, energetic, pioneering way. He is as appalled as I am by the vacuum in our politics, but his production seems to increase as things get worse. He began the sorry decade with his highly personal version of the life of Oliver Cromwell.[24] Although Hill regards God's Englishman as a truly Hegelian world-historical figure, he is no hero-worshipper and his Cromwell is very much the creature as well as creator of his times. It is not a biography in the full and definitive sense; Hill rightly regards Sir Charles Firth's biography published in 1900 as still the best. But Hill's effort is not only the most readable and provocative life; it also is a wonder of selective quotation from an eminently quotable man. Somehow Hill manages in this book to do exactly the opposite of his previously highly discursive, digressive circling about Puritanism – he encapsulates Cromwell's public person and the torrent of events of which he was a painful, symbiotic, triumphant part in some 250 pages that are neither simplistic nor boring. In a way, Hill has written a prolegomenon for the great biography which the subject deserves.

In 1972 appeared the book that for my students at least was like a breath of the invigorating air from the 1960s. *The World Turned Upside Down* is Hill's luxuriant celebration of all those religious crazies who populated English towns and some villages during the years of rebellion and revolution which are for Hill, in spite of his knowing better, the Puritan Revolution. It is so good a book it simply shouldn't be written about. It should be read. The stories, quotations, personality portraits, evocations of forgotten crises; the warm, tireless patience with which Hill threads his way through the mad theology of angry, inspired, hopeful and hopeless religiosity; the final effort to see all the intellectual and emotional chaos as illuminating and relevant to both their revolution and ours – well, somehow it works. It is a totally successful work of historical imagination. Hill followed it immediately (1973) with a thoroughly brilliant introduction to a Pelican edition of Winstanley's major writing and thus completed his perfect record of the revolutionary radicals – the rank and file who originated the democratic and socialist history of our civilization. Finally, or at least in a corpus of extraordinary quality, his *magnum opus* to date, there is Hill's version of John Milton to be considered.[25] The Milton Industry, which doesn't like to be called that, is naturally up in arms over a Marxist version of the making of Milton. Not since William Empson's apostasy, which was greeted by more frightened silence than the petty nastiness reserved for Hill, has the industry been so shaken. No matter; the book is a flaming wonder and will long outlive its critics.

The intention of his *Milton* is consistent with all Hill's research over the past two decades: it is to see Milton and his work as crucially the product of the Puritan Revolution, and particularly of the radical, democratic elements in that revolution. There is no way to summarize that argument. It has to be read in the richly rewarding detail of Hill's evocative, allusively complex argument. In all of his beautifully conceived essays on literary subjects, Hill has responded to the brilliant invocation from Yeats.

> O chestnut tree, great-rooted blossomer,
> Are you the leaf, the blossom, or the bole?
> O body swayed to music, O brightening glance,
> How can we know the dancer from the dance?

The 'dancer' which Hill presents in Milton is rescued from 'the Lady of Christ's' tradition. We are given instead the ambitious, bawdy, gambling, smoking, sword-bearing young man of reality. The domestic disasters of his relations with Mary Powell and his daughters are presented without anachronistic moralizing. Most original of all is Hill's portrait of Milton's courage and resourcefulness throughout the terrible years from the winter of 1659 to his death.

The 'dance', however, is Hill's great achievement; in a way, the apotheosis of his life's work. From his matchless evocation of the revolutionary years enriched by the miracle of 'teeming freedom', through the years of triumphant hope in service to the Commonwealth, the last-ditch courage of *The Read and Easy Way*, to the incredible final outpouring of genius in *De Doctrina* and the greatest poems – all wrenched from a world shattered, dangerous and despairing – Hill's historical skills and vision seldom falter. We are given a magnificent Samson who 'never resolved his tensions – between liberty and discipline, passion and reason, human love and God's providence', but who remained to the end a revolutionary who renounced miracles for 'patient, courageous, stubborn work on limited objectives'.[26]

If it were possible for a scholar to retire, Hill has certainly earned that dubious right. Instead he has wisely chosen to continue teaching – in the Open University, in forums as various as those of provincial and foreign universities, the Friends House in London, the Marx Memorial Library, the Folger Library, the Humanities Research Centre in Canberra, the New School for Social Research, and endless conferences. He also continues to publish major reviews in various journals, to counsel colleagues and students, and to produce splendid essays. 'A Bourgeois Revolution?' is one such, epigrammatic Hill at his best;[27] another contains 'a few suggestions' on the continuity of the English radical underground of ideas.[28] A lecture before a London 'workshop' in 1983 contains some of his wittiest and most trenchant writing.[29] Other fugitive and valuable pieces keep surfacing in print.[30] Perhaps the projected volumes of 'collected essays' will round up most things presently in existence.

However, despite his disavowel of major work in progress, Hill has just published a book more important in suggestions for future research than anything he has done in some time. *The Experience of Defeat* (dedicated to Norman O. Brown) contains some inspired writing on perhaps the most neglected subject in seventeenth-century historiography: the reactions of the Miltonians and related subversives to apocalyptic failure; above all, the reality – much concealed then as now – of the survival of the Good Old Cause.[31] Republicanism and radical religious ideologies did not perish in the triumphs of Restoration with its codes of repression.

Let me conclude with a few words of however inadequate summary of a body of work still very much alive and growing. The first and most obvious judgement to be made is that Hill has raised the English Revolution to the high historiographical level of the French and Russian revolutions. Forty years ago, I repeat, there was almost nothing done or in progress on the English Revolution. At this moment I suspect there is as much able work in progress on seventeenth-century revolutionary problems as there is on those of the eighteenth and twentieth centuries. Whether one is a philosophical purist above scholarship or, like Hill, is convinced that historical ignorance is politically dangerous, the new knowledge of the English Revolution, and its increasingly wide dissemination, is a major achievement.

Second, Hill has done more than anyone I can think of to make 'intellectual history' a viable enterprise. Even though in theory Marxists should write solidly rooted histories of ideas and ideologies – rooted, that is, in social realities – very few have been successful. Most are either too dogmatic or too ignorant, or both. Hill, it seems to me, has made this most problematic of the sub-disciplines of history respectable, and even exciting.

Third, and in my view most important, Hill has done a great deal to make Marxist history an intellectual alternative in a country long hostile to all forms of Marxism. The reasons for his success have partly to do with his concentration on religious history and his disarming affection for religious fanaticism; mostly, I suspect, it is his discovery of something that neither Bolingbroke nor Marx thought possible – that seventeenth-century English Christianity was socially progressive in both bourgeois and democratic terms.

But finally, perhaps, we come back in any estimate of Hill's work quite simply to its intrinsic value. He may no longer be the Master of Balliol College, but he is much more importantly and permanently a master of his craft. As Edward Thompson has said somewhere, he is the dean and paragon of living English historians. And if good history does indeed make good politics, his current depression over the socialist future of the country he loves may lift by as much as the rewriting of the past which he has inspired gathers momentum and another inch of progress is realized.

Notes

1. I have always thought Hill was the perfect successor to John Wyclif as the Master of Balliol; the present Master is A.J.P. Kenny, a prolific philosopher who was for some years a Roman Catholic priest, recently the author of *The Anatomy of the Soul*.
2. Marx wrote that History was the only true *Wissenschaft*, in German a word with a broader meaning than the English 'science', *Marx–Engels Werke* (Berlin, 1956ff.), vol. 3, p. 18.
3. Galbraith, *The Historian at Work* (London, 1962), p. 1.
4. Ibid.
5. Ibid., pp. 1–9.
6. Hill began as a private in Field Security Police and by 1943 was a major of infantry seconded to the Foreign Office.
7. This and most of such information in this essay has its source in talks and letters exchanged with Hill over the past thirty years. But see Eric Hobsbawm, 'The Historians' Group of the Communist Party', in Maurice Cornforth, ed., *Rebels and Their Causes*, (London, 1978).
8. Donald Pennington and Keith Thomas, eds., *Puritans and Revolutionaries* (Oxford, 1978).
9. Interview conducted by Sylvia Strauss of Keen College, New Jersey, 22 May 1976 at a conference on 'Three British Revolutions' in Washington, DC.
10. Hill, 'The English Revolution and the State', *Modern Quarterly*, new series, vol. 4, no. 2 (1949), p. 110.
11. Ibid.
12. Anderson, 'Origins of the Present Crisis', *New Left Review*, no. 23.
13. Ibid., p. 128.
14. Hill, *The Good Old Cause: The English Revolution of 1640–60*, Christopher Hill and Edmund Dell, eds., vol. I of *History in the Making Series* (1949); 2nd edn, Frank Cass, 1969, revised with a new introduction by Hill.
15. For recollections of that significant event, see *Past and Present*, no. 100 (1983).
16. Hill, *Puritanism and Revolution* (London, 1964): reprinted from *History*, nos. 141–3 (1956).
17. Hill, *Society and Puritanism in Pre-Revolutionary England* (New York, 1964).
18. Hill, *Intellectual Origins of the English Revolution* (New York, 1964).
19. For Kearney, Gweneth Witteridge, and T.K. Rabb on Hill's version of the scientific revolution in England, and Hill's replies, see *Past and Present*, nos. 27–31 (1964–5).
20. Hill, *Some Intellectual Consequences of the English Revolution* (Madison, Wis., 1980), especially pp. 34–5.
21. Hill, '"Reason" and "reasonableness"', the Hobhouse Memorial Lecture, 1969, printed in the *British Journal of Sociology*, vol. 20, no. 3 (1969); reprinted in *Change and Continuity in Seventeenth-century England* (Cambridge, Mass., 1975).
22. Concerned with the interesting vicissitudes of the Antichrist myths which he feels

'at all points ... tremble on the edge of major intellectual issues', *Anti-Christ in Seventeenth-century England* (London, 1971), p. 177.

23. *The Century of Revolution, 1603–1714* (New York, 1961) and *Reformation to Industrial Revolution* (New York, 1967).

24. *God's Englishman: Oliver Cromwell and the English Revolution* (New York, 1970).

25. *Milton and the English Revolution* (New York, 1977). Curiously, a structuralist critic of Hill's 'Old New Left' orientation appeared shortly thereafter: Andrew Milner, *John Milton and the English Revolution* (Totowa, NJ, 1981).

26. See vol. 1 of Harvester's *The Collected Essays of Christopher Hill* (Amherst, Mass., 1985) for the most recent publication of Hill's literary criticism. I owe the lines from Yeats's 'Among School Children' to Tryna Zeedyk.

27. In J.G.A. Pocock, ed., *Three British Revolutions: 1641, 1688, 1776* (Princeton, NJ, 1980).

28. In Maurice Cornforth, ed., *Rebels and Their Causes* (London, 1978).

29. See 'God and the English Revolution', in *History Workshop*, no. 17 (1984).

30. See Christopher Hill, Barry Reay, and William Lamont, *The World of the Muggletonians* (London, 1983) and J.F. McGregor and B. Reay, eds., *Radical Revolution in the English Revolution* (Oxford, 1984).

31. *The Experience of Defeat* (New York, 1984).

Christopher Hill and Historical Sociology

Mary Fulbrook

Christopher Hill is a professional historian. His historical vision is of a particular sort: concerned with grand social transformations, long-term world-historical developments, and the ways in which these were effected, lived and experienced by people in the struggles which create and constitute social change. His approach is thus one of direct relevance to sociologists; indeed it can be argued that there is in principle no difference between history and sociology when the two institutionally separated disciplines share a common concern with historical processes of societal change. History is not simply a practice of naive, 'atheoretical' narrative; nor sociology one of abstract theory (however much practitioners of each may from time to time suggest this to be so).[1] Moreover, Hill has an avowed theoretical stance, a stance which is claimed also by certain sociologists: Hill's work is located within the framework of Marxist concerns and debate. Hill's approach is of direct relevance to sociologists concerned to understand major patterns of social change.

Nevertheless, in certain respects Hill conforms to the conventions of the discipline of history rather than sociology. His focus is less on answering precisely posed theoretical questions, formulated in terms of relatively abstract concepts, than on the recovery and interpretation of substantive aspects of the past. Despite his overt avowal of Marxist sympathies and categories, Hill is remarkably unconcerned with self-conscious elucidation of his analytical framework and explanatory assumptions. His political values inform and stimulate his historical work, but he spends little time in analysis of the theoretical implications of his approach.

At the beginning of his first book, *The English Revolution 1640*, Hill made the following assertion:

31

The orthodox attitude to the seventeenth-century revolution is misleading because it does not try to penetrate below the surface, because it takes actors in the revolution at their face value, and assumes that the best way to find out what people were fighting about is to consider what the leaders *said* they were fighting about.[2]

Beginning from fundamentally Marxist assumptions about the period-ization of history, the importance of economic forces and class struggles, Hill has nevertheless devoted much of his subsequent work over the past forty years to analysis of what people *said* they were fighting about. Given his own theoretical lack of self-consciousness, Hill has not developed much by way of explicit statements of his treatment of ideology and ideas as compared with other approaches. This essay, in considering Christopher Hill's work in relation to the enterprise of historical sociology, will focus particularly on what has proved to be a fundamental problem in social analysis: the reconciliation of a commit-ment to a 'deep' understanding of history, penetrating beyond what participants themselves comprehend, with a serious treatment of the actors' ideas, a respect for the issues people said they were fighting about.

Interestingly, Hill's work has developed and changed considerably since his early, rather crude Marxism of 1940; and this development has called forth quite different reactions, even within the Marxist or *marxisant* tradition. On the one hand, Stuart Hall suggests that 'it was Hill's decision to treat the religious, ideological and intellectual dimen-sions of the "English Revolution" seriously in their own terms – and not simply as a simple reflection of economic forces – which saved his work from its earlier tendency to economic reductionism: saved it, that is, not from but *for* Marxism'.[3] Richard Johnson, on the other hand, asserts that the progression from *The English Revolution 1640* to *The World Turned Upside Down* represents a degeneration into what Johnson criticises as 'culturalism'.[4] This criticism is echoed in Milner's disagree-ment with Hill's interpretation of Milton as lying between two cultures.[5] Rather different reactions have emanated, more generally, from the non-Marxist, revisionist camp of historians. Here, the criticism of 'Marxist approaches' (not always explicitly identified with examples) is that they pay inadequate attention to people's ideas. Revisionists inveigh against what they take to be the teleology of Marxist history, as events 'inevitably' moved towards their historical goal, and participants were mere puppets of forces beyond their comprehension or control. The revisionist response generally has reference to the motives and intentions of actors, who, they point out, did not want to have a revolution.[6] In a rather separate and select camp of his own, Hexter (who disagrees with

revisionists) makes a comparable criticism of Hill: that Hill, an inveterate 'lumper', proposes theses and forces the evidence of contemporaries'
statements into support of his presuppositions without adequate attention to the real meaning and context of their words.[7] How, then, is Hill's
work to be interpreted – as a sophisticated and subtle Marxist treatment
of ideas; as an insipid culturalism; or as an exemplar of procrustean,
teleological lumping? And what are the implications of Hill's approach
for others who are concerned both to understand the broad patterns of
historical change and to listen to the voices of those who formed and
were formed by such change?

It will be impossible, in a brief essay such as this, either to do justice
to the full range of Hill's work or to propose exhaustive answers to these
questions. Rather, some suggestions will be made concerning the nature
and implications of Hill's treatment of ideas and culture in the context of
his wider historical and sociological vision, as informed and inspired by
his political values.

Hill's Vision of History and Society

Hill has a strong sense of historical periodization: there is no danger, in
reading Hill's work, of becoming lost in a meaningless flux of historical
events, unrelated except by 'coincidence', and memorable or less
memorable facts. (To this extent, Hill's vision has affinities with the
Whig view caricatured in Sellar's and Yeatman's *1066 and All That*:
'With the ascension of Charles I to the throne we come at last to the
Central Period of English History (not to be confused with the Middle
Ages, of course).'[8]) Hill believes that a decisive transformation took
place in the seventeenth century, from the feudal, agrarian, communal
society of medieval England to the capitalist, industrial, individualist
society of modern times. For sociologists reared on a variety of
'tradition/modernity' dichotomies, Hill's historical vision is appealing
indeed. When things changed, they all changed, as an interconnected
and coherent system; and this complex, world-historically important
transformation took place in the central period with which Hill is
concerned. Thus for Hill, 'the years between 1603 and 1714 were
perhaps the most decisive in English history':

> The transformation that took place in the seventeenth century is ... far more
> than merely a constitutional or political revolution, or a revolution in
> economics, religion, or taste. It embraces the whole of life. Two conceptions
> of civilisation were in conflict. One took French absolutism as its model, the
> other the Dutch Republic.... [Seventeenth-century changes] set England on

the path of parliamentary government, economic advance and imperialist foreign policy, of religious toleration and scientific progress.[9]

Hill's depiction of this great transformation is not one imbued with simple overtones of evolutionary progress. He evokes a certain nostalgia for the 'social cohesion and solidarity' of 'traditional' communities, which were replaced by 'the inculcation of an individualist morality', the hard ethic of modern capitalism. The 'bourgeoisie' may have been historically progressive, but the world they ushered in was in many respects harsher than the one which was dissolved. Hill's moral characterizations of his historical periods echo those of Marx: 'The bourgeoisie ... has put an end to all feudal, patriarchal, idyllic relations. It has pitilessly torn asunder the motley feudal ties that bound man to his "natural superiors", and has left remaining no other nexus between man and man than naked self-interest, than callous "cash payment".'[10] Yet for Hill, as for Marx, the modern capitalist world contains the potential for a fuller emancipation, and the earlier transformation represented a crucial step along the way. Hill's radical answer to the Whig version of history, summarized at the end of his textbook, *The Century of Revolution*, runs as follows:

> The struggle for freedom, then, in the seventeenth century, was a more complex story than the books sometimes suggest. The men of property won freedom – freedom from taxation and arbitrary arrest, freedom from religious persecution, freedom to control the destinies of their country through their elected representatives, freedom to buy and sell. They also won freedom to evict copyholders and cottagers, to tyrannize over their villagers, to hire unprotected labour in the open market.... The smaller men failed to win either the vote or economic security.

He continues:

> Freedom is not something abstract. It is the right of certain men to do certain things.... Only very slowly and late have men come to understand that unless freedom is universal it is only extended privilege.[11]

Similar themes provide the closing sentence of Hill's other general textbook, which covers a slightly longer time-span, *From Reformation to Industrial Revolution*:

> The Industrial Revolution was to give birth to a working class movement which would challenge private property in a rather more serious manner than More, would pick up ideas which Winstanley had thrown onto apparently stony ground during the English Revolution and would conceive of a society in which wage labour would be abolished and common freedom established.[12]

Part of Hill's aim in reconstructing the history of the seventeenth century is to rekindle the flame carried by the defeated radicals of England's partial, bourgeois revolution. Hill is carrying the torch for those struggling to achieve a more complete, truly human emancipation.

Within this general historical framework – a framework which embodies both a sociological and a moral vision – Hill's conception of society is one based on class conflict. This is a simple enough statement to make, but one which disguises considerable complexity and ambiguity. For Hill, like many good historians, is less concerned with theoretical purity than with attempting to comprehend more adequately what actually happened. This attempt cannot of course be undertaken without certain conceptual presuppositions, but Hill is less than explicit about what these are. Hill's empirical concerns have led in his work both to a number of acknowledged shifts in his substantive class analysis, and to some implicit inconsistencies and ambiguities.

Put very simply, Hill's model of society is a three-cornered one; but the three corners vary in content. In his earliest work, the model is the somewhat crude one of ruling, rising, and oppressed classes: old feudal aristocracy, historically progressive bourgeoisie, and exploited direct producers.[13] This model, as such, has disappeared in Hill's later, more refined analyses, but certain vestiges of it remain. Hill now emphasizes that the English Revolution originated as a split *within* the 'ruling class' (never very precisely defined), and can be characterized as a 'bourgeois revolution' only because of its *consequences* for subsequent economic and political development, irrespective of the historical *origins* of the event. In other words, Hill agrees with the revisionist attack on the concept of an intentional bourgeois revolution made by a rising class seeking consciously to appropriate more power for itself; but he disagrees with the revisionists' wilful refusal to acknowledge the fundamental historical significance of the event once it had erupted.[14] Yet while emphasizing now the importance of a split *within* a ruling class, for Hill this split is not (as with the revisionists) an arbitrary, personal and factional split; rather, it has to do with fundamentally different economic and political interests. The 'progressive' class is still there, combating the reactionary protectors of the old order; and the underdogs of history, the oppressed and exploited, are as important as ever. In the general, three-cornered model, the triangle has shifted sideways to insert the 'rising' class into the 'ruling' level. As Hill puts it in *The Century of Revolution*:

> There was rivalry between those who wanted to preserve a static hierarchical society and those who were busy shaping a more fluid society in which men of ability and means would be able to make their way to the top; below both

groups were those whose poverty prevented them, in normal times, even conceiving the possibility of altering the world in which they lived. In short, there was a quarrel between two groups of the ruling class; but looking on was the many-headed monster ...[15]

For Hill, adequate analysis of the origins and consequences of the English Revolution must take the changing sets of relations among these classes into account. While the Revolution originated as a split within the ruling class, the eruption of radical lower-class politics helped to determine the recombination of the different ruling-class fractions in 1660, against the threat from below, but on terms which were more favourable to the interests of the 'progressive' elements, thus ensuring the preconditions for the further development of industrial capitalism.

The three-cornered model is the crudest characterization of Hill's conception of society. As indicated above, his approach is frequently more complex than implied by his summaries of arguments. Hill is well aware of all the infinite detail of historical reality which renders its theoretical appropriation so inherently difficult and contentious a task. Particularly in a non-capitalist society – or a society in which capitalism had not yet become predominant, had not yet laid bare the naked cash nexus – status groups were at least as salient as classes defined strictly in terms of relationship to the means of production. This salience of status to contemporaries was mirrored in historians' controversies; and, as Hill perceptively points out, in his (1956) discussion of 'Recent Interpretations of the Civil War', the gentry 'were not an economic class. They were a social and legal class; economically they were divided. . . . It is not helpful to speak of the legal class as though it were in any sense an economic class.'[16] This awareness helps Hill in his later distinctions among different elements of the 'ruling class'. But his sensitivity to the importance of status as well as relationship to the means of production, combined with his class interpretation of culture, can lead to some very odd, theoretically apparently hybrid, definitions:

> In the middle class I include most merchants, richer artisans, the independent peasantry (yeomanry) and well-to-do tenant farmers. These were differentiated from the landed gentry and the ruling oligarchies of London and the bigger towns, on the one hand, by their lack of privilege; and from the mass of the rural and urban poor and vagabonds, on the other, by the possession of enough property to be economically independent. . . . These groups, increasing steadily in numbers, wealth and education, formed the Bible-reading class. . . . It was such independent men of small means who established the new ideology of the middle-class home, as against the great households (aristocratic, monastic) of the Middle Ages.[17]

These may well be historically enlightening characterizations, helping us to understand what was actually going on; but, in the combination of privilege and property, class is here not treated in the straightforward Marxist sense relating to structural aspects of the mode of production. To point this out is neither to criticize nor commend, but to raise a question about 'Marxist' approaches to non- or largely pre-capitalist societies, to which I shall return later.

Culture enters even more centrally into Hill's three-cornered model of society when he discusses the conflicts and tensions among the 'three cultures': the 'orthodox' culture of the 'hierarchy'; the 'Puritan opposition'; and the 'radical' third culture. It is on the relationship between this triangle of cultures and Hill's wider view of social conflict that a general interpretation of his theoretical approach hinges. The next section turns to examine in more detail Hill's treatment of ideas and culture in the context of his overall historical vision.

Hill's Treatment of Ideas

Hill cannot seriously be accused – as anti-Marxists frequently do accuse Marxists – of ignoring the roles of 'ideas' and 'great men' in historical change. Several of his books, and many of his essays, have to do with the ideas and actions of individuals – Lenin, Cromwell, Milton, and many others. Nor can Hill be accused of ignoring the strivings and not always coherently expressed aspirations of countless less prominent individuals and groups. (From some Marxist perspectives, he can even be accused of paying the overt ideas of such people, great and small, too much attention.) The problem is to sort out how exactly Hill relates his treatment of ideas to his conceptions of society and historical change. It seems to me that there are three main ways in which Hill analyses ideas; and that while these three ways are frequently conceived as belonging to mutually incompatible (or at least different) theoretical traditions, they are in fact complementary in Hill's work.

The three approaches may very broadly be characterized as: the 'consequences of ideas' approach; the *Wahlverwandschaft* or 'elective affinities' approach; and the retrospective 'functionalist' approach. These approaches are in fact overlapping in Hill's work, and are frequently found together in the same paragraph, or even sentence, as different aspects of Hill's attempt to illuminate our understanding of a particular phenomenon. Yet it is worth separating them out to examine their implications.

The 'consequences of ideas' approach takes ideas as historically given, and examines their consequences in different sets of conditions.

In his essay on 'Social and Economic Consequences of the Henrician Reformation', for example, Hill comments that 'it is indeed one of the many paradoxes of the English Reformation that in temporarily solving the economic problems of the ruling class it gave a stimulus to ideas which were ultimately to overthrow the old order'.[18] Part of Hill's project, in books such as *The World Turned Upside Down*, and *Intellectual Consequences of the English Revolution*, is to find out, as he implies at the beginning of the latter, 'what went wrong': to examine why certain radical ideas, with which he sympathizes, could not be successful under certain historical circumstances. Hill strongly believes in the historical importance of ideas; as he puts it in the Introduction to *Intellectual Origins of the English Revolution*, 'almost by definition, a great revolution cannot take place without ideas. Most men have to believe quite strongly in some ideal before they will kill or be killed.' However, he continues,

> Ideas do not advance merely by their own logic.... [T]he logical implications of Luther's doctrine could not be realized in practice in England until political circumstances – the collapse of the hierarchy and the central government – were propitious. Ideas were all-important for the individuals whom they impelled into action; but the historian must attach equal importance to the circumstances that gave these ideas their chance. Revolutions are not made without ideas, but they are not made by intellectuals.[19]

Thus when Hill pays serious attention to historically given bodies of ideas – which he does not wish to treat as 'merely a pale reflection of ... economic needs, with no history of their own' – he seeks to examine their consequences in the context of specific historical circumstances.[20]

Before turning to look at the ways in which Hill relates ideas to circumstances, it is worth pointing out that for Hill bodies of ideas need not be interpreted only in terms of the conditions of the present. Sometimes people are constrained by thinking in terms which are handed down, traditional frameworks, conventions and assumptions which are no longer appropriate or adequate to contemporary experience. It takes some time for these frameworks to be questioned, reinterpreted and developed; ideas can be 'constraining' as well as 'progressive' forces. And sometimes people's ideas leap far outside or 'ahead' of both received frameworks and present experience: *The World Turned Upside Down*, as its title implies, has much to do with ideas which attempted radically to rethink the nature of the world, to re-conceive the place of people in this life and the next, to conceive a new heaven and a new earth. Utopian as well as 'residual' ideas, leaps into the future, into the imagination and fantasy, as well as inherited concepts and unquestioned beliefs, are as important in Hill's work as ideologies which appear deeply rooted in the material conditions of contemporary life.

One particular way in which Hill attempts to make the linkage between bodies of ideas and social conditions, is to examine the social reasons why particular ideas might appeal to large numbers of people; and why ambiguous 'texts', or bodies of ideas, might be interpreted in one particular way rather than another. This is where the *Wahlver-wandschaft*, or 'elective affinities', approach enters in. To quote again from Hill's explicit statement introducing *Intellectual Origins*, it seems to Hill 'that any body of thought which plays a major part in history – Luther's, Rousseau's, Marx's own – "takes on" because it meets the needs of significant groups in the society in which it comes into prominence'.[21] A constant theme in Hill's work is stated already in his 1952 essay on 'Puritans and the Poor':

> It was, I believe, to the small employer that Puritanism especially appealed. The great feudal household, with its under-employed menials and hangers-on, had no labour problem; but the small craftsman or farmer offered less excitement and harder work to his prospective employees. He needed a body of ideas which would emphasize the dignity of labour for its own sake; which would be critical at once of the careless and extravagant rich and of the idle and irresponsible poor. He found both in Puritanism.[22]

Hill interprets Puritanism as directly related to 'bourgeois virtues' which were more likely to appeal to certain social groups than to others:

> These *bourgeois* virtues, which were also those inculcated by Puritanism, were less likely to be found in aristocratic families, with their traditions of ostentatious living, their troops of serving men, retainers, and poor relations, than among lesser gentry and yeomanry or small farmers.[23]

Hill devotes his book on *Society and Puritanism* to suggesting 'social reasons for which men could hold many of the traditional puritan beliefs'.[24] And he concludes that:

> To understand Puritanism we must understand the needs, hopes, fears and aspirations of the godly artisans, merchants, yeomen, gentlemen, ministers and their wives, who gave their support to its doctrines.... Puritanism was valid for them only when they felt it on their pulses. It seemed to point the way to heaven because it helped them to live on earth.[25]

Such an approach does not try to 'reduce' the reality of the religious ideas, but does try to render them more intelligible to later observers in terms of their relationships with other aspects of social experience.

Whether consciously aware of it or not, people found that certain religious ideas 'made sense' (or, in the Quaker expression, 'spoke to their condition'), because they related to real, material experiences of life, in the context of a particular social environment.

Intimately related to this attempt to elucidate 'elective affinities' between ideas and social experience is a rather more functionalist approach. It is here that analysis of Hill's work becomes more complex, for it is difficult to argue that a historian so sensitive to the actions and struggles of real people should fall into the sort of retrospective functionalism that bedevils certain forms of Marxism. I shall in fact suggest that Hill does not; nevertheless, he makes two sorts of apparently functionalist statements. One sort has to do with the 'needs' (whether perceived or otherwise) of particular classes ('real' interests?); the other has to do with the 'needs' of 'society'.

We have seen an example of the combination of a *Wahlverwandschaft* approach with a suggestion of class needs in the quotation from 'Puritans and the Poor', above. A similar suggestion of the useful functions of certain religious ideas for particular social groups is found in Hill's analysis of Sabbatarianism. The Sabbatarian ideas which Hill analyses were not themselves necessarily *propounded* by the 'industrious sort'; but because of the material, economic and political, links between preachers or lecturers and their congregations or audiences, the ideas of the intellectuals can be taken, Hill argues, as representing to a considerable extent what the audiences wanted to hear (and were prepared to support financially and politically). Hill claims that

> Protestants and especially Puritans elevated the Sabbath, the *regular* day of rest and meditation suited to the regular and continuous rhythms of modern industrial society: they attacked the very numerous and irregular festivals which had hitherto marked out the seasons. To celebrate a hundred or more saints' days in a year was all very well in an agricultural society like that of mediaeval England.... But an industrialised society, such as England was becoming in the sixteenth century, needs regular, disciplined labour.[26]

Leaving aside for the moment what begins to look like a societal functionalism at the end of this quotation, what are the implications of Hill's class analysis of Sabbatarianism? It seems quite clear (whatever the historical rights or wrongs of Hill's argument) that it is plausible to claim that small employers and industrious entrepreneurs would find it within their *perceived* class interests to oppose the endless irregularity of numerous saints' days and holy days. But a problem arises with the prohibition of work on Sundays, when on Hill's own account the religious ideas seem to correspond more to the 'real' (and unacknowledged) than to the 'perceived' interests of the class:

In the seventeenth century there was only one way in which the industrious sort could be protected from themselves: by the total prohibition of Sunday work, and of travel to and from markets; and by the strict enforcement of this prohibition, in the interests.of the class as a whole, against the many individual members of the class who would try to evade it.[27]

Without further explication of how this was supposed to operate, it does appear to fall into a problem of functionalism: assuming, from a particular standpoint, that certain of the ('beneficial') *consequences* of a phenomenon can be held to *explain* it. Hill here appears to be departing from his general emphasis on agency, and causal explanation, in favour of a class functionalism.

This apparent functionalism occasionally found in Hill's work appears not only with respect to class, but also in relation to 'society'. For example, after discussing 'traditionalistic' work attitudes, Hill suggests that an 'ideology advocating regular systematic work was required if the country was to break through this vicious circle to economic advance'.[28] In *The Century of Revolution*, Hill remarks that 'Discipline was something that concerned this world as well as the next. It is one of the many points at which Puritanism appears to serve the needs of early capitalism.'[29] At a more general level, Hill suggests that

Popery is suited to a static agricultural society, which offers the mass of the population no possibility of becoming richer than their fellows, and in which poverty is a holy state. Protestantism is suited to a competitive society in which God helps those who help themselves, in which thrift, accumulation and industry are the cardinal virtues, and poverty very nearly a crime.[30]

Thus Perkins's ideas, for example, were said to help 'lubricate economic processes'.[31] Hill links this stress on the 'societal' functions of certain cultural phenomena, however, very closely to his 'elective affinities' approach. Thus, again talking of discipline in his study of Milton, Hill reflects

on the social function of discipline. It helped to internalise the Protestant ethic. But this ethic of voluntary hard work, abstinence, accumulation, was naturally more attractive to the middle classes than to the working class. The former were more prepared to labour 'as ever in my great Taskmaster's eye' because they had never in fact known an earthly taskmaster.[32]

When Hill does talk in terms of functions and needs, it is not with an implied reification of the social whole, but rather with a very real sense of the particular social classes who would benefit by, or be attracted to, certain sets of ideas.

The linguistic appearance of functionalism at certain points in Hill's work is in fact something rather different, arising from his particular historical (and political) standpoint of interest. What Hill is centrally concerned with is the question of how we came to be where we are: how the society in which we have to live and struggle came to be as it is. Given this question, around which his historical work is structured, Hill *must* ask how the elements prerequisite for the development of modern capitalist society came to be present or to combine in certain ways. When Hill discusses the ways in which 'Puritanism appears to serve the needs of early capitalism', he is pointing up connections which retro- spectively appear to be important in the general framework of investi- gation. The statements suggesting 'functions', 'needs' and the like are in the nature of an argument about historical counterfactuals; what had to be present for something to occur, what conditions not obtaining would have led to alternative patterns of development. When Hill refers to functions, he is illuminating the material from a certain historical point of view; he is not in general suggesting that consequences can be viewed as causes. Nor, *pace* revisionists, is he suggesting that certain develop- ments were 'inevitable'; merely that they did occur, and given that they did occur, certain things seem to have played an important role. On the whole, Hill stays within an action-theoretical framework, in which different historical options are always open, if limited, as men and women seek to make their own history (though not, as Hill is sometimes better aware than revisionists, in conditions of their own choosing).

Hill's Approach: Interpretations

How does this treatment of ideas relate to Hill's general conception of history, sketched in the previous section? To start with, it must be noted that, apart from (very influential) general textbook treatments and brief essays, Hill's major concern has been less with economic–political than with social–cultural aspects of historical change. While he believes that all these changes are interconnected, his most detailed contributions have been in socio-cultural analysis. In many of his specialized works, Hill takes the economic background as given; for example, he reminds readers in the Preface to *Society and Puritanism* that he has not 'discussed at all the economic changes of the sixteenth and seventeenth centuries' but rather has 'taken them for granted'.[33] Similarly, he begins his book on *The World Turned Upside Down* with a sketch of the demographic and socio-economic changes which provided the context of the radicals' ideas, and a reminder that there was 'a greater back- ground of class hostility in England before 1640 than historians have normally recognised'.[34] Hill's particular interest in cultural questions is partly what has given rise to the classification of his work as 'culturalist'. But as Keith McClelland has pointed out in response to Johnson's discussion of culturalism, it is a mistake to see 'a concern with culture or experience, rather than with modes of production, as representing a theoretical break in itself. This is to confuse a description of what people are studying with a "theoretical" statement about how they might be doing it.'[35] Nevertheless, the question remains of the sense in which Hill's treatment of ideas and culture – perhaps at present the most ambiguous areas of Marxist theory – are 'Marxist' in relation to his general historical vision; and how Hill's treatment of these problems compares with other approaches in historical sociology.

Let me deal, first, with two related (but opposite) accusations, mentioned briefly at the start of this essay: the problem of 'culturalism', on the one hand, and of failing to give serious attention to the ideas of participants, on the other hand. According to Johnson:

> Marxist culturalism tends to reject two key aspects of Marx's original contri-
> bution to a developed historical method: the process of systematic, self-
> conscious abstraction; and the notion of social relations that are structured,
> have a logic or tendency or force of their own and operate, in part, 'behind
> men's backs'.

By contrast, Johnson asserts,

> Social processes cannot be (wholly) understood in terms of the recorded
> experiences of individuals or classes. Sometimes these lie at the very heart of
> inadequate explanations of the world. The object of an adequate history must,
> then, not merely be 'people' but the whole complex set of relations in which
> they stand.[36]

By these criteria, it is very difficult to see why Hill is presumed to have a purely phenomenological approach. For he neither entirely conflates culture with class (a problem to which I shall return in a moment), nor does he ignore the logic of processes 'behind men's backs'. Rather, Hill assumes these processes to be of fundamental importance in explaining why things eventuated in the way they did, irrespective of participants' understandings or intentions. This is a key feature of Hill's recent debate with revisionists. His 1980 Neale Lecture, 'Parliament and People in Seventeenth Century England', presents an account of the background to the English Revolution in terms of structural, social and political relations, which were as important as the beliefs and aspirations of participants. Hill has some pointed comments to make about historians who remain at the level of contemporaries' understandings:

> One useful consequence of Professor Elton's incursion into the seventeenth century is that he looks at its problems with the eyes of a man for whom the sixteenth-century consensus was normal. Failing to appreciate the underlying socioeconomic issues, he usefully reproduces the muddled thinking of the average early seventeenth-century M.P. But to echo the fumbling is not to write the history.[37]

And, later in the same essay:

> One of the things 'revisionists' most dislike is hindsight: they call it Whiggish to consider what happened next. But in discussing men fumbling with problems which their mental apparatus was incapable of solving, it does not help merely to report on their vain efforts to square the circle.[38]

Whether one agrees with these judgements or not, it seems clear that Hill is well aware that there is more to historical explanation than the reconstruction of the perceptions of participants. This latter task is important, and is one to which Hill has devoted a considerable amount of energy – particularly when the participants are those normally disregarded by historians, relegated to an irrelevant 'lunatic fringe' – but such reconstruction is intended by Hill as a supplement to, not a replacement for, a deeper socio-economic analysis.

While Hill is not a 'cultural reductionist' upwards, neither is he a 'class reductionist' downwards (if spatial metaphors may be used in this connection). Many of his writings, which are concerned less with theoretical precision than with historical reconstruction, give the impression that Hill assumes a close correspondence between 'culture' and 'class'. His stress on 'elective affinities', discussed above, suggests a strong case for an intimate fit between sets of ideas and social experiences, such that it appears almost inevitable that certain groups held certain outlooks. Moreover, at times when Hill speaks of the 'three cultures' (orthodox, Puritan opposition and radical), it does appear that he assumes a direct correlation with social groups ('conservative' ruling class, 'progressive' ruling class and exploited/oppressed classes). But when Hill's works are examined in more detail, it becomes apparent that he does not adhere to a class reductionist view, in two ways. First, the ideas themselves cannot be 'reduced' to their class carriers, or 'read off' in a mechanistic fashion from notions of 'class interests' or 'material' experiences. There are independent, partially autonomous intellectual traditions, in the context of which people select, interpret and creatively

debate with those aspects which are most relevant in given circumstances. And these cultural traditions do make a difference to the course
of events. Secondly, the fit between 'culture' and 'class', while suggestive, is not absolute: as at all times, people from the 'wrong' social
classes passionately believed in certain ideas, and tried to propagate
them among those in the 'appropriate' social classes to which they
should appeal (a recurrent problem for middle-class socialists). In
Society and Puritanism, for example, Hill points out in passing that
Puritan ideas appealed to many in the upper ranks of society, and that
aristocratic Puritans were of considerable importance for the history of
the movement. But it is Hill's concern in the book to explore 'the
formation of [a] wider climate of opinion', focusing particularly on the
'industrious sort'.[39] It is possible for critics such as Hexter to consider
this an exemplar of illegitimate 'lumping'; but all historians, whether
implicitly or explicitly, operate criteria of selection; and Hill is here quite
open about the particular historical connection he wished to explore,
without suggesting that it exhausted all there might be to say about the
origins, class bases or social connections and implications of Puritanism.

So the fit between 'culture' and 'class' is not absolute in either
direction: Hill neither believes that 'culture' summarizes all there is to
class relations and processes of social change (for much lies beyond the
comprehension of both participants and phenomenologically inclined
historians); nor that 'class' explains all there is to say about 'culture'.
There are no simple *a priori* assumptions or equations. As Hill said, in
an early essay, 'the connections of religion, science, politics, and
economics are infinite and infinitely subtle'.[40] And at the beginning of
Reformation to Industrial Revolution Hill makes it quite clear that he is
interested in the *interaction* among different elements: 'We cannot
change one variable without affecting all the others.'[41]

To say this is not to suggest that Hill is a complete pluralist, however.
While Hill is not explicitly concerned with theoretical debates about
'base' and 'superstructure', 'being' and 'consciousness', 'determined' and
'determining' and the like, he does operate with some strong background assumptions. Debates on these questions of 'materialist'
approaches have frequently been conducted more by way of biblical
exegesis, so to speak – rival readings of the sacred texts – than by way of
empirical, historical, investigation. (The latter particularly poses a
problem from certain epistemological positions held by some of the
contributors to the debate.) Hill, however, as a practising historian,
proceeds in accordance with Weber's concept of value-relevance:

> History has to be rewritten in every generation, because although the past
> does not change the present does; each generation asks new questions of the

past, and finds new areas of sympathy as it re-lives different aspects of the experiences of its predecessors.[42]

Assuming a legitimate division of labour among Marxist historians, Hill has been less concerned to tease out the intricacies and logic of economic change than to reconstruct for the present the radical or progressive ideas of the past. Hence, while Hill certainly does not share the assumptions of structuralist Marxists, he does tend to take for granted certain general Marxist assumptions about the fundamental importance and character of certain economic changes in the transition from feudalism to capitalism. Nor is Hill very concerned to theorize directly about politics and the state: he tends rather to assume that the state is in some way an instrument of the ruling class, and a focus of class struggle, both arising out of and affecting economic processes, creating or obstructing the conditions for economic change. These background assumptions form the framework for both Hill's textbook histories and his more detailed analyses of culture and ideas. The precise character, detail, theoretical acceptability and empirical adequacy of Marxist approaches to the state and to 'modes of production' have been the subject of controversies, among both Marxists and non-Marxists, with which Hill has not been directly involved. Whether his background assumptions are 'correct' or 'incorrect' is another matter; but they must be seen as setting the parameters when Hill speaks of complex 'interaction' among variables.

Yet turning to Hill's major substantive area of contribution, the picture is rather complicated. Recent debates among Marxists, reacting against varieties of 'economism', 'technological determinism', 'Stalinist orthodoxy' and so on, have sought to develop and clarify more subtle approaches to the analysis of ideas and culture. These attempts are related to debates over the status of Marx's own major analytic contribution: was it, narrowly, a political economy of the capitalist mode of production; did Marx fail to develop an adequate general sociology; how far is Marxism applicable to non-capitalist, non-industrial societies? The intrinsic importance of the supposedly 'superstructural' elements of law, politics, religion, in societies in which the 'economy' has not (as in capitalism) been specifically separated out and accorded apparent autonomy, has been noted and puzzled over.[43] Much of Hill's work could be taken as making a direct historical contribution towards resolution of these questions. Hill, for example, explicates in detail the political and economic location and role of the established state Church in early modern England, such that religion necessarily became the idiom for political debate. While the state Church enjoyed both a monopoly status and played such an important political role, yet was in such a contested economic and political position, it was inevitable that political and religious controversies should have been so intertwined.[44] The structural changes in the location of the Church in the course of the seventeenth century probably had far more to do with the presumed process of 'secularization' than did the later changes of urbanization and industrialization generally favoured by sociologists of religion. But reflection on this undoubted contribution, in the context of the wider debates about the scope of Marxism, raises some interesting questions.

Specifically, it seems to me that where Hill does make his most important contributions – where, in other words, he is engaged in teasing out empirical interrelationships, rather than in his general background assumptions – in these areas, Hill's work shows a remarkable theoretical convergence with Max Weber's general approach to the analysis of religion, ideas and society. Weber, of course, had rather different views on the state, power and economic processes than those embodied in Hill's background framework (not to mention rather different political values). But formal similarities in their approaches to the analysis of culture in non-capitalist societies cannot be overlooked.[45] Both Hill and Weber accept a certain autonomy for inherited cultural traditions, which provide the terms and context of debates. Given certain cultural traditions, the analysis of the particular interpretations of ideas selected and developed from a competing variety of possibilities must be undertaken with reference to the social, material, experiences of the groups to which they appealed.[46] (The notion I used earlier in this essay on Hill's approach, *Wahlverwandschaft*, is of course a concept favoured by Weber.) And then it is only by analysis of the struggles among competing social groups, in the context of specific historical circumstances, that one can adequately explain which sets of ideas will be historically 'victorious' (and with what ironies and unintended consequences). Ideas affect, and are affected by, social processes: both Weber and Hill reject any disembodied 'history of ideas' approach, as much as they reject any simplistic assumptions of monocausality. These similarities in the general theoretical approaches to culture in the works of Weber and Hill are all the more remarkable considering that the central difference between 'Marxist' and 'Weberian' approaches is frequently said to be in the role accorded to ideas. This convergence will be welcomed or rejected, depending on personal prejudice. But it does raise the question of what would be a distinctively 'Marxist' treatment of culture, given a particular form of Marxism that is of a non-functionalist and non-structuralist variety. If one reinterprets 'determination' as the 'setting of limits' and 'exerting of pressure' (as Raymond Williams does, and as appears to be the case in Hill's work), then there is little formal difference between this and the general approach suggested by Weber's work, whatever arguments there may be over particular substantive hypotheses. Moreover, when one recognizes the historical importance of 'superstructural' (religious, political) elements, and of status as well as relationship to the means of production, then this sort of materialist history begins to be as compatible with Weberian historical sociology as with Marxian political economy.

Hill's History and Historical Sociology

I have been concerned in this essay, not to evaluate the substantive adequacy of Hill's analyses, nor to comment on the details of his methodology, but rather to present as clearly as possible the general outlines of Hill's reconciliation of a commitment to a 'deep' under-standing of historical forces with a concern and respect for those who were the makers of history. Many comments could be – and have been – made about particular hypotheses set forward by Hill, and about his treatment of evidence in relation to his theses. Hill's interpretations have developed over time, incorporating new evidence, refining particular views, discarding others. His work has not said all that could be said, nor in as rigorous or systematic fashion as some might like: Hill's particular strength has been richness of illustration and evocation, rather than rigour of theoretical testing. In his chosen areas, Hill has perhaps done more to illuminate the connections between culture and class, and to shed twentieth-century light on what would otherwise have remained forgotten corners of our seventeenth-century heritage, than to develop systematic analyses of the structural conditions which helped to deter-mine particular outcomes. Hill has by no means presented the whole picture, and there are contestable details in those parts that he has done so much to illustrate. But one historian cannot do everything. It is the strength of Hill's work that he realizes that there *is* a whole picture, and that the parts are intrinsically interrelated: that no aspect can be isolated, and reified as a 'topic' of its own. It is the ways in which different elements interconnect that give them their particular historical signifi-cance and efficacy. Moreover, Hill realizes that in part these very interconnections are artefacts of our retrospective standpoint of interest: they are the relationships in which *we* are interested, from a particular point of view. So, just as there is no reification of isolated parts, there is also no reification of a functioning 'system' as a whole. For Hill, there is a value-related exploration of those connections that have contemporary significance, in the context of certain theoretical assumptions and explanatory framework. Within this framework, Hill's imaginative reconstruction, based on massive collection, selection, and presentation of evidence, has made a major contribution to the resuscitation and interpretation of aspirations, actions, and connections which in 'orthodox' histories had been disregarded.

How one wants to characterize Hill theoretically is a debatable matter. Given that 'Marxism' is not a monolithic entity, defined in terms of a particular set of unchallengable doctrines, but rather is a terrain of debate and controversy, frequently held together mainly by a common political commitment, then Hill might be called a socialist humanist. If one wants a narrower, or a more essentialist, definition of Marxism, then Hill's history is not of the sort that has on occasion been either defended or attacked as strictly Marxist. It is not an approach which assumes modes of production to have logics of their own, irrespective of human ideas and action; it is not teleological, nor functionalist, in general character. In many respects, Hill's contribution has not directly questioned or assessed certain of the underlying materialist assumptions on which it is based. Yet considering Hill's history in its own terms, not attempting to measure it against standards of orthodoxy or heresy, it has made a tremendous contribution to the theoretically informed reappropriation of the complex patterns of our past.

Notes

I am most grateful to Margot Heinemann for comments and discussions which helped greatly in the writing of this essay.

1. See, for example, Philip Abrams, *Historical Sociology* (Shepton Mallet, 1982).
2. Christopher Hill, *The English Revolution 1640* (London, 1940, 3rd edn, 1955), p. 6.
3. Stuart Hall, 'The Hinterland of Science: Ideology and the "Sociology of Knowledge"', in Centre for Contemporary Cultural Studies, *On Ideology* (London, 1978), p. 16.
4. See Richard Johnson, 'Edward Thompson, Eugene Genovese, and Socialist–Humanist History', *History Workshop*, no. 6 (1978), p. 99; Johnson, 'Culture and the Historians', in John Clarke *et al.*, eds., *Working Class Culture* (London, 1979), p. 63; Johnson, 'Histories of Culture/Theories of Ideology: Notes on an Impasse', in Michèle Barrett *et al.*, eds., *Ideology and Cultural Production* (London, 1979), p. 51.
5. Andrew Milner, *John Milton and the English Revolution* (London, 1981).
6. See for example Kevin Sharpe's Introduction to *Faction and Parliament* (Oxford, 1978); Conrad Russell's Introduction to *The Origins of the English Civil War* (London, 1973); and for my general analysis of their mode of argument, Mary Fulbrook, 'The English Revolution and the Revisionist Revolt', *Social History*, vol. 7, no. 3 (1982), pp. 1–16.
7. J.H. Hexter, 'The Historical Method of Christopher Hill', reprinted in Hexter, *On Historians* (London, 1979).
8. W.C. Sellar and R.J. Yeatman, *1066 and All That* (Harmondsworth, 1960), p. 71.
9. Hill, *The Century of Revolution, 1603–1714* (New York, 1966; 1st edn, 1961), pp. 1, 4–5.

10. Karl Marx and Friedrich Engels, *Manifesto of the Communist Party* (Moscow, 1952 edn), p. 44.

11. Hill, *Century of Revolution*, pp. 310 and 311.

12. Hill, *From Reformation to Industrial Revolution* (Harmondsworth, 1969; original edn 1967), p. 270.

13. See, for example, *English Revolution 1640*; see also Hill, *Lenin and the Russian Revolution* (Harmondsworth, 1971; 1st edn 1947).

14. See for example Hill, 'Parliament and People in Early Seventeenth-Century England', *Past and Present*, no. 92 (1981), pp. 100–124; Hill, *Some Intellectual Consequences of the English Revolution* (London, 1980), p. 34.

15. *Century of Revolution*, p. 105.

16. Hill, 'Recent Interpretations of the Civil War', in *Puritanism and Revolution* (London, 1965), p. 8.

17. *Reformation to Industrial Revolution*, p. 55.

18. In *Puritanism and Revolution*, p. 38.

19. Hill, *Intellectual Origins of the English Revolution* (Oxford, 1965), pp. 1, 3.

20. *Intellectual Origins*, p. 3.

21. *Intellectual Origins*, p. 3.

22. Hill, 'Puritans and the Poor', *Past and Present*, no. 2 (1952), pp. 37–8.

23. *Century of Revolution*, p. 16.

24. Hill, *Society and Puritanism in Pre-revolutionary England* (New York, 1967; 1st edn 1964), p. 509.

25. *Society and Puritanism*, p. 511.

26. *Society and Puritanism*, p. 146.

27. *Society and Puritanism*, p. 152.

28. *Society and Puritanism*, p. 125.

29. *Century of Revolution*, p. 84.

30. *Society and Puritanism*, p. 132.

31. 'Puritans and the Poor', p. 39.

32. Hill, *Milton and the English Revolution* (London, 1979; 1st edn 1977), p. 263.

33. *Society and Puritanism*, p. 11.

34. Hill, *The World Turned Upside Down* (Harmondsworth, 1975; 1st edn 1972), p. 19; see generally chs. 2 and 3.

35. Keith McClelland, 'Some Comments on Richard Johnson, "Edward Thompson, Eugene Genovese, and Socialist–Humanist History"', *History Workshop*, no. 7 (1979), p. 104.

36. Johnson, 'Culture and the Historians', p. 70.

37. 'Parliament and People', p. 108.

38. 'Parliament and People', p. 122.

39. *Society and Puritanism*, p. 135.

40. *Puritanism and Revolution*, p. 29.

41. *Reformation to Industrial Revolution*, p. 16.

42. *World Turned Upside Down*, p. 15. Compare Max Weber:

The cultural problems which move men form themselves ever anew and in different colours, and the boundaries of that area in the infinite stream of concrete events which acquires meaning and significance for us, i.e., which becomes an 'historical individual', are constantly subject to change. The intellectual contexts from which it is viewed and scientifically analyzed shift. The points of departure of the cultural sciences remain changeable throughout the limitless future as long as a Chinese ossification of intellectual life does not render mankind incapable of setting new questions to the eternally enexhaustible flow of life.
> Max Weber, *Methodology of the Social Sciences*, Shils and Finch, eds. (New York, 1949), p. 84.

43. See for example Perry Anderson's unsuccessful attempt to re-conceptualize pre-capitalist modes of production, and specifically feudalism, in terms of aspects of their

'superstructure': Perry Anderson, *Passages from Antiquity to Feudalism* and *Lineages of the Absolutist State* (London, 1974); and, for problems with this attempt, Mary Fulbrook and Theda Skocpol, 'Destined Pathways: The Historical Sociology of Perry Anderson', in Skocpol, ed., *Vision and Method in Historical Sociology* (New York, 1984), pp. 170–210.

44. See what is perhaps Hill's most brilliant book, *Economic Problems of the Church* (Oxford, 1956).

45. I do not mean by this specific substantive similarities in, for example, their interpretations of early modern Protestantism; I refer rather to the more general character of their theoretical approaches to culture. Weber's work is perhaps as ambiguous as Marx's; my own interpretation of Weber's sociology of religion is set out in Fulbrook, 'Max Weber's "Interpretive Sociology": A Comparison of Conception and Practice', *British Journal of Sociology*, vol. 29, no. 1 (1978), pp. 71–82.

46. Hill's *Society and Puritanism* fits very neatly with the sort of 'sociology of religion' approach outlined by Weber in *Economy and Society* (New York, 1968), vol. 2, ch. 6; and in Part 3 of Gerth and Mills, eds., *From Max Weber* (New York, 1958). Margot Heinemann has suggested to me that Hill's convergence with Weber may be related to the fact that Hill was greatly influenced by the work of Tawney. (Curiously, though, the similarities between Weber and Hill are *least* in their interpretations of early Protestantism.)

The World Turned Upside Down: A Retrospect

Barry Reay

I want to begin this paper with a discussion of some of the main aspects of the work of Christopher Hill, generally acknowledged to be one of Britain's greatest living historians. These facets – Hill as an implicit Marxist theoretical practitioner, Hill as a reconstructor of historical consciousness, Hill as a politically engaged historian, and Hill as a pioneer of seventeenth-century people's history – can be detected in the broad corpus of his work. We need to be familiar with them if we are to fully understand the context of the subject of this essay, his book *The World Turned Upside Down*.

> The founders of Marxism never expounded their materialist conception of history systematically. Believing as they did in the unity of theory and practice they conveyed their historical theories by writing history and not by writing about the writing of history.... Marxism as applied to history is a technique of analysis, a method of approach, not a dogma: and it is correspondingly difficult to summarise briefly without doing it an injustice. Its real test is in action, whether in the writing or the making of history.[1]

Hill wrote this in 1948 and forty years later he still adheres to it; the job of the historian is to write history not to write about the writing of it. Christopher Hill is a historian, not a historiographer. He would not, I fear, approve of this particular exercise. And yet, as E.P. Thompson has reminded us, Hill is a formidable explorer of Marxist categories – through historical practice rather than theoretical discourse.[2] His essay 'Protestantism and the Rise of Capitalism' (1961 and 1974) is a marvellously subtle account of the interaction between Protestantism and developing capitalism, an attempt indeed to marry Marx and Weber.[3] His remarkable piece 'The Norman Yoke' (1954 and 1958) and the book *Antichrist in Seventeenth-Century England* (1971) show the ways in which ideas are taken up, shaped, imbued with different meanings, and used by different groups in society.[4]

The Marxism of Christopher Hill and Edward Thompson, Richard Johnson has recently claimed, is 'culturalist' Marxism: neglectful of the economic side of history, distrustful of theoretical abstraction, concerned overridingly with culture and experience. The shift of Hill from an 'economistic' to a 'culturalist' Marxism, it is argued, can be seen by simply comparing *The English Revolution* (1940) with *The World Turned Upside Down* (1972).[5] Now it is true that *The World Turned Upside Down* is in Johnson's terms a work of culturalism. It is true that Hill, like Thompson, has spent a lifetime exploring the superstructural aspects of the Marxist basis/superstructure formula (though like Thompson he would probably now reject the basis/superstructure theory as too reductionist). Hill's work on religion in the seventeenth century meshes nicely with Thompson's analysis of the role of law in the eighteenth century – the latter dedicated his book *Whigs and Hunters* (1975) to Christopher Hill, 'master of more than an old Oxford College'. But if we examine Hill's work as a whole he can by no means be said to have neglected the economic base. There is his *Economic Problems of the Church* (1956, 1963 and 1968), a painstaking piece of empirical Marxist research, with, as the title suggests, an emphasis on the non-theological side of religious conflict. There is the *Century of Revolution* (1961, revised 1980), a textbook, structured chronologically 1603–40, 1640–60, etc., but also layered with separate chapters on economics, politics and the constitution, religion and ideas; hailed by Victor Kiernan as a vindication of the Marxist method.[6] And – after the publication of *The World Turned Upside Down* – we have his 1980 reformulation of England's seventeenth-century revolution as a bourgeois revolution; a revolution which made the bourgeoisie if indeed they did not make it.[7] If the term 'culturalist' has any meaning Hill is not a culturalist.

Edward Thompson has also suggested that Hill has shown us how to think differently about whole areas of early modern English history. ('He now seems to have been there all the time. But he wasn't.'[8]) This is true. Hill has set agendas, the terms of reference for debate. The obvious examples here are *The Intellectual Origins of the English Revolution* (1965, 1972) and the disputes over 'Puritanism and Science'.[9] However, it all began with *The English Revolution* (1940, etc.), the most influential Marxist account of England's mid-seventeenth-century crisis. It was, Hill has recalled, an angry essay, intended to shock. It was iconoclastic ('I knew that the word "bourgeois" was a red rag to English academics') and pitched against the dominant tone of English historical writing:[10]

the sort of history which Gareth Stedman Jones was gunning for nearly thirty years later in the pages of the *New Left Review*: 'a growing academic industry distinguished mainly by conceptual archaism and reactionary apologetics';[11] the type of history still extolled by John Kenyon and G.R. Elton.

The English Revolution is also an engaged piece of history. It 'was written in great haste and great anger, at a time when I assumed I was going to be killed in a world war which I thought could have been prevented if policies advocated for many years by myself and others had been adopted. So I regarded the essay as, in a sense, my last will and testament to posterity.' 'My virulence against Charles I was I fear caused by conflating him with Neville Chamberlain, just as my hostility to Laud was directed against the Tory school of historians.'[12] In his Pelican Classics edition of the writings of the seventeenth-century agrarian communist Gerrard Winstanley, Hill has suggested that Winstanley's writings 'may be of interest to those in the Third World today who face the transition from an agrarian to an industrial society'.[13] *The World Turned Upside Down* itself is very much a product of the late 1960s – although in my opinion reviewers and some readers have pushed the 'counter-culture' aspect of the book further than Hill would have wished. But there are certainly echoes of Marcuse; the stress on youth, solidarity, sexual liberation, the shattering of established values. Hill quotes him with approval: 'In the great historical revolutions the imagination was, for a short period, released and free.' He also rather uncharacteristically intrudes himself into the text to talk of nuclear bombs and the competitive society.[14]

Raphael Samuel has pointed out that so noticeable is the fusing of past and present in the work of Hill, one can, in certain key works, trace English political developments over the last five decades: 'triumphalist in 1940' in the *English Revolution*; affected by the student revolt of 1968 in *The World Turned Upside Down*; disillusioned, despairing, self-questioning in *Milton and the English Revolution* (1977).[15] His latest book is *The Experience of Defeat: Milton and Some Contemporaries*, written in Thatcher's Britain.

Finally Hill has injected some 'history from below' into the often staid and conventional history of the seventeenth century. This brings us again to *The World Turned Upside Down*, for although it contains elements of most of the facets of Hill's historical writing discussed so far, its main significance is as a work of people's history.

Writing this review has been a strange experience. It is well over ten years since I first read *The World Turned Upside Down* as an undergraduate, and it came (as I recall it) as something of a liberating

experience after several months of Elton and the Tudor constitution. I
discovered overnight that early modern English history could actually be
moving and exciting. So it is impossible for me to completely distance
myself from the book; it has those kinds of associations. However, I am
going to try to hold *The World Turned Upside Down* at arm's length and
attempt what can best be described as retrospective review, examining
the reception of the book, its arguments, its strengths and weaknesses,
and how it has stood up to the test of time and the impact of the
research which it played no small role in stimulating.

*The World Turned Upside Down: Radical Ideas during the English
Revolution* was first published in 1972, the first in a series on popular
rebellions edited by Rodney Hilton, a medievalist and like Hill a former
member of the Communist Party Historians' Group. Its companion
volumes are Hilton's *Bond Men Made Free* (1973), a book on medieval
peasant movements; a study of the Monmouth Rebellion of 1685 by
Robin Clifton (a former student of Hill's); and Dorothy Thompson's
The Chartists (1984). There were a few carping voices. 'I think we are
entitled to ask where all this discussion of obscure left-wing fanatics is
getting us,' wrote Kenyon in the *Spectator*.[16] 'What is the intellectual
value, especially for students, of studying nonsense?' asked A.L. Rowse;
such studies as Hill's 'merely fortify the prejudices of the inferior'. 'What
would Communist Russia say to such lunacy?'[17] But the overall response
was one of critical acclaim. Many 'will reckon *The World Turned Upside
Down* to be his best and most sustained achievement since *Economic
Problems of the Church*', wrote the anonymous reviewer in *The Times
Literary Supplement*.[18] Has 'claims to be regarded as Christopher Hill's
best book to date': Keith Thomas in the *New York Review of Books*.[19]
His 'best work so far', 'arguably his finest book', 'perhaps his finest
work'.[20] A book of 'marvellous erudition'; 'stirring'; 'memorable' in the
'learning, the penetration, the love and compassion which its author
brings to "those marvellous decades" and to the humbler sort of men
who found hope and utterance in them'.[21]

By academic standards Hill's book has sold well: 3,300 copies in the
Temple Smith hardback edition; 46,000 in the United Kingdom
Penguin edition published in 1975. A decade after its initial publication
it was selling at the rate of 3,000 copies a year.[22] In the winter of 1978–9
there was a play based on the book, performed at the Cottesloe in
London by the National Theatre. The British rock singer Billy Bragg has
a song called 'The World Turned Upside Down'. So the book's appeal
has not been limited to academic circles.

The subject matter of Hill's book was nothing new. *The World
Turned Upside Down* had many predecessors, for British communists
and socialists had long laid claim to the revolutionary Puritan and

Nonconformist tradition, and still do:[23] Eduard Bernstein's *Cromwell and Communism* (first published in England in 1930); Jack Lindsay's *John Bunyan, Maker of Myths* (1937); Henry Hollorenshaw's (that is, Joseph Needham's) *The Levellers and the English Revolution* (1939); D.W. Petegorsky's *Left-wing Democracy in the English Civil War* (1940); H.N. Brailsford's *The Levellers and the English Revolution* (1961), prepared for publication by Hill; A.L. Morton's *The World of the Ranters* (1970). Alan Cole's article 'The Quakers and the English Revolution' (1956) and Keith Thomas's piece 'Women and the Civil War Sects' (1958), both published in *Past and Present*, were of a somewhat less committed ilk; and there were many other works on the radicals, all scrupulously acknowledged by Hill. Bernard Capp's book *The Fifth Monarchy Men* appeared at the same time as *The World Turned Upside Down*. But it is Hill's book that has ensured that the radical popular revolt within the English Revolution has a place in any textbook dealing with seventeenth-century England.

Nor has the impact of *The World Turned Upside Down* been confined to historians of the seventeenth century, or indeed historians. A glance through the *Arts and Humanities Citation Index* and the *Social Sciences Citation Index* will show that while *The World Turned Upside Down* does not match Keith Thomas's *Religion and the Decline of Magic* (1971, 1973) and E.P. Thompson's *Making of the English Working Class* (1963, 1968) – two of the greatest works of English history produced this century – in terms of the sheer range of citations in scholarly works from different fields, it is still a widely read book, particularly when it is noted that it deals with a relatively short period of history in one country. *The World Turned Upside Down* has been cited in works dealing with a variety of periods and fields of history (medieval and modern, African and Asian) as well as in journals of sociology, law, medicine, education, science, and political, literary and feminist studies.

The World Turned Upside Down deals with the revolt within the English Revolution of 1642–60, with 'what from one point of view are subsidiary episodes and ideas in the English Revolution, the attempts of various groups of the common people to impose their own solutions to the problems of their times, in opposition to the wishes of their betters who had called them into political action'.[24] It begins with a section on social tensions in seventeenth-century England (the social basis for the ideology he discusses later) and with 'lower-class heresy', a tradition of scepticism and anti-clericalism. There was a class hostility, much underestimated by historians. 'Not far below the surface of Stuart society ... discontent was rife.'[25] In another chapter in this section Hill deals with what he calls the 'masterless men': vagabonds, the mobile and poor populace of London, itinerant traders, cottagers and squatters. He emphasizes the role of the woodland and pasture areas in the history of independence and insubordination. These were the areas of large parishes, loosely controlled manors, scattered settlements of cottager and squatter, of struggle against enclosure. They contrast strongly with the subservient arable regions with their close-knit, nucleated, 'field' communities under the watchful eye of manor and church. Hill also anticipates the role of the New Model Army (Parliament's army), mobile, ideologically motivated, linking together 'hitherto obscure radical groups'. Finally, Hill writes of the importance of the north and west of England, traditionally dismissed as backward and conservative, in providing many of the radicals who will appear later in his book. So the scene set in the initial chapters is one of mobility, independence, freedom from the traditional 'categories of a hierarchical agrarian society'. The groups and ideas dealt with in this section of the book make up the 'combustible material' which fuels the conflagration of the Civil War.

Hill sets the stage too for the vital role of religion in the generation of radicalism during the Revolution: the millenarian expectations of ordinary people; the role of the Bible. ('Men coming to the Bible with no historical sense but with the highest expectations found in it a message of direct contemporary relevance.')[26]

The section on the revolution within the Revolution begins with the Diggers or 'True Levellers', perhaps the best-known, certainly the most written-about, of the Revolution radicals. The Diggers were agrarian communists whose main spokesperson was Gerrard Winstanley. Winstanley provided the most coherent, thought-out, comprehensive critique of the ruling order and the most far-reaching solution to the injustices of the period: the abolition of private property.

The novelty of *The World Turned Upside Down*, however, is that it concentrates on the radicals of the second half of the Revolution: Ranters, Seekers, Quakers, and a whole range of popular messiahs and prophets. Such groups were a product of the Calvinist milieu. Calvin's theory of predestination, so influential in England, had dispensed with the old possibility of 'earning a place in heaven'. One was either among the elect or was damned to an eternity of torment; there was nothing that could be done about it. At the same time the doctrine of the priesthood of all believers rejected the mediation of priest and sacraments, setting men and women 'face to face with God'. Every believer has a 'priest in his own conscience'. It was important to preach the word. There were, Hill writes, 'inherent contradictions in combining a theology which stressed that the elect were a minority with a moral preaching designed to reach all men'.[27] The religious radicals of the Revolution can be seen as a product of this contradiction. Before 'I was chosen of God', wrote the sectary Lodowick Muggleton,

> my thoughts were troubled about salvation and damnation; and the dispute within me grew very great ... the motions of faith being so well grounded upon the Scriptures, did prove to my reason, that there was a necessity, that some men and women should be saved, and the greatest part should be damned; so that I saw there was a certain damnation and salvation, and both eternal; but which way to gain the one, and escape the other, I could not tell, or what course to take; loth I was to be damned to eternity; and how to gain the assurance of eternal salvation, I knew not, because it lay in God's prerogative power.... I saw my righteousness, nor prayer, nor any good deeds I could do, would not save me, if he had made me a vessel of wrath; so that my hope was cut off, and almost utter despair in the room; so that I wished in my heart that I had never been born; or that I had died in my mother's womb; for I did not desire so much to be saved, so that I could but escape being damned.[28]

Muggleton and John Reeve, the founders of the Muggletonian sect, reacted to the harshness of predestinarian theory and an associated fear of Hell and damnation by providing a variation on Calvinism: they had the power to recognize the blessed and the damned and to pronounce sentence accordingly. Ranters, Quakers, General Baptists and Gerrard Winstanley responded to the situation by rejecting the notion of predestination: 'God woulde have all men to bee saved.'[29] Particular (that is, Calvinist) Baptists and Fifth Monarchists presumably convinced themselves that they were among the elect, the saints.

The years of the Revolution were a time of immense speculation and questioning. Rice Jones of Nottingham reached a position where he thought in terms of an internal crucifixion and resurrection; 'there never was such a thing' 'as a Christ that died in Jerusalem'.[30] Jacob Bauthumley preferred to see God as 'one individed essence', 'in all Creatures, Man and Beast, Fish and Fowle, and every green thing, from the highest Cedar to the Ivey on the wall'.[31] 'Where is your God', asked John Boggis of Great Yarmouth (quoted with relish by Hill), 'in heaven or in earth, aloft or below, or doth he sit in the clouds, or where doth he sit with his arse?'[32] Thomas Webbe has reputed to have said that there was no Heaven but women and no Hell but marriage.[33] Laurence Clarkson believed at one stage that Hell, the Devil, and Heaven were 'all in the imagination'.[34] The Scriptures are to be treated as allegories and should be subjected to textual criticism.[35] Sin exists only in the imagination; there is 'no such act as Drunkennesse, Adultery, and Theft in God'. To the pure all things are pure. What 'act soever is done by thee, in light and love, is light, and lovely; though it be that act called

Adultery'. Till 'you can lie with all women as one woman, and not judge it sin, you can do nothing but sin'.[36]

Some themes emerge: an emphasis on the spirit within and the Scriptures, a rejection of the distinction between the priest and laity and of the whole concept of an established church, hostility to tithes, anti-Trinitarianism, mortalism, unorthodox ideas about Heaven and Hell, an advocacy of human effort as a means to salvation or at least an attempt to control if not to reject completely the doctrine of predestination, a call for liberty of conscience. Such discussion was not limited to the 1640s and 1650s; in *The World Turned Upside Down* and elsewhere Hill traces continuities, geographical as well as ideological, between the heretics of the sixteenth century and the radicals of the seventeenth.[37] But if we are seeking a sustained critique of traditional ideas, on all fronts, then we must turn to the revolution within the Revolution.

> There had been moments when it seemed as though from the ferment of radical ideas a culture might emerge which would be different from both the traditional aristocratic culture and from the bougeois culture of the Protestant ethic which replaced it. We can discern shadows of what this counter-culture might have been like. Rejecting private property for communism, religion for a rationalistic and materialistic pantheism, the mechanical philosophy for dialectical science, asceticism for unashamed enjoyment of the good things of the flesh, it might have achieved unity through a federation of communities, each based on the fullest respect for the individual. Its ideal would have been economic self-sufficiency, not world trade or world domination.[38]

The World Turned Upside Down is not really a book for sociologists or political scientists. Hill does not spell things out. His themes and sub-themes are nearly always implicit in form. Hence John Dunn's frustration in his *Listener* review, his comment that Hill is not 'totally successful in clarifying just what thesis he is intending to advance'.[39]

Structurally the book adheres to what Christopher Hill has called the 'three-handed struggle' between royalist, parliamentarian and radical in the English Revolution.[40] There are similarities with the late Albert Soboul's work on the *sans-culottes* of the French Revolution in that Hill advances the idea of a popular movement (or, better, movement from below) which is able to force the pace of revolution but which is ideologically at odds with both the old and emerging orders. However, *The World Turned Upside Down* is not a political history in the vein of much of the work of Soboul. It deals with ideas and doctrines rather than actual political dynamics and the repercussions of pressure from below: the *ideological* revolt within the Revolution rather than the political revolt within the Revolution. Hill covers the upside-down world of political, religious, economic and sexual radicalism. *The World*

Turned Upside Down is, as Dunn has observed, essentially a 'celebration' of this world. It does not, for the most part, explain what could be described as the dialectics of the revolt within the Revolution; reactions to radicalism from below, radicalism's actual impact on the politics of the period. What I have in mind here is the work of Brian Manning, another British Marxist, who has charted how pressure from below in the form of demonstrations and the emergence of radical forms of religion in the early 1640s terrified many of the nobility and gentry, welding together 'a party of order', the royalist party, a party which stood for stability and the preservation of hierarchy in Church and state.[41] Or, for a slightly later period, there is work on 1659, building on the ideas of Hill, which stresses the role of radicalism in stimulating a conservative reaction.[42] Hill touches on such matters in *The World Turned Upside Down*, but does not examine them in any depth. Still, as a 'celebration', Christopher Hill's book is a masterpiece. Powerful, moving, awe-inspiring in its grasp of primary and secondary literature, it does a wonderful job of rescuing those largely neglected in conventional accounts of the English Revolution.

Hill has another aim in *The World Turned Upside Down*, to tell us something about English society before and after the Revolution. Ideas that had always been around surfaced in the relative freedom of the English Revolution; we must use that period to throw light on the periods before and after that upheaval. This is of course more problematical. Was the Revolution a generator of radical thought or should we think more of continuity, a radical underground? Should we be stressing the novelty of the revolutionary situation or should we, to quote Hill in a more recent book, use the 'sudden Babel of unorthodoxy' between 1640 and 1660 to 'listen more carefully to the silences of the periods before and after'?[43] We still know surprisingly little about the silences. Derek Hirst has demonstrated that popular participation in the political process predated the Revolution. Perhaps 40 per cent of the adult male population had the vote by the mid seventeenth century. 'Those involved in the popular outbreaks of the 1640s had clearly had some form of political education beforehand.'[44] Other than that, little work has been done.

That ordinary women and men could and did (and do) resist, that they did not necessarily believe everything they were told, is a historical truth which needs to be reiterated. We should not be star-struck by the self-congratulatory image of the early modern English hierarchy. The ferment of the Revolution suggests that a 'class dominated society may contain an egalitarian society struggling to get out'.[45] Again we are in Hill's debt. But what we are also entitled to ask is how typical of popular thought and activity was the radical milieu? And there is a tendency in

The World Turned Upside Down, as Peter Burke has pointed out, in effect if not in intent, to conflate the radical with the popular. *The World Turned Upside Down* 'deals alternately with radical ideas and with the ideas of ordinary people, so that an incautious reader may very well be led to equate the two'.[46] Like Thompson's *Making of the English Working Class* there is all too little on popular conservatism or, in the case of *The World Turned Upside Down*, more traditional forms of popular protest.

Some of the lacunae have been filled since *The World Turned Upside Down* first appeared. By means of some innovative work with church-wardens' accounts, John Morrill has suggested that stubborn adherence to the rituals of the Church of England posed more of a challenge to reforming Puritans than the radical sects. He has not proved his case, but he has certainly established that popular Anglicanism is an important and neglected factor in the history of the Revolution.[47] There is also a growing literature on the Clubmen of the Civil Wars, popular traditionalists who in the mid 1640s banded together in their thousands to protect their communities against marauding armies and to defend traditional values and rights and 'the pure religion of Queen Elizabeth and King James'. They are a reminder that for large numbers of the common people local interests, community ties, were uppermost.[48]

Another aspect of popular activity which has been dealt with in more detail since the publication of *The World Turned Upside Down* is popular political ideology and protest as revealed in riot. There are now two good monographs and several important articles on riot in seventeenth-century England, what has been called the non-ideological, non-revolutionary side of popular protest: Buchanan Sharp's *In Contempt of All Authority* (1980) which deals with disturbances in the west of England; Keith Lindley's *Fenland Riots* (1982) which covers agitation against enclosure in the Fens; and the work of John Walter and Keith Wrightson on food riots.[49] Non-ideological is probably an inappropriate description, for there was a coherent rationale behind the riots of the seventeenth century. Rioters acted in defence of traditional rights and customs, such as the right to subsistence and the right of access to the common land. They were protecting the traditional economy against innovation; protecting standards and rights which the community thought were reasonable and just. Thus rioters were imbued with a strong sense of moral purpose. The ideology behind the riot, to quote Robert Malcolmson, was a mixture of 'custom, inherited expectations and moral evaluation', what E.P. Thompson has called the 'moral economy of the poor'.[50]

If we cannot say that the riot was non-ideological, we *can* say that it was non-revolutionary. The 'masterless men' of Christopher Hill's *The*

World Turned Upside Down are a far cry from the inhabitants of the Forest of Dean and the Fens who figure in the work of Sharp and Lindley. Rioters, although they did express class hatred, rarely articulated any notions of a radical restructuring of society of the sort to be found in the ferment of the 1640s and 1650s. They acted *in defence* of the status quo, persuading the magistrate to act against grain hoarders and speculators, fen drainers and enclosers. (Sharp calls rioting an 'extreme form of petitioning'.[51]) Historians usually remark on the orderliness and restraint of the rioters. There was never much chance for united insurrection – whatever the fears of the gentry – for grievances were immediate, localized and specific. Certainly there was, as Wrightson has put it, 'a strong element of negotiation in the tradition of riot'; rioters demanded that certain common rights be respected and that 'the authorities live up to the standards of their own paternalistic rhetoric'.[52] Occasionally, very occasionally it seems, rioters looked forward to a millennium in which the poor would 'enjoy their own'.[53] But generally, to quote Wrightson again, 'Riot posed no lasting threat in a society in which few ... imagined any alternative social order'.[54]

Historians have disagreed about the part played by this kind of behaviour in the events leading up to revolution. Sharp argues that apart from the fact that people used the upheaval of the Civil Wars as an opportunity to settle old scores, the riots of the Revolution demonstrated the 'indifference of many ordinary people in the West to the issues involved in the Civil War'.[55] His theme, then, is continuity of issues. Sections of the common people were concerned with disafforestation, food supply and enclosures during the Revolution just as they were before the upheaval. Manning argues, however, that such grievances merged with political and religious concerns to become an important factor in the drift to civil war. Rioters, he claims, identified enclosers with the regime of Charles I and tended later to see the royalists as the party of the landlords. He stresses popular support for Parliament, born of such tensions.[56] In contrast, Sharp maintains that rioters were hostile to landlords regardless of their political allegiances. The fact that many of such men of property happened to be royalist 'was quite incidental'.[57] Of course we do not need to plump for one or other of these interpretations. In fact Lindley has worked towards something of a synthesis. In some places in the Fens there was support for Parliament because of the King's support for the drainage and enclosing of the Fens and because the commons thought that Parliament might take action against the undertakers and enclosers. But generally the behaviour of the Fenland rioters supports the view 'that the bulk of the common people were indifferent to the great issues raised at Westminster'; 'for most fenmen their war was with enclosure, loss of common rights and enforced change, rather than with King or Parliament'.[58]

I have spent the last few pages discussing the book which Christopher Hill did not write, a cardinal sin for a reviewer. I now would like to deal more specifically with the book he did write. What, if any, are the internal weaknesses of *The World Turned Upside Down*? How has recent research modified its arguments?

When it appeared, reviewers made several criticisms of *The World Turned Upside Down*. One was that Hill had imposed too much order on the disparate groups he dealt with; it was all a bit 'too orderly and over-categorized' for the reviewer for *The Times Literary Supplement*.[59] Austin Woolrych saw dangers (as well as gains) in treating the radicals as though they constituted one 'brotherhood of social protest'.[60] Hill, to be fair, does refer to splits within the radicals and in fact relates these divisions to their defeat; but there is little doubt that the drift of his argument is towards unity rather than division, consistency rather than eclecticism. We should allow for inconsistencies. Bernard Capp has warned against 'imposing rigid categories on the mid-century flux of ideas'; he provides an example of a royalist, radical, episcopalian millenarian.[61]

Another criticism, which again Hill has anticipated, is what some historians have described as his tendency to over-explain popular protest; that he goes too far in rescuing the radicals from oblivion. Perhaps, suggests Gregor McLennan, who is by no means unsympathetic to the work of Hill, popular protest can at times be 'close to the "mindless" stereotypes beloved of conservatives'.[62] We should be wary of detecting rationality where it does not exist.

The wider issue of rationality is never really resolved in *The World Turned Upside Down*. Like Peter Worsley (and unlike Norman Cohn) Hill emphasizes the essential rationality of his popular religious movements in terms of their social situation.[63] In a sense we are back to 'culturalism': respect for the 'authenticity' and 'validity' of the thoughts and expressions of those being studied; Eric Hobsbawm's attempt to 'think and feel' himself 'into the skins' of his 'primitive rebels'.[64] Yet there is a certain tension in Hill's work very similar to the tensions in Hobsbawm's *Primitive Rebels*, which, despite its effort to meet the rebels on their own terms, still talks of them as 'pre-political', 'blind and groping, by the standards of modern [movements]'.[65] It is the same with Hill. 'The eloquence, the power, of the simple artisans who took part in those discussions is staggering.' 'How overwhelmingly right Milton's pride had been in the "noble and puisant nation, rousing herself like a strong man after sleep and shaking her invincible locks."'[66] Like beauty, madness is in the eye of the beholder. Madness itself may be a 'form of protest against social norms'; the lunatic may 'in some sense be saner than the society which rejects him'. 'We may be too conditioned by the way the world has been for the last three hundred years to be fair to those in the seventeenth century who saw other possibilities. But we should try.'[67] However, there are also vestiges of the old progressivist scientific Marxism, where rationalism is defined in twentieth-century Western, scientific terms, in terms of the development of 'dialectical science'. Many of the seventeenth-century radicals were 'ahead of the technical possibilities of their age'; 'Modern physics and chemistry are catching up with the dialectical element in their thought.' The revolt within the Revolution prefigures the Age of Reason. Radical thought trembles on the brink of secularism.[68] The forward-looking Winstanley is, as Keith Thomas puts it, the real hero of the book.[69] There is still this tendency to pick winners.

In his review of *The World Turned Upside Down* Thomas hinted that the section of the book dealing with the social context of radicalism did not cohere successfully with the section on ideology. This to my mind is the major weakness of the book. Throughout the volume there is a lack of precision about the identity of the radicals, a haziness concerning their social origins. The idea of linking land use with ideology, adopted by Hill though first proposed in England by Joan Thirsk and Alan Everitt, is an attractive one. David Underdown has had some success in linking the 'field: forest pasture antithesis' to popular allegiances in the Civil War.[70] But I think it would still be true to say that the hypothesis is yet to be proven. Land settlement may have some link with religious radicalism but there are many other factors which have to be taken into account.

We now know more about the social origins of the radicals of the upside-down world. The ideologists and leaders of the radicals and sectaries were often men or women of substance, alienated merchants, lesser gentry, wealthy farmers.[71] (The Leveller John Lilburne was known in Durham as a rack-renting landlord.[72]) But the rank and file was firmly of the 'middling sort': independent craftsmen and small traders, comfortable husbandmen, yeomen, and their wives, widows and daughters.[73] They were the less illiterate sections of the population, those who would have been included in a Leveller franchise. We should therefore think in terms of the Revolution radicals as predominantly of what were then called the 'middle sort of people', an amalgam of social groups stretching from the aspiring bourgeois to the lower-class elite, with interests which often clashed yet which could draw together in common 'hostility towards the nobility and gentry and richer classes'.[74] Then much of their ideology falls into place: the Fifth Monarchist and Leveller attack on monopolies and merchant oligarchies; the radical obsession with law reform; Quaker opposition to tithes; antipathy towards the monarchy, nobility and gentry. At the same time we can understand – with the notable exception of the Diggers – the radicals' attachment to private property. When they talked of reform they had in mind a nation of small producers with some limitations on the distribution of wealth. In one of the visions of the radical George Foster God appeared as a 'mighty Leveller', cutting down all those who 'were higher than the middle sort' and raising up 'those that were lower than the middle sort'. As I have suggested elsewhere, Foster's God personifies the social preoccupations of the revolution radicals.[75]

What of the future? There are signs that the history of seventeenth-century radicalism will soon be facing a revisionist revolt similar to that raging in Stuart parliamentary history. Here I refer to J.C. Davis's recent attempt to abolish the Ranters, one of the more sensational products of the world turned upside down. It is worth spending some time on his book, *Fear, Myth and History*, because it has been received as an explicit attack on the method and work of Hill.[76] Predictably, John Kenyon has greeted the 'abolition of the Ranters' with undisguised enthusiasm.[77]

The first point that needs to be made about Davis's work is that it builds upon the research of J.F. McGregor. Traditionally (in the work of Norman Cohn, G.F. Ellens, Hill and Morton) the Ranters were seen as a radical religious group which made a brief but dramatic appearance in 1649–50 during the English Revolution. But McGregor has argued that the Ranters were less a movement than a 'religious mood' and a few individuals who, although they differed 'in style and purpose', presented a 'reasonably coherent' doctrine: mystical antinomianism. McGregor has also suggested that to a large extent Ranterism was in the eye of the beholder: 'Ranters there may have been, but never so many as in the imaginations of those hostile observers on whose evidence we must generally rely.'[78] This work is crucial for Davis's thesis. (On rough count, McGregor is referred to, either in text or footnote, in 39 of Davis's 137 pages of analysis, and in 50 or more footnotes.) However, *Fear, Myth and History* takes McGregor's argument even further. There was no central core of Ranters, no Ranter theology; 'the Ranters did not exist'. At most, there were a 'few isolated individuals of heterogeneous persuasions'. They were a projection of deviance, 'a mythic projection'.[79]

If the Ranters did not exist, then why were contemporaries so exercised about them, and why did historians get things so wrong? Davis explains the seventeenth-century myth of the Ranters in terms of moral panic. The Ranters represented the anxieties of a particular historical moment, a collective recoil from the implications of revolution and the Puritan impulse, 'a projection reflecting contemporary anxieties and the desire for moral boundaries and conformity'. Reaction against the execution of a king, uncertainty for the future of religion, fear of social disorder, became fastened on to a group of manufactured deviants. The key to Ranterism, Davis argues, is not the activity of a few isolated individuals in 1649–50 but a panic in 1650–51. The twentieth-century myth, Davis claims, is the result of the 'egregious errors' of a group of historians 'predominantly of the left'. (His *group* is Hill and Morton!) According to Davis, they needed the Ranters to demonstrate a popular ideological revolution within the English Revolution, a challenge to bourgeois hegemony: if the Ranters did not exist 'they would have had to be invented'.[80]

What is wrong with all this? The last section of the book, on the twentieth-century historians, can easily be dispensed with. At the beginning of the book Davis pointed to the role of Cohn, McGregor and Ellens in the rediscovery of the Ranters, and to the counter-cultural mood of the late 1960s and early 1970s which found new relevance in the antinomianism of the English Revolution. By Chapter 6, however, Cohn and company have faded mysteriously from his argument and the whole affair has become a Marxist plot, the result of the baneful influences of the British Communist Party Historians' Group. The role of the student revolt of 1968 in stimulating interest in our radical past and the work of non-Marxists are conveniently forgotten: the Ranters are the invention of blinkered Marxists. (Incidentally, the disappearing Cohn article was published in the *right-wing* journal *Encounter*.) Apart from the dishonesty of the slide from Chapter 1 to Chapter 6, it is simply wrong to say that the Ranters are necessary for those who have a Marxist interpretation of Britain's past. The idea of a radical revolution within the wider English Revolution is not affected one jot by the presence or absence of the Ranters; they are but one aspect of a wider radical constellation. The cellulose in this chapter should be recycled.

As far as the seventeenth century is concerned, Davis provides a valuable, although not exactly novel, service in cautioning us against over-reliance upon hostile sources. He is right in his claim that we are all historiographical captives of the sensationalism of the anti-sectarian literature of the seventeenth century, both of its exaggerated reportage and its tendency to fit religious enthusiasm into neat sectarian boxes. But he goes too far. Laurence Clarkson's autobiography, he implies, cannot be used as a guide to his life because it was written when he was a Muggletonian – that is, it is biased. Thomas Edwards's *Gangraena* is not to be trusted as a guide to radical activity because it is hostile to radicalism. And yet many of the beliefs set out in *Gangraena* were expressed in radical pamphlets. John Holland's *The Snake of the Bottomlesse Pit*, a hostile source, claimed that the Ranters said that 'the

essence of God was as much in an ivie leaf as in the most glorious
Angel'; and we know from one of his own pamphlets that this was what
the 'Ranter' Jacob Bauthumley actually did say.[81]

Davis's forte is close textual analysis. He is persuasive with his
argument for the lack of theological coherence in what has traditionally
been assumed to be the Ranter core. (Although this does not mean that
the Ranters did not exist.) However, his obsession with the printed text,
with the signed, printed pamphlet as the only authoritative historical
source, useful only for the ideas of the person who actually signs that
pamphlet, leads him towards a kind of historical aridity. There is no
room here for the might-have-beens, little awareness of what are usually
called the silences of history. Ironically, outraged catalogues of errors
like *Gangraena* may have helped to spread the very ideas that they were
condemning. Davis debates the finer points of whether the core Ranter
writers stopped short of practical antinomianism: in Bauthumley's work
there was 'a paper-thin barrier' between theoretical and practical antinomianism.[82] What he cannot do is guarantee that the *readers* of
Bauthumley observed this same barrier. When reading *Fear, Myth and
History* it is easy to lose sight of the fact that the culture of seventeenth-
century England was substantially oral and that a great deal of debate
and exchange of ideas went on verbally, not in print.[83] Of course we are
not able to prove, nor should we assume, practical antinomianism. But
we should surely not rule it an impossibility just because the sources
claiming such behaviour are hostile or because no one wrote a pamphlet
about it.

This concentration on the analysis of pamphlets presents other
problems for Davis's argument. He has not used any manuscript
sources. He did not search the London court records for any possible
surviving indictments or depositions relating to alleged Ranterish
activity, or the Clarke Manuscripts for references to the alleged purge of
Ranters from the New Model Army. Nor did he consult the Quaker
letters of the early 1650s, which claim the existence of Ranters and
which, on occasion, set out encountered Ranter doctrine.

There are even difficulties with Davis's depiction of a panic in 1650–
51. Davis invokes the literature of folk devils and moral panics (Stanley
Cohen's classic study of Mods and Rockers), as well as material on the
manufacture of news. The reaction against the Ranters in 1650–51 is
described as 'the sensation'; there are references to the 'outpouring', the
'vigorous outpouring', of anti-Ranter pamphlets in what was, by seventeenth-century standards, 'a major press phenomenon'. What Davis is
actually writing about is a mere *ten* tracts produced in 1650–51, hardly a
sensation, even in seventeenth-century terms.[84]

In short, Davis has shown that the fears of the Revolution fastened upon a deviant group of the late 1640s, 'the Ranters'. He has not demonstrated that these fears created this group or that there was a mass panic. Davis has skilfully argued for a lack of theological coherence in the writings of several radical prophets traditionally associated with Ranterism. He has yet to persuade that they cannot best be described as Ranters. For all the argument in *Fear, Myth and History*, there was still a phenomenon in the late 1640s and early 1650s which contemporaries decided to call Ranterism. The Quakers encountered it. John Bunyan was troubled by it. The early Muggletonians moved among those whom they described as the 'Ranters people'. The Ranter *movement* may now have been buried once and for all, yet we are still left with what Hill once called the 'Ranter milieu'.

Perhaps 'revisionism' is a depressing note on which to end a paper on the 'world turned upside down'. But we can be sure that Christopher Hill's book will endure however much historians revise. For the greatness of the work is as a celebration of the upside down world where 'literally anything seemed possible'. 'It is remarkable', Raphael Samuel once wrote, 'how much history has been written from the vantage point of those who have had the charge of running – or attempting to run – other people's lives.'[85] Now the picture is less depressing. When we do have a comprehensive 'history from below' for the seventeenth century, it will be due in no small measure to the efforts of Christopher Hill.

Notes

1. C. Hill, 'Marxism and History', *Modern Quarterly*, vol. 3 (1948), p. 52.

2. 'An Interview with E.P. Thompson', *Radical History Review*, vol. 3, no. 4 (1976), p. 21. For a comprehensive introduction to British Marxist historiography, including the work of Hill, see H.J. Kaye, *The British Marxist Historians* (Oxford, 1984).

3. *Change and Continuity in Seventeenth-Century England* (London, 1974), ch. 3.

4. *Puritanism and Revolution* (London, 1968), ch. 3.

5. R. Johnson, 'Edward Thompson, Eugene Genovese, and Socialist–Humanist History', *History Workshop*, no. 6 (1978); 'Culture and the Historians', in J. Clarke, C. Critcher and R. Johnson, eds., *Working Class Culture* (London, 1979), ch. 2.

6. *New Left Review*, no. 11 (1961), p. 62.

7. 'A Bourgeois Revolution?', in J.G.A. Pocock, ed., *Three British Revolutions* (Princeton, 1980), ch. 2.

8. 'An Interview with E.P. Thompson', p. 21.

9. See C. Webster, ed., *The Intellectual Revolution of the Seventeenth Century* (London, 1974).

10. C. Hill, '*The English Revolution* Revisited', paper delivered at Humanities Research Centre, Australian National University, February 1981.

11. G. Stedman Jones, 'The Pathology of English History', *New Left Review*, no. 46 (1967).

12. '*English Revolution* Revisited'.

13. C. Hill, ed., *Winstanley: The Law of Freedom and Other Writings* (London, 1973), p. 10.

14. H. Marcuse, *An Essay on Liberation* (London, 1969); *The World Turned Upside Down* (London, 1972), pp. 336, 236–7.

15. R. Samuel, 'British Marxist Historians, 1880–1980', *New Left Review*, no. 120 (1980), pp. 55, 94.

16. J. Kenyon, 'Christopher Hill's Radical Left', *Spectator*, 8 July 1972, p. 55.

17. A.L. Rowse, *Discoveries and Reviews* (London, 1975), pp. 233–4.

18. *The Times Literary Supplement*, 18 August 1972, p. 969.

19. K. Thomas, 'The Ranters', *New York Review of Books*, 30 November 1972, p. 29.

20. R. Schlatter, in *American Historical Review*, vol. 78 (1973), p. 1054; R.C. Richardson, *The Debate on the English Revolution* (London, 1977), p. 104; A. Woolrych, in *History*, vol. 58 (1973), p. 291.

21. D. Caute, 'Three-Dimensional Men', *New Statesman*, 23 June 1972, p. 872; Richardson, *Debate*, p. 104; Woolrych, in *History*, vol. 58 (1973), p. 291.

22. I owe the information on sales to the kindness of Maurice Temple Smith, and Jenny Wilford (Press Officer, Penguin Books, London).

23. See Samuel, 'British Marxist Historians', pp. 42–3, 51–2; and (for a recent example) F. Brockway, *Britain's First Socialists* (London, 1980), foreword by Tony Benn.

24. *World Turned Upside Down*, p. 11.

25. Ibid., p. 17.

26. Ibid., p. 75.

27. Ibid., pp. 122–3, 127.

28. J. Reeve and L. Muggleton, *A Volume of Spiritual Epistles* (London, 1755), pp. 460–61.

29. *The Journal of George Fox*, N. Penney, ed. (New York, 1973), vol. 2, p. 149.

30. *Narrative Papers of George Fox*, H.J. Cadbury, ed. (Richmond, 1972), p. 51.

31. N. Cohn, *The Pursuit of the Millennium* (London, 1970), p. 304.

32. *World Turned Upside Down*, p. 141.

33. Ibid., p. 182.

34. L. Clarkson, *A Single Eye* (London, 1650), p. 10.

35. *World Turned Upside Down*, ch. 11.

36. Clarkson, *Single Eye*, Sig.A2v, pp. 7, 9–10; idem, *The Lost Sheep Found* (London, 1660), p. 25.

37. C. Hill, 'From Lollards to Levellers', in M. Cornforth, ed., *Rebels and Their Causes* (London, 1978).

38. *World Turned Upside Down*, p. 275.

39. J. Dunn, 'Triggers and Diggers', *Listener*, 3 August 1972, p. 152.

40. Hill, '*English Revolution* Revisited'.

41. B. Manning, *The English People and the English Revolution 1640–1649* (1976), chs. 1–5, 7–8, p. 111.

42. B. Reay, *The Quakers and the English Revolution* (London, 1985).

43. 'Why Bother about the Muggletonians?', in C. Hill, B. Reay and W. Lamont, *The World of the Muggletonians* (London, 1983), p. 11.

44. D. Hirst, *The Representative of the People?* (Cambridge, 1975), p. 105.

45. Hill, 'Why Bother about the Muggletonians?', p. 13.

46. P. Burke, 'People's History or Total History', in R. Samuel, ed., *People's History and Socialist Theory* (London, 1981), p. 7.

47. J. Morrill, 'The Church in England, 1642–9', in Morrill, ed., *Reactions to the English Civil War 1642–1649* (London, 1982), ch. 4.

48. For the growing literature on the Clubman, see D. Underdown, 'The Chalk and the Cheese: Contrasts among the English Clubmen', *Past and Present*, no. 85 (1979); R. Hutton, 'The Worcestershire Clubmen in the English Civil War', *Midland History*, vol. 5 (1979–80).

49. J. Walter and K. Wrightson, 'Dearth and the Social Order in Early Modern England', *Past and Present*, no. 71 (1976); J. Walter, 'Grain Riots and Popular Attitudes to the Law', in J. Brewer and J. Styles, eds., *An Ungovernable People* (London, 1980), ch. 2.

50. R.W. Malcolmson, *Life and Labour in England 1700–1780* (London, 1981),

p. 121; E.P. Thompson, 'The Moral Economy of the English Crowd in the Eighteenth Century', *Past and Present*, no. 50 (1971), p. 79.

51. Sharp, *In Contempt of All Authority*, p. 42.
52. K. Wrightson, *English Society 1580–1680* (London, 1982), p. 179.
53. Lindley, *Fenland Riots*, pp. 142–3.
54. Wrightson, *English Society*, p. 179.
55. Sharp, *In Contempt of All Authority*, p. 247.
56. Manning, *The English People*.
57. Sharp, *In Contempt of All Authority*, pp. 264, n. 9.
58. Lindley, *Fenland Riots*, pp. 142–3, 138, 160.
59. *The Times Literary Supplement*, 18 August 1972, p. 970.
60. Woolrych, in *History*, vol. 58, p. 290.
61. B. Capp, 'The Fifth Monarchists and Popular Millenarianism', in J.F. McGregor and B. Reay, eds., *Radical Religion in the English Revolution* (Oxford, 1984), p. 184.
62. G. McLennan, 'E.P. Thompson and the Discipline of Historical Context' in R. Johnson *et al.*, eds., *Making Histories* (London, 1982), pp. 114–15.
63. P. Worsley, *The Trumpet Shall Sound* (London, 1970); Cohn, *Pursuit of the Millennium*.
64. Johnson, 'Socialist–Humanist History', p. 84; 'Culture and the Historians', p. 64.
65. E.J. Hobsbawm, *Primitive Rebels* (New York, 1965), p. 2.
66. *World Turned Upside Down*, p. 293.
67. Ibid., pp. 13–14, 312.
68. Ibid., pp. 275, 299–301, 310, 313–19, 336.
69. Thomas, 'The Ranters', p. 29.
70. D. Underdown, *Revel, Riot and Rebellion: Popular Politics and Culture in England 1603–1660* (Oxford, 1985).
71. G.E. Aylmer, 'Gentlemen Levellers', *Past and Present*, no. 49 (1970); R.T. Vann, *The Social Development of English Quakerism* (Cambridge, Mass., 1969), ch. 2.
72. M. James, *Family, Lineage and Civil Society* (Oxford, 1974), p. 91.
73. See Capp, *Fifth Monarchy Men*, ch. 4; B. Reay, 'The Social Origins of Early Quakerism', *Journal of Interdisciplinary History*, vol. 11 (1980); idem, 'The Muggletonians: An Introductory Survey', in Hill *et al.*, *World of the Muggletonians*, pp. 49–53; J.F. McGregor, 'The Baptists', in McGregor and Reay eds., *Radical Religion*, ch. 2.
74. Manning, *The English People*, p. vi.
75. G. Foster, *The Sounding of the Last Trumpet* (1650), p. 17.
76. J. Kenyon, 'Justified Sinners', *Observer*, 14 December 1986, p. 23; B. Coward, 'Exaggerated Reports', *The Times Literary Supplement*, 6 February 1987, p. 143; E.P. Thompson, 'On the Rant', *London Review of Books*, 9 July 1987, pp. 9–10.
77. Kenyon, 'Justified Sinners'.
78. J.F. McGregor, 'Ranterism and the Development of Early Quakerism', *Journal of Religious History*, vol. 9 (1977); and McGregor, 'Seekers and Ranters', in McGregor and Reay, eds., *Radical Religion*, ch. 5.
79. J.C. Davis, *Fear, Myth and History* (Cambridge, 1986), pp. 124–5.
80. Ibid., pp. 95, 125, 134.
81. A.L. Morton, *The World of the Ranters* (London, 1970), pp. 70, 73.
82. Davis, *Fear, Myth and History*, p. 46.
83. See B. Reay, ed., *Popular Culture in Seventeenth-century England* (London, 1985).
84. Davis, *Fear, Myth and History*, pp. 76, 80.
85. R. Samuel, ed., *Village Life and Labour* (London, 1975), p. xiii.

How the Words Got on to the Page: Christopher Hill and Seventeenth-Century Literary Studies

Margot Heinemann

> The language appears to be the same, but ... the same words may describe quite different things. There was a Parliament in seventeenth century England, and a King; as we shall see, their functions were very unlike those of Parliament and Queen in England today. There were people called Puritans, but most of them were not killjoys or prudes. When Henry Vaughan sings 'How fair a prospect is a bright backside,' he doesn't mean what I suspect you may have thought. He is saying that it is nice to have a garden behind the house.
>
> Christopher Hill, 'A Different World from Ours', in *Seventeenth Century England: A Changing Culture* (Open University, 1980) p. 6.

A keen interest in literature has always coloured Christopher Hill's historical thinking, and the same is true of many of the pioneering English Marxist historians from Dona Torr and T.A. Jackson onwards. This was an advantage to their Marxism, says Eric Hobsbawm looking back, because it influenced them 'never to reduce history to a simple economic or "class interest" determinism, or to devalue politics or ideology'.[1] And it proved an advantage no less for literary studies. Much of the most distinquished Marxist literary commentary of recent years has indeed come from people who are primarily or partly historians – among them A.L. Morton, Victor Kiernan, E.P. Thompson, Jack Lindsay and Christopher Hill himself.

Some of these were left-wing students in the 1930s. Others, rather older, had links with the popularizing Marxist criticism of the 1930s and 1940s.[2] Leslie Morton had worked closely with Edgell Rickword, Montague Slater and Douglas Garman on *Left Review* and later on *Our Time*; Hill wrote on history and Rickword on Milton in a joint volume on *The English Revolution* (1940). In that time of crisis it seemed

73

urgent to reach ordinary non-specialist readers, to be accessible to the labour and working-class movement. Understanding literature was to give people confidence and vision to strive for a better world: and the sense of this potential audience set the style and tone of the critical work. It has been, I still think, a useful inheritance.

Christopher Hill does not, however, set up to be a literary critic in the accepted sense; indeed he rather insistently claims not to be one, on the grounds that 'such expertise as I have is not literary'. As he said with alarming modesty in a recent lecture on seventeenth-century radical prose to a literary audience: 'I am only a historian, so I shall say nothing about quality: the texts can speak for themselves. No doubt I let myself be influenced by content in a way that austere people like you will not.'[3]

This is not *only* a joke. If we think of literary criticism as exclusively concerned with close analysis of verbal texture, style and genre, leading perhaps to an attempt to establish a hierarchy of aesthetic values – the particular thing that university English departments claim to teach and history departments do not – we can see what he means, skilled and subtle reader though he is. And some university teachers do seem to think of it that way; for them anything else is sociology, not criticism. But the definition is absurdly narrow even for the over-specialized academic world: and outside it, in reviews or books for the general reader, modern media programmes, teaching in schools, the sterile demarcations are in practice increasingly being broken down. And while Hill has assimilated and learned much from critics with a different kind of expertise – for example Christopher Ricks, William Empson, Arnold Kettle, John Carey, A.J. Waldock, M.A. Radzinowicz, Rosemond Tuve – he has himself made a unique contribution not only to cultural history, but to enabling us to read seventeenth-century authors with as much interest as we read the living. Which means, of course, being engaged and 'influenced' by the content as well as the form.

True, as readers and students of seventeenth-century literature we are already provided with far more detailed historical and 'background' information than most of us know what to do with. Faced with so much erudition, it is a temptation to think we can simply send our students back to 'the words on the page'.[4] Let the poetry speak for itself in a plain text, and all will be well. The intention, as Hill has said, is admirable, but unlikely to succeed, at any rate with longer and more complex works (even if not everything needs the dense annotation it now gets). Literature *is* deeply concerned with ideas which enter into its form, and though we can be immediately struck or moved by parts of it (otherwise we would hardly care to explore further), yet to grasp the work as a whole we usually need to understand something of the ideas, which involves seeing them in their historical context. The alternative view, that we need not be much concerned with finding out the author's intention or meaning (which cannot be ours anyway), but only with the effect the text as it stands happens to have on us and the way we may decide to read it, is perhaps an understandable reaction against scholasticism. All the same, it is a counsel of despair and a high road to boredom. We can not become seventeenth-century readers, nor should we wish to. But awareness of how their situation and choices were different from ours does not make the works remote objects of antiquarian or sociological study; on the contrary, it sharpens our sense of human processes and possibilities.

What gives Hill's contribution to literary studies its unusual power is his ability to set a detailed, sensitive reading of the particular text within a clear general view of the processes of historical continuity and change. However skilled we are in close reading (as we need to be), it is impossible to make sense of Milton or Raleigh or Bunyan – or for that matter of Marlowe or Middleton – within a crude Roundheads-and-Cavaliers model of the history. Because of Hill's mastery of both historical evidence and imaginative literature, he is able to select the relevant fact or quotation in a way that avoids sinking the novel or poem under the weight of 'background' information,[5] yet lights it up for the reader. The accusation of 'lumping' with which J.H. Hexter attacked this necessary selective process seems in my own experience wholly unjustified. Whenever I have followed up Hill's glancing literary references, I have found them, even at their most unexpected, valid in context and revealing: one might cite the odd allusion to Tourneur in the essay on 'Clarissa Harlow and her Times',[6] or to Gerard Manley Hopkins in *Milton and the Puritan Revolution* (p. 96), as thought-provoking examples.

In literature as in history, each generation needs to reinterpret the past, because although the past does not change the present does. 'Each generation asks new questions of the past, and finds new areas of sympathy as it relives different aspects of the experience of its predecessors.... The interpretation will vary with our attitudes, with our lives in the present.'[7] We ought to be conscious that we too, as readers, are ourselves somewhere in history. Hill's questions, his areas of sympathy, have been especially important for my own and succeeding generations because he is concerned with the revolutionary process in all its complexity and contradictions, with the radical lower-class revolution that failed as well as the propertied one that succeeded; with people's dreams and visions of a more fulfilling life on earth as well as in Heaven; with the hard lives and difficult hopes of poor peasants and craftsmen and vagrants; with the magical promise of science and the longing for sexual fulfilment without fear or exploitation of women; with the long, often frustrating struggle to make freedom real for most people, which he traces back through Lollards and Levellers and which has manifestly not been completed anywhere yet. In this sense it is a socialist as well as a humanist approach.

One of Hill's important contributions has been to free students and teachers from the restrictive view of seventeenth-century literature that so many have absorbed while still at school from critical reading based on T.S. Eliot and F.R. Leavis and their followers, a view no less influential for being often assumed rather than explained, and hence not referable to historical evidence or rational argument. Ironically, Eliot and Leavis had originally appealed strongly to young radicals (like A.L. Morton and later Arnold Kettle) by articulating, in 'The Waste Land' especially, the sense of a capitalist culture doomed and breaking down.[8] Their negative view of revolutionary change in the seventeenth century was in part a reaction against complacent Victorian assumptions that it had been the seed-time of perfect liberty and progress. But they were expressing also their feelings of threat and deeper revulsion from the revolutionary movements of contemporary Europe, from socialism and democratic anti-Fascism as well as from Marxism. Cultural decline came to be attributed to the Civil War and the disruption of the traditional order by Puritan demands for individual freedom, and later by rationalism and materialism.

Eliot, still a great critic of seventeenth-century literature, frankly admitted that he read it in the light of his own prejudices, 'theological and political dispositions, conscious and unconscious'. The 'dispositions' are as clear in his essays on Lancelot Andrewes and Bishop Bramhall as in the more famous case of his antipathy towards Milton, a 'symbolic figure' in the Civil War that 'has never been concluded'.[9] Indeed they reach right down into his detailed literary comments and evaluations:

> Compare a sermon of Lancelot Andrewes with a sermon by another earlier master, Latimer. It is not merely that Andrewes knew Greek, or that Latimer was addressing a far less cultivated public.... It is rather that Latimer, the preacher of Henry VIII and Edward VI, is merely a Protestant; but the voice of Andrewes is the voice of a man who has a formed visible church behind him, who speaks with the old authority and the new culture. (*Selected Essays*, 1932, p. 320)

Andrewes's Jacobean sermons are here made out, anachronistically, to be the supreme expression of the *Elizabethan* Anglican Church, which 'in its persistence in finding a mean between Papacy and Presbytery became something representative of the finest spirit of England at the time'. In Andrewes we find 'that breadth of culture, an ease with humanism and Renaissance learning, which helped ... to elevate their Church above the position of a local heretical sect. They were fathers of a national Church and they were Europeans.' The Laudian Church thus becomes a *via media* rather than the authoritarian Rome-inclined ceremonialism that it seemed to Presbyterians, Independents and sectaries alike. And humanist learning becomes a special attribute of High Anglicanism, though in fact the 'mere Protestant' Milton had at least as much of it as Andrewes, and was in that sense equally European.

Above all, Eliot's way of reading was based on his political reactions to the late-capitalist crisis of the 1920s and 1930s – distrust of democracy and socialism, a longing for hierarchy and an authoritarian 'Christian society' against the free-for-all which he saw as leading to chaos.[10] So too his dislike of the 'inner voice' of revolutionary Nonconformity (which embraced Cromwell, the Quakers and Blake as well as Milton) not only matched but 'consciously or unconsciously' derived from his fear of egalitarian working-class politics in contemporary Britain:

> The inner voice ... sounds remarkably like an old principle ... of doing as one likes. The possessors of the inner voice ride twelve in a compartment to a football match at Swansea, listening to the inner voice, which breathes the eternal message of vanity, fear and lust. ('The Function of Criticism' (1923) in *Selected Essays*, p. 27)

Leavis, with less insight into his own thought processes, was equally elitist, but more inclined to present his findings as timeless non-political moral or aesthetic value judgements by 'those of us who are concerned to preserve the continuity of a higher cultural tradition'. Consistent in his hatred of modern 'mass civilization', he seems never to have felt much need to investigate how far the contrasting 'homogeneous' society and culture, which he inferred from artefacts like Cotswold cottages, folk-songs and the poems of Jonson and Thomas Carew,[11] had actually existed in the early seventeenth century (or ever). 'We ought to have known more,' concedes L.C. Knights, the most brilliant and historically minded of *Scrutiny*'s early contributors on this period. If they could have read Keith Thomas on the sufferings of the common people,[12] or Lawrence Stone on the crisis of the aristocracy,[13] they might, indeed, have been more inhibited in talking about the 'organic society'; but even that, he thinks, would not have altered their general conclusions.[14]

Hill challenged this (already establishment) slant in a sharp and witty review of the third volume of the *Pelican Guide to English Literature, From Donne to Marvell* (*Spectator*, 5 June 1956):

The title of this book is ... in itself something of a manifesto: many would call it 'The Age of Milton.' Most of the ten contributors are docile pupils of Mr. Eliot and Dr. Leavis. They follow fashion in disparaging Milton by comparison with the metaphysicals.

Milton and Bunyan accordingly get in not as central figures but as poor relations, and even then the stress is oddly placed on 'mysticism' in Milton and on 'painfully discovered' Roman Catholic and Anglican elements in Bunyan's thought, Tudor elements in his prose. Alongside this goes what Hill calls 'retrospective sycophancy' in some contributors:

> Is it useful literary criticism to say that Cavalier poets 'put the tone of the gentleman into poetry', that 'Andrew Marvell was a gentleman'? Can we really not appreciate Cavalier poetry without 'especially close sympathy with the social and cultural attitude and interests' of Charles I's court? ... George Herbert wrote his great poetry after he had turned away from the court: court taste probably accelerated the drama's deplorable slide into decadence under Charles.

The 'traditional values' so boldly assumed are not based on evidence. 'Laud's "great intellectual tolerance" had not been very obvious to the many protestants with whom he disagreed.' It's not just a question of differing interpretations of particular authors, however: 'failure to recognise the central position of the religious and political conflicts deprives the book of unity.' Only Pennington's essay on 'Political Debate and Thomas Hobbes' fully faces this issue.

Hill's confidence that all this represented a past and outmoded way of seeing seventeenth-century writing was, however, premature. Indeed this same *Pelican Guide to English Literature*, vol. 3, after being reprinted fifteen times, has been reissued in 1982 as the *New Pelican Guide*, vol. 3, supposedly 'completely revised and updated'. But despite minor modifications (extra footnotes, paragraphs rewritten here and there in a minority of the articles, a few new essays on marginal topics, a chapter on Milton criticism), substantially it is still the same book; and the editor of the series, Boris Ford, has defended this on the grounds not only that it still sells, but that the Leavis outlook is in no way dated and that the 'very rigorous, highly selective minority-oriented approach of *Scrutiny*' is still the right one.[15] Indeed the slogan of 'minority culture' (easily translated as 'more means worse') has even more resonance in the time of higher education cuts than it did in the expansionist days of 1956. And this is still what is presented to undergraduates and sixth-formers in the most easily available commentary on the seventeenth century.[16] The argument has to continue.[17]

Neither Eliot nor Leavis ever spelled out the history on which they based their confident judgements about traditional values and their nostalgia for the Christian society or 'organic society' allegedly lost in the seventeenth century. Hill's coherent counterstatement of literary and cultural change, on the other hand, though it is not fully developed in a single critical work, does exist, in a highly condensed form, in the 'Religion and Ideas' sections of *The Century of Revolution* and the corresponding sections of *From Reformation to Industrial Revolution.* Although the compression means that complex processes often have to be simplified, these brief outlines remain remarkably pregnant and suggestive. Moreover their positioning in the book (within each period in *The Century of Revolution* they follow sections on (a) 'Narrative of Events', (b) 'Economics', and (c) 'Politics') makes clear that literary analysis has to be seen as closely interrelated with, and indeed starting from, the analysis of economic change and social and class struggles – an obvious point Hill has sometimes been criticized by other Marxists for not stressing explicitly every time he takes up his pen. Some aspects of the analysis are explored in greater depth in the literary parts of *Intellectual Origins of the English Revolution* and *Some Intellectual Consequences of the English Revolution.*

The value of this clear overview (although it is often modified or extended in later writings, for instance in relation to the growth of science and the role of magic) comes out in his treatment of individual writers in articles and reviews over many years, including 'Society and Andrew Marvell' (1946); 'Clarissa Harlowe and Her Times' (1955); 'Henry Vaughan' (1969);[18] 'Bunyan and Rochester' [Appendix to *The World Turned Upside Down* (1972)]; *Winstanley* (1973); *Milton and the English Revolution* (1977); 'George Wither' (1980);[19] 'John Bunyan and the English Revolution' (1979). Since I wrote this essay, it has been summed up in the masterly introduction 'The Pre-revolutionary Decades', in *Writing and Revolution in Seventeenth-Century England* [*Collected Essays of Christopher Hill,* vol. 1 (1985)].

In Hill's view, conflict in society, deep and sometimes violent, is not incidental but the central context of seventeenth-century literature at least until 1688. In the pre-revolutionary period we could tell simply by reading the literature of the time that two sets of standards were in conflict (*The Century of Revolution,* p. 81) though after the first decade of James's reign, as the divisions in society became more acute and the censorship tighter, their expression was less public than it had been in *Dr Faustus* or *King Lear.* As the conflict became too intensely personal to be played out on the censored stage, it was more and more expressed in what we call metaphysical poetry. The essence of this kind of lyric is 'its paradox, its sharp antitheses, its clutch at connections apparently the

most incongruous, its agonizing soul-questionings and search for salvation, its sense of the contrast between subjective and objective, desire
and possibility'. In all this it belongs to a period of intense challenge to
traditional authority by new ways of thinking, the readiness to test
everything by reason and experiment, a scepticism seen as terrifying and
subversive by some writers and liberating by others.[20]

> In this broad sense we may speak of the lyric of conflict, whose characteristics
> are an awareness in the poet's mind of the new and troubling (especially the
> new scientific discoveries) as well as the old and familiar, and an effort to fit
> them into a common scheme – first by the violent and forced juxtaposition of
> Donne, then by the unresolved conflict of the later metaphysicals; until finally,
> after the victory of the new political and intellectual forces, we get a new type
> of poetry drawing on new philosophical assumptions, and disturbed by none
> of the doubts which have tormented the sensitive since the days of Shake-
> speare. The tortured conceit gives way to the neatly balanced rhymed couplet.
> (*Puritanism and Revolution*, p. 341)

Reading Elizabethan and Jacobean literature in this way works
strongly against recent representations of the Civil War as a kind of
accident, the result of short-term self-interest, political ineptitude and
random causes, with nothing at stake that could not have been settled by
sensible men sitting round a table in 1640 (a view Hill has strongly
contested). Profound divisions in thought and feeling among the 'natural
rulers' in court and country, and between them and the lower orders
whose fate was 'only to be ruled', can be traced over the half-century
before war broke out in the writings of Marlowe and Shakespeare,
Chapman and Greville, Drayton and Daniel, minor figures like Wither
and Hubert. Not only ideas but passions and loyalties are evoked in the
representation of inner and outer conflict – over the rights of monarchs
and aristocracy, religion and law, the power of commercial wealth, the
claims of honour, the luxury and arbitrariness of kings, even the
confrontation – in *King Lear* and *Coriolanus* – of arrogant rich and
hungry poor. As *Intellectual Origins* demonstrates, these divisions and
contradictions appear in the literature not only as conflicts between
social groups or classes, but within groups and within the minds of
individuals like Bacon, Raleigh or Greville. Once we realize that not all
Puritans or revolutionaries were killjoys who took William Prynne's
attitude to the threatre – a matter I have myself been stimulated to
explore by Hill's writings[21] – we find overwhelming evidence of social
crisis in the dissident plays of Middleton, Massinger and Brome, as well
as in the court's self-adoring and immensely expensive masques from
Jonson to Davenant. Pre-revolutionary England, as far as the literature

enables us to enter into its experience and ways of feeling, was manifestly not a harmonious 'Christian society' or 'organic society,' but one already felt to be riven by irreconcilable conflicts of principle and desire.

In contrast to the traditionalist image of the revolutionary years as at best a barren interruption of the great line of literature by Puritan dogmatism and fanaticism, or at worst a kind of second Fall of Man making irrevocable a general cultural decline,[22] Hill sees the period from 1640 to 1660 as one of intense intellectual activity, profoundly altering literary forms and concerns (even though the radical 'second revolution' failed and Milton and Bunyan had to write their major works in the enemy climate of the Restoration). The most striking stylistic legacy was the growth of plain prose, rapidly developed by the pamphleteers on both sides in the 1640s to reach a popular audience after the collapse of the royal censorship. In different ways Dryden and Bunyan were its inheritors.

Insights derived from Hill's study of the Ranter and antinomian ideas which surfaced in the mid century also suggest new and penetrating ways of reading Restoration and later literature. There were affinities between Ranters and royalists in their opposition to the protestant ethic: the wits of Charles II's court, insecurely restored to the highest positions in a society increasingly alien to them because increasingly commercial, were not above reproducing the ideas of Ranters and radicals (or the radical ideas of Hobbes) to shock the victorious bourgeoisie. The prose of Restoration comedy too draws on the popular style established in the revolutionary years, and the anti-clerical and irreligious ideas of the dramatists, as of Rochester's satires, are rooted in those of the Ranters. (Indeed Aphra Behn, one of the most iconoclastic, sets on stage a sympathetic Widow Ranter, a drinking, smoking, sword-fighting feminist.) This analysis of Restoration drama makes better sense than attributing its tone either to 'French influence' or simply to a reaction against Puritanism (though of course it was that too), or merely regretting that 'its attitudes towards experience are immature'.[23] Because this drama was restricted by the theatre monopoly to an upper-class audience, and hence not as dangerous as the old popular drama had potentially been, it could, as long as it kept off politics, be more openly cynical and morally sceptical.

After 1688, with the ending of what Hill calls the 'fruitful social tensions' which had fuelled the great drama and the epic, censorship was relaxed. The rise of a middle-class reading public made writers less dependent on patrons; sentimentalism and poetic justice in drama reconciled the commercial classes to the theatre. The sense of control of its own life by the victorious middle class corresponded to a new this-worldly realism (as in Defoe), its great achievement the 'realistically earthbound' novel. Puritanism lost its revolutionary fervour, the king-dom of Heaven was deferred to the next world, and the mechanical philosophy replaced the semi-magical universe of correspondences and analogies: 'It became normal for poets to find themselves alienated from their society, sometimes to the point of madness.'[24]

In working out this map Hill, unlike most literary historians, high-lights the role of the censorship as one of the crucial factors. With the expansion of printing and the cheap commercial theatre in the sixteenth century, the state-tuned pulpit was no longer the only way to stir ordinary people, and the need to control the unprecedented flow of ideas became much more urgent. 'The most important event in the history of English literature in the seventeenth century, in my view, is the collapse of the censorship in 1641' (*Essays in Criticism*, April 1982). The whole of pre-revolutionary literature, and indeed of post-Restoration literature too, looks rather different once we realize that it was produced under a strong political and religious censorship which put life and livelihood at risk, and that what was printed or staged was not simply what the writers thought and felt but what they were allowed to say. A quarter of a century ago, replying rather tartly to the argument that the court of Charles I was favourable to the full development of minor talents ('but not of major ones', growled Hill), he declared that 'the absence of censorship in the 1640s did more for literature than the court had ever done'. Not only was there a vast outpouring of books and pamphlets and newspapers on a scale never before possible, but writers could publish freely who had never before been able to do so.

The understanding of this partly determines how we should read seventeenth-century writers, and has undoubtedly influenced Hill in directing so much research, especially on Milton, to uncovering mean-ings deliberately made obscure at the time – the cryptogram aspect of literary study. This is one important reason for making a historical approach, as he sees it, rather than limiting consideration to 'the words on the page'.

> It seems to me that there is in effect a conspiracy between seventeenth century censors and some twentieth century literary critics who believe that a poem should speak for itself, divorced from history; who do not sufficiently consider the processes in consequence of which some words get on to the page and others get left off. (*Some Intellectual Consequences*, p. 47)

Thus one can not argue that Milton was not an anti-Trinitarian because he never published an anti-Trinitarian poem, when to do so would have been to risk imprisonment or even death. The same doubts apply to the great Elizabethans.

Those who want to find 'Christian humanism' in the writings of Shakespeare and his contemporaries can always find it; but it may be no more satisfactory as evidence of genuine beliefs than is Milton's orthodoxy. It was what men were allowed to say. (Ibid., p. 48)

Milton's is a unique case because it enables us to see, from the prose writings of the revolutionary years when he was relatively free to express his ideas, and from the later and unpublishable *De Doctrina Christiana*, just what it was that could not be said directly in the great poems. But, as I have argued elsewhere,[25] it is salutary too to remember that the Jacobean dramatists, for example, *could not* show a lower-class revolt as justified, or ridicule devout Anglican clerics (as distinct from papists or Puritans), rather than to assume that their minds were effectively blocked by the 'Elizabethan world picture' (actually crumbling at this time). A truly historical approach, here as so often, makes the writers and their view of reality seem closer to us than if we suppose them all to have completely internalised the Book of Homilies and the learned treatises of James I on witchcraft and the divine right of kings.

Hill's is very much a humanist criticism, in the sense that it is focused on people and their lived experience. This is not quite the bland platitude that it may sound, for much recent criticism has been self-consciously anti-humanist, and humanist criticism has indeed been rather unfashionable since Eliot laid it down that 'the more perfect the artist, the more separate in him will be the man who suffers and the mind which creates'. In some varieties of modern Marxist criticism too,[26] 'humanism' is seen as a trap to avoid, and the word is treated as necessarily implying belief in an unchanging metaphysical 'human essence', rather than defined in the historical terms of change and development. The human subject, as author or reader or narrator, is 'decentred', the bearer of an ideology which determines what we call his/her experience as well as the expression of it. The text, properly deconstructed, may reveal the ideology which underlies it, but not a 'real world' which is inherently unknowable. The universe, in this view, is literally made out of language; we can study words but not things. Yet as Raphael Samuel has put it in relation to history:

It is one thing to point to the displacement which took place in any process of thought, and to emphasise the mediations which separate representation and reality. It is quite another to resolve the problem by abolishing one of its terms entirely, by jettisoning the notion of the real.[27]

Hill's method, on the contrary, is to start from the situation of the writer and his audience, living and acting in a real economic and social world at a particular time, and locate tradition and ideology in relation to it. This is not just a question of humanizing the style, though it certainly does that: it radically affects the analysis. Conscious and informed as he is about the pressures and limitations imposed by existing habits of thought, he never treats the individual writer – still less the particular work – simply as determined by and embodying the consistent and coherent outlook of a social class, and is in no danger of collapsing literature back into the ideas which help to form and structure it.

Because he *knows* so much ('empirically,' as the theoreticists patron-izingly say) about how people at different levels lived and thought, Hill can bypass the 'argument within English Marxism' to some extent. He can show the pressure of tradition and custom in forming and limiting a writer's language and way of seeing, without needing to diminish the human subject as maker of the work and active agent in history. In his writing there can still be what Brecht calls 'famous forebears', working people who suffer and struggle, even sometimes heroic examples.

To 'deconstruct' a literary text to show how it distorts reality is at best only a beginning. The next (and more interesting) stage is to reread it to reveal not only the distortions, but the complex insights it offers into a real changing world of lived experience – a concrete, sensory and psychological world which the writers and their audience know, up to a point, better than we do, and which in some respects and to some degree we can still share. This is not naive romantic illusion; imaginative litera-ture may well evoke or represent aspects of material reality, feelings and fantasies, which accepted patterns of thought and morality normally ignore or suppress. Again, writers are not always consistent or coherent about their ideas and beliefs, which often muddle or break out of the firm and congruent 'traditions' the scholars have selectively established for them. Inner conflict, choice and action remain crucial for historical change. To use an analogy which comes ready to hand, Hill's Marxism is of the 'radical Arminian' rather than the 'high Calvinist' kind.

As well as re-reading what are regarded as classical texts, a Marxist approach will necessarily challenge the single 'great tradition' of aristo-cratic and high bourgeois culture, recovering alternative Utopian, scientific and popular traditions[28] and directing attention to the works of underrated democratic or satirical writers, as Hill has done with Marprelate and the Levellers, Winstanley and Thomas Scott. But this does not mean simply dividing seventeenth-century works into 'progres-sive' and 'reactionary'; for Hill is profoundly aware of the ironies of 'progress' at this period, its double and contradictory character, especially for those at the bottom of the heap, evicted peasants and debt-enslaved craftsmen. In 'Clarissa Harlowe and Her Times' (1955) he specifically draws attention to a central irony. 'Thanks to the courage of the religious revolutionaries, a society had been established in which the money power ruled', an increasingly commercial patriarchal society in which the oppression of women through property marriage was intensified. To understand how the system of land tenure had changed, how important the concentration of estates was to a gentry family out for political influence and noble status, makes the brutal selfishness of Clarissa's relatives and Lovelace's savage will to power more convincing and terrifying, and Clarissa is seen as heroic rather than merely prudish in her resistance. Her agony is related to the struggle of the isolated Puritan conscience, but reveals also (whether Richardson was conscious of it or not) the 'fundamental flaw' of a conventional Puritan morality in which men are more equal than women, a morality which was not to be overtly opposed till the romantic-revolutionary age.

The analysis of irony and 'doubleness' is clear in Hill's treatment of Marvell, beginning with a much-anthologized essay which at the time it was first published (1946) was very unusual in trying to link the particular qualities of his poetry, in form as well as content, to the social and political situations through which he lived and his response to them. Once the point has been made, indeed, it may seem obvious – that the tension between action and inaction, soul and body, retirement and worldliness, ideal and brutal reality, sexual passion and religious spirit can be related ('very indirectly,' as Hill says) to the irreconcilable conflicts of the revolutionary years; and that this is true not only of the political 'Horatian Ode' (with its astonishingly delicate balancing of 'ancient right' against the irresistible 'force of angry Heaven's flame', King Charles againt Cromwell), but also of poignant personal lyrics like 'The Declaration of Love' and the Mower songs, of formal country-house poems in the classical mode like 'Appleton House'. The witty self-mockery does not annihilate the real struggle, though, as Hill says, one of Marvell's attractive qualities is his humour, his 'refusal to take his agonies too seriously' – itself an aspect of the 'double heart'.[29] His later work has reinforced the analysis historically rather than changed it.[30]

Robinson Crusoe, again, has usually been regarded as a simple case ever since Marx used it in *Capital* to distinguish use-value and exchange-value. Here truly is the literature of capitalist individualism, its hero an exemplar of the Protestant virtues, achieving happiness through industry, thrift, overseas trade and colonization. And yet within this context Hill's careful reading[31] brings out complexities and ambiguities, implied criticisms of conventional bourgeois moral and religious assumptions. Thus Crusoe works out his own version of natural religion, making little difference between Protestant and Catholic where to do so would hinder colonization, and unconcerned about the forms of baptism and marriage – in this more a man of the Enlightenment than a traditional Puritan. So too Crusoe (and Defoe) records both sides of European commerce and colonization, its violent exploitation as well as its 'civilizing' role, yet seems undecided about slavery and the degree of coercion allowable against 'backward' Indians. Hill powerfully per-suades us to 'suspect that Defoe was more aware of the ambiguities and contradictions in Crusoe's attitudes than commentators have already allowed'. Approaching him from the seventeenth century, he does not 'necessarily expect Defoe to be consistent in his thinking': he learned his theology 'not from a few books but from a lifetime's immersion in a cultural environment of decaying Puritanism'. And he reminds us, without making it a single sufficient cause, of Defoe's earlier radicalism, when he joined Monmouth's rebellion and was lucky to escape a traitor's death. Great writers may be inconsistent, using different and perhaps logically incompatible value-elements from different ideological 'sets'. Moreover, ideas may change their nature over time: victorious Puritanism in 1719 is not the same as the militant millennial Puritanism of Milton's or Bunyan's day. Observation and practice in what (in spite of structuralism) has to be called the real world interacts with the way ideologies are combined or modified by the writer.

The historical dimension is necessary: to read even the most democratic of seventeenth-century works as if they were modern is usually to oversimplify and sometimes to reject them. How, for instance, are we to understand the contradictions in Bunyan, in whose writings class-conscious plebeian feeling and language go along with hellfire preaching, and unbending condemnation of sinners who think they can be saved by their own efforts – attitudes which many readers now feel they have to ignore if they are to respond to him at all?

Hill's searching analysis[32] relates these jarring elements through the changing social and religious experiences brought to bear on Bunyan throughout his life – the radical atmosphere he found as a young conscript in the New Model Army, in a garrison where Ranter and antinomian ideas were rife; the personal conversion to Calvinism, which coincides in time with the decline and repression of radical extremism in the early 1650s; the sectarian democracy of his Bedford church, where the congregation freely discussed as religious issues much that we would now call political;[33] the class purge of local and national government and persecution of dissenters after the Restoration, when 'the vision of a humanity that controlled its own destiny disappeared'. In this light, Bunyan's defiance of the judges who ordered him to stop preaching, and his long imprisonment, are seen as the obstinate defence not simply of an out-of-date covenant theology, but of new freedoms for the common people briefly won by the sects in the revolutionary years.

True, as Hill emphasizes, in *Pilgrim's Progress* the 'upside-down

world' of millennial justice to which the wayfaring Christian is journey-
ing has been deferred beyond the grave. Yet Bunyan's work remains
consistent and subversive in its sympathy for the poor and hardworking,
its contempt for idle 'lords and great ones', and its fighting spirit, forti-
fied by his conviction of salvation, which appealed to later generations
of radical working men who had little sympathy with his theology.

In *Milton and the English Revolution*, by far the longest, most ambitious
and most sharply attacked of his writings on literature to date, Hill
presents Milton not just as a fine writer but as 'the greatest English
revolutionary who is also a poet, the greatest poet who is also a revolutionary'. This is certainly how Blake and Shelley saw him, but it causes a
good deal of controversy now. It runs counter not only to the still
influential 'demotion' attack mounted in the 1930s by Eliot and Leavis
(with useful fictional help from Robert Graves) which made Milton
personally antipathetic, poetically insensitive and hollow, 'disastrously
single-minded and simple-minded' (Leavis), his sympathies narrow and
his theology 'repellent'. It is equally a challenge to more modern
attempts, notably by the later Eliot (1947), C.S. Lewis and C.A.
Patrides among others, to salvage as much of Milton as possible for
'orthodoxy'. By the time of Eliot's *Little Gidding* Milton and Charles I
had become 'united in the strife that divided them' – a turn which for
many moderns has made Milton even harder to read.

It is quite wrong, however, in Hill's view, to relate Milton to anything
so vague and generalized as 'the Christian tradition'. He was a radical
Protestant heretic, at a time when both innovative and conservative
thinking were normally articulated in Christian terms. The book
demonstrates not only the nature of the heresies (already studied in
depth by Saurat, Empson and others) but their connections with the
most radical social and political thoughts of the age, what Hill calls the
'third culture' – the popular heretical culture which rejected the ideas
both of court and established Church and also of orthodox Puritanism.
This demonstration is important because by the time Milton's secret
treatise *De Doctrina Christiana* was published in 1825, religious heresy
as such was no longer revolutionary, and without such interpretation its
embodiment in the great poems can seem irrelevant to the ordinary
reader, another pedantic monument to dead ideas.

For reasons of space I can touch only on Hill's re-reading of the late
poems, though his book makes one realize more than ever how
unsatisfactory it is to separate Milton's poetry from his prose writings.
Indeed a sharp separation between prose, in which one thinks, and
poetry, in which one feels but is not expected to think, does not work
very well for any period, and certainly not for the seventeenth century.

Milton wrote with his left hand for different audiences and different occasions; those who accuse Hill of reading poetry as if it continued the prose by other means are missing the point. It is, indeed, the requirements of rational argument that give rise to the characteristic long Miltonic verse paragraph, the structural unit of his epic poems.

Hill's original reading of the major poems starts from two hypotheses. First, that they are centrally concerned with the problems posed by the failure of the English Revolution, in whose disillusioned aftermath they were written. Secondly (and more controversially), that the way in which Milton works on these problems is related to his uneasy position 'between the second and third culture,' between the official parliamentary-Puritan milieu and that of the radicals, which includes lower-class sectaries, Ranters, antinomians:

> If we think of him as carrying on a continuous dialogue with the extreme radicals, it becomes easier to see him rejecting with his intellect ideas which were familiar to him and which one half of his being accepted.... He was not of the devil's party without knowing it: part of him knew that part of him was. (p. 243)

Moreover, the strict censorship under which he had to write and publish meant that his more subversive ideas were expressed obliquely, though they were probably clear enough to those of the 'fit audience though few' to whom he was most concerned to speak.

To read *Paradise Lost* in this way is not, as some of Hill's critics have argued, to treat the poem simply as political allegory, ignoring its human and religious dimensions. Their argument artificially divides the religious from the political, the Bible story from events analogous to it in later times. For Milton, the Fall was a historical event, but it was also a metaphor for man's failure to live up to his own standards:

> *Paradise Lost* tells an epic story which is also a true story; but the story sums up the whole of human experience, including the valuable experience recorded in the myths of classical antiquity. It is truth and myth at the same time, and on both counts it has something to say to God's servants who had been defeated in the English Revolution. (p. 344)

So it is not 'diminishing' to see Abdiel, the loyal angel, as standing where Milton wished to stand, or his debate with Satan as less universal because it embodies arguments that had raged among revolutionaries in Milton's own time. Heaven and Hell are both real and metaphorical, images of states of mind. To complain as Leavis did that the sufferings of the damned are not concretely and consistently portrayed is to demand that Milton should be like Bosch rather than like Marlowe. No doubt he still believed in a literal Hell, because it was in the Bible; but some radicals did not, and the belief in it as a place of physical torment was on its way out. His visions of joy and woe do not depend on the torture house at all.

'Out of the quarrel with others we make rhetoric, out of the quarrel with ourselves poetry.' It is part of the emotional power of *Paradise Lost* that evil in it includes so much that to Milton had once seemed good. The fallen angels have many royalist characteristics, of course, but Satan alludes also to some of the worst aspects of the revolutionaries – the avarice and ambition of the generals who betrayed the republic, the irreligious and divisive speculations of Ranters and other extreme radicals. In tempting Eve, Satan echoes many Ranter arguments.

'Satan then is not a flat allegorical figure, to be equated either with royalists, Ranters or major-generals. Milton saw the Satanic in all three' (p. 343). To put it another way, in imaginatively embodying the father of evil Milton drew – as he must – on his own deepest experience. Because he had been a rebel, he now needed to know what kind of rebellion was justified and what was not, what caused good men to fall. And he needed above all to work through to a renewal of hope: to the achievement of Paradise within, through continued effort which would be something more than passive acceptance of defeat:

> by things deemed weak
> Subverting worldly strong, and worldly wise
> By simply meek.

This explains the intensity of Milton's commitment to 'justify the ways of God to men'. If, like William Empson or some of his own Ranter and Seeker contemporaries, Milton had believed that the God whom most Christians worshipped was a wicked God, he would have had no motive to write the poem. But if he had not been aware that such ideas were held, if he had not himself been tempted to anger or despair of God – not just for Adam's fall, but for the failure of the Good Old Cause to which he and others had sacrificed so much – he could not have written it either.[34] The poem assumes, says Hill, the whole Interregnum discussion on the Fall, the doubts about God's justice recognized by others besides Milton. And he is right, I think, in seeing Milton as bitterly accepting (because he must) the Father whose will is fate and history, but feeling out of tune with him, and himself 'aspiring more and more to the position of union with the perfect man who becomes God's son by merit' – itself a heretical, anti-Trinitarian belief.

These insights help to illuminate, though not to smooth away, some of the contradictions and conflicts that have so often been felt as problematic and paradoxical within the poem – the heroism and attractive power of Satan; the double evaluation of sex and sexual love; the apparent cruelty, hierarchic absolutism and remoteness of God the Father: the desire for knowledge as the cause of disaster; the condemnation (in *Paradise Regained*) of classical learning as a snare. It is not merely a question, Hill suggests, of rationally discussing and choosing between two sets of ideas, but of a personality 'in some deeper way internally torn' between orthodox Puritan and extreme radical reactions. Here, as in the earlier comments on Marvell and Vaughan, personal and psychological conflicts are related to social and political ones, to the writer's practice in the real world.[35]

The criticisms of this interpretation have been of two kinds, those which challenge the specific historical points involved, and those which object to the whole way in which literature and history are shown as interrelated.

Do we really need, as Hill proposes, to modify our image of Milton the cloistered scholar (an image naturally dear to cloistered scholars) by assuming that he got his ideas 'not only from books but by talking to his contemporaries'? The fact that he held many heretical and subversive ideas in common with seventeenth-century radicals can now hardly be disputed: but after all most of these ideas (like most of those he rejected) were to be found in books to which he had access. What *is* disputed is that he must have known, must even have been influenced by knowing, that such ideas circulated widely, and among the lower orders as well as the educated. Yet this is surely crucial for reading the poems. For instance, there would have been little point in Satan, and later Eve under his influence, arguing like Pelagius if the 'popular Pelagianism of the sectaries' had not been a force in Milton's own time. Such ideas can indeed be traced back over a thousand years to the early Fathers; but it is the contemporary context that guides the selection.

Of course seventeenth-century writers usually buttress their most innovative arguments with appeals to ancient and classical authority: but this does not mean that they necessarily arrived at their views by consulting such authority. Milton in *The Tenure of Kings and Magistrates*, defending the execution of Charles I, supported his cause with quotations from Aristotle, Tertullian, St Basil, St John Chrysostom and St Gildas, but it would be naive to suppose that he wanted to defend it *because* he had read the early Fathers and been convinced by them. (Indeed Professor Hexter might well have accused him of source-mining and 'lumping' here.) Milton's classical reading provided him with endless examples and analogies both with the biblical account of the Fall and with his own bitter experience of failure and defeat; it did not originate the bitterness.

Although some reviewers have scorned the thought that the austere elitist Milton could have been in contact with radicals, some of them plebeian ones, who often discussed their ideas in alehouses, the book does incidentally produce quite a lot of evidence of such connections. Milton's doctor and friend Nathan Paget certainly had many radical, even Ranter and Familist books in his library. Cyriack Skinner, one of his closest friends, chaired meetings of the republican Harringtonian Rota Club which met alternately in a coffee house and a tavern. Isaac Pennington senior, leader of the London Puritans and father of Milton's friend, ran an ordinary. And Alexander Gil the younger, close to Milton from his schooldays at St Paul's and for many years after, was a drinking man and a frequenter of taverns (though it may comfort academic Miltonists to know that Gil, who was imprisoned in 1628 for drinking a health to Buckingham's assassin, committed the offence while on a visit to Trinity College, Oxford).

But of course Hill's argument doesn't *depend* on proving direct personal links between Milton and the lower classes or getting him into a pub. The point is that many of the ideas he uses were circulating in that world, whence anyone could pick them up – as indeed *Areopagitica* makes clear in describing the intellectual ferment in London in the 1640s. In later years he may well have had less sympathy and contact with plebeian radicals.

Hill has been criticized more seriously for seeing Milton as 'between two cultures' at all.[36] It is argued that in so doing he reads back the preoccupations of twentieth-century revolutionaries (basing their hopes on the revolt of the lowest class, the organized proletariat) into the quite different conditions of the seventeenth century, and hence overestimates the importance of plebeian radicals in what was straightforwardly a bourgeois revolution. On this view, if Hill had not been guided by his own socialist and libertarian concerns to explore in depth the activities of fringe groups like Diggers, true Levellers and Ranters, he would never have supposed that Milton paid much attention to their ideas. To present him as wavering between the culture of orthodox disciplined Protestant values, some of which we find repellent, and the libertarian and antinomian ones which may now seem more attractive, is to make him behave like a liberal don trying to cope with a 1968 student revolt, rather than the tough old providence-inspired revolutionary Independent that he actually was.

However, I do not think this argument stands in face of the evidence, and above all in face of what have always been felt as contradictions and paradoxes within the poems. It is obvious, of course, that the dominant structure of *Paradise Lost* is not pro-Ranter or antinomian, and Hill never suggests that it is. These ideas enter the poem as the doubts, the 'outcry against God' that has to be answered. They enter also as the passionate presumption and libertarian indiscipline of Satan, with which he later infects Eve. They are felt in the very difficulty Milton encounters in making a rational God sympathetic when he allows 'innocent frail man' to fall, and through devoted love to a woman at that. They are of course refuted within the poem, but after a struggle whose intensity goes well beyond the need to 'give the devil a run for his money' for dramatic effect.

As a privileged elitist intellectual, son of a usurer whose profits had financed his long apprenticeship as a poet, Milton's angle of vision was not that of small craftsmen or dispossessed peasants. He had a stake in inequality. Yet the evidence shows that he continued to uphold many of the radical positions (toleration, no tithes, no state Church) against the more consistently property-oriented government in the 1650s. He never reneged on the mortalist and anti-Trinitarian ideas he shared with men like Overton and Walwyn, even if he came to see Leveller intransigence as disastrous, and democracy as impracticable and dangerous to the Revolution.

However, I think the phrase 'a personality in some way torn' may have misleading connotations. For it is not a question, as Hill has amply shown, of Milton's purely individual hang-ups, but of a much wider unresolved and unresolvable conflict. If a contradiction really is insoluble, you don't have to be a particularly indecisive, marginalized or psychologically vulnerable person to be unable to solve it. The 'divided heart' is then the consequence of the divided world – in this case the divided world of the English revolutionaries – in which others besides Milton had to live.

The revolutionary ideals of the Independent/radical/Leveller alliance in the 1640s were such as the revolutionary government *could not* put into practice and survive with support from the 'natural rulers'. Cromwell resolved this one way, by settling for tithes, a state Church, some power for the magistrate in religious affairs, suppression of the army radicals. Many of the Leveller leaders, under the pressure of disappointment and anger, resolved it in another way, lapsing into indifference or hostility to the regime: Fifth Monarchists in yet another, hoping to introduce God's kingdom by force. Milton warned Cromwell of the dangers of tyranny in the *Second Defence of the English People* (which as Hill notes is by no means the uncritical panegyric it is sometimes made out to be), but would not openly attack him for fear of worse. Like Brecht's Mother Courage, the trader-mother, or Shen-Teh, the Good Person, quick-changing between golden-hearted whore and ruthless businessman, Milton was 'torn' by a contradiction no one could wish away, and which led directly to the Restoration and the defeat of his hopes. He reasoned through it to decide on priorities, mostly unpleasant, for rescuing God's erring people.

More fundamentally still, the whole approach to Milton's poetry by way of seventeenth-century England disturbs some scholars. The desire to see poetry as quite separate from other kinds of writing, wholly transcending experience and history, seems at least as prevalent among historians as among literary critics, perhaps nowadays even more so. Suppose Hill is right about all the political and heretical references he finds in *Paradise Lost*, why should this interest the reader? The poem is not *about* politics or heresies.[37] If an epic on Heaven and Hell can't be timeless and universal, independent of civil wars and executions of one's friends, soon nothing will be sacred. It is like arguing that Wilfred Owen's poems are parochialized[38] if, in responding to their universal protest against man's inhumanity to man, we recognize that they are also 'about' his experience in the Great War of 1914-18.[39]

Of those historians who read literature seriously, some are among our most valued scholar-critics (one thinks for instance of Veronica Wedgwood).[40] Others seem to look to it not as a way of understanding the past, which they feel they already sufficiently do on the basis of parish registers, parliamentary records and account books, but as a refuge from these things and a source of uplift. I have personally met a number who, having learned as undergraduates that literary evidence does not count, have spent their best years in seventeenth-century studies without ever reading a Jacobean play other than Shakespeare, let alone *Paradise Lost*, either of which they would regard as a difficult specialist exercise they would be wiser not to attempt. Among them are several who criticize Hill for dealing mainly with the printed sources.

In the end the test must be what happens when we go back to the poems. It seems to me that Hill's interpretation does alter and sharpen our reading, and makes more sense of many parts of them than any other I have come across. (This is not to say it is the only way they can be read, as Victor Kiernan's essay in this volume shows; Milton is vast and contains multitudes.)

It has been argued that people can appreciate the great poems without any knowledge of seventeenth-century history or politics. In my experience and that of the students I work with, this is only partly true. Lacking knowledge of the ideas and history involved, we are likely, if we are honest, to be impressed by *Paradise Lost* as a collection of magnificent bits – episodes, scenes and visions, individual similes and speeches – linked by long stretches of boredom and nullity. Dr Johnson's comment, 'None ever wished it longer than it is', came from the heart. 'The want of human interest is always felt. *Paradise Lost* is one of the books which the reader admires and lays down, and forgets to take up

again.'[41] For us, though not for Johnson (who would have had ideological difficulties about it), Hill's way of reading has revealed much
more of the human interest, which is social as well as personal, and
brought to life great tracts of the poem which appeared to be dead, so
that the intellectual and imaginative structure becomes impressive and
graspable as a whole. To take a single example, the last two books of the
poem provide, in this interpretation, not an anti-climactic plod through
history, but the meaning of the whole action, which is not only explained
but poignantly felt as we realize that Adam's situation here is also
Milton's and our own. Not even Hill's sympathetic understanding can do
quite as much for *Paradise Regained.* But his reading on these lines of
Samson Agonistes (which he's surely right in assigning, with M.A.
Radzinowicz and others, to a date after the Restoration) is the most
satisfying I know.

Hill's major share in creating the Open University's course on *Seventeenth Century England: A Changing Culture* (1980) is in one way the
culmination of a lifetime's work in relating history and culture. There
are now, of course, a great many courses at universities and polytechnics
which set out to make such interdisciplinary connections; but what can
easily result is either an attempt to force carefully selected literary works
into a historian's ready-made framework, or, more often, a loosely
connected series of lectures and assignments on particular themes and
works, frequently contradictory and accompanied by immense reading
lists, which open up the field but don't resolve any problems, leaving the
essential links to be made in the individual brilliant student's head, if at
all. To get beyond this is not easy. One would hope that this Open
University course, with its careful structuring, its closely reasoned
discussion of alternative views, its jargon-free explanations, and its
wealth of multi-media illustrations from architecture and painting, music
and drama, poetry and science, may suggest new possibilities and
encourage mixed groups of experts elsewhere to extend this kind of
approach to other themes and periods.

Christopher Hill as course chairman, in co-operation with Open
University staff already experienced in the design of mixed courses, not
only secured a respectable degree of unity and mutual acceptance of
criticism among a very diverse group (of whom I was occasionally one),
but himself took great trouble to find ways of presenting complex topics
without talking down, yet without overawing or paralysing part-time
students, some of whom would have had relatively little training in either
history or literature. The drafts of units (corresponding to lectures in
other kinds of institution) were circulated to all team members for
comment; and the first page of Christopher Hill's own opening paper set

the tone by reminding us that many things, including the meanings of words, might have changed since the seventeenth century, as the epigraph to this essay shows. After that, even the most owlish of us felt authorized to make a joke, if we could think of one. Through all the tedious business of pruning, adapting and mutilating the work of sensitive authors, Christopher Hill's patience and firmness were exemplary. One might like to think of the final product as one of his best monuments in literary studies, if he were not adding to them year by year. For of course no combination of specialist contributions from different disciplines can replace the insight into literature of a critic who is himself a great historian: the words mean more to him. Fortunately in recent years, since his retirement from the Mastership of Balliol, Christopher Hill has found time to publish a number of major literary pieces, and more and longer works are in prospect. His continuing fertility and originality is not just a happy accident, however, but the result of an approach that has always been popular as well as scholarly, based on the conviction that seventeenth-century literature has something important to say to the makers of history in our own time.

Notes

This essay was written some time ago, and unfortunately delayed in publication. Since then Christopher Hill has published not only *The Experience of Defeat: Milton and Some Contemporaries* (1984), but also a collection of his literary essays ' *Writing and Revolution in Seventeenth-Century England*' [*Collected Essays of Christopher Hill*, vol. 1 (1985)], which includes important new work on 'The Pre-revolutionary Decades' and 'Censorship and English Literature'. I have thought it best to publish my essay as it stands, and leave it to readers to follow up the ideas in these later writings, which develop but do not change Hill's fundamental approach.

1. 'The Historians' Group of the Communist Party', in *Rebels and Their Causes: Essays in Honour of A.L. Morton*, M. Cornforth, ed. (London, 1978).

2. The legend that Marxist criticism at this time was all crudely 'economist' can be tested by looking at the volumes of *Left Review*, or at Edgell Rickword's two collections of *Essays and Opinions* (Cheadle, 1974 and Manchester, 1978). There was some crudity, certainly, but not from *Left Review*'s leading contributors. See also *The Thirties: a Challenge to Orthodoxy*, John Lucas, ed. (Hassocks, 1978), especially A. Rattenbury's article on *Total Attainder and the Helots*; and the essay by David Margolies on '*Left Review* and Left Literary Theory', in Jon Clark *et al.*, eds., *Culture and Crisis in Britain in the 1930s* (London, 1979).

3. 'Radical Prose in Seventeenth-century England from Marprelate to the Levellers', F.W. Bateson Memorial Lecture, reprinted in *Essays in Criticism* (April 1982).

4. The objection to the 'words on the page' emphasis is not, of course, that it directs attention to what a writer actually wrote (as opposed to making more general observations about his ideas or place in literary history); but rather that it tends to treat the words on the page as more 'pure' than they ever can be, and in doing this more or less unconsciously smuggles into 'pure' criticism the critic's own extra-literary attitudes and prejudices.

5. This is, nowadays, a real problem. Faced with a scholarly work like Carey and Fowler's admirable edition of Milton, recommended for Cambridge students, where

roughly two thirds of each page consists of commentary, one is inclined to send them back to the plain text and risk misunderstandings. But this is not really a final solution, at least for longer and more difficult works.

6. *Puritanism and Revolution*, pp. 392–3.

7. *The World Turned Upside Down* (London, 1972), p. 13.

8. For Eliot's impact on leftward-moving intellectuals, and his complex and uneasy relationship with Marxism, see the admirable 'personal view' by A.L. Morton in *The Matter of Britain* (London, 1966), pp. 155–66. For Eliot's pronouncements of the early 1930s, see Arnold Kettle in Jon Clarke *et al.*, eds., *Culture and Crisis in Britain in the 1930s* (London, 1979), pp. 89-90. On the social thinking of Leavis and the *Scrutiny* movement, see Iain Wright's essay in the same volume (pp. 37–59) and Francis Mulhern, *The Moment of Scrutiny* (London, 1979).

9. 'Milton II' (1947) in *Poetry and Poets* (1957), p. 148.

10. See 'After Strange Gods' (1934) for an explicit statement of this outlook.

11. See, for example, 'The Line of Wit', in F.R. Leavis, *Revaluation* (London, 1936), which laments the later decay of 'the old fine order, what was referred to above as the (Caroline) Court culture', and comments on a love-lyric by Carew, of all people, as representative of the fine and delicate poise of that culture – 'something consciously both mature and, while contemporary, traditional'.

12. *Religion and the Decline of Magic* (London, 1971), ch. 1.

13. *The Crisis of the Aristocracy* (London, 1965).

14. *Sewanee Review* (Fall, 1981). In this important retrospective article, Knights cites D.W. Harding as having been critical from the outset of *Scrutiny*'s willingness to pronounce dogmatically on social issues without detailed research or expert opinion, on the basis of a few repeatedly quoted texts like *Middletown* or *Change in the Village*.

15. *London Review of Books* (7–20 October 1982), p. 4. See also the early controversy between Hill and Leavis in *Politics and Letters* (Summer 1947–8), in which Hill criticizes the 'smug snob attitude' that 'our cultural tradition' is 'by definition inaccessible to the masses of our fellow men and women', and that its continuity can therefore only be preserved by a self-certified group of the elect.

16. How closely this anti-revolutionary approach to seventeenth-century literature was always intertwined with contemporary class and political prejudice is evident, for example, in Geoffrey Walton's remarks defending the Cavalier poets, reprinted unaltered in the 1982 edition:

> The communications media harp continually on the simple human phenomena of social class and its injustices actual and potential, while on the other hand the permissiveness of our affluent society encompasses a cult of dreariness, not to say squalor. Personal elegance and courteous behaviour seem not to be conspicuously fashionable. (p. 205)

17. It should be said that the volumes of the *New Pelican Guide* vary greatly in quality and historical sense. Vol. 2, *The Age of Shakespeare*, for instance, is far less one-sided than this one.

18. Review of Ross Gamer, *Henry Vaughan: Experience and the Tradition* in *Science and Society*, no. 25 (1969).

19. In *English Renaissance Studies, Presented to Helen Gardner* (London, 1980).

20. Hill's admiration for Milton has never implied any devaluation of metaphysical poetry. He once quoted approvingly E.M. Tillyard's remark that the differences between Milton and the metaphysicals are differences of poetic personality rather than of quality, and that one of the obvious distinctions between, say, Donne's poetry and Milton's is the absence in Donne's of serious social and political concerns. (Review of Tillyard, *The Metaphysicals and Milton*, in the *Spectator* (23 February 1956).)

21. M. Heinemann, *Puritanism and Theatre* (London, 1980), pp. 18–47 and passim.

22. This is not an exaggeration. For example, in the original 1957 edition of the *Pelican Guide*, vol. 3, the only essay specifically on prose style dealt with Donne and Sir Thomas Browne. The *New Pelican Guide* of 1982 has an additional one by Ian Robinson, entitled 'Prose and the Dissociation of Sensibility', which unfavourably contrasts Dryden's prose with that of Shakespeare and the Authorized Version (designed one might have thought to serve rather different purposes), and shows its disastrous results in the form of

modern rational argument. 'If our world is that of modern prose it does suffer from a certain impoverishment: we are not, in Lawrence's phrase, so "vitally conscious" as our forefathers if our ordinary written language is without some of the essential powers of theirs.' Luckily the novel 'has rescued English prose from the dissociation of sensibility' to some extent. The phrasing calls to mind Frank Kermode's comment thirty years ago:

> One often hears the phrase 'dissociation of sensibility' used as if it stood for an actual historical event like, say, Pride's Purge; after it, feeling disappeared from certain mental transactions, leaving a rump of intellect, with which we have been transacting our business ever since. (*Kenyon Review*, Spring 1957)

Kermode's essay is still illuminating. But he was evidently wrong to think the doctrine was 'going out'; its attraction was as a reinforcement not only of symbolist poetics, but of antinomian irrationalism and mystification.

23. P.A.W. Collins in *New Pelican Guide to English Literature*, vol. 4, p. 121.

24. *Some Intellectual Consequences of the English Revolution* (London, 1980), p. 83.

25. *Puritanism and Theatre* (London, 1980), ch. 2 and passim.

26. For general discussion of modern Marxist and post-structuralist approaches to literature, see Janet Wolff, *The Social Production of Art* (London, 1981), and Catherine Belsey, *Critical Practice* (London, 1980).

27. Editor's Preface, in R. Samuel, ed., *People's History and Socialist Theory* (London, 1981), p. xiv.

28. See, for example, 'Pottage for Freeborn Englishmen', in *Continuity and Change in Seventeenth Century England*, (London, 1974), pp. 183–6, which draws on Massinger and Wither, Spenser and Herbert for evidence that wage-labour was generally considered to make a man unfree. See also the allusions to authentic Utopian traditions of the Peasants' Revolt by Shakespeare's plebeian rebels in *Henry VI* Part 2, in 'The Many-Headed Monster', ibid.

29. *Puritanism and Revolution* (1958), p. 342.

30. For example, 'Milton and Marvell', in *Approaches to Marvell*, C.A. Patrides, ed. (1978), pp. 1–30.

31. 'Robinson Crusoe', in *History Workshop*, no. 10 (1980).

32. 'Bunyan and the English Revolution', *Marxist Perspectives* (Fall 1979).

33. For instance, their hostility to the proposed revival of kingship led them to hold a day of praise to God when Cromwell finally rejected the Crown.

34. 'No Ranter could have written *Paradise Lost*. The tension would have been lacking.' *The World Turned Upside Down*, p. 325.

35. See the appreciative critical review by Quentin Skinner, *New York Review of Books* (23 March 1978).

36. See, for example, the final section of Andrew Milner's study, *John Milton and the Puritan Revolution* (1981), the most serious and interesting criticism of Hill's book so far.

37. Thus G.K. Hunter, a respected critic, in reviewing Hill's *Milton* in *Sewanee Review*, admits that *Paradise Lost* undoubtedly contains echoes of controversies that meant much to Milton and those for whom he wrote. 'But the mere reader may still ask what it has got to do with him.' Antinomian rhetoric, the slyness of politicians, the self-justification of tyrants are all closely observed. 'But the poetry seems to be no more singularly about these than about cooking or gardening.'

38. 'Parochial' and 'impoverishing' are Blair Worden's terms. 'When Hill decides that the reference to the persecution of the Church in Book XII of *Paradise Lost* is an "explicit reference to persecution in Restoration England", he not only parochializes the vision of a writer who took all history for his province. He fails to recognize the process by which art comes to transcend experience' (*The Times Literary Supplement*, December 1977).

39. It is only fair to note that W.B. Yeats said something rather like this when he excluded Owen from the *Oxford Book of English Verse* on the grounds that 'passive suffering is not a theme for poetry'. But most readers now think he was wrong.

40. See especially her *Poetry and Politics under the Stuarts* (1960).

41. *Lives of the Poets* (1969), vol. 1, p. 127.

Talking with Christopher Hill: Part I

Tim Harris and Christopher Husbands

How did you become interested in history and writing the sort of history you have been writing?

Christopher Hill: That's a very long and difficult autobiographical question. I suppose I started off by disliking a lot of the stereotypes that existed in the 1930s, when I became conscious of these things. It's difficult to remember now what sort of things did exist then; but thinking of the seventeenth century, the English Revolution – it wasn't called a revolution then – was discussed entirely in religious terms, or entirely in constitutional terms. The word revolution was pretty taboo, except as the Puritan Revolution. And I was interested in Marxism in the 1930s, and these two together made me want to stress parallels between the English and other great revolutions – the French, Russian, American and so on – and made me particularly anxious to react against the idea, still very prevalent, that English history was very different from history on the 'wicked continent', that in England we'd always had our own constitutional, peaceful, moderate progress by way of compromise, muddling through. So I started off rather wanting to overemphasize the revolutionary aspects of what happened in the seventeenth century. It seemed to me that this ought to be brought to the attention of historians who tended to be, I think, rather smug and insular. The first book I wrote, which often gets quoted against me now – *The English Revolution 1640*[1] – I wrote as a very angry young man, believing he was going to be killed in a world war, which I (and a lot of other people) had been foreseeing, and engaging in activities in the 1930s which we thought, rightly or wrongly, were aimed at preventing a world war. And then we got copped in it. I suppose that book, which was written very fast and in a good deal of anger, was intended to be my last will and testament.

Living with my last will and testament for the last forty years, I might have written it rather differently, if I'd realized I wasn't going to die, and the world wasn't going to come to an end. But that's why it was deliberately aimed at being rather provocative. I cannot say I thought that the understanding of what happened in the seventeenth century was going to transform political life in the twentieth. I think I assumed that what I saw as the defect in orthodox historiography in the 1930s resulted from a political smugness – an assumption that the English way was the right way.

University English history got set up in the late nineteenth century when it seemed plausible to believe that all history was a steady progress to parliamentary democracy and the British Empire. So England seemed different, and much more successful than anywhere else. We're not likely to fall for that illusion now! It still seemed possible down to the First World War and in the 1920s – which was simply a 'temporary setback' – to believe in this notion of progress. But it was really only from the crisis of 1931, and the slump of the 1930s, that people began to realize that history hadn't come to a stop with the British constitution. I think people still thought that the English model of parliamentary democracy was going to be the ideal to which all other nations would turn – but again, that hasn't quite worked out.

After 1940 it was a long time before you wrote anything else: not until 1956.

Hill: Well, it took quite a long time to pick up again after the war. Teaching was quite difficult, after six years. I remember a colleague who came back a year after I had, apologizing to his Balliol undergraduates for being rusty, and was told, 'Oh, don't worry, we saw Christopher Hill through that phase last year.' Obviously there was quite a long pick-up period. And I was fairly politically active in the Communist Party. I wrote a lot of more or less hack party stuff. But also I was collecting material all the time for *Economic Problems of the Church*,[2] which was the one that came out in 1956. There was a long pre-history to that. It was intended as one chapter of a larger work, but chapters are apt to overflow. So, for quite a long time, I got my perspective all wrong, and was collecting too much material for a much more widespread work, until I decided to concentrate on a much smaller subject. And though that was the next serious academic work, I did edit a collection of documents, with the later Labour Minister Edmund Dell, called *The Good Old Cause*,[3] which took quite a lot of time. It's true, though, it was a long time. I was forty-four before I wrote a serious academic work.

It's been said that your post-1956 works show a more sophisticated, less deterministic concept of the Revolution than did the pamphlet of 1940. Were you consciously refining your model?

Hill: Yes. There the discussions we had in the Communist Party Historians' Group had a great influence. It made me refine. We were all trying to refine. Those discussions were some of the most stimulating experiences I've ever had.

Who were the other members of the Communist Party Historians' Group?

Hill: I'm a bit embarrassed about that. A lot of them wouldn't want me to mention their names. There were some very surprising names, actually. A very, very eminent collection of historians: Eric Hobsbawm, Rodney Hilton, Victor Kiernan – I can mention those without embarrassment. But as for some of the others, I'd have to get their permission before I mentioned them. A lot are now very eminent professors, and are not keen on being reminded. They were very, very stimulating discussions. As a result, I was more aware of defects of the 1940 pamphlet, and I did quite consciously decide to change my vocabulary. In 1940 I more or less threw the word 'feudal' in people's faces, just to show them, and this clearly was an obstacle to communication, because medieval historians had their own very different definitions of the term, and just weren't prepared to accept the possibility that it might have other meanings. I quite deliberately changed my vocabulary in that respect and others. I hope we were all refining and improving all the time.

You see it as a refinement rather than as a break?

Hill: I do, yes, but how does one know? Other people have to answer that. If I changed my mind more than I think I have, I wouldn't be aware of it. If you compare with other historians, such as Eric Hobsbawm, I should think that the same sort of thing happened to them. It was a desire to communicate as opposed to slogan-shout, which was what I was doing in 1940. Again, the fact that it was my last will and testament had something to do with its strident tone.

I think a lot of historians have a stereotype of what Marxists are. Once the label 'Marxist' is attached to you, then the stereotype is attached as well. If I'm asked in public whether I'm a Marxist or not, nowadays I say, 'Well, it all depends on what you mean by Marxist.' Otherwise, if I say I'm a Marxist, I know the next question is going to be 'What do you do when you find a fact that doesn't fit into your preconceived hypothesis?' And by the time you get to that question, it's no good saying that you haven't got a preconceived hypothesis, because, if you say you're a Marxist, the chap who's asking you 'knows' you've got a preconceived hypothesis, and if you deny it, you're just establishing the other fact that everyone 'knows' about Marxists, which is that they're dishonest. But when I say, 'It all depends on what you mean by Marxism', I want an open-ended Marxism, dialectical rather than deterministic.

Nowadays many younger historians would argue that it is only possible to understand political history by looking at the broader social and economic context.

Hill: Yes, that is something that has happened in my lifetime. The social and economic context was studied, but if you look at the Oxford histories of England, they are three-quarters political history and have three or four chapters tacked on at the end, like a donkey's tail, about culture, religion and science – completely unrelated to the main text. Today, most historians feel that to understand any period you have to understand its literature, art, and science as well as what goes on at Westminster. There's a bit of a reaction now against this sort of an approach, and the 'revisionists' are trying to narrow it down again. But at least I think the question has been opened up, and it can no longer be discussed in the sort of smug, insular way that it was.

Of course, its easier, after all, to go in and study a set of constitutional documents than to look at the whole of society.

Hill: This raises the whole Hexter problem.[4] Clearly I and other historians of my generation have flopped into the opposite defect. Instead of being two narrow, we've tried to be too all-embracing, and have talked about things we didn't really know about. I've certainly talked about a lot of things I don't know enough about. When I'm attacked on this I try to reply that I was trying to open something up for discussion.

It seems to me that it's only worth writing history if you've got something new to say. If you think you've something you need to say, then you collect evidence which doesn't mainly contradict what you're trying to say – though one hopes one doesn't ignore the other evidence. You can't always make all the qualifications you'd want to make. I think you take for granted the existing state of historical knowledge, and try to insert something into it. Jack Hexter complains that I ignored the fact that Puritan preachers believed in Christianity, and that advocating Christianity was their primary function. I don't think that's the sort of thing it's necessary to state all the time. I was trying to pick out new elements in Puritan thought which did give little openings that could be forced wider by the people who listened to Puritan preachers or read them. It seemed to me that this was more interesting than drawing attention to elements in Puritan thought that are wholly conventional – which is of course 95 per cent of Puritan thought. The other 5 per cent seemed to me more interesting for what I was trying to do.[5]

Notes

This interview is reprinted from *University History: A Forum for Student Historians*, no. 1 (1980), pp. 5–15.

1. C. Hill, *The English Revolution 1640* (1940, Hill's essay first published separately, 1955).

2. C. Hill, *Economic Problems of the Church from Archbishop Whitgift to the Long Parliament* (Oxford, 1956).

3. C. Hill and E. Dell, eds., *The Good Old Cause: The English Revolution of 1640–1660* (London, 1949).

4. J.H. Hexter, 'The Historical Method of Christopher Hill', *The Times Literary Supplement*, November 1975, reprinted in his *On Historians* (London, 1979).

5. C. Hill, 'Protestantism and the Rise of Capitalism', in *Change and Continuity in Seventeenth-Century England* (London, 1974), pp. 81–103.

PART II

Society and Puritanism: Some Further Explorations

Above all, we must widen our view so as to embrace the total activity of society. Any event so complex as a revolution must be seen as a whole. Large numbers of men and women were drawn into political activity by religious and political ideas as well as by economic necessities.... No explanation of the English Revolution will do which starts by assuming that the people who made it were knaves or fools, puppets or automata.

Christopher Hill, *Puritanism and Revolution*
(2nd edn, New York, 1964), p. 31

Common Rights, Charities and the Disorderly Poor

Buchanan Sharp

One distinguishing mark of Christopher Hill's work has been his emphasis on the centrality of conflict as a fact of life in sixteenth- and
seventeenth-century English society. In particular, with regard to the
relationship between the respectable 'better sort' and the 'poorer sort',
Christopher Hill has always insisted on the existence of social polarities
which often took on the dimensions of class conflict. He has consistently
emphasized that from the second half of the sixteenth century onward
the better sort, especially those who were Puritan in religious persuasion,
strived to impose a discipline at once moral, social and labour – a
veritable reformation of manners – upon the recalcitrant poor.[1]

For a while during the late 1960s and early 1970s, with the rise of
what one historian has called 'the organic-functionalist approach' to be
found in many county studies, it looked as if conflict was going to be
written out of the social history of the Tudor–Stuart period and replaced
with the notion of community.[2] But more recently, the so-called county
community school has come in for trenchant criticism, particularly from
Professor Clive Holmes seconded by Christopher Hill.[3] One telling
criticism is that in identifying the county with the gentry and their
concerns this 'school' too readily assumes a common interest between
the better sort and the rest of the population, thereby perpetuating the
myth of a one-class society 'and the romantic image of communal
corporatism'.[4]

Beyond such criticisms, current scholarship has restored conflict to a
central position in the study of seventeenth-century society and has
extended it to the parish level. No matter what revisions of accepted
views will ultimately be required in this area of historical inquiry,
Christopher Hill's place will be secure as a pioneer of a trail of investigation that many others continue to follow.

One seventeenth-century development worth examining, for what it reveals about contemporary attitudes towards poverty and its causes and about social tension between the respectable and the poorer sort, is the enclosure or improvement of waste ground. It was axiomatic among statesmen and social commentators that unimproved waste and pasture fostered a population of idle, disorderly and beggarly poor. This belief justified enclosure that aimed to extend tillage and, in the process, not only eliminated disorder and idleness but also reformed the manners and behaviour of the poor who obtained allotments of land as compensation for loss of access to commons. The instrument of reformation is perhaps most clearly seen in those instances of enclosure where the compensation for the poor commoners took the form of the endowment of town or parochial charities managed by the better sort of the community. When the consequences for the poor of waste land's enclosure are examined, one encounters a phenomenon much like that dealt with in important recent work of David Levine and Keith Wrightson.[5] They have demonstrated that in a number of parishes, mainly in early seventeenth-century Essex, there emerged a self-conscious elite of substantial craftsmen, husbandmen, yeomen and some minor gentry who dominated the community through their monopoly of such positions of authority as jurymen, constables, churchwardens and overseers of the poor. These local notables not only distanced themselves from the traditional culture of their neighbours, in which they had once participated, but through their access to the church courts and the quarter sessions they tried to impose a reformation of manners, mainly through the suppression of alehouses, upon what they now regarded as the drunken and disorderly poor. In order to preserve their own dominant local position and the benefits they had obtained from the rising price of agricultural products, the members of the parochial elite increasingly identified themselves with the values of their social superiors.[6]

A similar social conservatism, manifested in a desire to maintain hierarchy and good order in the face of disorder and chaos, was a hallmark of sixteenth- and seventeenth-century opinion on enclosure.[7] Such opinion, to be found in pamphlets, proclamations and preambles to statutes, was clearly the expression of the dominant national political and intellectual elite, but it was shared by local elites at the county and parochial level. It is striking that certain themes and attitudes run through both condemnations of depopulation and approbations of improvement. Sixteenth-century opinion focused largely on the negative social and economic effects of depopulation and decay of tillage that were believed to result from the enclosure of arable land and its conversion to pasture for sheep and, later, cattle grazing. Other historians have dealt with the arguments against such enclosure often and well; only the briefest attempt will be made here to sketch the main points.[8]

The central message of sixteenth-century anti-enclosure literature was that the strength of the Commonwealth and the vitality and virtue of its inhabitants were grounded in tillage. Decay of tillage struck at the vitals of the Commonwealth. Since the supervising of animals on pastures required far less labour than tilling the soil, the conversion of arable to pasture deprived husbandmen of their livelihoods and drove them and their families to lives of idleness, vagrancy, beggary, drunkenness, and ultimately crime. Depopulation also deprived the King of tax-paying subjects and of a ready supply of stout soldiers who could be called upon to serve in times of national emergency for, in that often quoted phrase, 'shepeherdes be but yll artchers'. Finally, the shrinkage of arable made the commonwealth dependent at times on foreign suppliers of grain and therefore vulnerable to the vagaries of international markets and politics.[9] The suggested solution to these problems was simple. Although some commentators hoped for a change of heart and a re-dedication to principles of Christian morality on the part of grasping and hard-hearted landlords, most opted for the seemingly more practical solution of legislation to prevent depopulating enclosure and to compel the restoration to tillage of land recently converted to pasture.

Such opinions on the effects of enclosure are to be found in the writings of sixteenth-century moralists and social commentators as well as in the pronouncements of various Tudor governments. One particularly comprehensive statement comes from the preamble to the Enclosure Act of 1597, passed towards the end of one of the most severe periods of harvest failure and food scarcity in the sixteenth century.

Whereas the Strengthe and florishinge Estate of this Kingdome hath bene allwayes and is greately upheld and advaunced by the maintenaunce of the Ploughe & Tillage, beinge the Occacion of the increase and multiplyinge of People both for service in the Warres and in tymes of peace, beinge allso a principall meane that People are sett on worke, and thereby withdrawen from Ydlenesse, Drunkenesse, unlawfull Games and all other lewde Practises and Condicions of Life; And whereas by the same meanes of Tyllage and Husbandrye, the greater parte of the Subjectes are preserved from extreame povertie in a competente Estate of maintenance and meanes to live, and the Wealthe of the Realme is kepte dispersed and distributed in manie handes, where yt it is more ready to answere all necessary Chardges for the service of the Realme; And whereas allso the saide Husbandrie and Tillage is a cause that the Realme doth more stande upon it selfe, withowt dependinge upon forraine Cuntries either for bringinge in of Corne in tyme of scarsetye, or for vente and utterance of our owne Commodities beinge in over greate Abundance.[10]

During the first half of the seventeenth century, uncompromising blasts aimed at depopulating enclosure, as the root of social evil and as a threat to the stability of the Commonwealth, continued to be made in terms similar to those of the Tudor period.[11] In 1612, John Moore, minister of Knaptoft in Leicestershire, no doubt with the Midlands Revolt of 1607 fresh in his memory, wrote a stinging denunciation of depopulating enclosure and conversion of tillage to pasture. In the 1650s, he again thundered against enclosure, stimulated to the attack by the works of Joseph Lee, an advocate of the enclosure of both arable and pasture.[12] Moore condemned conversion of arable to pasture as the ruin of the husbandman and his family; it weakened the Commonwealth and created poverty and vagrancy. Depopulating enclosure also violated God's ordinance that tilling the soil was the duty of Adam's descendants. As a consequence of the Fall, the earth was barren by nature and unless 'Adam and his brood get their bread with the sweate of their browes, the earth will yeeld them nothing but briers, brambles, thornes and thistles. Force it they must by their great toile and travell [travail] or else it will not be fruitful.'[13]

In 1636, Robert Powell condemned conversion of arable to pasture largely in traditional terms.[14] He started from the position that after the Fall God enjoined Adam and his descendants to maintain agriculture by the sweat of their brows. Powell then approvingly surveyed the parliamentary enactments against enclosure listing the reasons why such laws ought to be enforced. According to him, the maintenance of tillage was necessary to England's strength and prosperity for a variety of reasons: to increase population for service in peace and war; to set people on work and draw them from idleness, drunkenness, and unlawful games; to provide the people with a competent estate and keep them from poverty; and to reduce the kingdom's dependence on foreign suppliers of grain in times of scarcity.

Later in the century, Henry Halhead attacked depopulating enclosure in terms similar to those of Moore and Powell but his emphasis on the poverty, disorder and decay attributable to enclosure is worth pointing out.[15] The growth in the number of idle poor, as a result of the conversion of arable to pasture, meant an increase in idleness, alehouse haunting, adultery, and felonies. Halhead believed that those engaged in husbandry were too busy to be tempted by the diversions of the alehouse: 'the ploughman's work is never at an end.' Another consequence of poverty and idleness was the difficulty that the Commonwealth experienced in finding strong and able men fit to be soldiers.

In his response to the argument that one of the benefits of enclosure for pasture was an increasing supply of wool to set the poor on work making cloth, Halhead made explicit certain assumptions about the social virtues attributable to tillage and its practitioners that were held by virtually all who wrote on both sides of the enclosure question. Halhead agreed that a growth in the wool supply resulted in increased employment in the cloth industry, but he regarded clothworkers as so poverty-stricken that they had nothing 'to lay up' for their posterity. Moreover, they were unfit to be able-bodied soldiers. In addition to their chronic poverty, cloth-workers were pinched and starved in years of food shortage or depression. 'And herein by the way the gatherers of the labours of the poor are like the task masters that exact more and more upon them. And when did you see any, out of their mean and meer labour, marry their children, and provide for their posterity in a comfortable manner.' The solutions to the problems of poverty were simple: to pass new laws against enclosure and to increase tillage at the expense of pasture. As a result, 'mankind the best of all the creatures would be nourished and bred up stronger and able to do more service to God and their country and have in their hand to lay up for their posterity'.

There is another seventeenth-century condemnation of depopulating enclosure worth noting for its statement of the social virtues associated with husbandry. In his *History of the Reign of King Henry the Seventh*, Francis Bacon discussed at some length one of the first anti-enclosure laws, the 1489 Act against pulling down of towns.[16] In praise of this statute Bacon pointed particularly to its provision 'that all houses of husbandry that were used, with twenty acres of ground and upwards, should be maintained and kept up forever'; he concluded that it was intended to reverse the decay of the yeomanry. The inhabitant of such a house of husbandry would not be 'a beggar or a cottager, but a man of some substance, that might keep hinds and servants, and set the plough on going'. The greatest benefit flowed to the kingdom itself, for by insuring that holdings were of sufficient size to maintain 'the yeomanry or middle people, of a condition between gentlemen and cottagers or peasants' the King increased his available military power:

> the principal strength of an army consisteth in the infantry or foot. And to make good infantry, it requireth men bred, not in a servile or indigent fashion, but in some free and plentiful manner. Therefore if a state run most to noblemen and gentlemen, and that the husbandmen and ploughmen be but as their workfolks and labourers, or else mere cottagers, which are but housed beggars, you may have a good cavalry, but never good stable bands of foot.

In the sixteenth and seventeenth centuries, there was always a body of opinion in favour of enclosure; its spokesmen were usually surveyors and champions of agricultural improvement such as Fitzherbert, John Norden and Walter Blith. They did not approve of depopulating enclosure or the permanent conversion of arable to pasture. Rather, they advocated the introduction of improvements like convertible or up-and-down husbandry. In such husbandry, animals were maintained on pasture as crucial to the fertility of the arable, and land was converted from pasture to arable and back again according to the dictates of fertility and to the demands of the market. To improve the management of the land, surveyors often advocated the consolidation into enclosed parcels of each tenant's strips of arable in the common fields and a similar consolidation of pasture into closes.[17]

Another advocate of mixed husbandry was Joseph Lee who in the 1650s crossed swords in print with John Moore over the issue.[18] It is clear from the controversy that Moore believed enclosure to be an evil in itself, which inevitably brought depopulation and attendant social disruption. Lee, on the other hand, believed that enclosure could be good or bad according to circumstances; it was possible to have enclosure without depopulation. Despite this major contention and other differences between the two men that Professor Joyce Appleby has recently examined, they also shared some striking similarities of outlook.[19] Both believed that the solution to the social problems of poverty, idleness and disorder lay in the preservation and extension of tillage. Joseph Lee emphasized that tillage is 'the staffe of a country' and was as strongly opposed as Moore to the permanent conversion of arable to pasture, describing it at one point as a canker.

Moore and Lee did differ on how to protect and increase the tillers of the soil. Moore's views were undoubtedly shaped by his experience in Leicestershire where there were frequent protests against depopulation. He blamed poverty on enclosure; for him the solution lay in the enforcement of laws against conversion of tillage to pasture. Joseph Lee saw poverty and underemployment in open field villages and believed the answer was to give every tenant, no matter how humble or how small his holding in the common fields, an enclosed parcel of ground which he would work and improve for himself. Thus 'the monarch of one acre will make more profit therof then he that hath his share in forty in common'. In his naive enthusiasm for the benefits of improvement, Lee was much like the reformers and intellectuals associated with Samuel Hartlib in the 1640s and 1650s. According to the most recent account of Hartlib's circle, one member, Gabriel Plattes, 'urged that the poor could be supported with ease, if they practised even the most simple and cheap improvements; and he calculated that whole families could subsist on extremely small plots of enclosed land'.[20]

In the seventeenth century, the wrath of the moralist and the policy of the Crown focused increasingly on unenclosed waste as the cause of poverty, vagrancy, disorder and other social evils that had been associated in the Tudor period with the grazier, the sheepmaster and the conversion of arable to pasture. The remedy lay in enclosure and improvement of waste. An earlier proposal for improvement dates from the middle of Elizabeth's reign. In 1576, Alderman Box of London proposed to Lord Treasurer Burghley the conversion of waste ground to tillage; his scheme was permeated with the sort of zeal and optimism that marked similar proposals in the next century.[21] The central aim was to increase the production of corn, 'knowinge that corne and all other victuall is scante and at great prise, and feared to be worse yf remedye be not hade'. Fertile ground lying waste and overgrown with brambles and briars needed to be brought under the plough. Beyond the production of corn, the cultivation of such ground would give employment to the idle poor who could barely subsist on the waste and who produced many children that lived by begging. In the alderman's view, the aim of charity was to provide the idle with work; he could not conceive of better work than to replace bitter weeds with sweet corn.

In his proposal Alderman Box put a great deal of emphasis on the increase in the value of land that would result from improvement. Ten acres of waste cleared, cleaned, ploughed and sown with corn would be worth more than one hundred acres of unimproved ground. This emphasis was doubtless intended to encourage the implementation of the plan. Box hoped that landlords would be encouraged to divide their manorial wastes into enclosed parcels and let them to their tenants in acreage proportionate to the rents they already paid for their existing tenements. To speed the work of improvement, Box thought that landlords should allow their tenants to take up a piece of waste rent free for two years. If after that time no improvements took place, the landlord could take back the parcel and convey it to another tenant. As a result of these efforts, in Box's words, 'so shall every man make the most and best of his grounde, for his own profyte, and the welthe of his country, and doe no wronge to any man but shall reape the frewt of his owne laboure'.

During the 1650s many proposals similar to Box's appeared in print. The advocates of enclosure, like its opponents, believed the root of social distress lay in overabundance of waste or pasture and lack of arable. In 1653, Adam Moore insisted that the enclosure and cultivation of wastes and common grounds were necessary to keep the populace from enduring the effects of high grain prices, which were intensified, in times of scarcity, by dependence on foreign supplies and by the sharp practices of 'the sharking engrosser and mercilesse hoarder'.[22] Like John

Moore and other resolute opponents of the conversion of arable to pasture, Adam Moore believed that God charged man with the labour of tilling the soil 'to keep it and dresse it for the comfort, encrease and preservation of His people committed unto it'. Moore, likening unenclosed waste to the Arabian desert and enclosures to the fruitful fields of Canaan, asked his readers, 'is it a better spectacle without your doors to see a confused common, fruitlesse, naked and desolate, or fields and vales of plenty storing your houses and countrey with food and wealth?'

Moore argued that enclosure of waste would not merely increase the productivity of English agriculture and enable the husbandman to be a Joseph providing against the seven years' famine, but it would solve the pressing problem 'that people are no where more penurious than such as border on Common lands'. In his view, cottagers and borderers on waste eked out a living through 'many strategems' such as pasturing a horse, a cow, some geese or swine, gathering firewood and killing game, but their lack of bread and their generally idle and debauched lives often led them to beg, wander, steal and murder. The solution was enclosure of the waste by a process virtually identical to that followed in contemporary disafforestation cases. The government of the day was to establish a commission in each country to oversee the business. Owners of waste ground, manorial lords and their 'able' freehold and copyhold tenants who could establish legally recognized claims to common were to receive compensatory allotments carved out of the waste in return for the extinction of their rights. Poor tenants, cottagers and borderers were, in charity, to be alloted a sufficient amount of land to rescue them from their penury; Moore believed that four acres each would suffice. The poor tenants would also have employment hedging, ditching, fencing and generally labouring on the enclosed parcels of their better-off neighbours. For the relief of the impotent poor, the enclosure commissioners would provide a portion of land separated from the waste and managed by the churchwardens.

As a result of improvement through the application of manure, marl, chalk or lime, Moore was convinced pasture and arable would be made more productive, the people and the Commonwealth stronger and more prosperous. The numbers and wealth of freeholders and other substantial taxpaying subjects would be increased and the revenues of the government thereby enhanced. And, of course, there would be stout soldiers; Moore, in recommending the husbandmen of Devon and their agricultural improvements as a model, observed that 'of such strength, spirit and the hardinesse are these people ... that in any martiall action for their countreys service, they can endure and perform as much or more than any people whatsoever'. But the leading beneficiaries were to be the poor cottagers and borderers on the waste who could now toil on their own behalf and gain their own bread. Consequently, the state would no longer need 'to make continual massacres of them [on the gibbet] for those misdoings which even their want of bread urgeth them to commit'.

The year before Moore's tract another, urging the enclosure of commons and waste, was published by Silvanus Taylor.[23] At the beginning there is the customary biblical invocation that, after the Fall, God thrust man out into a world of briars and thorns and enjoined him to make it fruitful by the sweat of his brow. It was thus the duty of Englishmen to turn the estimated one-sixth of England's land surface that was waste, choked with briar and thorn, into cornfields, improved pastures and fruitful orchards. Like Moore, Taylor regarded the unimproved waste as the maintainer of poverty; he refers to the poor commoner 'lazying upon a common to attend one cow and a few sheep, for we seldom see any living on commons set themselves to better employment'. Inevitably, the children of the poor were raised to lives of idleness, alehouse haunting, beggary and thievery. The reformation of the poor would be accomplished with the enclosure of the waste and the conveyance of an enclosed parcel to each poor commoner. Since Taylor believed that 'the two great nurseries of idleness and beggary, etc. in the nation are alehouses and commons', magistrates were to suppress disorderly alehouses, and workhouses were to be erected to employ the vagrant, the thief and the beggar.

In Taylor's plan, as in Moore's, the state was to appoint commissions in each county to carve up the waste. One-quarter of the land was to be set aside for the poor commoners in allotments ranging from twenty to forty acres depending on family size. This was certainly a more realistic estimate of the holding required to sustain a family than Moore's planned four acres. Such allotments, which required considerable labour, would eliminate idleness and compel the poor cottager and his children to work to sustain themselves. The rents from these holdings were to be used to build workhouses for the incorrigible poor. Any land left after the satisfaction of the poor commoners' needs was to be applied for the benefit of the impotent poor relieved by the parish. The remaining three-quarters of the enclosed waste were to be allotted to manorial lords and their freehold and copyhold tenants in compensation for loss of common rights. Taylor believed that, in addition to solving the problems of poverty, vagrancy and crime, the enclosure of forests would produce the usual benefits for the Commonwealth, including reduction of dependence on foreign corn and the addition of twenty thousand able men to the ranks of those suitable for military service.

There is one other pamphlet of the 1650s that forcefully advocated enclosure of waste ground and weaved together masterfully the significant arguments in favour of tillage as both the solution to the country's social problems and the means to strengthen the Commonwealth.[24] The aims of *Waste Land's Improvement* are succinctly put in the prologue as 'some hints touching the best and most commodious way of improving the forests, fenny grounds and waste lands throughout England, tending very much to the enriching of the Commonwealth in general, the prevention of robbery and beggary, the raising and maintaining of a public stock for the perpetual supply of armies and navies without taxations and excise, and also a way for satisfaction for part of the nation's debts and obligations'. Unlike other pamphleteers, E.G., the author of *Waste Land's Improvement*, does not invoke God's injunctions to the fallen Adam as justification for enclosure and improvement. He refers instead to unenclosed waste ground as 'howling wilderness' and 'like a deformed chaos'. Once enclosed, cleared of thorns and briars, fertilized and tilled, waste land would produce more bread corn for the poor, 'the staff of sustenance', and greatly increase the supply of cattle, flax and hemp that could also be raised there.

The means to waste land's improvement would be through Parliament asserting the state's title to all such land and acting as a public landlord. Parliament could then send out its agents to survey and enclose the waste, and let it out at reasonable rents with title reserved to the Commonwealth. The rents would go into the treasury to defray public expenditures and eliminate the need for taxation. In the author's view, the greatest achievement would be the elimination of poverty and social dislocation. The poor cottagers who lived bordering on the commons would be the first people offered the opportunity to take leases of the enclosed ground; those who took up leases could thus sustain themselves on their own holdings. The other poor who could not afford holdings would obtain work as labourers on the lands of freeholders and copyholders. The opportunities for land and work created by the enclosure of waste 'would be like unto, and instead of, a manufacture to set awork multitudes in all the corners of the nation; and more effectually yield a comfortable maintenance to the said country poor than the erected house [workhouses?] do unto the poor of the City'. At the same time, enclosure would 'lay the axe to the root' of most of the serious crimes that plagued the Commonwealth through the elimination of 'those vast, wild, wide forests which ... do administer liberty and opportunity unto villainous minds to perpetrate and commit their wicked and vicious actions'.

Sixteenth- and seventeenth-century opinion on both sides of the enclosure issue shared an assumption that the healthiest, best ordered and most prosperous commonwealth was one with the largest possible proportion of its population actively engaged in tillage – hard-working, sober, tax-paying yeomen and husbandmen who increased both their own substance and the general prosperity of a Commonwealth to whose defence they were ready to rise. The social commentators of the 1650s, who proposed the extension of cultivation at the expense of waste and the elevation of as many poor commoners as possible to the ranks of the husbandman with the object of eliminating the chaos of idleness, poverty, vagrancy, and crime, were in effect the advocates of a long-standing social vision that united them with their Tudor predecessors, despite the points of detail and substance that may have separated them.[25]

The attack on unimproved waste was not the only proposed or even the most widely publicized strategy for dealing with poverty. From the middle of the seventeenth century onwards there were vigorous discussions in print on the merit of erecting workhouses and other institutions for the employment of the poor.[26] Even Silvanus Taylor recognized that there was not enough waste to sustain all the poor as husbandmen and he proposed setting up workhouses to employ the able-bodied vagrant. None the less, the schemes of Taylor, Adam Moore and E.G. represented more than simply idle theorizing or wishful thinking. They were seriously intended and, as Charles Webster has demonstrated with regard to similar proposals of the 1640s and 1650s made by Samuel Hartlib and his associates, they were designed to be implemented once those in authority were persuaded of their utility.[27] The pamphlet *Waste Land's Improvement* was, for example, directed to Parliament at a time when proposals were being actively considered for the disposal of former royal forests. Furthermore, the programme advocated by Adam Moore in *Bread for the Poor* was based, as he noted, upon his experience in the county of Somerset. Moore had been one of the projectors for the ultimately unsuccessful scheme, begun in the reign of James I, to drain and enclose Sedgemoor in Somerset, fourteen thousand acres in extent. Early in the process, Moore and two of his partners wrote a justification of the improvement in terms that were later substantially restated in *Bread for the Poor*. Of course in his advocacy of Sedgemoor's drainage Adam Moore was not simply a public-spirited promoter of the Commonwealth's good; he and his partners hoped to obtain a grant of a thousand acres for themselves from the King's share of the drained marsh.[28]

Particularly in projects of the reigns of James I and Charles I, such as improvement of Sedgemoor and the enclosure of royal forests, are to be found evidence for widely shared assumptions about the nature of unenclosed waste. The pamphlets of the 1650s were not simply statements of a social ideal but rather reflected contemporary events; in fact they lagged behind events, for the substance of their proposals had already been implemented in a number of undeveloped lands, and was to be attempted in others during the Protectorate. The large-scale enclosures authorized by the first two Stuarts and the Protectorate were designed to benefit the Commonwealth mainly through the enhancement of its revenues. There can be no doubt that those projectors who, like Adam Moore, were advocates of improvement intended to profit from the outcome and offered self-serving justifications which shrewdly identified private interest with the good of the Commonwealth. None the less, the form that improvement took and the ways in which it was justified, reveal that the Crown, the greater gentry and the parochial elite, who either urged or willingly acquiesced in the process, shared the views towards the poor expressed by projectors and pamphleteers. Private interest, benefit to the Commonwealth and solutions to social problems were inextricably mixed.

There emerged from a series of surveys of Crown lands made early in James I's reign, proposals for the enclosure and improvement of wastes in which the Crown had demesne rights. On survey, it was found that the King received little income from his demesne woods and wastes in royal forests which were being despoiled by the poor who erected cottages and pastured a few beasts.[29] The surveyors, in pointing the finger at the poor cottages and their depredations, confirmed an attitude that was commonplace in official circles. In a document, prepared for the Privy Council's consideration in the wake of the Midlands Revolt of 1607, it was noted that 'the nurseries of beggars are commons as appeareth by forests and fens'.[30] In 1610, James I recommended a number of 'Articles of Reformation' to Parliament. One proposed the suppression of excess alehouses, 'the breeders and nurseries of thieves, rogues and vagabonds and maintainers of drunkards and dissolute, wicked and filthy livers amongst the common and meaner sort of people'. In another, which dealt with cottages, the King noted neglect in the enforcement of the Statute of 1589 that prohibited erection of cottages with less than four acres of ground attached. As a consequence, multitudes of cottages were being built on the wastes and commons in the vicinity of royal forests, chases and parks, and their inhabitants destroyed the King's woods and game. 'And such cottages generally are breeders, nurseries and receptacles of theives, rogues, and beggars and other malefactors and disordered persons.'[31]

The Statute of 1589 hearkened back to the Tudors' attempt to sustain the poor in tillage through legislative measures. The prohibition on erection of cottages, without the laying of four acres to each, aimed to prevent the growth of a population of idle and beggarly poor and 'was designed to preserve the principle that all countrymen should have some land for their essential support'.[32] James I returned to the reformation of manners in his Star Chamber speech to the assize judges before they went on the summer circuit of 1616.[33] He was particularly concerned with the large number of alehouses and recommended to the judges the pulling down of those that were infamous as haunts of criminals and as receivers of stolen goods and poached game. Another object of the King's ire was alehouses 'which are houses of haunt and receipt for debaushed rogues and vagabonds, and idle sturdie fellowes'. He also encouraged the judges 'to suppresse the building of cottages upon commons, which are as bad as alehouses, and the dwellers in them doe commonly steale deere, conies, sheepe, oxen, horses, breake houses, and doe all manner of villanies'.

Given James I's concern with matters such as disorderly alehouses, despoliation of woods, and the need to reform the behaviour of disorderly poor cottagers living on the waste, it is not surprising that in his reign serious consideration was first given to the enclosure of royal forests. In 1612, royal surveyors recommended the enclosure of 'wastes and common forest grounds and chases'. Their proposal was as grandly optimistic as any mid-century pamphlet in its claims for the benefits that would result. The King's revenues would be enhanced and fiscal demands on the subject reduced. Those subjects who took up tenancies and improved the enclosed ground would be more capable of supporting the King with taxes in time of war. The extension of tillage would create greater employment opportunities for the beggarly poor. In general, prosperity and food supplies would be increased.[34] In response to such recommendations, James I moved to disafforest and enclose a number of royal forests. It was a policy which continued and, in fact, peaked in Charles I's reign; it was revived again during the Protectorate.

The procedures followed were, in their essentials, much like those outlined in the pamphlets written in the 1650s. Commissioners surveyed the land, authorized either by the Courts of Exchequer and the Duchy Chamber of Lancaster under the monarchy or by Parliament during the Protectorate; they then compounded with those who had legally recognized claims to common on the waste. Manorial lords and their freehold and copyhold tenants who established claims were compensated with allotments of land. Compensatory allotments were also provided for the poor. The King's share of the waste was either let or sold in enclosed parcels to interested gentry, yeomen and husbandmen or the whole share was farmed to projectors who then disposed of it in smaller enclosed parcels.[35] The agricultural consequences of this process are well summarized in Eric Kerridge's book *The Agricultural Revolution*. In reference to the forests of western Wiltshire, disafforested in the reigns of James I and Charles I, he observes that in 1608 they contained 'tens of thousands of both timber trees and dotards and hundreds of acres of coppice'. By 1650, 'most of the woods had been cleared and the remainder thenceforth covered only about one-twelfth of the land'. Beyond the erection of fences and the cutting of trees, the improvers had to clear the land of stumps, brambles and briars. It was then ready to be brought into a system of up-and-down or convertible husbandry which raised its rental value twelvefold.[36]

Contemporaries also noted the positive results of enclosure. After the disafforestations of Neroche and Frome Selwood in Somerset, deponents in Exchequer suits pointed to the benefits that had flowed to manorial lords, freeholders and copyholders, and to the Commonwealth generally. Tillage had been greatly increased, pastures improved with the application of marl and lime, and the poor set on work. None of this could have happened if the land had remained forest.[37] In August 1639, John Smyth of Nibley wrote to his son who was employed as a commissioner for the disafforestation of The Forest of Dean, Gloucestershire. He advocated the enclosure of the ample waste ground at Slimbridge because commons in general attracted 'many poor people from other places, burden the township with beggarly cottages, inmates, and alehouses, and idle people; where the great part spend most of their days in a lazy idleness and petite thieveries and few or none in profitable labour'. The elder Smyth was convinced that enclosure was the answer to the problem for he observed that James I and Charles I 'reduced into severalty, and into smaller parcels let to private men's uses and farmers thereof' forests, chases, and waste grounds. This was to the benefit of Crown and Commonwealth 'both in the breed of serviceable men and subjects, and of answerable estates and abilities'.[38]

Emphasis on enclosure's advancement of both private interest and public good, much like that expressed in Smyth's letter, is also to be found in the Crown's attempts to gain support for its policy. Official pronouncements admitted that disafforestation would increase the King's revenue but also insisted that it was 'for the benefitt and ease of his loveinge subjects'.[39] What this intermingling of the public and private meant in practice can be illustrated in the case of Attorney-General Heath and Neroche Forest, Somerset. The disafforestation of Neroche began in 1627, presumably on Heath's urging. This would not only increase the King's revenues but also, in Heath's view, result in the improvement of tillage. In his advocacy the Attorney-General was a far from disinterested public servant. From Sir Robert Phelips he had purchased the manor of Broadway that included a thousand-acre common within the bounds of Neroche Forest. On disafforestation, Heath enclosed most of the common for tillage, no doubt in expectation of the sort of increase in rental value that Eric Kerridge describes as occurring with the improvement of former forest land.[40]

Despite the optimism of the improvers, the enclosure of waste ran into a great deal of opposition from those poor who were supposed to be among its beneficiaries. It has been asserted in what is the standard work on the history of English agriculture during the sixteenth and seventeenth centuries that 'the least contentious enclosures were those which effected no change in land use or else resulted in the conversion of pasture to arable', while 'the most contentious enclosures of all ... were those which led to the permanent conversion of arable to pasture'.[41] Although these assertions may be true for the sixteenth century, they need to be radically altered for the seventeenth. Admittedly, the Midlands Revolt of 1607 fits the traditional pattern, but in the seventeenth century the enclosure of waste for improved pasture and for conversion to tillage produced far greater popular protest than did the conversion of arable to pasture. In the years 1626–32, there were large-scale riots in five royal forests undergoing enclosure – Gillingham in Dorset, Braydon in Wiltshire, Dean in Gloucestershire, Feckenham in Worcestershire and Leicester in Leicestershire. Simultaneously, there were rumblings of discontent in the twin forests of Chippenham and Blackmore in Wiltshire, which had been enclosed late in the reign of James I and where there had been sporadic anti-enclosure violence ever since. On the eve of the Civil War, there were other disturbances in Needwood Forest in Staffordshire, and again in the Forest of Dean. During the Civil War and into the early years of the Commonwealth there were renewed riots at Gillingham, Braydon and Leicester, and disturbances in forests such as Frome Selwood and Neroche in Somerset and Duffield Firth in Derbyshire that had been peacefully disafforested in the reign of Charles I when opposition had largely been confined to petitions and legal obstructionism. During the Protectorate, a new crop of resentments were produced in reaction to governmental attempts to improve former royal forests; violence ensued at Enfield Chase in Middlesex and again at the forests of Needwood and Dean.[42]

The Crown was not the only landlord whose intention to extend cultivation at the expense of waste produced violent reaction, nor was enclosure of waste only a phenomenon of the Stuart period. Two episodes, one from the reign of Henry VIII and the other from the reign of Charles I, serve to illustrate the activities of prominent private or corporate landlords who pushed for improvement as much as the Crown. Some time in 1528, Lord Thomas Darcy, to whom Henry VIII had granted the park of Rothwell Hey in Yorkshire, began to enclose the land and convert it to tillage. At least in his own eyes, Lord Darcy moved with caution. In order to establish secure title to the park, he began an action in the Court of the Duchy Chamber of Lancaster against the neighbouring inhabitants who claimed common. During the legal proceedings an agreement was made between Darcy and some of the commoners that he would set aside two hundred acres of the park as a common for pasturing cattle and, in return, he would be free to enclose the rest. Two years later, in 1531, a Duchy of Lancaster commission awarded another thirty acres to the commoners who complained that two hundred acres were insufficient for pasturing their animals. Subsequently enclosure seems to have gone on apace. Then on 3 May 1532 a crowd of 250 people entered the enclosed ground and destroyed the fences and hedges. After this action they drove four hundred head of cattle into the enclosed ground to graze on the corn growing there. Two days later, after temporary enclosures had been erected to keep the cattle out, the crowd returned, cast down the enclosures once again and drove the cattle back on the property to feed.[43]

In response, Lord Darcy complained to the Court of the Duchy Chamber that the rioters were in contempt of previous court orders. In his bill of complaint, Darcy asserted that he was engaged in agricultural improvement to the benefit of poor men who had obtained holdings in the enclosed park and who were the real victims of the riots; the corn of the poor was consumed and trampled by the cattle driven through the gaps in the destroyed enclosures. He also pointed to the general benefit that improvement produced: 'a grett quantitie of the baren ground within the said parke at the gret costes and charges of the said lord were made tyllable.' Darcy also reasserted his title to the park and maintained that the commoners had no legal right to common; they had only a summer agistment for their cattle and for that privilege they paid regular sums of money to the landlord's agent. Their so-called rights were only allowed by the landlord's goodwill. In a passage that was to be all too typical of later legal judgements on common rights, Darcy asserted that the commoners 'beinge only tenantes at wyll, time makes no good prescription ne [nor] tytle unto the pretendyd commen'.[44]

In reply to Darcy's claims, the riotous commoners claimed full rights of common in the entire park. They also stated that they had never been parties to the previous agreements that set aside 230 acres for the commoners. In responding to Darcy's self-justification as an improving landlord concerned to extend tillage, the commoners appealed to contemporary governmental concern over depopulation. Their answer made the point that the defendants were two hundred poor goodmen and heads of households capable of providing and equipping fifty tall men for the King's service in time of war, but if they lost their rights of common they would be forced to sell their cattle and destroy their houses.[45] This revealing passage indicates not only that the rural population consisted of more than simply tillers of the soil but also that, even in the sixteenth century, agricultural improvement and disruption of rural life were not merely the consequences of the conversion of arable to pasture.

While pursuing his opponents through the Court of the Duchy Chamber, Lord Darcy also sought criminal prosecutions for riot in the local quarter sessions. The commoners claimed that Darcy had used his influence with local magistrates to have a privy sessions of the peace held at Pontefract Castle of which he was steward. There, a jury composed of his servants and tenants found indictments against the rioters. Although Lord Darcy denied such charges, there does exist a letter to him from Thomas Gryce, one of his agents in Yorkshire, which contains the statement that the common people so favour the commoners of Rothwell that it would be difficult to obtain a conviction of the rioters without 'special favour of the sheriff in the return of his impanell'.[46] Eventually, Darcy ground the commoners into submission. Sometime later, the commoners of Rothwell petitioned Darcy in abject terms. They admitted that they had 'cruelly and maliciously' destroyed the enclosures in pursuit of claims to rights that had no legal foundation. They begged his lordship's pity and forgiveness so he might lift the indictments that threatened to be their undoing.[47] Darcy was not to enjoy his triumph for long; at the end of June 1537 he was executed for his part in the Pilgrimage of Grace. If nothing else, the moral of this tale is that landlords who were religious and social conservatives were not necessarily paternalists and could easily be improvers.

Roughly a century later, a similar series of events occurred when in 1637 the Dean and Chapter of St Pauls, in order to eliminate despoliation by their manorial tenants, enclosed Caddington Wood in Hertfordshire and Bedfordshire. By agreement with the tenants, one-third of the wood, four hundred acres, was set out to the use of the Dean and Chapter while the other two-thirds were allotted in enclosed parcels to the tenants. The Dean and Chapter's share was leased to farmers who improved the land and planted oats. In spite of the apparently generous provision for the tenants, there was considerable discontent with the whole idea of enclosure. For two years those claiming common of pasture harassed the farmers, destroyed fences and hedges, drove in beasts to feed upon the standing oats and cut the harness of plough horses. On the intervention of the Privy Council a compromise was arranged; the Dean and Chapter obtained the right to enclose 150 acres, the vicar of Caddington got a ten-acre close, and the tenants were awarded the remainder of the wood as an unenclosed common.[48] In this instance, as in the case of Lord Darcy's treatment of the commoners at Rothwell, a supposedly conservative landlord can be seen participating in the rage for improvement.

The argument has already been made at length elsewhere that the rioters against the enclosure of royal forests were mainly cottagers and other poor commoners.[49] The reasons for this are not hard to find. As an Exchequer decree of 1668 noted with regard to the disafforestation of Neroche in Somerset, 'the poore of the said parish would be the greatest loosers by reason of the said dissafforestation for that by the inclosures they weare debarred from gathering drywood, feeding a cowe or horse, and the like'.[50] In rejecting enclosure, the poor commoners were also rejecting the role suggested for them, that of combination small holders and labourers on other men's holdings. The one- or two-acre compensation set aside at disafforestation for each poor cottager, lucky enough to obtain such, combined with his original garden or acre or two of pasture, was hardly enough to sustain a small holder. Whatever the remedial social ideals behind the Crown's enclosure of waste, they foundered on the rock of fiscal necessity; provision for the poor was niggardly.

But no matter the amount of land provided for the commoners they were not speeders of the plough, actual or potential. Their connection with agriculture was tenuous; at best they were occasional pastoralists running a few beasts on the open waste of the forest. In some forests, like Braydon, Needwood, and Rockingham, many of the poor cottagers depended on the open waste for their entire living; in addition to pasturage for animals there was game to be poached, and wood to build and warm a cottage. Among its cottager population every forest had its complement of workers in wood and animal hides. In other forests, such as Gillingham, Dean, and those of eastern Somerset and western Wiltshire, many cottagers earned their livings in a variety of trades connected with cloth-making, mining, iron-making and charcoal-burning. For such wage-earning cottagers access to common in open waste was perhaps not as essential to their livelihood as it was for the poor commoners with no trades, but it was none the less a prized part of their life and, in times of depression and scarcity, provided important income supplements.[51]

Whether the poor commoners would have been materially better off quietly accepting their one- or two-acre allotments is not at issue here. At stake was something more important and more intangible. The open waste, instead of the nursery of idleness and beggary that the improvers believed it to be, was really one important means through which the labouring poor preserved a measure of independence and self-respect. Christopher Hill has argued persuasively that the dwellers in forests and other wastes in the seventeenth century enjoyed a measure of freedom, including an ability to defy the law, generally unavailable to other ordinary Englishmen living in more settled parts of the country.[52]

Examples of this freedom are to be found in the difficulties that authorities faced in apprehending forest rioters and in the rioters' defiant, at
times extravagant, rhetorical outbursts against those identified with
enclosure, but there are others.[53]

In the early 1660s there was a lawsuit in the court of Exchequer to
determine if the lands of the former Chippenham Forest, Wiltshire,
owed tithes in the parish of Chippenham. Evidence was presented that
the officers of the parish and hundred of Chippenham had no authority
to execute writs or other process within the forest; this power lay with
the keepers and other forest officers. Thus, men had fled to Chippenham forest to escape conscription; one witness claimed to have sheltered
a number of such individuals who were fleeing from the Constable of
Chippenham. Officers who did enter the forest in the line of duty were
liable to be assaulted; even an important local figure like Sir Henry
Bainton was not immune. One witness deposed that, some time in James
I's reign, Bainton, a prominent Wiltshire magistrate, entered the forest
accompanied by the Constable of Chippenham in pursuit of a sheep-
stealer. The witness's father, deputy ranger of the forest, told Bainton
that he and the constable had no standing in the forest; they must bring
the right forest officer with them. Bainton replied using 'evil language'.
Thereupon the ranger drew his hanger and cut Bainton's horse about the
neck, forcing the justice to withdraw.[54]

One cautionary note does need to be sounded with regard to the way
some historians have characterized the freedom of cottagers. Not all
cottagers were wandering, masterless men who squatted on the waste,
lacked any real connection with the communities in which they found
themselves, and planned to move on again at the first available opportunity. It is true that the poor migrated into forest districts in order to
live off the abundant waste or to obtain employment in various forest
industries. In those instances, particularly where there was a great deal
of Crown demesne, the migrant poor simply erected cottages or cabins
without anyone's leave; the Forest of Dean provides many examples of
this process. No doubt there was migration into every forest, but in the
case of a place like Gillingham the recurrence, generation after generation throughout the seventeenth century, of about a dozen surnames
among many of both the better-off and the poorer inhabitants indicates
that much of the cottager population was the result of the community's
own natural increase. Furthermore, except in the case of Dean, it is
difficult to find cottagers without landlords. Many cottagers were listed
in manorial rentals as rent-paying tenants of ancient copyhold cottages
which had existed for generations. Other ancient cottages were held by
yeomen and husbandmen who sublet to the poor. Landlords from
among the yeomanry and husbandmen occasionally erected new

cottages which they let out, while poorer men, to help pay their rents, divided their houses and took in lodgers or inmates. But the best-recorded examples of newly erected cottages were those built by gentry landlords either on their own manorial waste or encroaching on royal demesne. Sometimes as many as sixty were built by one individual. Their inhabitants were rent-payers; only the poorest, usually widowed or disabled, lived rent free. This kind of cottage building can be regarded as an aspect of estate management, a seventeenth-century rural equivalent of slum landlordism.[55] Moreover, the freedom that cottagers enjoyed was economically precarious; livelihoods were dependent on the seemingly unchanging permanence of the unenclosed waste. Enclosure, instead of simulating cottagers to move on or to become contented smallholders, compelled them to resist alterations in their way of life.

During the first half of the seventeenth century the number of poor cottagers living in areas with abundant open waste grew rapidly. The evidence of rentals, surveys, Exchequer special commissions and depositions in lawsuits all testify to this.[56] At the same time, the respectable members of those communities with an increasing population of cottagers, even where their presence has been encouraged by enterprising landlords, came to regard their poorer neighbours as idle and dissolute alehouse-haunters and, with their families, potential charges on the poor rates. Frequent complaints came from forest areas that there were more poor people than the ratepayers could support.[57]

In particular, the large population of cottagers living in and around Frome Selwood Forest in Somerset, who worked in the cloth industry and were subject to the disastrous effects of periodic depression and harvest failure, became the objects of their better-off neighbours' animosity. A number of prominent local landowners erected cottages on the waste; Sir Thomas Thynne and Edmund Leversedge esq. put up at least sixty and rented them to poor men whose cattle grazed in the forest. Early in James I's reign, two Somerset yeomen sued Leversedge in Star Chamber for building cottages with less than four acres attached in violation of the terms of the Elizabethan Statute of 1589. In their bill of complaint the yeomen insisted that the erection of cottages had resulted in the parish being pestered with a great multitude of poor; if this was not stopped the parish and all neighbouring towns would be overwhelmed.[58] Also during James's reign, in the manor of North Brewham lying at the southern end of Frome Selwood, John Parrott, a poor man with the licence of the lord of the manor, Sir Charles Berkeley, and the quarter sessions – the legally approved method of obtaining exemption from the Statute of 1589 – built a cottage on the waste. A number of tenants from the nearby manor of North Petherton, who claimed common, pulled down the cottage. They asserted in their defence that Parrott, who must have run an alehouse, was suspected of entertaining 'lewd company' and, as a very poor man with four small children, was likely to become a burden to the parish and a great destroyer of the King's woods and deer.[59]

The respectable had come to identify the freedom of the poor dwellers on the waste as licence and their shifts to eke out a living as idleness. Thus in the course of the seventeenth century, the better sort began to distance themselves from the poor in a variety of ways including acceptance of enclosure as a positive social good that would eliminate, if not poverty, at least the attractiveness of their parishes to the poor. Limiting access to commons would enable control to be exercised over the poor. Elimination of the waste would prevent an increase in the numbers of idle and disorderly poor.

When the Crown enclosed waste, manorial lords and their tenants, yeomen and husbandmen, were amply recompensed with allotments of enclosed land in return for the extinction of their rights to common. This compensation – along with the frequently collusive nature of the lawsuits designed to establish the Crown's title and to confirm the enclosure agreements in disafforestation cases – allows one to speak of the local elite's acquiescence in enclosure. So too does the fact that it is extremely difficult to find gentlemen or yeomen among convicted or known rioters. No doubt such men were willing to benefit from any concessions of further compensation that the Crown made in the face of riot, but their active participation is hard to discover and evidence of their reputed behind the scenes leadership is non-existent.[60]

Respectable forest inhabitants not only avoided participation in riots, but they distanced themselves from the sorts of people who might engage in disorder. The best evidence for this comes, most appropriately, from the Forest of Dean which, with its abundant waste and employment opportunities in wood-working, iron-making, and mining, had a very large population of poor cottagers. In 1616, a jury of inquisition, undoubtedly composed of the better sort of Dean's inhabitants presented to a special commission looking into spoil of woods that seventy-nine cabins and cottages inhabited by 340 men, women and children had recently been erected in the coppices enclosed for timber. According to the presentment, these cottagers used the King's woods to bake and brew for victualling. In their victualling houses they harboured many lewd and disordered persons who robbed travellers in the forest.[61] Early in Charles I's reign, before the riots of 1631, some people calling themselves the miserable inhabitants of the forest petitioned the King, pointing out a variety of ways in which the woods were being despoiled to the hurt of the royal revenue. One was a result of cottage and cabin building by strangers, 'whoe are people of very lewd lifes and conversations, leaveinge their owne and other countryes and takeing this place for a shelter as a cloake to their villainies. By which unruly crue your Majesties woods and tymber trees as [are] cutt downe and ymbezeled and your Majesties game of deere much disquieted and distroyed.' Probably of more immediate significance to the petitioners was their belief that such poor people after living for a while in the forest would look to the parish for support 'or els they will run away and leave their children upon the country'.[62] After the riots of 1631, the miserable inhabitants again petitioned the King distancing themselves from the lewd people who erected cottages and cabins and apologizing for the riots, 'seeing that this soddaine commotion was done by the meaner sorte'.[63] There is, finally, the testimony of Thomas Yerworth, yeoman, who, upon examination before Attorney-General Heath on his know-ledge of the Dean rioters, dismissed them as 'very beggerly and naughty people and such as he never saw or tooke notice of'.[64]

One other way in which the respectable distanced themselves from cottagers, while at the same time exercising a measure of control over them, was in the administration of charities. On some occasions when a forest was enclosed, a parcel of ground was set aside for the support of the poor, usually the poorer commoners but sometimes including the poor relieved by the parish. Such a grant was intended as compensation for loss of common and took the place of the one-acre parcel granted to each poor cottager at other disafforestations. While the property was intended to aid the poor commoners, they did not obtain direct control over it. Invariably the land was conveyed to trustees who would qualify as members of the parochial elite as defined by Levine and Wrightson. The trustees managed the property in the best interests of the poor; this meant leasing it out and distributing the income to those eligible to receive it.

There were three charities established on the disafforestation of Braydon in Wiltshire: twenty-five acres for the poor of Purton Stoke; twenty-five acres for the poor of Leigh; and one hundred acres for the poor of Cricklade and Chelworth.[65] In each instance, the Court of Exchequer commissioned a group of local gentlemen to meet with the 'cheife inhabitants' to inquire into the best course for managing the property and to determine which persons were 'fit' to manage it. Their recommendations were then confirmed by a decree of the court. Those entrusted with the management of the hundred acres for the poor of Cricklade and Chelworth were the bailiff and constables of the borough of Cricklade and the churchwardens and overseers of the poor in the parishes of St Sampson and St Mary's. The annual income from the property was to be distributed as follows: one-half in equal sums to eight poor but industrious men or women willing, but not quite able, to maintain themselves through labour in their callings so that they could reach self-sufficiency and be no further charge on the parish; one-quarter to bind out as apprentices three poor children likely to become charges on the parish or, if such could not be found, the money to be used to help poor apprentices set up as journeymen; the final quarter to be distributed as alms to the impotent poor.[66] The management of the twenty-five acres allotted to the poor of Leigh was entrusted to the two closest justices of the peace, the constables of the hundred of Highworth Cricklade and the churchwardens and tythingmen of Leigh. The income from the property was to help support thirty poor commoners who were named in the confirming decree; they were to be replaced as death or other cause removed them from the list of eligibles.[67] The twenty-five acres for the relief of the poor of Purton Stoke were entrusted to the churchwardens and overseers of the poor in Purton parish who distributed the income from the land to those in need.[68]

The best-documented forest charity is that established at Mere following on the disafforestation of Gillingham. At the time of enclosure, Exchequer special commissioners set out one hundred acres as a common to compensate the freeholders and copyholders of Mere, but no separate provision was made for the poor commoners. Finally in the 1650s, after years of complex legal manoeuvring and intermittent rioting, the grantees of the forest agreed to set aside eighty acres for the benefit of the poor of Mere. The agreement, confirmed by a Chancery decree, conveyed to thirteen trustees, all gentlemen and yeomen, the title to the eighty acres which they were to manage in the interest of the poor; in the course of time when eight of the trustees had died the remaining five were to appoint eight more.[69] Except for the expressed purpose of relieving the poor of Mere, this charity was bound by no other limitations. There survives an account book which runs from its inception in 1656 to 1739. Over that period, the annual yield of the eighty acres was around forty pounds. The disbursements hold no surprises. Twice a year there were interest-free loans made to poor tradesmen and numerous grants of five or ten shillings to poor men and women, including many widows. In addition, there were substantial sums spent to bind out poor children apprentices and occasional amounts to those suffering from the disastrous effects of fire or sickness.[70]

On the surface, the forest charities seem quite routine and unremarkable endowments typical of the period. In fact, they represent a significant development in the social history of their communities. Through enclosure the poorer sort had been cut off from access to the waste; instead of being compensated with a common for their own use they now had to depend upon charity to help supplement their wages and bridge the gap between income and expenditure. In place of independence sustained by access to the common, the labouring poor were reduced to partial dependence upon charity administered in their name by their more respectable neighbours. The meaning of this process can be illustrated by one small example. Early in the accounts of the Mere forest charity there are entries of monies disbursed for the purchase of coal to be sold to the poor at twopence per peck. Clearly the purchase and sale of coal was to replace the poor gathering their own wood in the now enclosed and improved forest. Similarly, on the disafforestation of Leicester, forty acres were set aside to be administered by the corporation of the borough of Leicester with the profits to go towards the purchase of fuel for the town poor who had once gathered their own in the forest.[71] As a consequence of enclosure and the establishment of charities, the respectable had been permanently intruded between the poor and the common which symbolized their independence.

There can be little doubt of the contempt in which charity trustees held the poor. During Queen Anne's reign the Attorney-General, on behalf of the poor of the township, sued the trustees of the Mere charity for violating the terms of the trust. According to one witness, when Edward Cornelius, a gentleman and trustee, was told that the poor wanted an accounting of the profits of the eighty acres he responded that he would put a mark next to the names of those who made such a demand so that they would receive nothing from the charity during his lifetime. He is also reported to have declared that he would bestow charity on anyone he wished, including the poor of Bristol; 'the poor of Mere should not have a groat of it though they starved'. When Henry Clarke, another trustee, had been asked on a different occasion to go downstairs at the Ship Inn and give an accounting to the poor who were gathered there, he replied: 'it was not safe to go downe to them for he had heard that some of them had threatened him.' When urged a second time he exclaimed, 'What! Would you have me putt off my hatt to them?' Another witness deposed that Clarke told him, 'I scorn to give an account to such poor rascals.'[72]

The respectable, like the pamphleteers who advocated agricultural improvement, doubtless looked on unenclosed waste as unformed chaos and on the disorderly, idle, alehouse-haunting poor like the briars and thorns growing there. Just as enclosure provided the opportunity to uproot the briars and turn the waste to fruitful and productive tillage, so the poor would be uprooted and improved. Some would be turned into productive smallholders, the rest could labour and be sustained where necessary by the disciplined administration of charity. In 1653, Joseph Lee observed that, while open waste harboured a great population of poor, in those places where the poor were few in number they were better relieved.[73] Enclosure of waste largely eliminated the attractiveness of a forest area to in-migrants and the establishment of forest charities closed the parish to outsiders. That this was a deliberate intention on the part of the respectable is revealed in the negotiations for the establishment of the Mere Forest charity in the 1650s.

Early in 1652 when agreement had been reached for setting up the Mere charity, complications arose. At the time of disafforestation, one hundred acres were allotted as a common to compensate the freeholders and copyholders of Mere. As part of the agreement that established the eighty-acre forest charity it was also settled, between the fee farmers of forest and the better sort, that the hundred-acre common could be enclosed and divided among the freeholders and copyholders. This decision was unsuccessfully opposed by some inhabitants of the parish, no doubt the poorer commoners, who wanted the hundred acres and the poor's eighty acres to be used together as one common. In the end the points made by Richard Greene, counsel for the better sort of the parish, prevailed. He argued strenuously against a common for two reasons; managed as a charity the income from the land would help to defray the parish's poor relief costs and, more crucially, enclosure was a necessity because 'increase of commons doe increase not lessen poore'.[74]

Enclosure and the establishment of charities can be regarded as one solution to the problem of high poor rates that were the bane of respectable inhabitants in parishes with a considerable expanse of open waste. Conventional views on poverty and its causes were ultimately reflected in the Settlement Act of 1662, which aimed to reduce the mobility of the poor who attempted to settle where there was 'the largest commons or wastes to build cottages, the most woods for them to burn and destroy, and when they have consumed it, then to another parish, and at last become rogues and vagabonds'.[75]

What of the response of the poor commoners to the transformation in their position? There were of course the recurrent riots: the massive riots when enclosures were first made and riots ten or twenty years down the line when favourable opportunities presented themselves during the distractions of the Civil War and Interregnum. As late as 1671, there were disturbances against the continued enclosure of Mailescott Woods in the Forest of Dean, whose original enclosure in the reign of Charles I had sparked the outbreaks of 1631.[76] At Mere in the early 1650s there were riots against the enclosure of the eighty-acre poor plot and again in the years 1657–59 the fences were broken down and cattle driven in. As late as 1693 a single inhabitant is reported to have destroyed fences.[77]

The poor also had recourse to the law and in this, as in the periodic outbreaks of violence, revealed that they had long memories. Two Exchequer law suits of the early eighteenth century indicate that for the parochial elite forest charities had become simply another means available to relieve the poor with no particular significance attached to them. On the other hand, for the labouring poor each charity had specific meaning which was expressed in the special circumstances of the original grant. In their view, the charity represented compensation that was granted to the poor commoners living in particular places; it was not simply a charitable endowment for relief of the parish poor.

In a case brought earlier in the reign of Queen Anne by the Attorney-General on behalf of the poor of Mere against the trustees of the Mere forest charity for mismanagement, one of the central charges against the defendants was that they applied the proceeds of the eighty acres indiscriminately to the relief of any and all parochial poor. The thrust of the plaintiffs' case was that, before disafforestation of Gillingham, the poor householders of Mere township, that is those not dependent on alms or the parish, had exercised right of common in the forest; the profits of the eighty acres were designed to aid them alone, in compensation for their loss of common. Instead, the trustees had been applying the income from the rents to relieve the poor generally, impotent as well as able-bodied, throughout the parish of Mere, including those of Zeals township whose inhabitants had never enjoyed rights of common in the forest.[78] This was the echo of an argument lost in the 1650s. Then, some inhabitants of Mere had fruitlessly argued that the poor plot, along with the hundred acres allotted to the freeholders and copyholders, ought to be used as one common by the poor and all other commoners, since both properties represented compensation for loss of common rights. The triumphant position in the 1650s, and the one which the trustees supported, was that the eighty acres were for the relief of the poor in the parish and therefore all who bore part of the burden of the poor rate should share in the relief provided by the charity, including the inhabitants of Zeals.[79] That behind this lawsuit lay the memory of the common is further indicated by one of the other charges against the trustees: they permitted the ploughing up of part of the eighty acres to the impoverishment of the soil. The response of the defendants, who admitted the charge, must have been particularly galling to the poor, who wanted a common pasture; they allowed thirty acres of the land to be ploughed and marled 'of advantage to the said lands so that the same will thereby hereafter be of greater improved yearly value'.

In 1734, the poor of Purton Stoke enjoyed a small legal triumph. They obtained a decree in the court of Exchequer that prohibited the trustees of the twenty-five-acre poor plot, obtained at the disafforesting of Braydon, from applying the proceeds to the indiscriminate relief of the poor in Purton parish. The income was henceforth to go to those whom the original grant intended to benefit, the poor commoners of the hamlet of Purton Stoke who lost common rights on disafforestation. The inhabitants of the hamlet were also authorized to choose fifteen new trustees to manage the land.[80]

This process, whereby the better sort extended control over the waste and the poor through enclosure, was not confined to forests. It can be found, for example, in struggles over town commons. At Malmesbury, Wiltshire, in the reigns of James I and Charles I there was a long contest between the corporation and the poor inhabitants for access to a six-hundred-acre common called the King's Heath. The aldermen carved out a number of closes totalling one hundred acres from the Heath for their own private use, and thereby excluded the poor from commoning there. In compensation, the aldermen paid an annual rent of twenty pounds for charitable purposes, ten pounds to support a schoolmaster, and ten to relieve five poor inhabitants. But the poorer inhabitants wanted their common pasture; they rioted against the enclosure and also got involved in a series of inconclusive lawsuits with the aldermen.[81] A similar conflict seems to have taken place at Hertford in the early 1630s and, no doubt, social tensions between the poor and the better sort underlay many of the struggles over borough commons in the period.[82]

There are many ironies inherent in the general encouragement to enclosure of waste in the seventeenth century. Arguments that were used in the sixteenth century to oppose enclosure were mobilized in the seventeenth to justify it. In an age whose charity, it has been forcefully argued, was rationally designed to make the poor more self-reliant, enclosure of waste reduced a good many to partial dependence upon hand-outs.[83] What the pamphlet writers and those in authority, from the Crown down to the parochial elite, perceived as the idle and dissolute lives of the poor commoners living on the waste, can also be viewed as part and parcel of the labouring poor's independent existence and a means of supplementing wages. In an age reputed to be marked with economic projects designed to enhance the independence and prosperity of the poor, one of the biggest projects of all, enclosure of waste, had the consequence of depriving the poor of an important part of their livelihood.[84]

It may be that, in the second half of the seventeenth century, formally administered poor relief, private charity, lower grain prices, and the increased employment opportunities of the sort outlined in Joan Thirsk's *Economic Policy and Projects*, along with the slowing of both inflation and population increase, improved the lot of the labouring poor. None the less in the process of waste land's enclosure they lost some part of their long-standing independence. It was lost not in the name of a labour discipline that looked forward to the eighteenth-century factory, but in the name of social stability and good order grounded on an ideal of a rural-agrarian society of stout and prosperous tax-paying husbandmen and yeomen. If, as some have claimed, and the evidence in its support seems persuasive, the decades between the 1620s and 1650s were lean and hungry times of depression, plague, scarcity and social conflict, then the pervasiveness of this ideal of prosperity and stability, also characteristic of hard times in the sixteenth century, is understandable.

Notes

1. The theme runs through much of Christopher Hill's work, but it can be conveniently sampled in the essay 'William Perkins and the Poor', in *Puritanism and Revolution* (New York, 1964), pp. 215–38 and chs. 4, 6, 7 and 12 of *Society and Puritanism in Pre-Revolutionary England* (New York, 1964).

2. The expression comes from J.S. Morrill's review article 'Provincial Squires and Middling Sorts in the Great Rebellion', *Historical Journal*, vol. 20 (1977), p. 233.

3. C. Holmes, 'The County Community in Stuart Historiography', *Journal of British Studies*, vol. 19 (1980), pp. 54–73; C. Hill, 'Parliament and People in Seventeenth Century England', *Past and Present*, no. 92 (1981), pp. 100–24.

4. Holmes, 'The County Community', pp. 72–3.

5. K. Wrightson and D. Levine, *Poverty and Piety in an English Village: Terling, 1525–1700* (New York, 1979); K. Wrightson, 'Two Concepts of Order: Justices, Constables and Jurymen in Seventeenth Century England', in J. Brewer and J. Styles, eds., *An Ungovernable People* (London, 1980), pp. 21–46, and 'Alehouses, Order and Reformation in Rural England, 1590–1660' in E. and S. Yeo, eds., *Popular Culture and Class Conflict 1590–1914* (London, 1981), pp. 1–27.

6. Wrightson and Levine, *Poverty and Piety*, pp. 176, 184.

7. For seventeenth-century ideas on good order see K. Wrightson, 'Two Concepts of Order', passim; K. Wrightson and J. Walter, 'Dearth and the Social Order in Early Modern England', *Past and Present*, no. 71 (1976), pp. 22–42; C. Hill, 'The Many-headed Monster' in *Change and Continuity in Seventeenth Century England* (Cambridge, Mass., 1975), pp. 181–204.

8. For example, in W.R.D. Jones, *The Tudor Commonwealth 1529–1559* (London, 1970), and J. Thirsk, 'Enclosing and Engrossing', in *The Agrarian History of England and Wales* (Cambridge, 1967), vol. 4, pp. 200–25.

9. This is based upon a reading of the following materials: the pamphlets and statutes gathered together in R.H. Tawney and E. Power, eds., *Tudor Economic Documents* (New York, 1963), vol. 1, pp. 1–90, and vol. 3, pp. 12–81, and in A.E. Bland, P.A. Brown, and R.H. Tawney, eds., *English Economic History: Select Documents* (London, 1914), pp. 260–77; the proclamations in P.L. Hughes and J.F. Larkin, eds., *Tudor Royal Proclamations*, 3 vols. (New Haven, 1969), and *A Discourse of the Commonwealth of This Realm of England*, M. Dewar, ed. (Folger Library, 1969). The quote comes from Tawney and Power, *Tudor Economic Documents*, vol. 3, p. 55.

10. Tawney and Power, *Tudor Economic Documents*, vol. 1, p. 84; see also p. 89 for Cecil's concurring sentiments.

11. See the convenient list in E.M. Leonard, 'The Inclosure of Common Fields in the Seventeenth Century', *TRHS*, 2nd series, vol. 19 (1905), p. 143, n. 1.

12. John Moore, *A Target for Tillage* (London, 1612), *The Crying Sin of England* (London, 1653), and *A Scripture Word Against Enclosure* (London, 1656). See also the two statements against enclosure from the same period in *Records of the Borough of Leicester, 1603–1688*, H. Stocks, ed. (Cambridge, 1923), pp. 396, 428–30.

13. Moore, *A Target for Tillage*.

14. Robert Powell, *Depopulation Arraigned* (London, 1636).

15. Henry Halhead, *Enclosure Thrown Open* (London, 1650).

16. Francis Bacon, *Moral and Historical Works* (London, 1909), pp. 359–60.

17. E. Kerridge, *The Agricultural Revolution* (London, 1967), ch. 3.

18. Joseph Lee, *Considerations Concerning Common Fields* (London, 1653) and *A Vindication of the Considerations Concerning Common Fields* (London, 1656).

19. J. Appleby, *Economic Thought and Ideology in Seventeenth Century England* (Princeton, NJ, 1978), pp. 59–63.

20. C. Webster, *The Great Instauration* (London, 1975), p. 472.

21. Tawney and Power, *Tudor Economic Documents*, vol. 1, pp. 72–7.

22. Adam Moore, *Bread for the Poor* (London, 1653).

23. Silvanus Taylor, *Common Good* (London, 1652).

24. E.G., *Waste Land's Improvement* (London, 1653), conveniently reprinted in J. Thirsk and J.P. Cooper, eds., *Seventeenth Century Economic Documents* (Oxford, 1972), pp. 135–40.

25. For arguments in favour of the continuity of the Commonwealth idea into the seventeenth century see Jones, *The Tudor Commonwealth*, pp. 224–7, and J. Thirsk, *Economic Policy and Projects* (Oxford, 1978).

26. C. Wilson, 'The Other Face of Mercantalism', *TRHS*, 5th series, vol. 9 (1959), pp. 81–101; Appleby, *Economic Thought*, pp. 129–57; V. Pearl, 'Puritans and Poor Relief: The London Workhouse 1649–1660', in D. Pennington and K. Thomas, eds., *Puritans and Revolutionaries* (Oxford, 1978), pp. 206–32.

27. Webster, *The Great Instauration*, pp. 465–83.

28. BL, Royal MS, 17A XXXVII, ff. 17–33, 'An apology of the King's agents for the enclosure of Kinges Sedgmoore in the county of Somerset'; T.G. Barnes, *Somerset 1625–40* (Cambridge, Mass., 1961), pp. 150–51.

29. PRO, L.R. 2/194, fo. 277, 'abuses and wrongs done to His Majesty in his forests', 27 April 1609; BL, Cotton MS Titus B.IV, ff. 332–3, 'abuses observed by the surveyors of the woods', undated but early in James I's reign; Bod. Lib. Ashmolean MS 1148, ff. 255–6, 'a report by John Norden on the New forest'; BL, Lans MS 166, fo. 354, 'a report on the waste of woods in Dean forest', 11 March 1610/11.

30. Thirsk and Cooper, *Seventeenth Century Economic Documents*, p. 107.

31. E.R. Foster, ed., *Proceedings in Parliaments, 1610*, (New Haven, 1966), vol. 2, pp. 279–82.

32. Thirsk, 'Enclosing and Engrossing', p. 228.

33. C.H. McIlwain, ed., *The Political Works of James I* (New York, 1965), p. 342.

34. Thirsk and Cooper, *Seventeenth Century Economic Documents*, pp. 116–20.

35. This somewhat simplifies a complex process; for a fuller account see B. Sharp, *In Contempt of All Authority* (Berkeley, 1980), chs. 4–6.

36. Kerridge, *The Agricultural Revolution*, pp. 215–16.

37. PRO, E.134/1654/5/Hil.1, deposition of Hugh Vincent, husbandman in Berkeley vs. Maddox; E.134/1658/Mich.17, deposition of John Symes esq. in A-G vs. Hertford.

38. Thirsk and Cooper, *Seventeenth Century Economic Documents*, pp. 122–3.

39. The quotation comes from the opening of PRO, E.125/7, ff. 75–84, decree disafforesting Feckenham, Worcestershire, 23 June 1629. Similar statements can be found in E.126/3, ff. 209–21, decree in the Leicester forest case, 7 February 1627/8 and S.O.1/3, pp. 266–8, signet letter authorizing the disafforestation of Dean, Gloucestershire, 26 March 1639.

40. PRO, E.112/240/207, bill in Heath vs. Broome, Trin., 1639; Barnes, *Somerset 1625-40*, pp. 156–9; Kerridge, *The Agricultural Revolution*, pp. 215–16.

41. Thirsk, 'Enclosing and Engrossing', pp. 208–9. Thirsk's views seem to have changed considerably when a few years later she discussed the enclosure of waste in 'Seventeenth-Century Agriculture and Social Change', in J. Thirsk, ed., *Land, Church, and People* (Reading, 1970), pp. 167–9.

42. Sharp, *In Contempt of All Authority*, chs. 4 and 9; D.O. Pam, *The Rude Multitude: Enfield and the Civil War* (Edmonton Hundred Historical Society, Occasional Paper no. 33, 1977). A similar but even more complex relationship between improvement of

waste and violent popular response can be traced in the fens of East Anglia, for which see now K. Lindley, *Fenland Riots and the English Revolution* (London, 1982).

43. This and the following paragraphs are based on Darcy's papers in PRO, S.P.1/235, ff. 223–30; S.P.1/236, fo. 233; S.P.1/237, ff. 47–52, 74, 147–224, 240–61; S.P.1/238, ff. 79–84, 118; S.P.1/241, fo. 99. They are calendared in *Letters and Papers of Henry VIII, Addenda* (London, 1929), vol. 1, pp. 189–90, 228, 249, 252, 266–72, 275–7, 293–4, 299, 421–2.

44. PRO, S.P.1/237, ff. 222–4, Darcy's answer to a bill of complaint by tenants of the lordship of Rothwell.

45. PRO, S.P.1/237, ff. 179–88, answer of inhabitants of Rothwell to a bill of complaint by Lord Darcy.

46. PRO, S.P.1/237, fo. 151, Thomas Gryce to Lord Darcy, 22 June 1532.

47. PRO, S.P.1/241, fo. 99, petition of the tenants of Rothwell to Lord Darcy. This document is undated and its dating to the year 1537 by the editors of *Letters and Papers Henry VIII* seems too late to me.

48. PRO, S.P. 16/368/80, petition to PC from the Dean and Chapter of St Paul's, 30 September 1637; no. 81, draft of PC order, 30 September 1637; S.P. 16/423/103, Sir Francis Crowley *et al.* to PC, 14 June 1639; P.C. 2/49, pp. 39, 45, 84–5, 92, 208, 229–30, 236, 307; P.C. 2/50, pp. 560–62.

49. This is one of the central themes in Sharp, *In Contempt of All Authority*, on which this paragraph is largely based.

50. PRO, E.126/9, ff. 323–6, decree confirming the grant of 162 acres for the poor of Combe St Nicholas on the disafforestation of Neroche, 23 April 1668.

51. For other evidence on cottagers see P.A.J. Pettit, *Royal Forests of Northamptonshire 1558–1714* (Northants Rec. Soc., 1968), ch. 8, V.H.T. Skipp, 'Economic and Social Change in the Forest of Arden, 1530–1649', in J. Thirsk, ed., *Land, Church and People* (Reading, 1970), pp. 84–111, and *Crisis and Development: An Ecological Case Study of the Forest of Arden 1570–1674* (Cambridge, 1978).

52. C. Hill, *The World Turned Upside Down* (New York, 1972), pp. 32–45.

53. Sharp, *In Contempt of All Authority*, ch. 4.

54. PRO E.134/15 Chas 2/Mich. 32, depositions taken by commission in Hales vs. Cannaway, 15 September 1663; E.134/16 Chas 2/Eas. 13, depositions in same case 8 March 1663/4. See also S.P.29/303/180, 7 March 1671/2 for a report that in order to avoid wartime service hundreds of sailors sought sanctuary in the weald of Kent.

55. The evidence in this paragraph is drawn largely from Sharp, *In Contempt of All Authority*, chs. 4–8. The sources for the erection of cottages by prominent landlords relate mainly to Selwood Forest in Somerset and Wiltshire and the twin forests of Chippenham and Blackmore in Wiltshire and are as follows: PRO, STAC 8/76/5, and 88/8; E.112/131/282; E.134/7 Chas.1/Mich.20; E.178/4577, mm.23–5.

56. See especially the works of Pettit and Skipp cited in n. 51 above.

57. Wilts. R.O., Q.S. Recs. Great Roll, Eas. 1625, no. 136, petition to JPs from the parishioners of Purton; see also the orders relating to the relief of the poor in the Forest of Dean in PRO, Assizes 2/1, fo. 274, 29 February 1675/6 and Gloucs. R.O., Q.S. Order Book, fo. 34, Trin., 1673; fo. 104, Epiph. 1675/6; fo. 181, Mich. 1678; fo. 211, Eas. 1680.

58. PRO, STAC 8/88/18, bill and answer in Coles vs. Leversage, 21 May 1603. See also E.112/131/282, information and answer in A-G vs. Seymour, Mich. 1624.

59. PRO, STAC, 8/76/5, bill and answer in Berkeley vs. Tynnye, 4 February 1624/5.

60. Sharp, *In Contempt of All Authority*, ch. 5.

61. PRO, E.178/3837, mm.40–44.

62. PRO, S.P.16/44/45, petition from the inhabitants of the Forest of Dean to the King, 1630? This may be the petition mentioned below in n. 63 as of midsummer last.

63. Berks, R.O., Trumbull Add. MSS 37, petition of the inhabitants of the Forest of Dean to the King. I am grateful to Professor Thomas G. Barnes for a copy of his note on this document, part of a collection once in the temporary custody of the Berkshire R.O. but now unavailable.

64. PRO, S.P.16/195/5, examination of Thomas Yarwood, yeoman, 24 June 1631.

He signs his name Yerworth.

65. PRO, E.126/3, ff. 378–85, decree disafforesting Braydon 10 June 1630; E.178/2470, order on allotments in Braydon, Mich., 1630.

66. PRO, E.125/13, fo. 386, order authorizing commission to set out the plots for the poor 13 February 1633/4; E.178/2470, return of commission's proceedings, 15 April 1634; E.125/15, ff., 103–4, decree confirming those proceedings, 21 June 1634.

67. PRO, E.125/21, ff. 240–42, decree confirming proceedings of the commission on the twenty-five acres for the poor of Leigh, 27 October 1637.

68. Wiltshire R.O. (Bassett Down MSS), 1390/Box6/Bundle T, Exchequer decree on the poor plot at Purton Stoke, 10 June 1734.

69. Som. R.O. (Alford and Kirke MSS), DD/HLM, Box 2, papers relating to Gillingham Forest, Chancery decree, Mich., 1653 and indenture of 2 December 1656. In Wiltshire R.O. (Troyte-Bullock MSS, formerly at Zeals House), 865/613, accounts of the Gillingham Forest charity, 1656–1739, there are loose pages on which some of the instruments relating to the establishment of the charity were copied in the nineteenth century. For more on the conflict at Mere and Gillingham in the 1640s and 1650s see Sharp, *In Contempt of All Authority*, ch. 9.

70. Wiltshire R.O., 865/613.

71. Wiltshire R.O., 865/613, accounts for the half year ended 29 September 1659 and the half year ended 29 September 1661; PRO, E.126/3, ff. 209–21, decree disafforesting Leicester, 7 February 1627/8; *Records of the Borough of Leicester, 1603–1688*, pp. 247 and 253.

72. PRO, E.134/3 Anne/Trin. 19, depositions in A-G on behalf of the poor of Mere vs. Clarke *et al.*, trustees.

73. Joseph Lee, *Considerations Concerning Common Fields* (London, 1653).

74. Wiltshire R.O., 865/286, Richard Greene to Richard Major, 23 March 1651/2; 865/613, loose nineteenth-century copies of the foundation documents of the forest charity in the account book, 1656–1739; Som. R.O., DD/HLM, Box 2, Chancery decree, Mich., 1653.

75. *Statutes of the Realm*, 13 and 14, Ch. II, c. 12, 1662.

76. PRO, P.C. 2/63, fo. 67, PC to JPs near the Forest of Dean, 30 November 1671; K.B. 9/927/230, Latin information against twenty-four named Dean rioters, Hil., 1671/2.

77. Som. R.O., DD/HLM, Box 2, Chancery decree, Mich., 1653; the following accounts in Wiltshire R.O. 865/613, contain references to the destruction or repair of enclosures: Mich., 1658; Lady Day and Mich., 1659; Mich., 1693.

78. PRO, E.112/907/11, information and answers in A-G vs. Clarke *et al.*, Trin., 1702; E 134/3 Anne/Eas. 28 and Trin. 19, interrogatories and depositions in the same case. I could not find a decree in this case but I suspect it was dismissed or dropped because the evidence revealed that the trustees acted within the terms of the original benefaction.

79. See n. 74 above.

80. Wiltshire R.O., 1390/Box 6/Bundle T, Exchequer decree, 10 July 1734.

81. The conflict at Malmesbury can be followed in the following: PRO, STAC 8/93/2, Cowper vs. Elkington 23 January 1612/13; STAC 8/130/2 and 3, Elkington vs. Palmer, 1 February 1607/8; STAC 8/138/8, Evans vs. Elkington, 27 April 1608; STAC 8/290/22, Webb vs. Cowper, 23 January 1612/13; E.112/254/42, A-G vs. Arch, Mich., 1631; E.112/254/45, A-G vs. Hobbes, Hil., 1631/2; E.134/9 Chas. I/Mich. 75, depositions in the same case; *Acts of the Privy Council 1613–14*, pp. 92–3, PC to sheriff and JPs of Wiltshire, 21 June 1613.

82. PRO, S.P. 16/143/41, undated petition to PC from the poor inhabitants of Hertford; *Acts of the Privy Council 1630–31*, p. 286, PC to mayor and burgesses of Hertford, 6 April 1631 and p. 333, PC ruling on the dispute, 18 May 1631; for other conflicts over borough commons see E. Kerridge, *Agrarian Problems in the Sixteenth Century and After* (London, 1969), pp. 98–9 and D. Hirst, *The Representative of the People?* (Cambridge, 1975), pp. 46–60 and appendix 2.

83. I am thinking mainly of the voluminous work of W.K. Jordan.

84. So it is described by Thirsk in *Economic Policy and Projects*.

The Prophet and Her Audience: Gender and Knowledge in The World Turned Upside Down

Phyllis Mack

When a seventeenth-century Englishman was confronted with the shocking spectacle of a woman preaching in public – and there were hundreds during and after the Interregnum – what did he see and hear?[1] A Baptist minister, listening to Sarah Latchett preach against him in his own church, was contemptuous: 'It were fitter such an Idle Housewife were shipt, and sent to Bridewell to work, then to go about railing at people.' A lawyer, listening to a dispute between Mary Mollineux and a cleric about the payment of tithes, was bemused: 'I wonder you should trouble your Self to Discourse with that Woman! She hath so much learning, it makes her mad.' A religious sectarian, confronting a former disciple who had since become a prophet, was outraged and judgemental: 'I do pronounce Susannah Frith cursed, and damned, soul and body, from the presence of God, elect men, and angels, to eternity.' A Quaker, writing to the minister Margaret Fell, was abject and reverent: 'I behold thee in the invisible ... seeing thy hand stretched forth to me, to draw me nigher and nigher unto thee.' A husband, writing to the magistrates of Boston about his wife, the prophet Mary Dyer, was uncomprehending and desperate:

> 'Tis true, I have not seen her above this half year, and cannot tell how, in the frame of her spirit, she was moved ... to run so great a hazard to herself ... Let not your love and wonted compassion be conquered by her inconsiderate madness; Oh! do not deprive me of her, but I pray give her me once again. .... Pity me![2]

'A ranting woman', 'A grave and motherly woman', 'a filthy spirit', 'a Mother of Israel', 'a silly old woman', 'a goat rough and hairy', 'a Woman clothed with the Sun', 'An old Trot': there was enormous variation in the tone of contemporary writings on visionary women, from the satirical sniping of playwrights like Ben Jonson and Thomas Heywood and the authors of astrological almanacs, to the ponderous introspection of Puritan spiritual treaties, to the purple prose of some mystical philosophers. There was also great variation in the attitude of audiences toward individual women, ranging from veneration to cynical amusement to outright sadism. My own reaction as a historian was a powerful urge to impose order; I wanted to know what made observers finally decide that a particular individual was a prophet, a witch or a pitiable lunatic. As an historian who is also a student and admirer of Christopher Hill's work on the radical sects, my obvious first step was to examine the relation between radical prophecy and class hostility.

Women prophets were both unlettered servants and respectable matrons, and a gentlewoman like Margaret Fell was relatively immune to the savage physical abuse meted out to other prophets. But all visionary women were subject to confiscation of property and imprisonment, and all were identified, in both popular and learned opinion, with the mob; the 'giddy' or 'promiscuous' body of the people.[3] Women prophets were ridiculed as 'tub-preachers', laundresses who turned their washtubs upside down to use as pulpits, inciting the mob to rebellion and themselves to sexual orgies; and in fact, much of the most powerful Quaker women's preaching was overtly hostile to the interests of the propertied classes. Grace Barwick travelled 150 miles to warn the officers in the parliamentary army:[4]

> There is a great darknesse over you ... and I feele a renting and tearing ... it is high time to remove the oppression of *Tithes* ... there is a weight of blood cruelty and injustice lying under this great Mountain, and it is time to be cast down ... and the people eased from it: ... and the people loves Liberty, and however that shall come to them, it will be thankfully received, whether by a Law or contrary to a Law.... It is not the changings of Government into new titles and names, but it is truth and perfect freedom that the best of men delights in, and it is that, that will satisfy the hungering people.

Even when women prophets were royalist or apolitical, they still reinforced, in words and manner, the popular image of the prophet as social reject. 'The Wisdom of God is ... wonderful in the Choice which He makes of instruments, to Manifest himself by,' wrote the middle-class Jane Lead. 'He takes up an ordinary Plowman [and] a Woman to be a ... Savior in Israel, when no man was found, and a few fishermen.'[5] Barbara Blaugdone, a schoolteacher with aristocratic friends and independent means, insisted on preaching only in places where she was not respected. One can only speculate on the impression she made as she harangued the public in Bridgewater, having slept in a pig-trough the night before.[6]

Starting with Professor Hill's model of a society divided into two increasingly polarized groups, elite and popular, where the treatment of female visionaries was a means of articulating class relationships and resolving social and economic tensions, I then addressed the issue of gender, and speculated that misogynist attitudes lent added energy to the hands that held the whips or signed the death warrants of uppity popular women, while the tradition of positive feminine symbolism (wisdom as the virgin Sophia or the church as the Woman in the Wilderness) made visionary women important to other elite men as a means of authenticating their own policies and beliefs. For people (usually women) were often imbued with spiritual power at the very moment when that power could be co-opted by others (nearly always men) who were still more powerful.[7] Elinor Channel, a poor woman with several young children, was struck dumb when her husband refused to let her go to London to prophesy about the restoration of the monarchy. When she finally *did* reach London, still unable to speak, she was abused by a mob because she behaved like an idiot. She was discovered wandering in the streets by Arise Evans, who published her royalist verses as a framework for his own opinions. Claiming he had recognized in her an 'angel of God', he wrote: 'It must be more of God than we are aware of ... that by this Dumb Woman, God will put all vain talkers to silence.' Elizabeth Poole prophesied in support of Oliver Cromwell in 1648, after which Colonel Rich remarked: 'I cannot but give you that impression that is upon my spirit in conjunction with that testimony which God hath manifested here by an unexpected Providence. What she hath said being correspondent with what I have made [known] as manifested to me before.' Christian James, a young woman from Cornwall, 'died' and came briefly back to life, admonishing all to repent and live in harmony; her verses were then published by the local magistrates, to be sung to the tune of 'In Summertime'.[8] All of this is not to say that women visionaries were the victims of cold-blooded manipulation; probably Colonel Rich and the magistrates in Cornwall were genuinely relieved to learn that God had sanctioned their values and activities through the mouths of his weak vessels.

They might have also been relieved to be able to mediate at least one prophet's performance, because they lived in a society where women in general were perceived as more visible, more mobile, and more aggressive than before. Some were resisting the ceremony of churching as a remnant of medieval superstition and the greed of the clergy; others were leading food riots or were active in the protests of the 1640s.[9] There is also evidence that women's economic activities in midwifery, dairy farming and small trades were becoming more visible in some areas of the country, and that in those very areas rituals expressing sexual hostility were more prominent.[10] In a world that seemed full of masterless men and women, the apparently masterless, untethered female prophet must have been seen by many as the ultimate threat:

> When ladies ride abroad with waxed boots, and men thresh with their Cloaks on; when the pot freezes in the Chimney-corner, and Puss sits with her arse to the fire; When women go abroad and fetch home wood, and men sit at home by the fire side and burn it: When isesickles hang at peoples noses, and women cannot catch them a heat with scolding; when all these signs come to pass, you may be confident of cold weather.

This from an almanac of 1664.[11]

Having established a parallel between behaviour stemming from social and economic tensions and anxiety about gender roles, I concluded that the desire to control both women and the mob fused to create an explosive and largely hostile reaction to militant female prophets; a disquieting picture for contemporaries, but a coherent and tidy model for the historian, particularly a historian like myself, anxious to reconcile an analysis based on the horizontal divisions of class and status with one focusing on the vertical division of gender. As I continued to read and ponder the sources, however, my tidy synthesis of class and gender began to come apart in my hands, for while it was true enough that women and the labouring classes were identified symbolically in anti-sectarian propaganda and in the words of some male and female prophets, the equation broke down altogether when I looked more closely at sectarian writings themselves.

Given the widespread perception that women prophets were both sign and symptom of social breakdown and political rebellion, one might reasonably infer that the most radical groups, those who sought to turn the social and clerical hierarchy upside down, were the ones most willing to see truth in the words and deeds of women prophets and to champion the equality of all women. Professor Hill and others see the ideological peak of seventeenth-century radicalism coming with the Levellers and the True Levellers or Diggers; these groups were the most eloquent defenders of the labouring classes and the ones with the most well-developed political programme. While the vast majority of Englishmen defined 'the people' as consisting only of male property-holders, the Diggers, led by Gerrard Winstanley, advocated absolute equality of servants and masters, male and female, in a democratic, communistic society. 'And by people', writes Hill, 'Winstanley really did mean all the people.'[12]

My own reading of the sources indicated that there were important differences among radical groups on the question of women as prophets. In fact it was precisely the most radical of the radical sects (radical in Professor Hill's terms, that is) whose programmes were least concerned with women, visionary or otherwise; it was the sects or groups or individuals which had the least articulated political programme and the most mystical theology – the Ranters, the Baptists, and above all the Quakers – which were most willing to integrate women into their activities. The problem of accounting for these differences in attitude led me to a further analysis of the gendered language of radical political discourse during the Civil War.

The Diggers preached that men and women might both achieve the perfection each had enjoyed before the Fall; Winstanley argued repeatedly that both men and women had the capacity for perfection, and that corrupt earthly power does not know 'that their wives, children, servants, subjects are their fellow creatures, and hath an equall priviledge to share with them in the blessing of liberty'.[13] But Winstanley also envisaged a law of freedom which combined a radical insistence on the needs and rights of the weak with an utterly conservative scenario of the beginnings of patriarchal authority: Adam, the first father, was also the first ruler, because his children needed and accepted his authority in order to insure their own preservation. 'By this choice, they make him not only a Father, but a Master and Ruler. And out of this root springs up all Magistrates and Officers.'[14] Winstanley railed against the community of women supposedly practised by other sects, chiefly in order to preserve the patriarchal family as the cellular basis of society and authority.

> In a private Family a Father, or Master, is an Officer ... he is to command [his children] in their work ... he is either to reprove by words, or whip those who offend.... That so children may not quarrel like beasts, but live ... like rational men, experienced in yielding obedience to the Laws and Officers of the Commonwealth.[15]

Professor Hill is surely right to view Winstanley's advocacy of universal human rights as immensely creative, in that he attributed virtues to the poor which most theorists applied only to property-holders.[16] Winstanley's programme for women was also partially progressive. Rather than define a married woman as a legal nonentity, Winstanley gave her a certain independence; she might choose whom to marry, and 'The wife or children of such as have lost their Freedom, shall not be as slaves till they have lost their Freedom, as their parents and husbands have done.'[17] This said, we must still observe that Winstanley's social philosophy, while radical in terms of class relationships, is conservative to the core in terms of gender; in his utopia, women are not even given authority over the freshness of the meat they put on the table:

> No Master of a family shall suffer more meat to be dressed at a dinner or supper, then what will be spent and eaten by his household.... If there be any spoil constantly made in a family of the food of Man, the Overseer shall reprove the Master for it privately; if that abuse be continued in his family, through his neglect of family government, he shall be openly reproved ... before all the people ... the third time he shall be made a servant ... that he may know what it is to get food, and another shall have the oversight of his house for the time.[18]

Winstanley's patriarchalism looks more striking when set beside Puritan views on the domestic authority of the good wife, including the duty to teach and prophesy within her own home; it looks even more striking when set beside Quaker treatises on women preaching, Quaker measures on protecting women in trades, Quaker views on education, and Quaker reverence toward many female prophets.[19] Listen to William Caton, writing to the Quaker leader Margaret Fell about his plans to travel as a missionary to Scotland:

> Therefore do thou ask Counsel of thy heavenly father concerning me, and let me hear from thee ... whether that thou wouldst have me to go ... for I know that whatsoever thou shalt speak to me, it will be unto me as from the mouth of the Lord, now dear heart I know thou hast the tongue of the learned, therefore speak a word unto me in due season ... thy paper was read in meeting ... and truly my heart was much broken to hear thy voice, it was so pure and pleasant to my ears.[20]

A few months later Caton wrote to her,

> who art Ordained of God to feed his Lambes, to water his tender plants, to bind up the brokenhearted, to strengthen the weak, and to speak Comfortably to his people ... yea often both night and day I behold thee in the Invisible, which sees they glory and they beauty and thy garment of praise.... I thus behold thee in the invisible ... seeing thy hand stretched forth to me, to draw me nigher and nigher unto thee, that thou mayest take part with me of my sufferings.[21]

Why did Diggers and Quakers differ so profoundly in their vision of the role of women? Their attitudes could not have been rooted in the class background of their adherents, since Quaker yeomen and artisans were not that far removed from the servants, labourers and small householders who made up the Diggers.[22] Nor were these attitudes related to their awareness of sexual injustice; Fox and Winstanley were both articulate critics of the oppressed position of women in their society. Their different vision of gender roles derived instead from their differing approaches to the problems of knowledge and salvation. As Professor Hill has stated, the Diggers were pantheists and materialists of a kind. They believed that knowledge came through the senses, and that the physical universe, while filled with spiritual meaning, was not subject to unpredictable intervention by spiritual forces; it could be appreciated and comprehended by reason alone. Materialism, for these men, meant mind over matter; Reason was God. By 'Reason' Winstanley did not mean the wisdom taught in universities or the ethereal concepts learned in church, but the 'laborious Knowledge' that comes from practical education; husbandry, minerals, the ordering of cattle, the 'secrets of nature'. 'And thus to speak, or thus to read the *Law* of Nature (or God) as he hath written his name in every body,' wrote Winstanley, 'is to speak a pure language ... giving to every thing its own weight and measure. By this means, in time men shall attain to the practical know-ledge of God truly ... and that knowledge will not deceive a man.'[23] The Diggers were also relatively secular in their priorities; their goals focused on the transformation of society rather than transcendence of wordly concerns or personal, spiritual insight. As the Digger song, quoted by Professor Hill, went, 'Glory *here*, Diggers all!'[24]

The Quakers also believed that salvation gave women and men a true understanding of the natural world through the senses.[25] And, like the Diggers, Quakers were socially conscious and socially aggressive, as an Anglican minister found out when a female prophet yelled at him to 'Come down, you painted beast!' Quakers suffered by the thousands for non-payment of church taxes and for preaching against the corruption of the clergy and aristocracy. But Quakers were less preoccupied with social structures, whether in protecting them or turning them upside down, than the Levellers or Diggers. They also placed less trust in reason as *the* guide to truth, but emphasized the unpredictable, emotional and mystical character of human insight. When Judith Zinspinning arrived from Holland to preach in 1663, she used an English translator, but the Quakers asked to hear only the Dutch even though they couldn't understand a word she said. They knew well that the prophet's deeper message was nonsense; literally non-sense.[26]

How did these very different approaches to the problem of know-ledge relate to attitudes about gender? My impression is that contem-poraries lived in at least two mental worlds, each with its own set of assumptions about gender relationships. Spiritually, women were believed to be powerful, in some ways more powerful than men. The kind of power or energy associated with this female spirituality was more akin to the power Freud ascribed to sexuality than it was to the diluted piety of an eighteenth-century pillar of the Church. Spiritual power infused and energized the body; it was polymorphous; and it was morally ambiguous, either godly or demonic. The kind of power and virtue associated with the *political* sphere, in which women were virtually absent in any official capacity, was power of a very different sort; self-conscious, self-controlled, practical and tough. Queen Elizabeth presented herself in public as an exemplar of feminine virtue, her breasts exposed to reveal her as the chaste, nursing mother of her people, but when it was necessary to instil confidence in her subjects at moments of national crisis, she assured them that, although a weak woman, she had the 'heart and stomach of a King'.[27]

For Winstanley, as for more mystical thinkers, the sun represented the masculine light of Reason; the moon and earth, the dark, fleshly, feminine side of existence:

> the Moone is the shadow of the Sun, in regard they have been led by the powers of the curse in flesh, which is the *Feminine* part; not by the power of the righteous Spirit which is Christ, the *Masculine* power ... King imagination ... rule(s) over the created flesh, which is the feminine part, and will not allow it to obey the sun of righteousness, which is called conscience.[28]

'And this shall be your mark,' Winstanley wrote to the prophet Eleanor Davies, 'that you have lost the breeches, your Reason, by the inward boiling vexation of your spirit ... and that inward power shall chaine you up in darkness, til Reason, which you have trampled under foot, come to set you free.'[29]

I do not quote these obviously metaphoric utterances in order to expose the soft underside of Winstanley's radicalism; on the contrary, this kind of statement allows us to understand how the thinking of the most socially conscious man or woman was skewed by the categories – whether conscious or unconscious – by which he or she perceived and ordered reality. For Winstanley did say that women might preach; 'that man or woman that sees the Spirit, within themselves ... is able to make a Sermon, because they can speak by experience of the light ... within them'.[30] But the kind of knowledge in which women were believed to excel had little or no place in Winstanley's conception of nature, which one scholar has described as Baconian; nor would it have had much to contribute to the life of his egalitarian and orderly utopia.[31]

Please note that no one, in either of these groups, was challenging traditional stereotypes of the nature of womanhood. It was rather that those who thought most creatively about women's participation in religious and social life had a view of knowledge which harmonized with traditional views of women as both intensely physical and intensely imaginative or spiritual; as, if you will, more unstructured than men. George Fox, who believed that salvation gave men and women automatic and direct knowledge of the workings of nature, enabling them to speak with God's voice, could envision women as healers, teachers and ministers – as mothers in Israel.[32] Gerrard Winstanley, who wanted to understand nature through reason and education, envisioned a sort of postal system, whereby new information would be carried from one community to another; it was inconceivable, given contemporary values, that he could have imagined women as postmasters. (The irony is that the Quakers actually did have an informal but effective international postal system, and it was organized and directed by a woman, Margaret Fell, who used her house at Swarthmore as a clearing house for letters, and who corresponded herself with almost every leading male and female Quaker.)[33]

Contemporary values also implied that women's spiritual power was never unequivocally benign. The epistemology of the Quakers not only allowed for the prominence of women in the spiritual and practical life of the community; it also implied that women might as easily be witches. Martha Simmonds, formerly a respected Quaker minister, was accused of witchcraft by her own people after she and some other Quakers staged an imitation of Jesus' entry into Jerusalem. In the miraculous episodes which George Fox recounted in his journal, the witches and possessed people he discovered and cured were almost invariably female.[34] In this regard it makes little sense to argue that some religious groups 'liked' women more than others; rather, they embued women with a spiritual potential which was always fluid and potentially sinister. The more materialist sects ignored women as either prophets *or* witches, arguing, as did the most advanced thinkers and physicians of the time, that witchcraft was a fantasy because the devil would hardly deign to make himself known through the vehicle of a silly old woman.[35]

Perhaps there was a fundamental contradiction in the very notion of a rationally organized society, whether hierarchical or democratic, energized by occult spiritual forces. Visionary men like George Fox might have been seen to resolve this contradiction by embodying both unrestrained spiritual energy and practical leadership; visionary *women*, active in a period of extreme political upheaval and intense political consciousness, made the contradiction more explicit. Winstanley resolved the problem by viewing women as equal but passive citizens of a community rationally structured down to the smallest aspects of domestic life. The Quakers resolved the problem by propounding a view of knowledge in which moral integrity, emotion and spirituality were conflated; as one Quaker put it, 'where righteousness and Peace kisseth each other'.[36] They also adhered to a communal structure so minimal that the flow of spiritual authority was relatively unrestricted; servants, artisans and gentry, both male and female, might become weighty Friends.

The Puritans demonstrate even more clearly the difficulty of resolving inspiration and rational organization; indeed, their fixed standard of authority and behaviour in family, congregation and community was ultimately irreconcilable with their ideal of spiritual fluidity in the Elect's relationship to God. Puritans shared, indeed they probably inspired, the Quaker emphasis on Paul's doctrine that before God there is neither male nor female; both groups viewed the wife as an affectionate partner in marriage and embraced the custom of informal prophesying by both men and women. But unlike the Quakers, Puritans were also intensely concerned with issues of hierarchy and structure. Hence their complicated church structure dominated by male ministers, elders and deacons. Hence also their fear that a member of the Elect might slide into the sin of presumption, falling from there into the worse sin of infallibility, finally hurtling downward into the pit of antinomianism, the heresy for which Anne Hutchinson had been banished in 1637 and the heresy with which female visionaries were invariably associated.[37]

A Puritan watching and listening to a female prophet, say, Mary Dyer attempting to preach on the way to her own execution or the elderly Elizabeth Hooten haranguing the magistrates of Boston, would have seen at least two things: a woman speaking in public who was not a queen, which was unambiguously wrong, and a woman speaking what may have been holy words, which – if they *were* holy – was unambiguously right. Indeed, the Puritans displayed almost as much confusion as fanaticism in their cruelty toward Quaker women. At least one Puritan was driven to despair by confusion over the meaning of Quaker prophecy; 'Sometimes she would hate Quakers, sometimes plead for them: some time, weeping tears, she could of herself, speak not a word to any; some time [she would] weary others with much speaking.'[38] It is curious that, as much as the Puritans feared Quaker female prophets, they only pricked a few of those who came to Massachusetts for witches' marks. The prophet Mary Dyer was actually reprieved by the magistrates just before her execution; by her own voluntary reappearance to preach in Boston after her release, she virtually forced her own head into the noose.[39]

Even the Quakers had increasing difficulty as they struggled to reconcile their so-called feminine elements – whether found in the prominence of female adherents, in the emotive writing and behaviour and androgynous religious symbolism of men like George Fox, or in the fluid relationships that characterized the group as a whole – with the constraints of a rationally organized community and church. After the Restoration, efforts to bring Quakerism into the social and political mainstream included the establishment of a network of autonomous women's meetings. The overall, long-term impact of these women's meetings on the public lives of Quaker women was probably positive, but the immediate impact was to channel women toward the traditionally feminine activities of overseeing children's education, regulating marriages and visiting prisoners, and to limit the appearance of women, particularly young women, as preachers or public Friends. In 1708 the Quakers of the Westminster monthly meeting noted that 'A paper was brought in from one Mary Willis and read, wherein she condemned herself for ... suffering the agitation spirit to come upon her. She is advised to forbear imposing her preaching upon our public meetings for worship until Friends are better satisfied.'[40]

Christopher Hill has shown us the importance of class relationships to an understanding of seventeenth-century popular religion, and for this we are all in his debt. We also confront a new and challenging project; that of tracing the complex and changing relationship between class and gender as significant categories of analysis. What *does* seem clear at this point is that the crisis of knowledge and the conflict among social groups which exercised both religious philosophers and unlettered servants during the seventeenth century was bound to resolve itself to the disadvantage of women as sources of both spiritual and secular authority – as it did in the later Quaker movement and in society at large – so long as women remained exclusively associated with the qualities of intuition, enthusiasm and unrestrained spiritual and emotional energy; qualities which were deemed irrelevant or dangerous by conservative magistrates and businessmen and radical thinkers alike. In the new age of limited ecclesiastical power and unlimited economic expansion, some members of the labouring classes would respond to the visionary leadership of the Shaker Ann Lee or the Methodist Ann Carr, but in the middle and upper classes God's grace would be experienced, not in a hot gush of mystical revelation, but in the steady drip of a measured, moderate and entirely reasonable piety, intoned and explicated by the ordained male minister.[41]

Notes

I would like to thank Joan Scott, Margaret Hunt, Christopher Hill, and John Elliott for helpful conversation and criticism. Thanks also to the Rockefeller Foundation and the Institute for Advanced Study, Princeton, for providing a supportive atmosphere in which to pursue this study.

1. On women as prophets, see Phyllis Mack, 'Women as Prophets during the English Civil War', *Feminist Studies*, vol. 8, no. 1 (Spring 1982), pp. 19–47. Over four hundred women prophesied at least once during the second half of the seventeenth century, about 375 of whom were Quakers.

2. Roger Hayden, ed., *The Records of a Church of Christ in Bristol, 1640–1687* (Gateshead, 1974), p. 30; Mary Mollineux, *Fruits of Retirement: Or, Miscellaneous Poems, Moral and Divine* (London, 1702) n.p.; Elizabeth Stirredge, *Strength in Weakness Manifest*, reprinted *The Friends Library: Comprising Journals, Doctrinal Treatises, and Other Writings of Members of the Religious Society of Friends* (Philadelphia, 1838, 1st edn 1746), vol. II, p. 201; Lodowijk Muggleton, *Spiritual Epistles* (London, reprinted 1820), p. 80, quoted in *Dictionary of Quaker Biography*, MSS, Friends House, London, under the heading, 'Frith, Susannah'; William Caton to Margaret Fell, London, March 1656/7, Swarthmore MSS, vol. 1, p. 316; William Dyer to Governor Endicott of Boston, before her execution in 1660 (quoted in James Bowden, *The History of the Society of Friends in America* (London, 1850), vol. 1, pp. 199–200).

3. On the association of women and the poor, see Christopher Hill, 'The Poor and the People in Seventeenth-Century England', *History from Below: Studies in Popular Protest and Popular Ideology in Honour of George Rude*, Frederick Krantz, ed. (Montreal, 1985), pp. 75–93.

4. Grace Barwick, 'To All Present Rulers, Whether Parliament, or Whomsoever of England' (London, 1659). On the link between occult magic and radical politics, see P.M. Rattansi, 'Paracelsus and the Puritan Revolution', *Ambix*, vol. 9, no. 1 (February 1961), pp. 24–32; Michael MacDonald, *Mystical Bedlam, Madness, Anxiety and Healing in Seventeenth-Century England* (Cambridge, 1981), pp. 230–31; Christopher Hill, *The World Turned Upside Down*, (New York, 1972) (hereafter *WTUD*), pp. 24, 73–5. On the link between women and political rebellion, see Hill, *WTUD*, pp. 82–3, and Keith Thomas, 'Women and the Civil War Sects', *Past and Present*, no. 13, April 1958, pp. 42–62.

5. Jane Lead, *The Wonders of God's Creation Manifested in the variety of Eight Worlds: As they were made known experimentally to the Author* (London, 1679?), Preface.

6. Mabel R. Brailsford, *Quaker Women 1650–1690* (London, 1915), pp. 175–6.

7. Mack, 'Women as Prophets', pp. 32–3. For an excellent theoretical discussion of this position, see I.M. Lewis, *Ecstatic Religion: An Anthropological Study of Spirit Possession and Shamanism* (Harmondsworth, Middlesex, 1975, 1st edn 1971). 'Thus if possession is the means by which the underdog bids for attention, witchcraft accusations are the countervailing strategy by which such demands are kept within bounds ... for these upstart controllers of spirits are, by their very power over the spirits, suspected of causing what they cure' (pp. 121–2).

8. Elinor Channel, 'A Message from God, By a Dumb Woman', Arise Evans, ed. (London, 1653); on Poole, C.H. Firth, ed., *The Clarke Papers: Selections from the Papers of William Clarke* (Westminster, 1894), vol. 2, p. 152; 'A Wonderful Prophecie, declared by Christian James' (n.p., n.d.), broadside.

9. On churching, see Dorothy Ludlow, '"Arise and Be Doing": English "Preaching" Women, 1640–1660', PhD dissertation, Indiana University, 1978, pp. 56–62. On popular protest, see Barry Reay, ed., *Popular Culture in Seventeenth-Century England* (London and Sydney, 1985), Introduction, p. 12, and the essay by Buchanan Sharp, 'Popular Protest in Seventeenth-Century England', on pp. 274, 285, 290. Lyle Koehler states that in New England, the number and seriousness of crimes committed by women increased during this period. There were also more cases of women requesting divorces, licences to sell alcoholic beverages, and women committing suicide (*A Search for Power: The 'Weaker Sex' in Seventeenth-Century New England* (Urbana–Chicago–London, 1980), pp. 229, 254).

10. On dairy farming, see David Underdown, 'The Taming of the Scold: The Enforcement of Patriarchal Authority in Early Modern England', in *Order and Disorder in Early Modern England*, Anthony Fletcher and John Stevenson, eds, (Cambridge, 1985), pp. 135–6. Christopher Hill writes that aristocratic theatre was cynical and contemptuous in its attitude toward women, probably because of rising middle-class households where the wife was the junior partner in the business (*WTUD*, pp. 247–8). There was also a scheme

to incorporate the midwives of London, which was turned down by the College of Physicians (J.H. Aveling, *The Camberlens, and the Midwifery Forceps. Memorials of the Family and an Essay on the Invention of the Instrument* (London, 1882, 34ff). Wallace Notestein remarks on the numbers of accused witches who were teachers (*A History of Witchcraft in England from 1558 to 1718*, 1911, reprinted 1965, pp. 211–13, 223–4). W.K. Jordan notes that while there was little legal improvement for women in London from 1480 to 1660, the actual rights of women were increasing in all urban communities, and that there was a rapid gain from the 1620s through 1650. In London and Bristol, most charitable activities were handled by women (*Philanthropy in England 1480–1660: A Study of the Changing Patterns of English Social Aspirations* (London, 1959), pp. 28–30).

11. 'Poor Robin's Almanac' (London, 1664), 'Signs of Cold Weather', n.p. Satirical almanacs and other popular writings often used female figures as symbols of social breakdown. The pamphlet '*Hic Mulier*; or, The Man-Woman' stated, 'since the days of Adam women were never so Masculine: ... from the Mother to the youngest daughter; ... Masculine in Mood, from bold speech to impudent action; and Masculine in Tense, for without redress they were, are, and will be still most Masculine, most mankind, and most monstrous' (London, 1620; quoted in Katherine Usher Henderson and Barbara F. McManus, *Half Humankind: Contexts and Texts of the Controversy about Women in England, 1540–1640* (Urbana and Chicago, 1985), p. 265).

12. Hill, 'The Poor and the People', p. 89; Hill, *WTUD*, ch. 7. For an overview of the radical sects, see Frances Dow, *Radicalism in the English Revolution 1640–1660* (Oxford, 1985), p. 79: Dow agrees that Winstanley's beliefs 'mark the peak of radical, innovative tendencies in the history of political, religious and social thinking in the 1640's and 1650's'.

13. Gerrard Winstanley, 'Truth Lifting Up Its Head Above Scandals' (London, 1649), quoted in T. Wilson Hayes, *Winstanley the Digger: A Literary Analysis of Radical Ideas in the English Revolution* (Cambridge, Mass., 1979), p. 115.

14. Gerrard Winstanley, *The Law of Freedom in a Platform or True Magistracy Restored* (London, 1652), in George H. Sabine, ed., *The Works of Gerrard Winstanley* (Ithaca, NY, 1941), p. 532.

15. Winstanley, *Law of Freedom*. On Winstanley's patriarchalism, see also J.C. Davis, *Utopia and the Ideal Society: A Study of English Utopian Writing 1516–1700* (Cambridge, 1981), p. 197.

16. Hill, 'The Poor and the People', p. 87.

17. Winstanley, *Law of Freedom*, pp. 597–9.

18. Winstanley, *Law of Freedom*, pp. 599–600.

19. Quakers were opponents of book-learning as it was commonly taught. George Fox's programme for Quaker schools was that 'whatsoever things was civil and useful in ye creation' should be taught to boys and girls. He wanted a garden planted 'with all sorts of physical plants for lads and lasses to learn simples there, as well as the nature of flowers, roots, plants and trees' (Geoffrey F. Nuttall, '"Unity with the Creation": George Fox and the Hermetic Philosophy', *The Puritan Spirit* (London, 1967), pp. 140–41).

20. William Caton to Margaret Fell, Sunderland, August 1655, Swarthmore MSS, vol. 1, p. 316.

21. William Caton to Margaret Fell, London, March 1656/7, Swarthmore MSS, vol. 1, p. 316.

22. On the Quakers, see Richard Vann, *The Social Development of English Quakerism, 1655–1755* (Cambridge, Mass., 1969). On the Diggers, see Hill, *WTUD*, p. 97.

23. Winstanley, *Law of Freedom*, pp. 564–5, 577–9. Also see Hill, *WTUD*, pp. 115–20, on Winstanley's reliance on the senses and his use of biblical stories as metaphors for practical human truths.

24. Hill, *WTUD*, p. 120.

25. Nuttall, 'Unity with the Creation', pp. 134–43.

26. Brailsford, *Quaker Women*, p. 237.

27. Quoted in Louis Montrose, '"Shaping Fantasies": Figurations of Gender and Power in Elizabethan Culture', *Representations*, vol. 2 (1983), p. 77. On Elizabeth's symbolic costume, see pp. 63–4.

28. Gerrard Winstanley, 'Truth Lifting Up its Head Above Scandals' (London, 1649),

quoted in Hayes, *Winstanley*, p. 114. See also pp. 66, 69, 101.

29. Winstanley to Eleanor Davies in Pirton, Hertfordshire, 1650, Paul H. Hardacre, ed., *The Huntington Library Quarterly*, vol. 22, no. 4 (August 1959), pp. 345–9. Winstanley actually became an employee of Eleanor Davies after his attempt to establish a Digger commonwealth had failed. Although he was aware of her fame as a prophet, his relationship with her was apparently limited to an argument over payment of his wages.

30. 'The New Law of Righteousness Budding forth, in restoring the whole Creation from the bondage of the curse' (London, 1649), quoted in Hayes, *Winstanley the Digger*, p. 132.

31. Conversation with James R. Jacob.

32. Fox wrote, 'it was showed me how all things had their names given them, according to their nature and virtue,' *because* he had been 'renewed into the image of God by Christ Jesus, to the state of Adam, which he was in before he fell' (quoted in Nuttall, 'Unity', p. 140).

33. On Margaret Fell and the Swarthmore correspondence, see Isabel Ross, *Margaret Fell: Mother of Quakerism* (York, 1984, 1st edn 1949).

34. *Journal of George Fox*, John L. Nickalls, ed. (London, 1975), pp. 18, 42, 43.

35. This was the most common 'progressive' argument against witchcraft. Reginald Scott wrote, 'First, that the glory and power of God be not so abridged and abased, as to thrust into the hand or lip of a lewd old woman' (*The Discoverie of Witchcraft* (London, 1686, 1st edn 1584), quoted in Sidney Anglo, ed., *The Damned Art: Essays in the Literature of Witchcraft* (London, 1977), p. 108). Also see Notestein, *Witchcraft*, pp. 179–80, quoting a popular parliamentary paper, 'Moderate Intelligencer', saying the same thing. Muggleton wrote, 'there is no other devil, or spirit, or familiar spirit for Witches to deal withal, or to work any Enchantments by, but their own imagination' (Lodowijk Muggleton, *A True Interpretation of the Witch of Endor*, 5th edn (London, 1856, 1st edn 1669), p. 1).

36. Swarthmore MSS, Epistle of James Nayler, 1653, vol. 3, p. 72.

37. The historiography of Puritanism reflects the confusion of Puritans themselves about the relative importance of Church structure, dominated by men, and spontaneous, emotional worship, in which both men and women participated as equals. Elizabeth Gilliam emphasizes the degree to which Puritan ministers took women seriously in their personal correspondence and spiritual treatises ('Women and Melancholy', unpublished dissertation in progress, Yale University). For the opposite view see Katheleen Davies, 'The Sacred Condition of Equality – How Original Were Puritan Doctrines of Marriage?', *Social History*, vol. 5, (May 1977), pp. 563–80. On the tension implied in the half-way convenant, see Michael J. Colacurcio, 'Visible Sanctity and Specter Evidence: The Moral World of "Young Goodman Brown"', *Essex Institute Historical Collections*, CX (no. 4, October 1974), pp. 259ff. For an interesting discussion of the way this tension was resolved in Puritan sermons and child-rearing practices, see David Leverenz, *The Language of Puritan Feeling: An Exploration in Literature, Psychology, and Social History* (New Brunswick, NJ, 1980).

38. John Hull, 'Memoir and Diaries', p. 192, quoted in Koehler, *Search for Power*, p. 253.

39. William C. Braithwaite, *The Beginnings of Quakerism*, 2nd edn (Cambridge, 1955), p. 404.

40. Quoted in Amelia Gummere, *Witchcraft and Quakerism: A Study in Social History* (Philadelphia, 1908), p. 17. On women's meetings, see William C. Braithwaite, *The Second Period of Quakerism*, 2nd edn (Cambridge, 1961), ch. 10, 'Women's Meetings and Central Organization', pp. 269–89.

41. On the relation of religion to the world of business at the end of the seventeenth century, see Margaret C. Jacob, *The Newtonians and the English Revolution 1689–1720* (Hassocks, Sussex, 1976).

On the Rant

Edward Thompson

Professor J.C. Davis has written a book to show that the Ranters did not exist.[1] There was no Ranter sect, no organization, no acknowledged Ranter leadership. Those alleged to be leaders did not agree with each other on some points of doctrine; or they denied that they were Ranters; or they quickly recanted; or (like Laurence Clarkson, or Claxton, who acknowledged in his autobiographical *The Lost Sheep Found* that he had been known as the 'Captain of the Rant') might have been falsifying their own record for the sake of better setting off their new convictions (Clarkson had become a Muggletonian). Accusations of drinking, swearing and sexual libertinism against the Ranters can be dismissed as the lampoons of opponents or the sensationalism of the 'yellowpress'. Accounts of Ranter beliefs and practices coming from Quakers, Baptists and other observers are valueless as evidence, being doctrinal polemics or lampoons. Davis demonstrates all this with tedious repetition and a swaggering pretence of rigour. He rounds it off with sixty pages of reprints from the worthless and salacious 'yellowpress' anti-Ranter tracts. This is like tying a large lead weight to the neck of whatever weakling kitten of the imagination has survived immersion in the tedium of his text, and sinking it finally to the bottom of the pond.

How, then, did it come about that both contemporaries and subsequent historians have supposed that there were Ranters? Two answers for that. First, in the disturbing times of 1649–51, a fictional, mythic image of Ranterism was projected, as a kind of moral *grande peur*. Once the Ranter bugaboo had arisen it was found very serviceable as a threat, or as a smear, in controlling doctrinal deviance or in effecting the consolidation of discipline in other sects. Secondly, the revival of interest in the Ranters since 1970 is explained in terms of the supposed 'goals' of the Communist party Historians' Group in 1946–56, the realization of

153

which may be seen in A.L. Morton's *The World of the Ranters* and Christopher Hill's *The World Turned Upside Down.* At the same time, these and other historians wished to find precursors for the anti-hegemonic 'hippie' culture of the late 1960s, and Norman Cohn (whose membership of the Communist Party Historians' Group has gone unrecorded) wished to clobber that culture, and to show the way in which millenial Ranting led on to totalitarianism. So the old bugaboo was dug up and dressed in modern jeans.

What is silly about all this is that Davis has set up a historiographical bugaboo of his own. To 'rant' was a term of insult, and 'Ranter' was, like 'loony Left', a term invented by opponents. It is not likely that Coppe or Bauthumley or Richard Coppin would have assented to the sobriquet. As for the historians, perhaps Cohn, in *The Pursuit of the Millennium*, was a little credulous, since his thesis required that millennial sects be seen at their most crazy. But Morton, Hill and others have always been at pains to make it clear that there was never a Ranter sect. 'It is extremely doubtful whether there ever was a Ranter organisation' – thus Hill, who also comments on the 'very wide discrepancies' between the theology of such men as Salmon and Bauthumley and 'the licentious practices of which rank-and-file Ranters were accused'. Nor does Hill ever pretend to some uniformity of Ranter doctrine. *The World Turned Upside Down* and *The Experience of Defeat* derived their richness of texture from their scrupulous attention to diversity among these unclubbable heresiarchs. As for Morton's *The World of the Ranters*, this also insists that the Ranters were never a sect: 'there is no evidence for any formal organisation or generally received body of doctrine.' The 'literature about the Ranters is uniformly hostile and frequently nothing but the lowest type of gutter journalism', 'pamphlets of the lowest, muck-racking type' (that is, Davis's 'yellowpress'). Morton considers, on the basis of such evidence as Clarkson's *The Lost Sheep*, that the accounts of Ranter licence 'may not be entirely without foundation', but he, like Hill, handles all accounts with caution.

A historian who might with reason feel a sense of grievance at Davis's historiographical bugaboo is Frank McGregor, whose unpublished thesis on the Ranters (Oxford, 1968) has been pillaged by Davis wholesale, yet who gave to him the most interesting part of his case. For McGregor, in several articles, has himself developed the argument that George Fox and others used the odium of Ranterism as a useful disciplinary control, and, in the case of early Quakerism, this 'undoubtedly contributed to the victory of group discipline'. But while Davis takes over this finding, he reproves and even scoffs at McGregor ('juvenilia of an early thesis') because his other conclusions are less convenient. Not only does McGregor identify a core of authentic 'Ranter' texts (by Coppe,

Bauthumley, Salmon and perhaps Clarkson), but he concludes that Ranterism did exist as 'a loosely co-ordinated campaign', a 'mood', and a 'movement of enthusiasm', whose presence may be located rather exactly in 1650–51. This is perfectly consonant with Ranterism's other function as an instrument of discipline – a bugaboo – which belongs to the years *after* 1651. Indeed, the uneasy memory of the excesses of enthusiasm of the *annus mirabilis*, 1650, with its heresiarchs, prophets and messiahs, with John Robins and Thomas Tany, with its 'witchcraft fits' and speaking with tongues, provided the odium of example which sobriety needed.

Davis has therefore written a book which is silly and unnecessary. No one has ever pretended that the Ranters were organized, as Puritanism's Militant Tendency. Hill, Morton and McGregor have already developed all that is valid in Davis's case, with more learning and attention to text than he can muster. Professor Davis's rehearsal of cautions as to the unsatisfactory character of the evidence as to Ranterism might – although familiar to scholars – have been worth writing up as an article. But the evidence as to a brief but infectious moment of Ranter enthusiasm comes from so many sources and has been endorsed by so much reputable scholarship that it is merely perverse to deny it.

Davis has written a work of anti-history, which discovers no new sources, throws no new light on obscure places, but whose object is to destroy the findings of scholarship and leave in their place nothing but a knowing sneer. No doubt, with time and patience, the slashed canvas will be restored by experts on Commonwealth intellectual history, of whom I am not one. My excuse for intervening is a long interest in the antinomian inheritance, as it extended through the eighteenth century. One of Professor Davis's disabilities is an insensitivity, or lack of interest, in theological discriminations. He constructs a 'paradigm' of Ranterism in the crudest terms: 'a shared pantheism, rejection of moral values and scriptural authority, associated significantly with atheism, mortalism or materialism, gave them a common identity.' Antinomianism is described, equally crudely, as involving the 'rejection' of sin, repression and Hell, and involving, in practice, the 'flouting of moral conventions, systematic impiety and pantheistic complacency'. Having set up these blunt criteria, Davis is able to show that each one of the supposed Ranter leaders did not unambiguously meet them, and hence to exonerate them all.

Antinomianism, in Davis's text, is an intellectually null heresy which can be identified only if it gave rise to fornication, blasphemy, or 'atheism', or to a manifestly radical social stance. But antinomianism is more interesting than that, has more scriptural and intellectual authority, and can be more fundamentally unsettling to the equipoise of orthodoxy. The heresy can be derived from many sources (including gnostic and Behmenist), but it may also (less esoterically) find authority in St Paul's Epistles to the Romans and to the Galatians. These passages, which originated in Paul's polemics against the slavish observance of Jewish ceremonial and ritual regulations, might be taken to have a much wider significance. The Mosaic Law was seen, not only in its ceremonial edicts but also in its moral commandments, to be the necessary rules of government imposed upon a faithless and unregenerate people: 'The law was our schoolmaster to bring us unto Christ, that we might be justified by faith. But after that faith is come, we are no longer under a school-master' (Galatians, 3, 24–5). Christ, by his sacrifice upon the Cross, in fulfilment of God's ancient covenant with man, 'hath redeemed us from the curse of the law' (Galatians, 3, 13). Thereafter it is not by 'the works of the law' but by 'the hearing of faith' that believers may be justified (Galatians, 2 and 3, *passim*). Believers are 'delivered from the law' (Romans, 7, 4–6).

This is not all that St Paul said, nor is it without ambiguity. Those with a nicely discriminating palate might classify the tenets of some Commonwealth enthusiasts as solifidian rather than antinomian: they rested more upon Lutheran premises of 'free grace' than Calvinist premises of 'election'. The solifidian premise rested particularly upon Romans, 3 (23–5, 28):

> For all have sinned, and come short of the glory of God;
> Being justified freely by his grace through the redemption that is in Christ Jesus;
> Whom God hath sent forth to be a propitiation through faith in his blood.
> Therefore we conclude that a man is justified by faith without the deeds of the law.

The zealous life of theological private enterprise which was thrown open by the English Civil Wars allowed hundreds of humble experimenters in doctrine to fashion eclectic systems, now drawing upon Calvin and now upon Luther, now upon Joachim of Fiore and now upon Boehme. The results are not likely to satisfy Davis's crude criteria.

It has long been supposed that, in the brief climax of the Ranters, antinomianism in one form or another assumed epidemic proportions. In this moment, the doctrine of 'free grace' seems more significant than the doctrine of election. Both Morton and Hill suggest that John Saltmarsh (whom Davis does not mention) had a profound influence upon the Ranter moment. In Saltmarsh's *Free Grace* (1645) Christ's blood was shed for all mankind, and all the sins of believers were 'done away on the Crosse'. 'The Spirit of Christ set a *beleever* as *free* from

Hell, the *Law*, and *Bondage*, as if he was in *Heaven*, nor wants he anything to make him *so*, but to make him *believe* that he is so.' The Gospel is 'a *perfect law* of life and *righteousnesse*, or *grace* and *truth*; and therefore I wonder at any that should contend for the ministry of the *Law* or *Ten Commandments* under Moses'. It was as a preacher of 'free grace' that Clarkson first made his mark. James Nayler, who is sometimes taken as the leader of a 'Ranting' tendency in early Quakerism, was equally known as a defender of 'the universal free grace of God to all mankind'.

Davis passes by, with one glancing reference, Christopher Hill's substantial demonstration that John Milton was influenced by the Ranter 'milieu', and that he trod 'a perilous path on the fringes of antinomianism'. Yet, how else are we to understand Michael's doctrine in Book 12 of *Paradise Lost*: 'Law can discover sin, but not remove.'

> So Law appears imperfect and but giv'n
> With purpose to resign them in full time
> Up to a better Cov'nant.

Christ, by his sacrifice, fulfilled the old Mosaic Law, delivered mankind from its curse, and:

> to the Cross he nails thy Enemies,
> The Law that is againt thee, and the sins
> Of all mankinde, with him there crufici'd,
> Never to hurt them more who rightly trust
> In this his satisfaction.

Henceforward those who are justified by faith (but not by 'legal works') enter upon a state of grace, subject to no laws save 'what the Spirit within/Shall on the heart engrave'.

Davis also appears to scoff at Christopher Hill's 'categoric' assertion that Bunyan 'moved in Ranter circles in his youth' – an assertion documented in *The World Turned Upside Down* by fourteen references to Bunyan's *Works*. The testimony of Baxter, Bunyan, Muggleton, George Fox and all Quakers, is disallowed because this served the polemical purposes of marking out the permissible boundaries of sectarian doctrine. This (which was McGregor's old thesis) may indeed be true, but it by no means disproves the reality of a Ranter 'moment'. It is notorious that in sectarian history (whether religious or secular) some of the fiercest polemics are between groups which draw upon a common inheritance and share certain premises. In its earliest years Quakerism was involved in unseemly polemics with the Muggletonians, in which each side accused the other of having gathered up former Ranters among their adherents. I cannot see any reason why this may not have been true of both, since both originated in the Ranter 'moment' and both defined their doctrines and practices in part as a *rejection* of Ranter excess.

Indeed, in those early years there was little attempt to deny that former Ranters had converted. Muggleton, in *The Acts of the Witnesses of the Spirit*, described how, in 1652, 'these Ranters were the most Company we had at that time', and they used to club 12d. per week 'to have Discourse with us'; the meetings took place in a victualling house in the Minories, at a 'Meeting of the Ranters' in Aldersgate Street, and elsewhere. In 1654 Reeve was writing of those called 'Ranters' as a 'generation deceived' – yet 'there are many of the tender spirited elect of God among them' whom the Lord in due time will call back again (*Sacred Remains*). Two years later John Reeve was writing to Christopher Hill (that scholar of astonishing longevity, who was then earning his living as a heel-maker in Maidstone) describing how 'one of the Chief speakers of the Ranters' had been converted to the truth of the Commission (this was almost certainly Laurence Clarkson), as a result of which Reeve had just been visiting half a score of 'his people' – husbandmen and tradesmen in Cambridgeshire – and had brought them to 'this truth' (*Supplement to the Book of Letters*).

The case of the early Quakers is more sensitive, because it touches on delicate points of doctrine. If there was a central Ranter tenet it was perhaps a mystic pantheism, which took God as dispersed throughout all creation: 'They had no other God but a spirit without a Body, which they said was the Life of every thing' (*Acts of the Witnesses*). They 'glory of a union with a God or Christ within them, calling themselves eternity, or everlasting love, and one pure being with the Creator' – or so John Reeve wrote in 1654. For some early Quakers also God was 'an infinite Spirit, that fills Heaven and Earth, and all Places, and all Things', whereas 'as touching Christ's Flesh, we are Bone of his Bone, and Flesh of his Flesh, and we have the Mind of Christ' (Samuel Hooton in *The Neck of the Quakers Broken*). However George Fox interpreted these beliefs, there were contemporary observers who insisted that many Quakers held themselves to be vectors of the divine spirit in the most literal sense. These believers, like the Ranters, saw the faithful as the embodiment of the divine, or as 'my one flesh'. In a passage of Alexander Ross's *A View of All Religions* Quakers are made to say that 'some of them are Christ, some God himself, and some equal with God, because they have the same spirit in them which is in God'; that 'Christ hath no other body but his church'; and that 'we are justified by our own inherent righteousness' – so that many believed that they 'cannot sin'.

None of these beliefs is disreputable, although Ross did add some sillier comments, such as that Ranters are 'a sort of beasts' and that the 'lives and demeanours' of Ranters and Quakers are 'much alike'. Muggleton's testimony on this was precisely the opposite. He also denounced the libertinism of some Ranter practice, 'where all was good, lying with their Neighbour's Wife, deflouring Virgins, couzening and cheating'. But those former Ranters who jointed the Society of Friends were, for this reason, ever-anxious to demonstrate their conversion by 'their Exactness of Life, and good Conversation'. When the 'melancholy Devil' of Quakerism cast out 'those merry Devils which they had upon the Rating-score', then the 'greatest things that I have heard the Quakers do, is to find Fault with a Piece of Ribbon, or Gold-button, or a Band-string'. In this interpretation we cannot understand early Quakerism if we erase the Ranters from the record, because Quaker sobriety in life, dress and manners was precisely a signal to the world that they had repudiated Ranting excesses – but not necessarily Ranting doctrine, for they would still have 'the Quaker's Bodies to be Christ's Flesh and Bone': 'The Quakers Principle', declared Muggleton in *A Looking-Glass for George Fox*, 'is but the Ranters refined into a more civil Kind of Life. For the Ranters were so grossly rude in their Lives, that spoiled their high Language, and made People weary of them; but the Quakers that were upon the Rant are the best able to maintain the Quakers Principle of Christ within them.' Other contemporaries concurred. According to Baxter, '*Quakers* ... were but the Ranters turned from horrid Prophaneness and Blasphemy to a Life of extreme Austerity on the other side. Their Doctrines were mostly the same with the Ranters.'

I am not a specialist in this period and I cannot hazard what the truth as to Ranter behaviour may be. But if they were, as Davis has it, 'no more than a mythic projection', then this projection cast extraordinarily long shadows. It is found, both as influence and rejection, in Quakerism, in Baptism, in Milton and Bunyan, and in a hundred other places. Something like a 'Ranter' tradition keeps turning up in the eighteenth century, both as polite mysticism and Behmenism (by way of Dr John Pordage, an associate of reputed Ranters) and in little churches and sects in London: Seekers, Ranters, Salmonists, Coppinists (who republished works of Richard Coppin), and such eccentrics as the 'Sweet Singers of Israel' described in 1706 as 'very poetically given turning all into Rhime, and singing all their Worship. They meet in an Ale-house and eat drink and smoak. ... They hold that there is no Sin in them.'

The doctrine of justification by faith, in its antinomian inflexion, was one of the most unsettling and potentially subversive of the vectors which carried the ideas of Commonwealth heretics through to the nineteenth century. It troubled early Methodism; and A.L. Morton was right to argue that the inheritance of antinomianism came down to William Blake even if his suggestive *The Everlasting Gospel* simplifies what was inherited. This is one among several reasons why an obscure impulse remains of historical significance.

It may not matter much whether there were real self-confessed Ranters and Ranter Meetings or not. But it seems improbable that the Ranters were invented simultaneously by Fox, Bunyan, Baxter, Muggleton, Reeve and scores of others only to advance their own sectarian disciplinary purposes; nor in order to advance the goals of the Communist Party Historians' Group three hundred years later. *The World Turned Upside Down* and associated scholarship by several hands seem to me to be among the most creative historiographic impulses of recent years. This work has disclosed to the non-specialist new worlds of thought and has helped us to regard intellectual history in new ways.

Of course this work is not privileged. It carries no immunity from criticism, nor would its authors ask for this. Yet it merits respect, and for this reason I dislike the tone of Professor Davis's work. While pretending to respect Hill, Morton and their colleagues, they are addressed as ideologues or charlatans. The fact that this meagre bit of anti-history has come from a prestigious university press and has been received with acclaim by several reviewers is a comment, not on its merits, but on the uncreative mediocrity of these latter days.

Note

1. J.C. Davis, *Fear, Myth and History: The Ranters and the Historians* (Cambridge, 1986).

Milton in Heaven

V.J. Kiernan

Milton belongs to the English Revolution;[1] but no simple explanations of him and his writings can be drawn from this. It may be no less relevant to say that he belonged to the time of an early experiment in revolution, in many ways premature. The events of the 1640s may be seen as hurried on, in advance of the maturing of economic conditions and of classes, by a ferment of ideas still very largely religious, as Milton's political thinking continued to be all his life: in this sense the old title of 'Puritan Revolution' has some validity. With so much of unreadiness and unclarity, the unfolding of events could not be other than very complex, often erratic; what could be achieved was bound to be far less than idealistic hopes had looked forward to. On the more progressive wing a coherent movement emerged only briefly, with the Levellers. Millenarian fervour ended in nothing more than a scattering of small sects and congregations.

Milton in any case was himself too complex, and too much a self-directed individual, to make a good party man; more so than the run of intellectuals who provide the catalyst for revolution but then find no congenial party or class to work with. An inspired writer cannot be the straightforward exponent of the aspirations of any class. He has of course his own social affiliations, but as an imaginative artist he stands partly above or outside them. More than in any current programme Milton believed in lofty and somewhat abstract principles. We are nearing the Age of Reason when we hear him say that 'the law is, above all, right reason',[2] or that reason is 'the best Arbitrator, and the Law of Law itself', overriding any statute (*Prose Works*, vol. 3, p. 403). He appealed to a still higher and more indefinable authority in the law of Nature, 'the only law of laws truly and properly to all mankinde fundamental' (*PW*, vol. 3, pp. 412–13).

161

On the religious plane he was moving towards a creed mainly of social ethics, leaving doctrine to free private choice. He was not obsessed with anxiety about personal salvation, like so many others of his time.[3] Desire for literary immortality may have given him a substitute. Man, instead of God, was on the way to becoming the measure of all things. Even the most sacred ordinance is designed for 'the good of man, yea, his temporal good not excluded' (*PW*, vol. 2, p. 623). The supreme Gospel law is 'to command nothing against the good of man' (*PW*, vol. 2, pp. 638–9). Politically, Milton was an elitist, desirous of an aristocracy of merit, or as we have learned long after to call it a 'meritocracy'. When force was required, it might have to come from the masses, whose tumults might be evidence of tyranny which God meant to overturn. It was 'this iron flaile, the People' that got rid of evils like the Star Chamber (*PW*, vol. 3, p. 391). But Milton's faith in the commonalty quickly waned, and more habitually he drew a line between the inconstant populace and 'the middle class, which produces the greatest number of men of good sense and knowledge of affairs' (*PW*, vol. 4, p. 471). He was against exorbitant wealth, as likely to provoke discontent (*PW*, vol. 7, pp. 445–6), but still more as morally corrupting; he was more concerned to depress the rich than to raise up the poor, and not clearsighted about the need of the poor for bread-and-butter reforms, or about the want of these as a cause of their political instability.

Milton saw the Civil Wars not directly as class division, but in terms of the country's division into enlightened areas like his London, and the benighted north and west, 'those cold and dark provinces of ignorance and leudness' (*PW*, vol. 3, p. 529). But the parliamentary regions proved far less enlightened than he supposed them. After Charles's execution he was disgusted by the welcome given to the royalist tract *Eikon Basilike* by 'an inconstant, irrational, and Image-doting rabble … a credulous and hapless herd, begotten to servility' (*PW*, vol. 3. p. 601). By contrast with such degradation he was understandably impressed by the New Model Army, in its best days, as England's defender against royal despotism and religious intolerance, and as a fusion of ordered discipline with ardent idealism.

Along with the army he admired Cromwell, its great captain, who alone was strong enough to protect the country against its many perils. He did so with misgivings; but he was ready to confess a reluctant admiration for Julius Caesar, usurper but man of destiny (*PW*, vol. 4, p. 449). Yet in the end he was reduced to thinking of the whole glorious endeavour at national renovation as futile, or too hasty: it was 'liberty sought out of season, in a corrupt and degenerate age'.[4] What he had to say of the Commonwealth was almost unrelievedly bad; so bad that it is hard to see with what logic he could blame the man in the street so furiously for turning away from it and welcoming back the monarchy. After that he could think only of the failure of the revolution as a crusade, oblivious of the extent to which it had satisfied the material aims of the better-off groups active in it, and put England ahead of nearly all other countries.[5]

In the exhilaration of 1641 Milton talked of some day pouring out in verse his full thanks to God for England's deliverance. The master-poem thus foreshadowed may have been embarked on in 1658, when the republic was nearing its deathbed; it was to be no joyful outpouring of thanks but an apologia for a God who seemed to have abandoned his chosen people. To find his answer Milton, typically of a writer who took himself and his country's fate so portentously, had to ascend into Heaven, descend into Hell, converse with angels and archangels. He had always wanted to be a truly national poet, with Arthur and Alfred among subjects formerly contemplated.[6] But his horizons, cultural and religious and political, were international: the mission he believed England to have been entrusted with was no narrowly self-centred one, like that of the chosen people of old. With *Paradise Lost* he was rising to a universal theme, and one in vogue at the time among European authors from Holland to Italy. Indeed the fable of war in heaven may be said to have haunted the mind of a continent perpetually torn by strife. In the early fifteenth century, in the midst of the Hundred Years War, an illustration in the *Tres Riches Heures* of the Duc de Berri showed Lucifer plunging down into the pit.[7] Duhrer drew St Michael, in mid-air, transfixing with his spear a Satan turned into a weird dragon-like creature. A century later Le Brun painted Michael hurling Satan and his crew Hellward.

However boldly adapted and enlarged, the Old Testament story could not provide a mirror of the events England had been passing through; but the turbulent emotions they had stirred up could find room in it, and what Milton took to be their essential meanings be given expression like vast, sombre shadows thrown on the clouds. *Paradise Lost* is more drama than narrative, full of opposites, of conflicting beliefs and irreconcilable demands. In this unique poetic legacy the English Revolution benefited by having been so incomplete and many-sided, and leaving so many unsolved problems to set imagination to work. Its French successor, by comparison, was too much a finished task, a *pièce bien faite*, the visible displacement of one social and political order by another, to bequeath to Frenchmen – though it did bequeath to some foreigners – much of the dream-stuff of poetry.

Milton is easily recognized in his Abdiel, the faithful seraph who alone in Satan's host refuses to join him in treason; or again in Raphael, sent to warn Adam of betrayal at hand as the poet before the Restoration warned England. Many who knew Milton must have expected the work to enshrine his conclusions about the times they had passed through, and he must have expected to be read in that light. His old colleague in the service of the Commonwealth, Marvell, who had made his peace with the new government, began a set of complimentary verses by acknowledging a fear beforehand that Milton might overturn 'sacred truths' like blind Sampson groping among the temple pillars – more really, we may suspect, a fear that the poem would be a political manifesto in disguise; and as if anxious to steer clear of any political bearings it might have, Marvell turned away to a defence of it on the harmless issue of its unrhymed verse. It would in any case have been impossible to publish a poem with a tithe of the overt political meaning of *Absalom and Achitophel.*

As it is, to try to pick a way through so many obscurities and ambiguities may seem as foolhardy as Satan's journey to earth. It is temptingly easier to fall back on an interpretation of the poem as a projection of Milton's inner self, a revelation of a contradictory personality.[8] Unquestionably collective experience can only become poetry by being filtered through the emotional complex of an individual's mind. But to see no more in *Paradise Lost* than a mind's workings, even Milton's, is to impoverish it very greatly. No epic can grow out of one individual's responses to life. It is true that England's next and last genuine epics, after a long further advance of individualism, would have for subjects Wordsworth's retrospect of his passage through early life, and Byron's camouflaged one of his. But both *The Prelude* and *Don Juan* were concerned with their authors' interactions with their era, and the first owes very much of its grandeur to the French Revolution, the second a great deal of its acid to the Napoleonic Wars and the Europe they left behind them.

In the midst of telling Adam that he can describe happenings in Heaven only in figurative terms, Raphael incongruously interjects a thought of Milton's own that maybe things heavenly and earthly are after all not very dissimilar (*Paradise Lost*, Book 5, lines 574–6; compare 6.893). In the poem at any rate similarities between them abound, and, most frequent, reminiscences of the England of the past two decades. Angels flock together 'in multitudes', just like Londoners, to hear the latest news from abroad (*PL*, 5.21ff.); and Milton's sturdy sense of material realities lends a fluctuating quality to his celestials, sometimes incorporeal spirits (1.423ff.), sometimes men with wings, who celebrate an occasion with song, dance, feasting and drinking (5.618ff.). Most insistent of all is the fact of Heaven being, like England of late, a vast armed camp. Milton was no egalitarian; his spirits pay all 'honour and obedience due' to their superiors.[9] Yet angelic natures might have been expected to allow of a society self-running and frictionless, without formal organization. Instead we find a totally militarized realm, its whole population inured to arms, as well versed as Fluellen could desire in the disciplines of the wars.

These angels are enrolled in 'regiments', often mustered for active service, put on guard duty in the style of Civil War patrols (4.778ff.); off duty they pile their arms and practice 'heroic games' (4.549ff.) like the Trojans in the *Aeneid* – a model that Milton must not seldom have had in mind. Their commander in chief, Michael, wields a sword 'with a huge two-handed sway', bestowed on him 'from the armoury of God' (6.251,321). Next to him in 'military prowess', in God's own estimation, is Gabriel (6.45–6). When Christ sets out at God's command to create the universe he is accompanied by a powerful escort of angels and chariots from the same armoury, where for ages 'myriads' have been stationed in readiness for this 'solemn day' (7.199ff.). Satan's opening moves have to look for an army plot (5.659ff.). He is the rebel 'General,' the 'Emperor' (we may take this to signify *Imperator* (1.337,378), an 'experienced' commander whose banner is hung with 'trophies' (1.568,539); in what unimaginable campaigns he had earned his soldierly repute we are left to guess). No severer condemnation of his revolt can be pronounced than that it is a violation of 'military obedience' (4.955).

No explanation is forthcoming as to why Heaven has been marshalled on those lines. None could be wider of the mark than to suppose God wishful to breed in his subjects 'a timid slavish mind'.[10] Milton's republicanism had its roots in early Greece and Rome, in the 'fierce democraty' of Athens[11] above all, where citizen soldiers guarded their native liberties. There was a vein of the soldier in his own make-up; he could compare himself as a controversialist to a tactician profiting by 'military advantages', catching his enemy off guard, busy with foraging or watering (*PW*, vol. 1, p. 872). In his plan of education martial exercises had a daily place, with wrestling and fencing, manoeuvres on foot and later on horseback, training in 'ancient and modern strategems, tactics, and warlike maxims' (*PW*, vol. 2, pp. 409, 411–12) – a regular blueprint for an Officers Training Corps. Now that England's star had set he could take comfort from memories of its departed Ironsides; he was besides compelled to realize that the Good Old Cause had never been able to count on more than a dwindling minority, and had only been sustained by armed force.

Loyalty, self-command, courage, were sovereign virtues with him, and an army can display them more conspicuously than any other human association. Liberty stood equally high, but could easily be reconciled with willing service and devotion to duty. Some tincture of these life-giving qualities survives even in the rebel host after its rout. It is quickly rallied again, once more a battle-hardened army with united purpose and trust in its leaders. Michael may predict that the mutineers will fall out and 'mingle broils' in their new abode (*PL*, 6.277); but there is no sign of this happening. Ardour is undamped, discipline unshaken; the rank and file are 'yet faithful' to a commander worthy of them (1.611).

Pride in arms, *esprit de corps*, Milton could approve of unrestrainedly; as to their employment on the stricken field he was more hesitant, as many others have been. He could not miss the lesson of the Civil Wars that no victories can guarantee final success. Scenes of fighting were indispensable to an epic, he must have felt when he began the poem; later on in it he speaks of war as having been deemed hitherto the sole heroic theme, but not really deserving first place (9.1ff.). Abdiel cannot help thinking it 'brutish' and 'foul' to have to overcome force by brute force, and before battle makes a last effort to bring Satan to his senses by the weapons of 'reason' (6.124–6). Still, contemplating the clash of arms from the distance of earth from Heaven, and with the comfortable assurance of nobody getting killed, Milton could feel its excitements as wholeheartedly as Shakespeare did. He describes it with Homeric gusto, and a realism bordering at times on the grotesque, collisions on English soil floating before his mind's eye. His loyal angels march to battle in 'quadrate' order (6.61ff.), the square formation which was to be part of European warfare into the nineteenth century; on occasion these winged 'Saints', as they are often called, outdo the Ironsides by wheeling in 'cubic phalang' (6.398–9). Sometimes they are mounted on fiery 'steeds' (6.391), of undescribed breed; they are encumbered with armour (6.595ff).

Hitherto with these warriors fighting had been Homerically simple. Satan bears a huge spear and shield (1.284ff.), the opposing chieftains meet hand to hand. But now new methods are called for to force a decision. It speaks for Milton's sense of the barbarity of war that he should ascribe to Satan the invention of gunpowder, made out of ingredients to be found in the soil of Heaven as of earth, and cannon (6.470ff.). A youthful sequence of Latin epigrams on The Gunpowder Plot shows the impression made on him by explosives, a demonic power steadily expanding in the world, able as Marlowe with fine hyperbole had written to 'make whole cities caper in the air'. There is a thunderous simile early in *Paradise Lost* of guns bombarding a city (2.922–5). Gazing ahead at the same invention to be made one day on earth, Milton predicts that it will be the work of an evil man 'intent on mischief' (6.498ff.).

Satan's battalions too come forward in square formation, this time with their novel artillery concealed in the middle (6.550ff.): again, a common marching formation of European troops for many years to come. Their firepower proves irresistible. Christ has to appear on the scene as *deus ex machina*, or rather *in* a machine, a ponderous self-propelled war-chariot rolling across the firmament, to rout the foe with his Father's thunderbolts (6.749ff.). We hear of 'linked thunderbolts' (1.328), reminiscent of cannon-balls chained in pairs; even these miraculous weapons take a familiar shape in Milton's mind. Further progress in technology is hinted at when Moloch in the council in Hell proposes to utilize Hell's own 'Tartarean sulphur and strange fire', and out of them forge instruments to storm Heaven with (2.60ff.).

Warfare above and below stairs might be much of a muchness; who the etherial combatants really were, and what they were fighting over, is harder to decipher. Milton himself could look at them variously, from different angles. Hill is of course right in saying that Satan, in particular, cannot be identified with any single human figure or party.[12] He has a dramatic identity of his own, while he catches the accents of heterogeneous earthly protagonists. It might even be said that all the *dramatis personae* of Milton's England were being confronted with their satanic features in a single evocation: all were in one way or another guilty of the ruin that had fallen on the country, by their self-seeking, thirst for power and pelf, defiance of moral law and neglect of what they owed to the community. In the end, with ambitious generals and feather-pated mobs helping royalist intriguers to restore Stuart despotism, the evil tendencies of all had coalesced into one.

But it is obviously in the royal camp that Satan must be looked for first of all. Milton was not being too fanciful if he thought of Charles starting a counter-revolution in 1642, rather than of Parliament starting a revolution; 'new monarchy', he held, was emulating continental absolutism and challenging old constitution and organic law. Charles moved northward to raise his standard at Nottingham. In religious tradition the inhospitable north was the lair of the powers of evil; and as Hill notes,[13] stress is laid in the poem on Satan's base being 'the quarters of the north' (5.683ff.). It is to start his rebellion there that he draws his followers off from what may be called the capital. It was folly in him to dream that he could overcome a God able to raise 'incessant armies' against him 'out of smallest things' (6.137–9), just as Parliament raised forces from the mass of humble folk despised by haughty Cavaliers. His followers are 'a godless crew' (6.49; compare 6.811), as Cavaliers always appeared to Roundheads – a not very appropriate expression when we have just heard some of them disdain to be 'less than Gods' (6.366; compare 6.452), a title all of them often claim.

The highly wrought account of Sin and Death building a causeway across Chaos to earth (10.235ff., 282ff.) must have put some early readers in mind of royalist *émigrés* and agents stealing into England to spread corrosion. Vanquished on high, Satan triumphs here below, just as the never-beaten army of the republic succumbed to deceit and demoralization. All these associations could contribute to a composite discord of rampant egotism and faithlessness. The long catalogue of fallen angels who are to become the false gods of idolaters (1.381ff.) must have a general reference to the moral failings which have been England's downfall: the sin of greed, especially, pursuit of 'the precious bane' and of luxury and ostentation whose evil genius is Mammon (1.678ff.). Hypocrisy was a vice Milton had seen much of in the Commonwealth, and thought of bitterly as the only one which baffles detection (3.682ff.). Satan is the first who ever 'practiced falsehood under saintly show' (4.122), but in this he is to have numerous English imitators. In their delineation of worldly self-seeking under the canting Puritan mask, Milton the disappointed republican and Walter Scott the troubadour of royalism are curiously alike.

But all these things together scarcely add up to the titanic and terrific embodiment of pride, grandeur, resolution, intellect, which is Milton's Satan before his decline into a baffled schemer; a warrior-statesman who leaves far behind every tragic hero of the Elizabethans, even Shakespeare's. It must owe some features to Milton's own stormy nature, which he must have had to struggle all his life to subdue, and which could vibrate to all the temptations held out by Satan in *Paradise Regained.* His was a confused, tumultuous time of change, when men felt themselves hurried forward into a frightening or intoxicating future, trying to hold on to whatever of their past they thought precious. For the dissension and disruption that were the keynote of the time, war in Heaven offered an ultimate symbol; for the driving-force of human will-to-power there could be none better than this Nietzschean superman, Satan. There had been a strong dash of 'Satanism' in Marlowe's heroes,[14] Tamberlane at their head with his boundless designs, ruthless self-assertion, destructiveness, along with a romantic streak and a kind of perverted self-righteousness or sense of mission. In both him and Satan can be discerned the energy, drive, leadership, immorality, of a class – with members on both sides in the Civil Wars, though more on the parliamentary – thrusting its way to dominance in a new age of expanding opportunity in England and in the world; of a new order which was to establish itself in England, and by imitation of England the world, in spite of many setbacks, and many crimes, by historical *merit*, of survival of the fittest. Personifying all this, Satan may be called the Spirit of the Age.

Milton admitted that God can be only incompletely understood, and not by 'nature or reason alone'. In *Paradise Lost* God, like Satan, is a shifting complex of diverse elements. He is irascible Old Testament greybeard, and inscrutable abstract purpose. In the former capacity he is capable of 'laughter', practises statecraft like any flesh and blood monarch (*PL*, 8.78, 237–41), descends to Eden to converse with Adam (8.311ff.), and later on, forgetting that he is omniscient, comes down on earth incognito to see what his subjects are up to (12.48–50), like a Caliph going about Baghdad in disguise. With the alternative conception Milton was approaching the borderline where God would begin to be relegated by deism to a polite distance. This depersonalized deity, audible only as a voice 'From midst a golden cloud' (6.27–8; compare 10.31–3), again has a twofold aspect.[15] He may be a distillation of Reason and Justice, emblem of human hopes, or an arbitrary, incomprehensible sovereign, emblem of human fears.

Milton could be strongly attracted to the thought of supreme, unchallengeable power. He was, after all, a contemporary of Hobbes and the Leviathan, absolute monarchy approaching its zenith, Lady Macbeth's daydream of 'sovereign away and masterdom' fulfilled; and for all educated men the Roman Empire was still standing as the grand monument of authority, if also as warning against its abuse. An irresistible will guiding the universe was a security against the squabbling and muddling of men's attempts to work together for good. It was a reassurance that above and beyond all life's enigmas and reverses there is a guarantee that somehow right must prevail. Psychologically, the contrast between Milton's unbending republicanism and his readiness to yield to divine omnipotence may suggest that only one who feels the seduction of power can resent power so keenly; much as, it has been said, to feel real dislike of cruelty a man must be conscious of a trace in himself of the cruelty latent in all of us.

When God summons a 'synod' it is not with any notion of inviting discussion, but simply to announce his intentions, as he does after the sin of Adam and Eve; condescension goes far enough for the audience to be addressed as His 'sons', and to be told that by gaining knowledge of good and ill Adam has become 'like one of us' (11.67ff.). He has already, however, on an earlier occasion, in his finest speech, revealed a decision to abdicate after the Day of Judgement (3.333ff.). Rule over a transfigured Heaven and earth will cease to be required: the sceptre will be laid aside, like Prospero's magic wand, it may have occurred to Milton to think. Absolute monarchy going on for ever, even in heaven, would be too much from him. He is looking forward to a new departure analogous to the withering away of the state towards which his political thinking may be said to have pointed. It will be something like abandonment of a Jacobin-style dictatorship, needful today for ruthless suppression of opponents. Or in view of the military composition of the present regime, it might be likened to the disbanding of an army, after long and arduous service, and release of its veterans to the freedom of civil life. It is then only, we may be inclined to add, that God will justify his ways, better than any apologist can do for him. He will be proving himself, in Empson's words, 'an emergent or evolutionary deity', one day to dissolve into the landscape.[16]

Meanwhile his sway is voluntarily submitted to by all the right-minded. In making this the keystone of his whole argument, Milton was boldly grappling with the thorny question of free will. As Weingarten wrote, religious England in the seventeenth century was not preoccupied with doctrine nearly so deeply as with Church management, but there was one salient exception, the Reformation dogma of predestination.[17] The treatise on *Christian Doctrine* which Milton went on composing at the same time as *Paradise Lost*, though it had begun earlier, shows him moving very far away from orthodoxy: the two works must have encouraged each other in this direction. It is impossible to square *Paradise Lost* with Trinitarian teaching. In *Christian Doctrine* he is very conscious in particular of how much of 'the outcry against divine justice' was aroused by the flagrant injustice implied in Calvinist teaching that God compels us to be good or bad, and then treats us accordingly (*PW*, vol. 6, p. 397). He argues against it lengthily, as contrary to Scripture, and depriving moral conduct of 'all man's freedom of action and all attempt or desire on his part to do right' (*PW*, vol. 6, p. 157). In the public mind impatience of old dogmatic fetters must have reinforced dislike of the Presbyterian clerical mercenariness of which Milton was so censorious: both grudges must have helped to chill attachment to the Commonwealth, and open the way to Restoration. For him as a political animal, such practical considerations outweighed any scholastic abstractions.

Already in 1644, in the *Areopagitica*, Milton had maintained that God gave Adam reason, and with it freedom, and observed that 'We ourselves esteem not of that obedience, or love, or gift, which is of force' (*PW*, vol. 2, p. 527). Now in *Paradise Lost* God assures His Son that He has endowed both angels and men with freedom of choice. Compulsory allegiance, merely mechanical, has no value to him. Fallen angels cannot plead 'predestination' or 'absolute decree': he foreknew their fall, as he now foresees man's, but it was their own fault (*PL*, 3.92ff). Some of them, down in Hell, debate this philosophically, 'in wandering mazes lost' (2.561); Milton dismisses all such speculation, and turns his eyes away from the logical difficulties of his position, really much the same as the *media scientia* put forward by the Spanish Jesuit Molina to reconcile divine foreknowledge with human liberty. For Milton what matters is the practical question of men's behaviour; he was more drawn to conundrums of the material universe, like the design of the solar system, than to subtleties of metaphysics. Adam's freedom of choice is insisted on afresh, in the most positive language (10.9ff, 34ff). Only 'voluntary service', of man or angel, Raphael tells him, is acceptable to God (5.520ff.).

In such passages we are made to feel how demeaningly plebeian or servile any doctrine of Necessity must have appeared to a temper like Milton's, aristocratic and self-reliant, prepared to answer the call of duty but not to be dragooned. Hill observes that it was an idea suited to brief situations of crisis.[18] More generally, it may be called the thinking of an early, fledgeling bourgeoisie, learning to walk in leading-strings, or nascent groups of the bourgeois genus, such as Scotland did not outgrow before the eighteenth century; whereas an adult, confident bourgeoisie must prefer a philosophy of freedom, harmonizing with its social-economic outlook, its open door for aspiration and competition. In England this stage was now being reached; 1660 was a compromise with the court party, not a surrender to it. In religion, in advance of politics, it could be proclaimed that man is born free; with the corollary that if he goes astray he must not blame his maker, or, as the cynic Edmund says in *King Lear*, explain 'all that we are evil in by a driven thrusting on'.

The other face of freedom is reason, which ought to govern all from highest to lowest, even though its application to celestial affairs must seem enigmatic. Very much like an enlightened despot of the next century, God identifies his will with 'right reason', which Satan is setting at nought (6.41–3). Genuine strength must depend on reason and virtue, Abdiel – seeing no possible discrepancy between the two – believes: hence Satan, 'unsound and false' in 'reason', must be at bottom weak, as later on proves true (6.114ff). Adam shows more insight when he points out to Eve that while the will is free because directed by reason, reason is not infallible, but may be deceived (9.351ff.). In Eden, Eve tells the Tempter, 'Our Reason is our law' (9.654), but she finds his eloquence very reasonable (9.872), and quickly reasons herself into infidelity. As a sort of umpire or higher court of appeal Milton invokes Nature, as the Age of Reason was so often to do. Again, what Nature has to do with Heaven is not clear, but both Abdiel and Michael think of it as desecrated by Satan's revolt (6.114ff., 267).

God's bestowal of free will belongs to his more open self; there are times when, as the unfathomable, he reverts to a more autocratic style – an octave deeper so to speak than the rhetoric of Shakespeare's mightiest Julius.

Necessity and Chance Approach not me, and what I will is Fate'

(7.172–3). Foreseeing and foreordaining seem at these moments much closer. 'All they request was my decree,' God tells Christ in answer to his petition on behalf of man (11.47). Prayer can be efficacious, Adam learns, but not against God's 'absolute decree' (11.141ff., 311–14). Free will has its limits in the heavenly dispensation; but so it has, of course, in the doings and happenings we encounter every day. In one aspect God stands, as Hill remarks, for 'the historical process'.[19] Every defeated party is likely to be reduced to pitying itself as hapless victim of fate and its unaccountable operations. God feels no sadness, only anger, at the falling away of so many long-dutiful angels.

Of his more overbearing acts the appointment of Christ as viceroy of heaven seems the crowning example. Christ's proper mission will be on earth, as mediator between God and man; it is hard to find any imperative function for him on high. It may look as if God is already at this stage paving the way for a partial retirement from office; but in fact he has to remain throughout the towering central figure of the drama, with his son very much a compliant deputy, for otherwise Milton would be evading the task undertaken in his opening lines.[20] We are told that Christ is to unite Heaven more closely and happily (5.826ff.), which implies that – like Commonwealth England – it has not been sufficiently happy and united hitherto, under God's direct rule. The installation as 'viceregent' was of Milton's own devising, and he must have had a reason for it. Very likely it was to provide a plausible explanation of Satan's revolt.[21] God's minatory language in informing the angels of His unalterable 'decree' (5.600ff.), and as it were daring them to object, sounds as if his aim is to provoke resistance, or at least to test obedience to the furthest. There is a curious resemblance to the Islamic story of Iblis, or Satan, refusing to bow before newly created Adam, as Allah's angels were very unreasonably ordered to do. It would be interesting to know whether the tale had reached Milton.[22]

Even here, he cannot help bringing in the wholesome middle-class touchstone of merit, to justify God's seemingly capricious decision. Christ is to reign 'by right of merit', Heaven is told (6.41–3). As he has only just been 'begotten', his deserts have to be taken on trust. But Milton always wants to exhibit moral worth in practical form. Christ displays it, when war breaks out, by assuming the role of conqueror, the Michelangelesque aspect of irresistible power that the poet could not help applauding (6.723ff., 801ff.), able to sweep away all opposition as the Good Old Cause had failed to do. Virtue may be strength, as he wants to think, but it is helpless against Satan's artillery; and the failure of the good angels, unprovided with up-to-date armaments, brings out as God meant that it should the superior quality of Christ and his right to the title of 'anointed King' (6.669ff., 718). After his victory all the faithful hail him as 'Worthiest to reign' (6.888). In much the same fashion every crowned head of Milton's day felt obliged to show his mettle by winning a battle.

God and Nature equally enjoin on us obedience 'When he who rules is worthiest,' Abdiel urges. Servitude is service of the 'unwise' or unworthy, or the unworthier part of oneself (7.174ff.). It is not unjust, he has argued earlier, 'to bind with laws the free': God's will is unsearchable, but experience teaches that it shapes all things for our good (5.818ff.). Milton sounds as if he is trying to convince himself, as he must have had to do when accepting, against the grain, the political necessities of Cromwellian rule. Satan's counter-arguments have more of clamant conviction, and he is a *tragic* figure because he and his fate stand for something of intense concern to Milton himself. He talks in the strain of Cassius: 'Liberty and Heaven' ought to be one and the same, though he too is no Leveller; 'orders and degrees' are quite compatible with freedom (5.792–3). Heaven has always been a monarchy, but God's action has in some way disturbed what might be called the balance of the constitution, or what he calls 'the fixed laws of Heaven' (2.18). 'New laws' are being imposed, which affect their allegiance (5.679–80). He speaks for 'A third part of the Gods, in synod met', who cannot admit 'omnipotence' in any.[23]

Though Satan is so ready to count heads and votes, it is only he and his fellow Grandees who can regard themselves as Christ's 'equals', and plead 'reason' and 'right' against being subjected to him, in derogation of the 'imperial titles' by virtue of which their place is 'to govern, not to serve' (5.794ff.). His rank-and-file following, though only indistinctly seen at the back of Milton's stage, are not so much a *mobile vulgus* stirred up by demagogy as a loyal train animated by sincere attachment. In the Civil Wars royalist levies were quite often tenants or retainers taking up arms at the bidding of landowners in something like the old feudal style. In Cornwall, a royalist stronghold, 'in Sir Bevil Grenville's regiment every man was his tenant or servant'.[24] Hitherto the political geography of Heaven has been that of a loose combination of provincial governorships or satrapies. But now this easy-going arrangement is to be superseded, and centralized authority inaugurated with authority concentrated in the hands of Christ, who is expected to begin with a tour of inspection of all the regions (5.692–3), like a chief minister or grand vizier.

A similar centralizing process had been going on in Europe for a long time, and was reaching its climax during Milton's lifetime, crushing resistance in France, Germany, the Hapsburg empire, Sweden, Catalonia. Also in the British Isles, it might be added, where an integral part of what was happening was the establishment of firmer English control over Ireland and Scotland, as over Wales in the previous century. This was a desideratum of both monarchy and the newer interests opposed to it; the latter could not want to see it achieved by the Crown, because it would strengthen the Crown against them, but once in the saddle they would implement it more thoroughly for themselves, as the Commonwealth did. In this context Satan can be taken as exponent of the ideas of magnates jealous of encroachment on their local autonomy, like the northern earls who rose against Elizabeth in 1569, or the kindred spirits who took the lead in national minority movements. His 'royal seat', a splendid palace or fortress on a northern mountain, suggests thoughts of Scotland, a country cordially disliked by Milton; so does the name he now, 'Affecting all equality with God', confers on his eyrie, 'The Mountain of the Congregation', by way of challenge to God's own residence on its 'holy Mount' (5.760ff., 6.743). One of Milton's last-minute arguments against bringing back the Stuarts was that it would mean the loss of the northern kingdom, England's now by right of conquest, a conquest no English King had ever been able to carry out (*PW*, vol. 7, p. 424).

A curious controversy in the poem falls into place here. When God presents Christ to the angels as their overlord, he tells them that he has begotten his Son 'this day' (*PL*, 5.603). But Abdiel insists that all the angels were created through the instrumentality of the Son.[25] This contradiction may be got round, laboriously, by resort to a pre-existence of Christ as Logos. 'In the beginning was the Word.' But the hard-headed Satan refuses to believe that he was 'the work of secondary hands', and goes on to assert that he and the rest were never created at all (5.853ff.): he seems to assume (the wording is unclear) that they came into being by spontaneous generation, as of Lucretian atoms joining. This was a Manichaean tenet, not shared by Milton.[26] Satan himself wavers. In the speech on Mount Niphates he knows that God created him; later on he is once more sceptical (4.43; 9.146–7). It was an argument of some European feudatories obstructing royal authority, and of the imperial knights in Germany defying the princes, that they had not been ennobled by the Crown, but came of lineage as old as the reigning family, and were entitled to a status of their own; a favourite thesis notably of the highest grade of the feudal nobility of Aragon, the *ricos hombres de natura*, ever recalcitrant and ready to assert, like Satan, 'Our puissance is our own' (5.864). But there is a relevance also to Commonwealth England, and the appointment of Cromwell as Protector in 1653. Army chiefs who took this with an ill grace might well reflect that they owed their positions to their services to Parliament and nation, not to this upstart. It is indeed a measure of Milton's genius, the intensity of his imagination, that he was able to weld together such disparate things of his time into poetic meanings for all time.

Reading Satan's thoughts from afar, God accuses him of aiming at supremacy, not merely at independence in the north (5.724ff.). After his failure Satan admits that his ambition was to rise one step higher, and make himself the highest (5.50–51). He makes no effort to conceal his love of power, his passion to 'reign'. Of his three titles to the leading place in Hell he puts first his old exalted rank, his 'just right'. But a defeated chief cannot play the despot, and his other claims are the 'free choice' of his party, and 'merit' displayed in council and in battle (2.18ff.). He is 'Dictator', but in the Roman constitutional sense, and one who holds regular consultations. On his side, unlike God's, much frank discussion takes place, greatly to the benefit of the narrative and its dramatic shape. At the end of the first day's doubtful encounter he gathers his 'companions dear' for a nocturnal council of war (6.413ff.). Hell knows 'sovereign power', but a collective one whose decisions are taken by 'Satan and his peers' (1.753,757). In the grand conclave these thousand 'Lords' keep their full stature, while the rest are, as if symbolically, shrunk down to pygmies small enough to crowd into the hall as spectators (1.792ff.). But representatives of each regiment are summoned, 'By place or choice the worthiest' (1.757ff.), like the 'Agitators' of the New Model; and the multitude of inferiors who are compared to bees conferring on their 'state-affairs' (1.775–6) might still more accurately have been compared to a crowd of Londoners. We hear of 'the popular vote', and it is with votes 'Consenting in full frequence' that Satan undertakes his journey to earth (2.313, 129–30).

In the official proclamation on the war with Spain Milton bracketed the Reformation and the discovery of America, as two comparably far-reaching events.[27] Another part of what was going on in his lifetime was the further expansion of Europe, and not a few touches in the poem sound like echoes of strife in the borderlands. Non-European peoples were being subdued by Europe's fire-power, or its superior fire-power when they had guns of their own, as Satan's cannon-balls were outranged by Christ's thunderbolts. A reference to 'the Grand' in Hell holding their 'dark Divan' (10.427, 457) links the rebels with Christendom's old enemy the Turks; and their withdrawal into the interior of Hell has just been compared with a Tartar retreat from the Russians into inner Asia (10.431ff.), with all those remote places – Cambalu, Agra, Samarkand – whose strange names fell so thrillingly on Milton's ear (11.385ff.).

Everywhere the story is pervaded by the storm and stress of unruly energies in conflict, a world in the grip of change. Michael predicted feuds in Hell; Satan thinks earth and mankind are being created to make up for the loss of subjects God has suffered, but at a safe distance from

Heaven lest excess of population should give rise to 'new broils there' (2.833–7). This carving of a second universe out of Chaos has a look of colonization; the old Anarch who presides over Chaos is compelled to keep guard on his frontiers and try to preserve what is left of his dominions, jeopardized by 'intestine broils' (2.998ff.) such as aided Europe to overrun its multiplying possessions, or England to overrun Ireland. God's purpose in the creation was indeed to show that he could easily make up for the loss of subjects inflicted on him by the rebellion (7.150ff.; compare 9.143ff., 177). It is rumoured in Heaven that all the stars are to be peopled (7.621–2). Earth is a new realm of God's 'empire' (7.555); but he is at once challenged there, as in Heaven lately, by Satan, 'the great Adventurer' setting out from his own territory in quest of 'foreign worlds' (10.440–41).

To clothe imperialism in this diabolic shape was not too far from the realities of history. Milton's view of it was to be sure very one-sided; he fully approved of the bloody subjugation of Ireland, but some ingredients in the overweening pride and lust of domination epitomized by Satan must have derived from the Roman Church and its champions, their Catholic and Most Christian Majesties, with eyes fixed on mastery in Europe and beyond and subversion of true religion. In this light we may consider earth's creation as the God-guided advent of Protestantism, especially of Protestant England, to balance the relapse of papist Europe into idolatry.

Mankind as makeweight for loss of angelic population is another hint of the slight gap separating the two races. 'Thou madest him a little lower than the angels,' Milton had read in *Hebrews*, chapter 2. Satan acknowledges in Adam a heroic opponent, impressive in person, courage, and intellect alike (9.482ff.). God's plan is for him and his descendants to rise gradually in the scale, qualifying themselves 'by degrees of merit' for citizenship of Heaven (7.156ff.). From the other side the gap is narrowed by Christ's promised assumption of humanity: he will continue 'Both God and Man', and deity thus be humanized (3.313–17). Between this sanguine prospect, and recoil into the deepest disgust, Milton alternated in a way in keeping with an epoch of towering hopes and searing disappointments; Hamlet and Lear likewise saw their fellow creatures as compounds of angel and beast.

There may be other suns and moons, Raphael conjectures, shining with 'male and female light': the 'two great sexes animate the world' (8.148–51). He might have been drawing on the Chinese concept of *yin* and *yang*. Half the conversation which fills Book 8 is about astronomy, half about sex, the two topics Adam is most eager to discuss with his celestial tutor. Milton's vein of sturdy materialism and 'modernism' comes out strongly in the large part played in Eden by sexual enjoyments, even though his praise of 'wedded love' upholds the Puritan ideal of marriage against 'court amours', aristocratic vice (4.750ff.). But like so much else of its epoch, the Puritan and Miltonic ideal was a half-way house between old and new, and the past asserted itself in the fixed notion that woman, however improvable, remained inferior, and subordinate to man. It was shared by most of the sectaries and radicals of Milton's time;[28] in this respect there was a falling back from Shakespeare, who was not clouded by religious prepossessions. Milton is unlikely to have approved of the attempts of some women of Leveller persuasion to take a hand in political affairs during the Commonwealth.[29]

So far as Eden is concerned, much is made of Adam's rank as earthly viceroy, a parallel with Christ's regency over Heaven, or – underlining the kinship between their acts of disobedience – with Satan's former governorship. As in Heaven, there seems no practical ground for this parade of authority. In a realm with only two inhabitants and a troop of well-behaved animals, Adam is to exercise 'Absolute rule', to which Eve joyfully submits (4.288, 440ff.). It is her part to sweeten her lover's self-esteem by looking up to him reverentially as also her lord and master, even as God's image. Yet her docility is only captivating to him because free and unconstrained, thereby betokening the strength of the impression his personality makes on her. He is too civilized to obtrude his authority, and it is because he only admonishes and does not compel that Eve falls into sin. There is an evident congruity between this attitude and that of God in granting free will to his creatures. He may be or talk at times like a tyrant, but he wants veneration and gratitude as well as submission. In Eden, it seems, a sexual substratum of Miltonic theology is revealed.

Eve's sin is a double disobedience, to God and to her husband: the two sides of her offence are given about equal weight. The People has often been conceived as a feminine entity, and there are similarities between Milton's view of it and of women. The foolish ought always to be governed by the wise (*PW*, vol. 4, p. 425–6). Woman should be ruled by man, the masses by the elite; both, in short, by John Milton. Eve was deaf to Adam's warnings, and had open ears for Satan's beguilements, just as England was deaf to Milton's preaching of how base it would be 'to be stroked and tam'd again' into 'Norman villenage', by the 'glozing words' of deceivers (*PW*, vol. 3, p. 581).

Many leading men of the Commonwealth ended as renegades from the Good Old Cause; and it was not the populace alone which was ready to hail the vulgar royal pomp which 'Dazzles the crowd and sets them all agape' (*PL*, 5.357). It may not be pressing analogies too far to see in Eve's fantasy, kindled by her dream and Satan's flattery, of rising to a more godlike status, the hankering of rich burgher wives for a place in the aristocracy; and Milton must have known not a few cases of men led astray by the vanity and conceit of their wives, as Adam – less discreditably – was led astray by Eve. He had professed deference to God's 'sovran will', as the highest law of everything (7.78–80). In secular language this can be taken to mean that the individual must rise above warping egotism, accept the restrictions of social duty, discover his final purpose somewhere outside himself.

For private consolation for the misconduct of his ideal consort, Milton fell back on the less rarified charms of polygamy, as sanctioned by the habits of the patriarchs, even though Solomon must be admitted to have 'exceeded the limit' (*PW*, vol. 6, p. 367). Baulked of his vocation to teach and guide mankind, the philosopher was day-dreaming of the polygamist's undisputed sway over his harem. Dr Johnson indulged in the same fancy, a cherished one to judge by his fury with Boswell for laughing at it. Blake had some similar wishfulness; perhaps another last infirmity of noble minds.

Adam faces exile with fortitude, and in the end he succeeds in working out his redemption. But there is very little sign, in the visionary panorama of the future revealed to him by Michael, of his descendants following his lead. They may still be endowed with free will, but no more than feebly and flickeringly; the impression of unfreedom is deepened by the future being no longer a secret known only to God. Foreknowledge and fore-ordinance are harder than ever to distinguish. We see history unrolling very much as Hobbes saw it, full of savagery and rapine. Michael comments on how admiration is given to strength, mistaken for valour, and on how glory is earned, 'with infinite man-slaughter', by conquerors who ought to be regarded as 'destroyers', 'plagues', instead of demigods (*PL*, 11.683ff.). For Milton war is losing more and more of its glamour. Men deserve their subjection to these 'violent lords' because they allow themselves to be enslaved by their own 'inordinate desires' and 'upstart passions'. (Polygamy has no place among these, apparently.) Or entire nations may 'decline so low' that even if not deprived of freedom by force they may forfeit it by 'justice and some fatal curse annexed' (12.79ff.). The illustration appended, for the censor's benefit we may guess, is the not very pertinent one of the progeny of Noah's disrespectful son Ham, the 'vicious race' of Africa; but the real allusion must be to England throwing away its freedom in 1660.

Thus Milton seems to be justifying God's way no better than with the bleak verdict that men fare no worse than they deserve to. No progress, no evolution, emerges from the record, only a handful of virtuous men here and there keeping their heads above the flood of wickedness. A more positive note is struck near the end: by simple, humble reliance on Providence these few may hope to find goodness 'Still overcoming evil', weakness strength, and 'suffering for Truth's sake' opening the path to 'highest victory' (12.561ff.): But Milton was far less close to the Shelley of *Prometheus*, or to Gandhi, than to Stoicism, and his words seem to relate more to the impregnable integrity an individual may attain than to any reclaiming of mankind. Many humanists had found the Stoic ethic admirable, and felt it to be compatible with Christianity.[30] In *Paradise Regained* the prime virtue of firm individual endurance of all trials is still more emphatic. And whereas at the outset of that poem there could still be hope of an Eden recovered 'to all mankind', the closing promise by the angelic choir is of a new paradise for 'Adams and his chosen sons' – the elect alone (4.614).

Yet as Hill writes, Milton's poems are apt to end on a note of quiet serenity, of human life continuing in spite of all calamities.[31] There was in him a tenacious instinct of life, rather than faith in life, untranslatable into any language. Hopefulness, it would appear, if not happiness, kept breaking in. He was not altogether isolated or forgotten after 1660, and he himself can never have forgotten his apocalyptic glimpse of an elysium of the far future when Heaven's sceptre will be laid aside, and those who have earned it will taste an existence of joyous activity, no more spiritual trance but 'golden days, fruitful of golden deeds' (*PL*, 3.337). It was a vista far more like a socialist utopia than a conventional Christian Heaven.

To smelt a complex of antiquated myths into a philosophical poem was an enterprise which could not avoid many contradictions. Milton was in manifold ways a product of two eras, an uneasy blend of old and new, undergoing the painful tensions of a society between the two, each containing both good and bad in a way that only men born much later, and brought up on the fruit of the tree of historical knowledge, can try to disentangle. But it is in the twilight at the ending of one age and the dawning of another, when imagination is stirred by the uncertain light, swallowed into the vortex of change, that superlative artistic achievement has oftenest seemed to come about. To possess the required emotional depth a work must have foundations in the past; to have an equal vitality it must feel the magnetic pull of a future half real, half guessed. These two consciousnesses working together gave us *Paradise Lost.*

Notes

1. Christopher Hill's book on Milton is one that only a lifetime of penetrating study of every facet of seventeenth-century England could have made possible. He ends by saying that each fresh reading of a poem like *Paradise Lost* kindles fresh impressions. The subject is indeed inexhaustible, which may serve as excuse for venturing on a few further reflections here.

2. *Complete Prose Works of John Milton*, D.M. Wolfe, ed. (New Haven, Conn., 1953), vol. IV, p. 492.

3. C. Hill, *Milton and the English Revolution* (London, 1977), p. 460.

4. *Prose Works*, vol. 5, p. 448. Compare A.L. Morton: 'The paradise which Milton lost ... was the early promise of the revolution' (*The English Utopia*, 1952, London, 1969, p. 89).

5. *Prose Works*, vol. V, pp. 442–50, a digression in the *History of Britain* from the description of the country's condition at the end of Roman rule. Compare D.M. Wolfe, *Milton in the Puritan Revolution* (New York, 1941), pp. 282ff.

6. J.H. Hanford, *John Milton, Englishman* (London, 1950), pp. 120, 124.

7. Referred to and reproduced in Marina Warner, *Joan of Arc* (London, 1981), pp. 99ff.

8. Hanford, *John Milton*, pp. 229, 231; it is this line that he broadly follows.

9. *Paradise Lost*, Book 3, lines 736–8. Compare Wolfe, *Milton*, p. 265: '*Paradise Lost* is essentially undemocratic in tone.'

10. W. Empson, *Milton's God* (London, 1961), pp. 110–11.

11. *Paradise Regained*, Book 4, line 269.

12. Hill, *Milton*, p. 343.

13. Ibid., p. 371.

14. There is force in A.L. Rowse's dictum that Milton was closer in spirit to Marlowe than to Shakespeare: *Milton the Puritan* (London, 1977), p. 250.

15. Milton's presentation of God is sometimes close to Luther's strict distinction between God as knowable and humane, and as unknowable and not measurable by human morality; see *The Bondage of the Will*, trans. J.I. Packer and O.R. Johnston (London, 1957), pp. 170–71.

16. Empson, *Milton's God*, pp. 130, 133. He finds a pantheistic flavour in the passage, and points out a borrowing from *1. Corinthians*, ch. 15.

17. H. Weingarten, *Die Revolutionskirchen Englands* (Leipzig, 1868), pp. 419, 437.

18. Hill, *Milton*, p. 270.

19. Ibid., p. 368.

20. One of the rare points at which one must disagree with Hill is his view that in *Paradise Lost* God has little part to play, and is overshadowed by his son (*Milton*, p. 357).

21. D. Saurat, *Milton, Man and Thinker* (London, 1924), p. 209.

22. See my essay 'Iqbal and Milton', in *Iqbal Commemorative Volume*, A.S. Jafri and K.S. Duggal, eds. (Delhi, 1980). It is intriguing to learn from Hill (*Milton*, Appendix 3) that the library of a close friend of Milton contained nine works of Raymond Lull, an early student of Islam as well as of alchemy.

23. Empson, *Milton's God*, p. 46, draws a parallel with the parliamentary denial of Charles I's divine right.

24. H. Green, *Guide to the Battlefields of Britain and Ireland* (London, 1973), p. 154.

25. Empson, *Milton's God*, ch. 2, has a good deal to say on this issue.

26. *The Prose Works of John Milton*, ed. J.A. St John (London, 1848), vol. 4, p. 184.

27. Ibid., vol. 2, p. 236.

28. Hill, *Milton*, p. 118.

29. On some of these episodes see J. O'Faolain and L. Martines, eds., *Not in God's Image* (London, 1973), ch. 10, section 5.

30. F. Wendel, *Calvin*, trans. P. Mairet (London, 1965), pp. 28–9.

31. Hill, *Milton*, p. 52.

William Dell, the Universities and the Radical Tradition

Peter Burke

> But all their works they do for to be seen of men: they make broad their
> phylacteries, and enlarge the borders of their garments.
> And love the uppermost rooms at feasts, and the chief seats in the
> synagogues.
> And greetings in the markets, and to be called of men, Rabbi, Rabbi.
> But be ye not called Rabbi. ... Neither be ye called Masters: for one is
> your Master, even Christ.
>
> Matthew 23.5–10: Authorized Version

One of Christopher Hill's outstanding achievements has been to put the
seventeenth-century English radicals back on the historical map, to
remind us of the existence and significance of a group which included
not only Levellers and Diggers, but fascinating lesser-known figures
such as John Warr, who advocated the reform of the law, and William
Dell, who recommended the reform of education.[1]

Were these ideas of reform worked out for the first time in the mid
seventeenth century, in reaction to the circumstances of the English
Revolution? Or do they represent the surfacing, in a period when
unorthodox ideas could at last be expressed safely in the open, of a
radical tradition which had long run underground? In what sense, if any,
were these revolutionaries traditionalists?

These are large and difficult questions, questions which Christopher
Hill has himself discussed on more than one occasion.[2] In returning to
them here I shall confine myself to one man, William Dell, who has
become something of a focus of interest in recent years, and to one
issue, the reform of universities.[3]

Dell's criticisms of the university system were expressed in three
works of the early 1650s: *The Stumbling-Stone* and *The Trial of Spirits*,

sermons preached at Cambridge, and *A Plain and Necessary Confutation*, replying to criticisms of these sermons by the Master of Pembroke. The *Confutation* includes a section on the 'Right Reformation of Learning', and also – in its 1660 edition – a new 'Apology' to the reader in which Dell restates his case.[4]

Dell's attitudes can best be summarized in his own vivid phrases. The universities, he asserts, are the home of 'false teachers'. These men teach false doctrine, 'only the outward letter of the Word' and not its spirit, and they teach for the wrong reasons, for 'their own profit and advantage'. The university is responsible for this situation because, 'through power received from Antichrist', it gives degrees in divinity, 'chiefly for money'. So the false teachers 'get to themselves titles and degrees in the university, for their pretended knowledge in divinity above other Christians; and by these degrees they get the uppermost seats in the synagogues and greetings in the markets, and are called of men Doctor Doctor'. (Here Dell is paraphrasing Matthew 25 on the scribes and pharisees, quoted as epigraph to this essay.) This reverence for the false teachers is 'a dangerous snare to simple people, causing them to receive all for good doctrine that is delivered by such men'.

Dell believed that the universities were still strongholds of popery, witness their customs and their curriculum. 'Many of the selfsame outward and antichristian forms and follies still remain in them, more than in any other people in the nation, again even unto their hoods, caps, scarlet robes, doctoral ring, kiss, gloves, their doctoral dinner and music.' As for the curriculum, there was too much 'wrangling, jangling, foolish and unprofitable philosophy'. There was also too much concern with pagan antiquity. 'The universities are built on the philosophers and heathen; Plato and Aristotle being the chief corner stones.' (The reference to Plato was as unusual as that to Aristotle was commonplace – but then Dell was a colleague of the Cambridge Platonists.)

Dell did not oppose learning altogether – or even universities. 'I am not against human learning upon all accounts, but do allow human learning (so it be sober and serious) in its own place and sphere.' He thought the universities had a function as 'schools of good learning for the instructing and educating youth in the knowledge of the tongues and the liberal arts and sciences, thereby to make them useful and serviceable to the commonwealth'. They should teach not divinity but logic, arithmetic, geometry, geography, medicine and law, and they should not be confined to Oxford and Cambridge. It would also be desirable to see colleges 'dispersed through the cities and towns of the commonwealth'.

Views similar to some of Dell's had also been put forward long before the 1640s, as he knew very well. He was not content to argue from reason and the Bible alone, but quoted authorities in his support;

patristic, medieval and modern writers, from Augustine to Zwingli. How well read a man Dell was, it is difficult to tell, for he did not normally give non-biblical references in his printed sermons.[5] However, in his works of 1653–4, he does sometimes quote passages in Greek; he shows familiarity with the ecclesiastical histories of Socrates and Sozomenus as well as the better-known Eusebius, and on occasion cites Joachim of Fiore and *The Ploughman's Complaint.*[6]

This use of authorities is problematic. It is not clear whether Dell quoted authorities because he took them seriously, or simply because he thought his listeners would take them seriously. It was ironic, to say the least, that he should have given learned references in a criticism of the function of learning in the study of divinity, or based himself on tradition when advocating a radical reform of universities. In any case, the authors he quoted did not always support his case, while some of the closest analogies to his position can be found in authors he did not quote. Dell appealed to Wyclif, Hus and Luther, great authorities in Protestant England, but doubtful allies of his cause. 'If any think', he wrote, 'I have too deeply censured the universities; let them know, that I have done in this matter, but as Wyclif, Hus, Luther, and several others ... have done before me.' He did not mention Karlstadt, or the Anabaptists, or the Brownists. We have thus to place Dell relative to two radical traditions rather than one; the first relatively orthodox, in the sense that the Church of England, correctly or incorrectly, laid claim to it; the second unorthodox, and so in a sense subterranean, although it was transmitted by printed books as well as by word of mouth.

To begin with 'orthodox' radicalism, the tradition of protest and reform which had been appropriated for Protestantism and Reformation. Of the great trio ('Wyclif who begat Hus, who begat Luther, who begat truth'), it was the radical Master of Balliol who was closest to the radical Master of Caius.[7] The treatise by Wyclif to which Dell refers, *The Mirror of the Church Militant* (*c.*1379), discusses what is wrong with universities in the context of a critique of Church endowments, and takes the form of a dialogue between Truth and Falsehood. Truth has two basic points to make about universities. The first is that Christ did not ordain them or their degrees. The second is that a simple uneducated person, by the help of God's grace, can do more to build the Church of Christ than many graduates.[8] There are no practical suggestions for reform, and of course no attack on scholasticism, but Wyclif's chapter and Dell's sermons might still be described as alike in spirit.

Wyclif's ideas were well known in Bohemia at the time of the Hussite revolution; indeed, most of the surviving manuscripts of *The Mirror of the Church Militant* were apparently copied there.[9] It is scarcely surprising, then, to find Wyclif's remarks on the universities elaborated in the

Hussite treatise *On the Kingdom of Antichrist*, which asserts that the mysteries of Scripture are not revealed to the wise of this world, but to the simple and childlike, and also that many doctors and masters belong to the mystical body of Antichrist – and here the author quotes Matthew 23 on the scribes and Pharisees. The appeal of this passage to Dell will be clear enough. He quotes it and ascribes the treatise to Hus (as did Otto Brunfels, in whose edition he read it). However, it is now believed to be the work of an earlier Bohemian radical, Matthew of Janov (*c.*1355–93).[10]

The case of Luther is rather more complicated, because Luther's attitude to universities was, like his attitude to institutions in general, somewhat ambivalent. There was a strong anti-institutional streak in Luther, who was prepared on occasion to call such outward forms the work of Antichrist; but he was also prepared to acquiesce in the foundation of a new institution, the Lutheran Church. He argued the priesthood of all believers, yet wanted a learned ministry. In his *Response to Ambrogio Catharino* (1521), which Dell quotes, Luther did indeed attack the universities as part of the rich, powerful, pompous, superstitious, diabolical ecclesiastical system, as well as criticizing them for teaching the dogmas of the Pope in the place of the Word of God. There are passages in the same vein elsewhere in Luther's writings, and Dell knew some of them, although he did not refer to the most important one, in *The Address to the Christian Nobility of the German Nation* (1520). Here Luther declared that what the universities wanted was 'a good strong reform' (*einer guten, starken Reformation*), because they were dominated by the ideas of 'the blind heathen master Aristotle'.[11] On the other hand, Luther did not reject the robes, rituals and degree-granting apparatus of the universities. On the contrary, he was shocked by the repudiation of all this on the part of his colleague Andreas Bodenstein von Karlstadt.

Whether or not Dell's *Stumbling-Stone* and *Trial of Spirits* caused any sort of sensation when they were preached in the university church in 1653, there can be little doubt of the dramatic nature of the incident in which Luther and Karlstadt were involved 130 years before. Karlstadt was dean of the theology faculty at Wittenberg University. On 3 February 1523, he refused to 'promote' any more degrees. Luther recorded that he was present at the degree ceremony that day and heard Karlstadt utter these 'sacrilegious words': 'I am prudent but impious because I promote degrees for two florins', and quote Matthew 23, 'be ye not called Masters'.[12]

Karlstadt's own writings of this period make his position a little clearer, and suggest (as the passages in Wyclif and Matthew of Janov are too brief to do), that he was responding to the problems of university life in his own day. He criticized the competitive ethos of the universities, where the Scriptures were studied simply for the sake of knowing them better than other people did. He was equally scathing in his comments on the importance given in the universities to status and power. 'For the sake of academic glory we kneel down, pay fees, and give expensive banquets, because this gives us authority over other people.'[13] Karlstadt's reaction was to reject the rat-race, to exchange his academic dress for peasant clothes, his official titles for that of 'brother Andrew', and the university for the rural parish of Orlamünde. Meanwhile, in Wittenberg, Luther waited for the fuss to die down and then asked the Elector to introduce doctorates again.[14]

'Oh, how like is John Lilburne to John of Leyden,' exclaimed Thomas Edwards in his diagnosis of the 'gangrene' of heresy, and 'M. Dell to Thomas Muntzer!'[15] He was of course trying to smear his opponents by associating them with rebellion and community of goods and women. All the same, there is something in his parallel with Anabaptism. Dell's views, including his views on universities, do have analogies in the 'radical reformation' of early sixteenth-century Germany, although Karlstadt is a closer parallel than Müntzer. Some of the German Anabaptists also criticized universities, or at least referred to them in the course of more general denunciations of human learning. Hans Hut cursed the universities of Paris and Wittenberg – in Hut's eyes Luther was making the same mistakes as his opponents – while Gabriel Ascherham attacked sophists and scholars and asked what use universities had been in the last fifteen hundred years in bringing people to the kindom of God.[16]

Whether Dell knew the writings of Karlstadt or the others it is difficult to say; he was obviously not going to give opponents like Edwards more ammunition by quoting passages like those above. However, he can hardly have been unaware of the Anabaptist opposition to learning, more radical than his (for they rejected human learning altogether), but part of a similar stress on the opposition between outward and inward, flesh and spirit. What is more, there were human links between them and him; the Elizabethan separatists. Robert Browne, Henry Barrow, John Greenwood, and Robert Harrison were all Cambridge men. They too were described by their enemies as Anabaptists.[17] They too wished to purge the Church of England of the remains of popery, and they too were critical of universities.

Browne's *Treatise upon the 23 of Matthew* (1582) – that chapter again – is an attack on would-be learned preachers for their spiritual pride:

For so soon as they have stood up in famous places, and showed their university degrees, and how well they become their hoods, or their scarlet gowns, and what standing in Cambridge, and reading they are in the tongues and doctors: there may then be none like them: then must you needs call them Rabbi, Master Doctor, My Lord's Chaplain, Master Preacher, and our Divinity Lecturer.

Browne also criticized universities for their concern with 'vain logic' and 'heathenish' learning, notably the study of Aristotle.[18]

Barrow's *Plain Refutation* (1591) is a more general critique of the clergy of the Church of England, including some sharp thrusts at 'university divines' as supporters of 'Antichrist's ruinous kingdom'; corrupting the Bible by their commentaries, studying Aristotle and other pagan writers, and disciplines which are 'profane, curious, unfit for a Christian', and participating in 'trifling ceremonies ... in their scarlet gowns, hoods, habits, caps, tippets etc'. Barrow was accused by the Master of Peterhouse of advocating the abolition of Oxford and Cambridge. However, the *Plain Refutation* does not condemn 'lawful arts or necessary sciences', indeed expresses the wish that 'the tongues and other godly arts were taught, not in the universities or a few places only, but ... at the least in every city in the land'.[19]

These last points are of course rather similar to Dell's own remarks on secular education, remarks which I have not yet attempted to place in any tradition. Christopher Hill has compared Dell's ideas with those of the Baconian reformers John Hall and Noah Biggs, while Charles Webster has compared him to Comenius, Dury, Hartlib and John Webster and again suggested his 'Baconian inspiration'.[20] Since the evidence for Dell's views on secular education consists of no more than a few paragraphs, firm assertions would be out of place, but I am not altogether happy with these comparisons. Dell's concern with what is 'useful and serviceable to the commonwealth' does indeed fit the Baconian paradigm, but Bacon had no monopoly of the argument from utility, and Dell's choice of subjects to be taught in the reformed university is not particularly Baconian. He has nothing to say about experiment, but he does mention mathematics, both arithmetic and geometry. Unlike Webster, with whom he is sometimes grouped, he does not refer to chemistry. A reminder that Dell was his own man, and that attempts to place individuals in intellectual traditions have only a limited usefulness.

To write intellectual history as if it were a kind of genealogy is to caricature it. Wyclif did not beget Hus, nor Hus Luther, nor did Luther (or Karlstadt, or Barrow, or Bacon) beget William Dell. Ideas are formed in response to situations.[21]

How, then, should intellectual historians deal with traditions? There is no consensus on the problem, and no space here to develop an argument, but it may be worth mentioning two suggestions. One stresses factors which are within the individual's control, the other factors which are not. The first suggestion emphasizes the fact that situations change, so that following a tradition means not following it; to say the same thing at a different moment is to say something different.[22] The second suggestion emphasizes the fact that individuals often have access to more than one tradition. They can appropriate elements from the traditions they find most relevant to their experiences, and they can rework the tradition they prefer in order to communicate fresh meanings.[23]

Both suggestions, or approaches, help in the understanding of the anti-intellectual (or anti-rational) tradition within Christianity, in which Dell stands. It goes back a long way. Some fathers of the Church, such as Clement of Alexandria, asserted that the best state of mind for a Christian was a childlike, passive, uncritical one, and this is perhaps what Christ meant when he told his disciples to be like little children.[24] This idea has appealed to many Christians since, but it has had different meanings at different times, and it has been worked into a variety of anti-rational world views.

In the late Middle Ages, for example, now that universities had developed and had been endowed in order to train the clergy of an increasingly rich, powerful and bureaucratic Church, the rejection of learning – by Waldensians, Lollards, and Hussites – took on an anti-clerical, anti-institutional meaning which it had lacked in the age of the fathers. The scribes and Pharisees, that traditional symbol of hypocrisy, now seemed an appropriate metaphor for university teachers. This image of proud men in gowns and hoods was still relevant in the sixteenth century, but superimposed on it was another image, of teachers teaching wrongly, engaging in sterile disputations and taking Aristotle too seriously. This was a humanist criticism of universities, associated with Petrarch and Valla in particular, but it was appropriated by Luther and others (Barrow, for example), for their own purposes. Karlstadt's criticisms by contrast were more medieval in inspiration, like those of the Anabaptists; but in restating the traditional opposition between flesh and spirit they too were saying something new, because they were turning Luther's arguments against Luther himself. As for Dell, he was well aware, as we have seen, of the radical traditions in which he stood, but his criticisms of universities gained a new meaning from the fact that they were made at a time of political revolution when the dream of 'universal reformation' seemed to be coming true at last.

Notes

1. C. Hill, *The World Turned Upside Down* (London, 1972), especially pp. 241f.; idem, 'The Radical Critics of Oxford and Cambridge in the 1650s', in *Universities and Politics*, J.W. Baldwin and R. Goldthwaite, eds. (Baltimore, 1972), pp. 107–32.

2. C. Hill, *Milton and the English Revolution* (London, 1977), ch. 6; idem, 'From Lollards to Levellers', in Maurice Cornforth, ed., *Rebels and their Causes* (London, 1978), pp. 49–67.

3. On Dell, R. Schlatter, 'The Higher Learning in Puritan England', *Historical Magazine of the Protestant Episcopal Church*, no. 23, 1954, pp. 167–87; L.F. Solt, 'Anti-intellectualism in the Puritan Revolution', *Church History*, no. 25, 1956, pp. 306–16; idem, *Saints in Arms* (Stanford, 1959), especially pp. 8, 13, 30f., 94; R. Greaves, *The Puritan Revolution and Educational Thought* (New Brunswick, 1969), especially pp. 42f., 133f.; E.C. Walker, *William Dell, Master Puritan* (Cambridge, 1970); C. Webster, 'William Dell and the Idea of University', in *Changing Perspectives in the History of Science*, M. Teich and R. Young, eds. (London, 1973), pp. 110–26; idem, *The Great Instauration* (London, 1975), especially pp. 181f., 197f.

4. W. Dell, *The Stumbling Stone* (London, 1653); idem, *The Trial of Spirits* (London, 1653); idem, *A Plain and Necessary Confutation of Divers Gross and Anti-christian Errors ... by Mr Sydrach Simpson* (London, 1654); idem, *Several Sermons* (London, 1709) (including the 1660 'Apology').

5. Dell quotes twenty authors, besides the Bible, in his *Select Sermons*, but he tended only to quote when discussing educational reform. His will left 'all my library of Latin and Greek books' to his son John (Walker, *William Dell*, p. 179), but did not indicate any titles, and there is no book in either of his colleges, Emmanuel or Caius, which is known to have been his. My thanks to J.H. Prynne, Librarian of Caius, for help with this question.

6. *The Prayer and Complaint of the Ploughman unto Christ* (n.p., 1531). The text, which is in Middle English, includes yet another paraphrase of Matthew 23: 'Lord thou sayest ne be ye nat cleped masters, for one is your master and that is Christ' (sig. E. verso).

7. It may be a mistake to assume that the John Wyclif who was Master of Balliol was the same man as the heretic. There is a similar problem of 'nominal record linkage' in the case of Dell himself, who was conflated by J.B. Mullinger, in the *Dictionary of National Biography*, with Laud's chaplain and only separated sixty years later, by H.R. Trevor-Roper, as he then was.

8. J. Wyclif, *Speculum Ecclesie Militantis*, A.W. Pollard, ed. (London, 1886), ch. 26.

9. Ibid., p.v.

10. *De Regno Antichristi*, ch. 14: edited by O. Brunfels (Strasbourg, 1524) as a work by Hus, but attributed to Matthew of Janov in his *Opera* (Hildesheim and New York, 1967).

11. M. Luther, *Ad Librum Magistri Ambrosii Catharini Responsio* (Wittenberg, 1521), reprinted in the collected edition of his works (60 vols., Weimar, 1883–1980), vol. 7, pp. 739f.

12. *Liber Decanorum Facultatis Theologiae Academiae Vitebergensis*, C.F. Förste-mann, ed. (Leipzig, 1838), p. 28n.

13. Translated from the passage quoted in R.J. Sider, *Andreas Bodenstein von Karlstadt* (Leiden, 1974), p. 177n.

14. Karlstadt was in Strasbourg in 1524, as was Brunfels, who in that year published his edition of 'Hus' (see above, note 10). Coincidence?

15. T. Edwards, *Gangraena*, part 3 (London, 1646), p. 262.

16. C.P. Clasen, *Anabaptism: A Social History* (Ithaca and London, 1972), pp. 316f.; G. Ascherham, *Unterschied Göttlicher und Menschlicher Weisheit* (1544), reprinted *Archiv für Reformationsgeschichte* 34, 1937 (see especially p. 28).

17. For example, by R. Some, *A Godly Treatise* (London, 1589), dedication.

18. *The Writings of R. Harrison and R. Browne*, A. Peel and L.H. Carlson, ed. (London, 1953), pp. 173–4, 181. The relevance to Dell of the ideas of the Elizabethan

separatists on education was brought out by H.F. Kearney, *Scholars and Gentlemen* (London, 1970), ch. 4.

19. *The Writings of H. Barrow*, L.H. Carlson, ed. (London, 1966), pp. 211f.

20. C. Hill, *The World Turned Upside Down* (London, 1972), p. 244; Webster (1973), p. 123.

21. Argued in B.I. Schwarz, 'The Intellectual History of China', in *Chinese Thought and Institutions*, J.K. Fairbank, ed. (Chicago, 1957), pp. 15–30.

22. Argued in J.R. Levenson, *Confucian China and its Modern Fate* (London, 1958), introduction.

23. Adapted (appropriated?) from *Resistance through Rituals*, S. Hall and T. Jefferson, ed. (London, 1976), especially pp. 176f.

24. G. Boas, *Essays on Primitivism in the Middle Ages* (Baltimore, 1948), pp. 25, 121f.

PART III

Atlantic Projections

Yet nothing ever wholly dies. Great Britain no doubt fared the worse in some respects for rejecting the truths of the radicals in the seventeenth century, but they were not utterly lost.... The broadside ballad of 1646, *The World is Turned Upside Down*, may well have been the old song of that name which was popular in the eighteenth century. It is said to have been played, appropriately enough, when Cornwallis surrendered to the American revolutionaries at Yorktown in 1781.

Christopher Hill, *The World Turned Upside Down*
(London, 1972), p. 307

All the Atlantic Mountains Shook

Peter Linebaugh

I have called this essay 'All the Atlantic Mountains Shook' because I wish to suggest profound and hemispheric events that originate beneath the surface of things and which are not confined to any particular nation but arise from all four corners of the Atlantic – North and South America, Europe, and Africa. Appearing at the beginning of Book 2 of William Blake's poem 'Jerusalem', it is a phrase of the revolutionary two decades ending the eighteenth and beginning the nineteenth centuries when those events were adumbrated in social practice. In his prophetic poem 'America', etched in 1793, the year that the British military made an armed bid to crush Toussaint L'Ouverture and the Dominican slave rebellion, Blake envisioned an Atlantic utopia:

> On those vast shady hills between America & Albion's shore,
> Now barr'd out by the Atlantic sea, call'd atlantean hills,
> Because from their bright summits you may pass to the Golden world,
> An ancient palace, archetype of mighty Emperies,
> Rears its immortal pinnacles, built on the forest of God.

Blake interprets the American, French, and Dominican revolutions by referring to the ancient myth of Atlantis. That myth has had various meanings. In Plato's *Timaeus* and *Critias*, Atlantis represented a huge island whose demiurgic and patriarchal society the Athenians had conquered in pre-Solonic times. Almost two millennia later at the beginning of the seventeenth century Francis Bacon represented Atlantis as a ceremonial, patriarchal laboratory, a kind of Los Alamos, where the exploration of nature was described in the imagery of conquest and rape. Blake rejected the implications of both these versions. The belief that the earth once had a different arrangement of continents

193

and oceans became the basis for imagining, not a legendary or future conquest, but an anti-imperialist peaceable kingdom.

Blake's knowledge of social contradiction was expressed in utterances wherein geography, history, morality, sexual generation and mythology were strikingly mixed in what might be called an interdisciplinary discourse that simultaneously challenged imperialism and empiricism. A few lines later the poem 'America' continued:

> Must the generous tremble & leave his joy to the idle, to the pestilence,
> That mock him? Who commanded this? what God? what Angel?
> To keep the gen'rous from experience till the ungenerous
> Are unrestrain'd performers of the energies of nature;
> Till pity is become a trade, and generosity a science
> That men get rich by; & the sandy desart is giv'n to the strong?

The 'Atlantic Mountains' provided a mythological suggestion of the unity and universality of a humanity divided by oppression, by science as a means of conquest, and by the 'laws' of political economy. Bacon's 'New Atlantis', by contrast, represented an oppressor's synthesis of Christianity and Platonic lore whose purpose was the creation of a society for 'the Enlarging of the bounds of Human Empire, to the Effecting of all Things possible'.[1] The 'meaner sort' played no role and the women kissed the hem of the garments of the men. Bacon, the empiricist of imperialism, and Blake, the prophet of classless humanity, were class as well as philosophic foes. Bacon was a high and mighty Lord Chancellor of England, William Blake a low and humble artisan, who none the less could write, 'The Prince of Darkness is a gentleman and not a man: he is a Lord Chancellor.' Bacon's 'Atlantis' received prompt realization in the foundation of the Royal Society (1660), the pinnacle of scientific cosmopolitanism in the Age of Mercantilism. Blake's visions of Atlantic destruction and redemption were the product of the Age of Revolution and have since belonged to an arcane tradition that has had its connections, however, with strands of 'proletarian internationalism'.

Thompson and Hobsbawm

One of these Blakean strands wound its way through the Communist Party Historians' Group that met in England during the late 1940s and early 1950s to which both Edward Thompson and Eric Hobsbawm belonged. Two of the most important productions of this group included Thompson's *The Making of the English Working Class* (1963) and

Hobsbawm's essay on 'The Crisis of the Seventeenth Century'.[2] By discussing that essay and comparing it with the first chapter of *The Making*, I can both define the problem that I wish to address and suggest some of the conditions for its solution without having to unravel the obscurities of Blake's Atlanticism or the opposing conception delineated in Bacon's 'New Atlantis'.

In 'Members Unlimited', the first chapter of *The Making of the English Working Class*, the organization and principles of the London Corresponding Society (1792), traditionally called the first independent working-class political organization in Britain, are described and linked with a debate almost 150 years earlier. Then, in 1647, the elected representatives of the rank-and-file soldiery confronted the 'grandees' of Oliver Cromwell's New Model Army in an extraordinary debate about the theory and practice of democracy.

Thompson in pointing out the similarity between these two confrontations – 'It is the old debate continued,' he wrote, 'the same aspirations, fears and tensions are there' – was himself contributing to a venerable tradition which finds in the Levellers' experience the beginning of modern democracy. There is a parallelism between such an invocation practised since at least Chartist times and the seventeenth-century practice of invoking the 'Norman Yoke' which attributed the origin of oppression and bondage to the invasion of William the Bastard in 1066. The parallelism expresses an impulse not so much of the English 'love of tradition', though there certainly can be nativist connotations to it, as of a persistent class-conscious and extra-academic pride in the history of previous struggle.

Of course, the parallel cannot be taken very far. What I wish to call attention to are two consequences of this particular way of posing the problem. First is the question of internationalism. Second, the question of tradition and continuity. The point of making the comparison across 150 years was to set out from the beginning the independent nature of the English debate from that of the French Revolution. Doubtless, this chapter and the following ones succeeded in this goal; the success, however, was not without its costs, the chief of which was the relative neglect of the international, especially the Atlantic, context of growth and development of the English working class. That problem, as I shall show, is closely related to the problem of continuity. It is a huge leap, this 150 years, from the Putney Heath mass meetings of haggard and determined soldiers to the Strand tavern of the Corresponding Society and the hopeful world of the London artisan. In making the leap Thompson does not ignore the intervening years. When the debate resumed in the 1790s, it did so 'in a new context, with new language and arguments, and a changed balance of forces', he wrote.

To explain the 'new language and arguments' he examines the complexities of three traditions: that of Dissent, that of the 'free-born Englishman', and that of the eighteenth-century mob. While each of these has stimulated considerable later investigation, I think that in outline his account of these traditions still stands.[3] They do not, however, explain the 'changed balance of forces'. Since that would require an investigation into material life and the mode of production, to leave the investigation after considering only the religious, political and 'subpolitical' traditions is clearly inadequate to the problem. Moreover, these do not explain, nor are they intended to, the duration of the pause between Putney and the London Corresponding Society.

Of course history is more than a discussion or a debate. 'The first premise of all human history is, of course, the existence of living human individuals. Thus the first fact to be established is the physical organization of these individuals and their consequent relation to the rest of nature.'[4]

It is interesting that from quite another framework altogether Eric Hobsbawm found himself wrestling with a similar problem of delayed or arrested development in his article 'The Crisis of the Seventeenth Century'. But where Thompson was concerned about the transmission of tradition, Hobsbawm was concerned about economic development; where Thompson applied his vision with unwavering concentration on English experience, Hobsbawm's ranged far and wide across the Channel and the oceans; where Thompson's touchstone lay in the past with the Putney debates, Hobsbawm's lay in the future in the notion of the 'Industrial Revolution'. While each wrote with different implicit assumptions about historical change, they converged on this problem of arrested development.

Why did the expansion of the later fifteenth and sixteenth centuries not lead straight into the epoch of the eighteenth- and nineteenth-century Industrial Revolution? Hobsbawm asked. 'What, in other words, were the obstacles to capitalist development?' To the larger question he answers with an exploration of the contradictions within the home, the European and the international markets. These inhibited the development of the social division of labour, the opportunities for mass production and the expansion of 'supra-local exchanges'. In eastern Europe a large number of food producers actually withdrew from the economy of money. The diminution of the supply of American bullion signalled an end to the period of colonial plunder and aggravated a price depression of prolonged consequence within Europe. The advance of technical innovation was halted. 'Once the decline had begun, of course, an additional factor increased the difficulties of manufacture: the rise in labour costs.'

At that point the working class, the producers of social wealth, the lower orders, the proletariat (it is not necessary to be pedantic in our choice of words) enters the 'crisis of the seventeenth century', not – be it noted – as the obstacle to 'capitalist development', but as a cost, and merely an incidental one at that. In a way this manner of entrance has some consistency to it, because the underlying model of development is one that places the sphere of circulation (trade, commerce and exchange) ahead of the sphere of production in explaining change. Thus, the seventeenth-century crisis as a crisis of circulation.

Yet when he writes that 'the major achievement of the seventeenth-century crisis is the creation of a new form of colonialism', he is emphasizing the decisive importance of the plantation. Considered also is the putting-out system; again, not with regard to the characteristics of the working people thus organized, but rather as a successful dissolvant of the corporate organization of guild production and of those rural relations which had effectually blocked the infiltration of commodity exchange, what Winstanley called 'the crafty Art of Buying and Selling'.

Summing up, we can see two approaches represented by Thompson and Hobsbawm to the problems of, first, the working class and, second, the apparent pause in English development in the late seventeenth and early eighteenth centuries. Thompson considered the English people as the bearers of an oppositional tradition, stored up within themselves, modified by social practice, goaded by new forms of oppression, which re-emerged in the 1790s. Although it is hardly given any social or material determinants, its historic importance is (as it were) expressed in Blakean leaps of the popular intellectual tradition whose power is undeniable but whose actual situation within the materiality of international life is left vague. Hobsbawm's view of labour is presented indirectly. If for Thompson the proletarian body is presented as speech and mind, for Hobsbawm it is expressed as stomach and hand. Labour to him forms, first, a potential market and so its unity appears as 'demand'. Second, it appears as a factor of production, but even here the general framework imposes its own limitations upon how that 'factor' is considered. Despite this, the framework at least leads us to production and invites us to consider the unity that trade or commerce brings about between widely different modes of production. While he offers the possibility of an Atlantic perspective to an English problem, there is a metropolitan and Baconian objectivism to his conception of living labour such that, as Walter Rodney has pointed out, he marginalizes the massive exploitation of Africans and American Indians.[5] As to the delay in development, Hobsbawm thinks that 'the stormy pace of economic development towards the end of the seventeenth century "ought" to have brought about industrial revolution much sooner', but he eschews

an explanation of the time-lag. Thompson mentions a number of
contingencies arising from the corruption and venalities encouraged by
the ruling and propertied classes.

In the remainder of this essay I shall discuss the relationship between
the evolving radical traditions that were largely English to the developing modes of production that were largely Atlantic. In so doing, I shall
propose that just as the accumulation of international capital depends on
the exploitation of Atlantic labour, so 'pauses' or 'arrests' in the process
of accumulation are the results of the many-sided oppositions of living
labour brewing within and among the modes of production. Furthermore, the interruption of the discussion begun so promisingly at Putney
took a form in which the forces creating that discussion were pulverized
and scattered to the four winds. These carried them far and wide. They
regained their strength in wholly new circumstances and returned in a
kind of Atlantic dialectical movement.

Beyond the Putney Debates

'A spontaneous outbreak of democracy,' Professor Brailsford called the
debates.[6] Besides the theoretical arguments, there was the painstaking
organizing work of the Levellers behind them. The elected representatives of the soldiers, 'Agitators' they were called, provided the world
with a new kind of leadership. The meeting itself was called to demand
arrears in pay. Agitators and soldiers, furthermore, refused to go to
Ireland until their demands were met and the question of the government of England settled. Those great debates thus arose in the context
of a pay dispute, a possible mutiny (made actual two years later), and
the first faint whiff of an anti-imperialist struggle. This unheard of
power, first, to elect representatives, second, to force a debate with the
grandees, third, to collect pay, and, fourth, to refuse service in Ireland,
was short-lived, two years long, but long enough to provide a haunting
memory to many generations of the English military establishment.

It was unsuccessful in taking state power: the chopping-block and the
gallows remained the property of the grandees, so it has been said that
the democratic forces were immature: a coalition of confused groups,
led by the radical petty bourgeoisie. And as C.B. Macpherson has shown,
the political or parliamentary vision of the Levellers was far less embrac-
ing than might be supposed because the franchise they advocated fell
very short of universal suffrage.[7] However, why should we measure the
importance of a popular movement by the *étatiste* criterion of its ability
to govern? If these discoveries tended to minimize the democratic
importance of the popular movement in one direction, the publication of

Christopher Hill's *The World Turned Upside Down* tended to expand it in another. This showed how the Seekers and the Ranters, the 'true' Levellers as well as the regular Levellers, the Muggletonians and Grindletonians, the preachers and prophets, the dreamers and activists, actually belonged to a wide movement that questioned all kinds of authority: of the law, of the King, of Scripture, of property, of patriarchy. The antinomian tradition was identifiable and widespread without being confined to a particular sect. It asserted that, first, God has no other existence but in each and all created things, second, the moral and ceremonial law is the result of a curse that has been lifted and, third, the destruction of Babylon and the building of Jerusalem is at hand.[8] At its most far out, among the Ranters for instance, the movement expressed a naive communism and plebeian materialism that advocated 'wanton kisses' and 'swearing i'th light, gloriously'.

The tradition was much richer than we thought. The social groups which thrust forward the spokespersons and leadership of the radical movement consisted of the masterless, who have been divided into these groups: (a) vagabonds and sturdy rogues, (b) the mass of the London proletariat, (c) the sectaries who might have been small propertyholders, (d) the itinerant population of small traders, (e) the cottagers and squatters of commons and wastes. In addition to this sort of classification, we may add others of region – the 'dark corners of the land' in the west and north – and of ecology – the wealden and pasture areas whose communities preserved their independence long after those in arable zones had succumbed.[9] Recently it has been shown that even the most general and apparently abstract of denominations such as the 'people' and the 'poor' have particular, concrete meanings. In the seventeenth century each of them denominated distinct and antagonistic social forces, the former being associated with the yeomanry, tradesmen and artificers and the latter with a larger mass of those expropriated from all forms of property.[10] Our argument need not depend on the precise definition of the stratifications within these groups. We are interested in their fluidity and the social dynamics that set them in motion. Besides masterlessness, what characterized these groups was their mobility, their freedom and their footlooseness.

Now, what I think needs adding to the view that we have thus far – leaders preaching, publishing, petitioning the radical traditions here, carefully defined social grouping hearing and receiving the antinomian traditions there – is the reciprocal nature of the interaction. This would allow us to examine independently of the fate of specific intellectual traditions, such as the Familists and Anabaptists and behind them the Lollards, the experiences of the volatile masses that gave birth to them, in the first place.

Vagrants and the Contradiction of Primary Accumulation

The Alpha and Omega of capitalist production consists in the meeting of two kinds of commodity owners: on the one hand, the possessor of the means of production and the means of subsistence; and, on the other, free labourers, the sellers of their own labour-power. It thus presupposes the complete separation of the labourers from all property by which they can realize their labour. In the sixteenth century primary accumulation consisted in the divorce of the producer from the means of production: 'their expropriation', wrote Marx, 'is written in the annals of mankind in letters of blood and fire.' The process was accomplished by the abolition of private armies and feudal retainers, by the closing of the monasteries, by the rooting out of itinerant friars, pardoners and beggars, the result of the medieval system of charity; and, finally, the enclosure of arable lands, the eviction of smallholders and the displacement of rural tenants led most directly and profoundly to capitalist production.[11]

Unable to find profitable employment, without land, credit or occupation, this early proletariat was thrust upon the roads and ways where it was subject to the merciless cruelty of as severe and terrifying a labour and criminal code as had yet appeared in modern history. This was the period of the criminalization of all forms of necessary labour outside of the ambit of producing surplus value. In the sixteenth century the major statutes against robbery, burglary and stealing were created. A nomadic, roaming people, the gypsies offered an example of living without land or master. They brought morris-dancing to England, and they provided an image of freedom. Menace, sharp practice and an idea of wandering brotherhood are suggested by three Romany words, 'cosh', 'gyp' and 'pal'. The laws against the gypsies were terrible: forfeiture of goods and chattels, banishment, and no legal defence. By an act of Mary, to remain in England longer than a month became a capital offence. An act of Queen Elizabeth enlarged the earlier laws to include those who 'in a certain conterfeit speech or behaviour' disguise themselves as Egyptians, illustrating the profoundest fear of dissimulation.

The laws against vagabondage provide us with a Foucault-like index of the growing attack on the corporal person. Under Henry VIII vagabonds could be whipped, have their ears cut off, and be hanged; under Edward VI they might have their chests branded with the letter 'V' and be enslaved for two years; under Elizabeth I they could be whipped, banished to galley service, or the House of Correction. The criminal code elaborated under Edward VI was scarcely less vicious against the propertyless and what Autolycus called 'snappers-up of unconsidered trifles'. The Statue of Artificers and the Poor Law, likewise, were huge efforts to legislate taking hire.[12]

Cruel, comprehensive and pitiless as this legislation was, howsoever many were hanged each year (the magnitude was in the hundreds), or howsoever many masterless men were rounded up in the Privy Searches that periodically terrorized the population (the magnitude was in the thousands), the proletariat retained its independence, its intractability and its wits. We can see this in the coney-catching pamphlets of Thomas Dekker and Robert Greene. It infuriated that Kentish squire, Thomas Harman, whose *Caveat for Common Cursitors* provides, in spite of itself, so many instances of daily victories which intelligence won over brute authority (similar in that respect to the signifying monkey and trickster of slave tradition). In the glossaries of cant or thieves' talk we are given a veritable dramatis personae of those rejecting wage-labour: the Abraham-man, the palliards, clapperdudgeons, whipjacks, dummerers, files, dunakers, cursitors, Roberds-men, swadlers, prigs, anglers, fraters, rufflers, bawdy-baskets, autem-morts, walking morts, doxies and dells. A.L. Beier's study of vagrants confirms what is suggested here, namely, that this wandering population consisted of men who mostly had had settled occupation. In addition to servants and labourers, he notes the prominence of cloth-workers and victuallers.[13] The flow between intermittent employments (these were greatly enlarged with the growth of the putting-out system) and the life of the road was so swift and fluid that the attempt proves vain which fixes a man or woman in one or other social category in that fast-moving and turbulent stream.

Sir John Popham, Chief Justice of the King's Bench between 1592 and 1607, listed thirty different types, falling into five main groups. First, there are the chapmen, the tinkers and pedlars, the men and women whose little transactions provided the commerce of the proletarian micro-economy. Second were the discharged or wounded, or pretended discharged and wounded, soldiers and sailors, whose labours provided the basis of the expansionist macro-economy. Third were the remnants of the surviving substructure of feudal benevolence, the procurers, the proctors, the pardoners. The entertainers of the day, the jugglers, fencers, minstrels, keepers of dancing bears, athletes and players of interludes made up the fourth group. Fifth, in mentioning those feigning knowledge of a 'crafty Scyence' like palmistry or physiognomy, or the fortune-tellers, or 'persons calling themselves Schollers', he designated those who supplied the intellectual and philosophical wants of the people whose ideas Dame Frances Yates and Keith Thomas have taught us to treat respectfully. Finally, Popham's preamble named, all wandring persons and common Labourers being persons able in bodye using loytering and refusing to worke for such reasonable wages as is taxed or comonly given in such Parts where such persons do or shall happen to dwell or abide, not having lyving otherwyse to mayteyne themselves.

Thus, falling within the statutory meaning of 'sturdy rogue and beggar' are all those rejecting wage-labour as well as those whose activities comprised the culture, tradition, and autonomous self-understanding of this volatile, questioning and unsteady proletariat. To the ideological opposition to wage-labour, here is the sign of the experience of opposition. It provided the soil in which the more arcane traditions, such as antinomianism, could find a warm environment during the winter of Tudor repression.

The first-time offender against the Beggar Act was to be stripped and whipped until his back became bloody. Second-time offenders were to be banished from the realm, beginning the English policy of transportation. It ought not to be surprising to learn that John Popham had a prominent interest in the Virginia Company or that the next generation of his family played a decisive part among the Puritan grandees of the West Country.[14]

The Atlantic Diaspora

The traditions opposing the inward bondages of the Protestant work ethic as well as the outward bondages of wage-labour were dispersed across the Atlantic in a white face, just as a century later, modified by fresh experience, they would return in black face to help revivify the movement in England. The dispersal of the active part of the English proletariat should be seen as double-sided: as the riddance of danger, 'the fewell and matter of insurrection', and as the basis of a new mode of production, the plantation. Robert Johnson in 1609 expressed the relationship in these words:

Two people are especially required herin, people to make the plantation, and money.... For the first, we need no doubt, our land abounding with swarms of idle persons, which having no means of labour to relieve their misery, do likewise swarm in lewd and naughty practices, so that if we seek not some ways for their foreign employment, we must provide shortly more prisons and corrections for their bad conditions.[15]

Usually, the diaspora is divided into two sorts of people: those who were in some sense political exiles which would include the revolutionary sectaries, the Quakers, the Monmouth Rebels, the veterans of the New Model Army, the Irish, and the Scottish convenanters, and a larger 'unpolitical' mass of people who departed as indentured servants or as transported felons.[16] The distinction was made by the Chesapeake planters and it has been rigidly maintained by historians. I wish to argue that the Agitator, the Ranter and the Rogue did not have such a mutually opposing social existence. In fact they shared common experiences in their enemies like Popham, Cromwell or Ireton, in their travelling on the highways of the country, in the hand-to-mouth existence of the London suburbs and in their voyage across the Atlantic.

A study of the seventeenth-century migrants to the Chesapeake shows that, like sixteenth-century vagrants and migrants, most were single, young and male. They tended to come from areas where the cloth trade was depressed or where agriculture had changed to throw off the young, or from London, or the areas of deforestation. The same study says these indentured servants were from the 'middle ranks' of society, but the evidence for this is unpersuasive.[17] The 'data base' of this study (the term is appropriate given the abstracted empiricism of the approach) consists of seventeenth-century Bristol indentures. These describe the sort of people who were far from the 'middle ranks', if by that term is meant either the tradesmen whose existence pre-dated the nineteenth-century 'middle class', that is the bourgeoisie, or the wealthier end of that complex hierarchy of crafts that indisputably constituted one of the structures of the social division of labour. They were, on the contrary, 'propertyless wage-earners and piece workers' (according to Dr Buchanan Sharp's study of the same area) whose experience prior to emigration was that of rioting against enclosures, high food prices and the expropriation of common rights, and participation in the Western Rising and the 'Club' movement of the Civil War.[18] Perhaps it would be anachronistic to take the 'sturdy rogue and vagabond' with his Tudor caparisons into the plainer life of the seventeenth century. Perhaps the 'indentured servant' ought to become the new concrete universal of the English proletariat as he at least (very few were women) was a climber of the 'Atlantean hills'. Neither term, however, can be construed to mean the 'middle rank'.[19]

Cromwell's God, we should not forget, was a God of work and of conquest: of Jamaica, of Scotland and, as shall not be forgotten, of Ireland. From Dublin in 1649 he wrote after the surrender of a hundred-odd Irish soldiers that he had the officers 'knocked on the head, and every tenth man of the soldiers killed, and the rest shipped for Barbadoes'.[20] William Petty, who followed in the train of the English marauders with his surveying equipment (so that there would be no complaints when it came time to slice up the baloney), later estimated that, between 1651 and 1654, 40,000 Irish people were transported. 'To frie the kingdom of the burden of many strong and idle beggars, Egiptians, common and notorious whores and thieves and other dissolute and louse persons' was the purpose of the first Scottish act of transportation.

Indentured servants, banished ranters and Irish rebels: not the stuff for that malleable labour market of late mercantilist dream. Let us consider what else happened to them on the western side of the Atlantic. Henry Whistler in 1654 wrote of Barbados: 'This Island is the dunghill whereon England doth cast forth its rubbish: rogues and whores and such like people are those which are generally brought here.'[21] Perrot, the bearded ranter who refused to doff his hat to the Almighty, ended up in Barbados. The street preacher and pantheistic materialist, Joseph Salmon, went there in a Zen-like search for 'nothing'. In the early stages anyway the Irish took the lead in forming maroon colonies with the African slaves. The radical hero of the servant class was Cornelius Bryan, an Irishman, mutineer, plotter and speaker of profanities against the planters.[22]

On the eastern shore of Virginia, the years following the Revolution saw an intensification of labour (even introducing night work in the tobacco cultivation) among the ex-convicts, the New Model Army veterans, the Irish and the sectaries. Doug Deal has written that the 'physical violence, verbal abuse, work slowdowns, sabotage, and running away by servants all became much more common after 1660'. Several areas existed where Quakers, renegades, Nonconformists, adventurers, servants and slaves, of both sexes and all races, could drink, smoke, carouse, fight and make music. In 1666 an African slave and an English servant ran away from their respective plantations. Before leaving his, the slave made sure, if he took nothing else, to take his master's fiddle. The Gloucester County plot of 1663 and Bacon's Rebellion of 1676 'convinced the planter class that it could no longer afford to continue to import large numbers of labourers from the British Isles', it has recently been concluded.[23] As late as 1683 it was reported by a young squire that 'Carolina and Pennsylvania are the refuge of the sectaries, and are in such repute, that men are more easily induced to be transported thither than to the Islands.'[24]

Among the 'lobster backs' of the New Model Army that captured Jamaica there were radicals. Some of these stayed on joining the intensely egalitarian (and cruel) buccaneers who had established among themselves and the areas they influenced, like Tortuga, northern Hispaniola and the Mosquito Coast (Nicaragua), an autonomous and mutualist tradition. After Henry Morgan sold out to work for Charles II and the Duke of York, the zone of these freebooters moved north and east to the Carolinas and Bahamas. Until the cycle of repression initiated by Walpole in the early years of his administration put an end to them, the men and women (Mary Read, Ann Bonney) who sailed 'Under the Banner of King Death' created a social existence that was, as Marcus Rediker has convincingly shown, collectivist, egalitarian and anti-authoritarian, comparing itself to Robin Hood and venerating the memory of the Revolution.[25] Christopher Hill hears echoes of Milton and Winstanley in Defoe's *A General History . . . of the Most Notorious Pyrates* (1724) which besides emitting those sounds was dead set against the slave trade.[26] In 1720 some pirates who had sailed on the *Flying Dragon* settled in Madagascar. James Plantin was one of these. It was reported that he lived at a place which he had 'given the name of Ranter Bay'.[27]

Of course, not all of the transatlantic British, Irish and Scottish migrants were revolutionary sectaries and schismatics. However, some were and others had been. The organizational form and ideological coherence that had flourished in determinate historical forms in England during the Revolution (or before it) could not be maintained as such in the 'New Worlds'. Those, like the Quakers, who did preserve a semblance of organizational continuity did so partly at a cost of distancing themselves both from their revolutionary heritage and from mass experience of the new kinds of labour. Others, such as the early Seekers and (most notoriously) the Ranters eschewed organization and prided themselves on their mole-like burrowing within the soil of mobile labour. As early as 1646 a hostile observer had written, 'they have many depths, wiles and methods which I know note, nor can finde out; there are many windings and turnings of the serpent, crooked goings, in and out, off and on, here and there, which I cannot trace'.[28] Some of the 'turnings of the serpent' can be traced, if not directly, then indirectly. Quakers, for instance, remained in dialogue with their early progenitors, the Ranters and the Seekers. John Burnyeat travelled in Virginia in 1672, where he had a dispute with a 'fifth-monarchy-man'. In 1680, Joan Vokins, a Quaker who travelled in England, Ireland, America and the West Indies, found herself troubled by the Ranters at general meetings in Oysterbay and Rhode Island.[29]

Even if it was a hostile relationship, we can see that the antinomian tradition persisted in an active and self-conscious way. It also continued, albeit in a subdued and marginal form, within the Quakers. John Hepburn in *The American Defense of the Christian Golden Rule* (1715) listed a number of 'excellent souls' who 'came out of Old England, that have kept their Integrity'. They detested the planters who bedizened 'their Carkasses with poslt and powdered Hair, with Ruffles, and Top-Knotes, Ribbands and Lace'. George Keith was disowned by the Friends for writing *An Exhortation and Caution to Friends Concerning Buying or Keeping of Negroes* (1693). Benjamin Lay, the cave-dwelling vegetarian, became an abolitionist. He appeared at a Philadelphia Quaker meeting wearing military uniform and a sword beneath his sombre Quaker garb. He carried a hollowed-out Bible in which he concealed a bladder of pokeberry juice. He rose during the meeting casting off his outer clothes, and stated that 'it would be as justifiable in the sight of the Almighty if you should thrust a sword through their [slave's] hearts as I do through this book'. Whereupon he pierced the book with his sword, spilling the red liquid all over the astonished Friends. He had once been a common sailor and had learned first hand about the slave trade. In *All Slave-Keepers That Keep the Innocents in Bondage, Apostates* (1737) he ranted against the 'Covetous, Covetous, the Covetous Earthly minded Idolater'.[30]

Thus, the defeated, the victims, Irish tories, Scottish covenanters, Quakers, sectaries, Ranters, Seekers and radicals – an antagonistic conglomeration of widely different linguistic, geographic and cultural origin – found themselves sharing an experience of valiant resistance to the English adventurers and grandees who had flung them to the edge of the map. There they shared an experience of survival in a strange ecology, a new kind of co-operation on the plantation, as well as the possibility of creating a life where, in Winstanley's words, 'There shall be no Tyrant Kings, Lords of Manors, Tything Priests, oppressing Lawyers, exacting Landlords, nor any such like pricking bryar in all this holy Mountain of the Lord God our Righteousness and Peace.'[31]

The Slave Trade and Pidgin English

The Atlantic diaspora was no more successful in producing a stable basis of capitalist accumulation, or a solution to the 'seventeenth-century crisis', than was the bloody code against the Tudor vagabonds, whose nomadic and roguish unavailability for wage-labour was a decisive and generally unmentioned cause of the crisis in the first place. The English Revolution, despite the defeats of the radicals and the victory of the militant bourgeoisie, demonstrated some limits to the exploitation of people and the land. Those were its most lasting and universal victories. English capitalism was thereafter driven elsewhere for people whose labour it could exploit (Ireland, Africa), and for land whose resources it could ravish (Ireland, America). Indeed, the two wings of the English bourgeoisie were ready to bury the hatchet when it came to this. While Cromwell was busy on one side of the Atlantic capturing Jamaica, his erstwhile opponent at the Battle of Marston Moor, Prince Rupert, was busy on the other side of the Atlantic in Gambia inquiring into slavery.

Upon the restoration of the Stuart monarchy in 1660, Prince Rupert helped direct his cousin's (Charles II's) money into the slave trade; he helped charter the Royal Adventurers a few months after Charles II landed in England; and he helped beat the Dutch at sea, thus securing the African coast. The King's brother, the Duke of York, put his mark upon the trade by requiring that the slaves be branded with a 'D.Y.' upon their foreheads. The 'cabal' invested heavily. So did John Locke. George Downing was a key figure in the early days. In 1645 he wrote of the barbados planters, hungrily, 'they have bought this year no lesse than a thousand Negroes, and the more they buye, the better able they are to buye'. This second graduate of Harvard and ship's chaplain served Charles II by an embassy to the Hague whose purpose was to provoke a war for the slave trade. His treachery and servility were rewarded with a knighthood and his avarice led him to the speculative building of a Whitehall street that still bears his name. These are only sordid indications about the closet politics leading to this trade. Let us leave the capitalist side of the history.[32]

By the end of the seventeenth century we may distinguish four ways by which capital sought to organize the exploitation of human labour in its combination with the materials and tools of production.[33] These were first, the plantation, in many ways the most important mercantilist achievement; second, petty production such as the yeoman farmer or fortunate artisan enjoyed; third, the putting-out system which had begun to evolve into manufacture; and the mode of production which at the level of circulation united the others, namely the ship. As modes of production I wish to consider them not as sources of wealth or means of value-creation, nor as stages of economic growth, and still less as means of satisfying human wants. I consider them only as a framework of human interaction, a framework both conducting and moulding human experience. They thus cease to be the technical infrastructure of economics and become instead 'the public realm' of working-class self-activity. Each of them organized human labour differently. Thus the plantation provided the first site in modern history of mass co-operation. Petty production remained the setting of resourcefulness and independent individualism. Manufacture and the putting-out system created the fragmented, detail labourer whose 'idleness' became the bane of the eighteenth-century political economist. The ship whose milieu of action made it both universal and *sui generis* provided the place where the articulation of disciplinary rules and the ratio of variable to constant capital (men to equipment) forebode the factory of the future.

'Long before the Industrial Revolution of the early nineteenth century which ushered in the factory system,' one scholar has written, 'the seamen had been working under many of the same characteristic features which have now become so well known in connection with factory production; and even though their settings were so different as to obscure or to hide the likeness, in essentials they were the same.'[34] The large capital outlay, the division of labour, the regimentation and repetition, the close supervision, the working in groups and the removal from home are the characteristics sailoring had in common with the factory. The ships' holds carried the congealed labour of the plantations, the manu-factories and the workshops to their new destinations. The rolling and pitching deck was the uncertain stage upon which the international sea-faring proletariat told its stories to one another and sought for itself its historic role.

The ship carried congealed labour; it also carried living labour: ships of transported felons, of indentured servants, above all, of African slaves. The ship was not only the means of communications between continents, it was the first place where working people from the conti-nents communicated. All the contradictions of social antagonism were concentrated within its timbers. Imperialism was the main one. What-ever highpoints stood out in the sun of European imperialism, they always cast an African shadow: it was not just his cabin boy who was black, Christopher Columbus's pilot, Pedro Nino, was an African. *The Mayflower* as soon as it discharged the famous Pilgrims sailed for the West Indies with a cargo of people from Africa.[35] Forced by the magni-tude of its enterprises to bring huge and heterogeneous masses of men and women together aboard ship to face a deathly voyage to a cruel destination, European imperialism also created the conditions of the circulation of experience within the huge masses of labour that it had set in motion. People will talk.

The people packed in the slavers spoke many languages. In 1689, the year that the two factions of the English ruling class under the constitu-tional tutelage of John Locke learned to speak a common language, Richard Simson wrote of his experiences in the South Seas:

> The means used by those who trade to Guinea, to keep the Negroes quiet, is to choose them from several parts of ye Country, of different Languages; so that they find they cannot act joyntly, when they are not in a Capacity of Consulting with one another, and this they cannot doe, in soe farr as they understand not one another.[36]

To communicate they had to develop a language of their own, and as often as not this was the oppressor's language. The English was not Dr Johnson's, it was Jack Tar's, and Jack Tar, as Jesse Lemisch has said, was a foul-mouthed speaker of the 'very shambles of language'. The mariners spoke 'a dialect and manner peculiar to themselves', said a writer in the *Critical Review* (1757). Ned Ward in the *Wooden World Dissected* asserted that the language of a ship's master was 'all Heathen Greek to a Cobbler'. A student of seventeenth-century ships' logs has shown in sixty densely worded pages how very different was maritime phonetics from that of the landsman.[37] What is perhaps most impressive about eighteenth-century sea glossaries is what is left out. In general they are technical and disciplinary manuals of instruction.[38] Sometimes, though, they are hints of other worlds like these:

quashee   a Negroe seaman

manany   someone who puts off work

Captain's cloak   the 36th article of war giving the captain powers of punishment in cases not expressly provided for

Fiddlers Green   paradise for seamen dying ashore

A combination of, first, nautical English, second, the 'sabir' of the Mediterranean, third, the hermetic-like cant talk of the 'underworld', and, fourth, West African grammatical construction, produced the 'pidgin English' that became in the tumultuous years of the slave trade the language of the African coast.

It was a language whose expressive power arose less from its lexical range than from the musical qualities of stress and pitch. Some African contributions to maritime and then 'standard' English include 'caboodle', 'kick the bucket', and 'Davy Jones' locker'.[39] Where people had to understand each other pidgin English was the lingua franca of the sea and of the frontier. Inasmuch as all who came to the New World did so after months at sea, pidgin or its maritime and popular cognates became the medium of transmission for expressing the new social realities. By the mid eighteenth century there were pidgin-speaking communities in Philadelphia, New York and Halifax. In 1722 Philip Ashton was asked by some pirates 'in their proper Dialect ... If I would sign their Articles'.[40] Pidgin became an instrument, like the drum or the fiddle, of communication among the oppressed: scorned and not easily understood by 'polite' society.

It has been estimated that by the end of the eighteenth century fully a quarter of the complement of the Royal Navy consisted of men of African origin, an astonishing figure and yet not considered implausible by Professor Walvin.[41] The ship, if not the breeding-ground of rebels, became a meeting-place where various traditions were jammed together, an extraordinary forcing-house of internationalism. African, Briton, quashee, American (not to mention Portuguese, lazar and Spanish) would have co-operated, for their lives depended on it, in the rigging and on the decks in the fo'c'sle and the mess. Shipboard co-operation plus a libertarian, anti-slavery ideology provided the background to the many instances of trans-continental, multi-racial struggles of the maritime proletariat. In 1747 white and black mariners battled the press-gang in Boston for three days, and again in 1767–8.[42] The first battle of the American War of Independence was led by just such a quashee, Crispus Attucks. He stood at the head of 'a motley rabble of saucy boys, negroes and molattoes, Irish teagues and outlandish jack tarrs', wrote John Adams. Olaudah Equiano, a Padmore-like figure of the eighteenth century, derived his own extraordinary abilities doubtless from his language and musical talents. In Africa he heard many tongues. It was the same in Jamaica, but there on Sunday afternoons the slaves of different languages met to communicate by dance and music. In the 'Wilkes & Liberty' days of London he studied the French horn! In the Bahamas the 'melodious sound of the catguts' brought him together with the free blacks. He was a lucky man in that during the Middle Passage he was able to handle the quadrant and to learn some English. Later fellow mariners like Richard Baker, an American, and Daniel Queen, an Englishman, taught him a trade and the language of Milton.[43] From them he learned something of what it meant to be 'free born', for he was soon objecting to every untried punishment on the grounds that it was not meted by 'judge and jury'.

The Boomerang

'Judge and Jury', 'No Standing Army', the law expressed in English not Latin: these were some of the abiding political achievements of the English Revolution and the party of the Levellers, just as restrictions upon unfettered capitalist use of the land and limitations upon the rate of exploitation of the 'free-born Englishman' were material achievements of the broader movement from which the Levellers arose. The more radical tradition that had partly been responsible for these latter accomplishments did not recover easily from the Atlantic diaspora or the repression of the Restoration. A quietistic turning to the Kingdom Within was one path, that might occasionally spawn the odd fish, like Benjamin Lay. An aggressive interpretation of the doctrine of the Elect that turned it into the self-justification of capitalist entrepreneurs or into the niggardly doctrines of Ben Franklin's 'Poor Richard' was another. Even the Quaker's 'inner light' found its outer, objective correlative in the glint of gold. Against these we must place a third – the submersion of the communitarian and antinomian traditions within the rivulets of local communities and within the long, heaving swells of the Atlantic.

There these traditions were not entirely dormant. Further research is likely to show that this was a light, winking sleep.[44]

We see it among the Spitalfields weavers when they rose against the engine-loom in 1675 or in the support they gave to the concentration of Anabaptist meeting-places in Spitalfields. We see it in Bedlam (a likely place!) where Ned Ward heard an inmate 'holding forth with as much vehemence against kingly government, as a brother of Commonwealth doctrine rails against plurality of livings'. We see it in taverns: in Aldersgate Ned Ward heard a tavern politician, 'a rattle-headed prattle-box set up to reform the Church, new-model the Government, and calumniate the best of Princes'.[45] We see it in Newgate chapel during the sermons for the condemned when the malefactors sometimes set up a Ranter-like counter-theatre of laughter, profanity and song.

Very often the tradition was associated with the heroes of the under-world. Jack Sheppard, the great gaol-breaker, was compared to a Leveller. Dick Turpin, the highwayman, inspired a large number of expressions of militant hatred of oppression.[46]

Doubtless, a sharp eye could see the thin filament of this tradition elsewhere. Like the red 'Rogue's thread' that ran through the cordage and sailcloth of HM Naval Stores, it was more a mark of identification than of power. We should, also, guard against disembodying or de-contextualizing these survivals for they lived only to the extent that they allowed themselves to be modified in the changing productive arrange-ments of life. Because the transformation of material and social relations attendant upon these changes in production, principally the wage, is the subject of a story I am telling elsewhere, here we may sum them up in words of Tom Paine, the Edmund Hilary of the Atlantic mountains: 'When the rich plunder the poor of his rights, it becomes an example to the poor to plunder the rich of his property.'[47] Tom Paine was born in a Quaker family. He worked as a stay-maker, first in a rural, proto-industrial setting, then in a London manufactory whose workers had struck against the fourteen-hour day, to escape which he tried unsuccess-fully to sign aboard the terrible privateer, *Captain Death*, and then successfully aboard the *King of Prussia*. 'A maritime life is a kind of partial emigration', he wrote later. It was the ship, therefore, that mediated his transformation from an urban craftsman in London to a world-shaking trans-continental revolutionary in America.[48]

It is true that London was an industrial city, the centre of a huge textile industry and hundreds of crafts. Primarily, however, its huge eighteenth-century growth was the result of its function as a port. As the port expanded so did its river and maritime populations. Smollett, Didbin and Marryat suggest that it was the richest of the Atlantic pidgin communities. Certainly it contained a larger black population than any city outside of Africa. Wherever you looked you saw black faces. At Bartholomew Fair Ned Ward shows us two female rope dancers: one Irish, another African. Oil paintings show the ubiquity of the African servant in the households of the aristocrats. Isaac George, a New England mariner, son of a Guinea man, made more than ten Atlantic crossings before he was hanged at Tyburn for robbing a surgeon of his implements.[49] The black population was about 20,000, or something less, by the 1760s when it was able to set Granville Sharpe in motion. It was concentrated in maritime and servile occupations. Black communities existed in Paddington, Whitechapel and St Giles-in-the-Fields.

Always, it was a reminder of liberty and, if Hogarth is anyone to go by, the association was with English liberty and mass revolt: in the eighth plate of *Industry and Idleness* he shows an African serving-man caught between the dagger of Wat Tyler's assassin (Sir William Walworth) and the gluttonous appetites of London vicars, lawyers and physicians. It is an apt, if portentous image of the first of four phases in the history of the London black population. The first period was a period of integration. It is expressed powerfully in the *Letters* of Sancho, who was born in the Middle Passage, became butler to the Duchess of Montagu, whose service he was forced to leave because, having developed a 'convexity of belly exceeding Falstaff', he could no longer stand. A fearful man, an exquisite flatterer, withdrawn from the affairs of the street, he had proposed various humanitarian schemes such as that to increase employment in the shipyards by reducing the Civil List, but his heart was in books where he shared the latitudinarian broad-spirited ineffectuality of Parson Adams or Uncle Toby.[50]

The second phase of the history was that of consolidation and the beginning of what has been called 'proto-pan-Africanism'. A Fantee man, Ottobah Cugoano, was the first ex-slave and African to call for the total abolition of the slave trade. He was instrumental in the formation of the London African Association and a leader of the abortive expedition to Sierra Leone, the first of the 'Back-to-Africa' movements. His *Thoughts and Sentiments* (1787) contains the thundering language of the revolutionary Puritan preachers as well as abiding statements of pan-Africanism. In this he developed an Atlantic perspective upon the unfolding of revolutionary events, an oceanic perspective that may be compared to that of W.E.B. DuBois who saw a connection between the abolition of American slavery and the Paris Commune of 1871. As part of his answer to the scribblers hired by the West India interest, Cugoano referred to a well-known print of the time called *The World Turned Upside Down.* It depicted a pig roasting a cook, a horse saddling a rider, and the like. 'It would be a most delectable sight,' said he, 'when thieves and robbers get the upper side of the world to see them turned down.

The complicated banditries of pirates, thieves, robbers, oppressors and enslavers of men are those cooks and men that would be roasted and saddled. ... It certainly would be no unpleasant sight to see them well-roasted, saddled and bridled too; and no matter by whom, whether he terms them pigs, horses, or asses.'[51] It was a venerable, working-class theme.

Christopher Hill remarked in the conclusion to *The World Turned Upside Down* (1972) that 'nothing ever wholly dies' and he noted that his title was a phrase that appeared occasionally among the eighteenth-century Shakers. Two hundred and one years ago, when Cornwallis surrendered at Yorktown, a tune of that name was played during the capitulation ceremonies.[52] Thomas Spence, revolutionary agrarian communist, composed a broadside of that name in 1805.[53] Cugoano thus drew upon a profound tradition stretching back to Merlin's prophecy, to Lear's fool, to the Geneva Bible, and to the revolutionary writings of the English Civil War. If it was the defeat of one English army in the mutinies of 1649–50 which produced the circumstances which brought the ideas of democracy to the West Indies and America in the first place, it was these same ideas which 150 years later, first in North America and then in Santo Domingo, inspired those who brought about the defeat of two other British armies. Perhaps they consoled themselves with the sentiment that Goethe uttered to the defeated Prussian soldiers at Valmy (1792): 'From this place, and from this day forth, commences a new era in the world's history; and you can all say that you were present at its birth.'

The third phase is that of the abolitionist movement in England. It was led by Equiano. I mean not only did he lead the English black community and travel all over to do this, he was also the wire-puller, the petitioner, the worrier who at least in the early stages encouraged Clark, the Quakers and the London Corresponding Society. His achievement is still sorely neglected by historians of the anti-slave-trade movement. By 1768 the black community was known for its militance, its refusal to support or accept slavery in any way, and its harbouring of international rebels; such anyway is the impression that the police leave. John Fielding wrote, 'There is great reason to fear that those blacks who have been sent back to the Plantations ... have been the occasion of those ... recent insurrections in the ... West Indies.'[54] The political and social presence of a population of ex-slaves, experienced in the insurrectionary tradition of anti-slavery as well as the internationalism of several sea voyages, gave to the more well-known middle-class movement its ballast and sail.

The abolition of the slave trade (1807) was the crowning achievement of this movement. Of course, the victory belonged partly to the struggle of the 'Black Jacobins' of Santo Domingo.[55] Together they presaged an end to slavery and the transformation of that triangulation of struggle that the blacks in London especially had supported at the apex.

Forthwith, the London black community, or at least its political cadre, threw itself into the working-class reform movement of England. It offered its rich and secretive traditions of conspiracy and ability – for the black face, like Proteus, could act as a mask – to communicate with all kinds of people. Robert Wedderburn, a tailor, son of a West Indian slave, led London's radical Spenceans after Evans was jailed in 1817. He believed in the Hebrew law of the Jubilee and the commonality of land under Moses and Alfred. He opened his own chapel in Hopkins Street in 1819 and became known for the vehemence of his anti-Christianity. He was an activist among soldiers, sailors and (significantly) the Irish labourers at Maudslay's engineering works in Lambeth. He was a leading tactition of the insurrectionary movement and was later associated with Carlisle and republicanism. William Davidson, a cabinet-maker and former mariner, was also an ex-Watsonite. He was an expert in weaponry, organizing a depot in Spitalfields. He was one of those who plotted to assassinate the entire Cabinet while it was at dinner. For this the Jamaican was hanged on May 1 1820, and with the other Cato Street conspirators he died 'like a hero'. Both men were 'old Jacks' with connections to the radicalism of the 1790s, both to the London Corresponding Society and to the Irish rebels of 1798. Their relations with Toussaint L'Ouverture and the great war in Haiti need to be explored. We may conclude this sketch of the fourth phase of the London black history with a mention of William Cuffay, another Jamaican, an activist in the London tailor's strike of 1834, a leading London Chartist, an organizer of the Orange Tree conspiracy of 1848, for which he was transported to Botany Bay. The boomerang continued to hurtle around the globe.[56]

The association between sailors and black freedom fighters persisted through the nineteenth and twentieth centuries. Denmark Vesey, the leader of the plot of 1822, had sailed in the Caribbean and had soaked up the experiences of the Haitian revolt. It was Irish sailors in Baltimore who first told the young ship's caulker, Frederick Douglass, about northern freedom. Stanley, a black sailor, gave Douglass his sailor's uniform and papers providing him with his disguise for his trip. Alone and desperate in New York, it was to a fellow sailor that he entrusted his plight.[57] In the 1920s the revolutionary newspaper *The Negro Worker*, on which George Padmore worked, was passed from hand to hand by black sailors in Hamburg, Marseilles and African and North American ports.[58] The ship remained perhaps the most important conduit of pan-African communication before the appearance of the long-playing record.

Some Conclusions

Thompson and Hobsbawm with their colleagues in the Communist Party Historians' Group posed the problem of a seventeenth-century arrest to the development that had begun so vigorously in the sixteenth century. One of them presented the delay as the cessation of the English working-class discussion of democracy. The other presented it as the temporary failure of west European (especially English) capitalism to industrialize. In this essay I have tried to suggest that what from a European viewpoint might appear as a 'delay' could, from an Atlantic perspective, appear as the oceanic generalization of the theory and practice of antinomian democracy. Moreover, the 'crisis' of the seventeenth century was an index of the widespread refusal of wage-labour. The imperfectibilities of the 'free labour market' became the driving force of Atlantic imperialism. When the countries on the limit of the empire exploded in slave revolts and revolution, the dispersed traditions returned and were reawakened in London within whose alleys and courts dwelt a proletariat which by the 1790s was both Atlantic and international.

Throughout I have chosen to analyse the mode of production as the setting where the working class transforms capitalist accumulation and exploitation (the terms are inseparable) into its own terms of discussion and struggle. The obstacles in the way of this transformation, the twin ogres of war and starvation, I have not stressed. In this view there is no problem of 'arrested development' or of a pause in an international discussion. That it had seemed so to the creative minds of the English Communist Party Historians' Group can be explained in a variety of ways which we cannot fully explain here beyond mentioning two considerations. First, it should be said that for the Marxist intellectuals of the post-war period the dominant experience was the collapse of the popular-front, anti-fascist alliance. To them the question of proletarian internationalism appeared less as the self-activity of the anti-colonial masses than it did as the domination of the Moscow International which saw the anti-racist, anti-imperial movement only as an incident of the 'national struggle'. Second, during this period English Marxist intellectuals accepted technicist models of 'economic development' which included a series of historical steps or stages whose inevitable progression was by no means closed to historical interrogation but which nevertheless were seen primarily as evolving structures that attacked, rather than caused, material scarcity.[59]

The recent wave of municipal insurrection within England under the leadership of the descendants of West Indian slaves makes it more difficult to regard material scarcity as a condition of only an early stage

of social evolution. Furthermore, it makes it difficult to accept a conception of working-class internationalism that depends only on the co-
operation of geographically distinct national units. The 1981 revolt in
Brixton invites us to search the past for alternative conceptions. Blake's
Atlanticism offers one that is still of interest because it fiercely opposes
the elitist scientific view of Bacon whose schematic followers turned
'generosity [into] a science/That men get rich by' and because the
African and ex-slave experience infused his vision of human love.

One of his 'Songs of Innocence' expressed the divinity of human life
in the form of maternal instructions of friendship to African and English
children. In the 'Song of Liberty' that concluded *The Marriage of
Heaven and Hell* human liberation is described as the hope of a militant,
revolutionary and anti-imperialist birth. To be put into effect, the hope
awaits only the rising of Londoner, Jew and African. To Blake the order
of the oceans and the continents was not fixed by latitude and longitude.
Nor was the order of the centuries fixed in a linear temporality. Still less,
of course, did revolutionary redemption depend on the secular analysis
of an invariable sequence of modes of production within a 'world-
system'. Yet, his tremendous powers of dissociation of the disciplines of
Enlightenment rationality produced a conception of the universality of
human potential that harked back to 'The Everlasting Gospel' of the
English Revolution and that alone permitted expression of the particu-
larities of trans-continental working-class co-operation which those
other systems could not. In his Lambeth artisan's chamber Katherine
Blake cooked at a fire and William Blake sat at his table before a
window overlooking the Thames and the Surrey hills.[60] There he
engraved the powerful images of enslaved African beauty that illustrated
Captain J.G. Stedman's *History of the Revolted Negroes of Surinam*.
There he composed that remarkable prophecy some of whose chapters
C.L.R. James and Walter Rodney have chronicled.[61]

> Let the slave grinding at the mill run into the field.
> Let him look up into the heavens & laugh in the bright air;
> Let the inchained soul, shut up in darkness and in sighing,
> Whose face has never seen a smile in thirty weary years,
> Rise and look out; his chains are loose, his dungeon doors are open;
> And let his wife and children return from the oppressor's scourge.
> They look behind at every step & believe it is a dream.
> Singing: 'the Sun has left his blackness & has found a fresher morning,
> And the fair Moon rejoices in the clear and cloudless night;
> For Empire is no more, and now the Lion & Wolf shall cease.

Notes

This article first appeared in *Labour/Le Travailleur*, no. 10 (Autumn 1982), pp. 87–121. It was originally drafted for presentation at the World Turned Upside Down Conference, November 1981, organized by the Philadelphia Centre for Early American Studies. I would particularly like to thank Marcus Rediker and Christopher Hill for their critical encouragement at that time. Philip Corrigan, Del Pedro, Kimberly Frarey, Leslie Farhangi, Gary Harriman, Stanley Engerman, Doug Deal, Bethia Linebaugh, Neil McMullin, Bruce Levine, Mike Zuckerman, Ferruccio Gambinio, Dale Tomich, Gary Garton and Bryan Palmer offered valuable and encouraging suggestions.

1. Francis Bacon, *New Atlantis*, G.C. Moore Smith, ed. (Cambridge, 1929), p. 35. The Ecology Movement and William Leiss, *The Domination of Nature* (Boston, 1972), have offered the profoundest criticism of Bacon.

2. E.J. Hobsbawm, 'The Crisis of the Seventeenth Century', *Past and Present*, nos. 5 and 6 (1954), reprinted in Trevor Aston, *Crisis in Europe, 1560–1600* (London, 1965).

3. The first two of these traditions has received less attention than the third which has been well served in E.P. Thompson, *Whigs and Hunters* (London, 1975), Doug Hay *et. al.*, *Albion's Fatal Tree* (London, 1975), and John Brewer, ed., *An Ungovernable People* (London, 1980). These contributions must modify the traditions at least as they were adumbrated in *The Making of the English Working Class*.

4. Karl Marx, *The German Ideology* (Moscow, 1968), p. 31.

5. Walter Rodney, *How Europe Underdeveloped Africa* (London 1972), p. 101.

6. H.N. Brailsford, *The Levellers and the English Revolution* (London, 1961).

7. *The Political Theory of Possessive Individualism* (London, 1962).

8. A.L. Morton, *The Everlasting Gospel: A Study in the Sources of William Blake* (London, 1958), p. 34.

9. Christopher Hill, *The World Turned Upside Down* (London, 1972).

10. See Christopher Hill, 'Parliament and the People in the Seventeenth Century England', *Past and Present*, no. 92 (August 1981), and Conrad Russell, *Parliaments and English Politics 1621–1629* (Oxford, 1979).

11. Karl Marx, *Capital*, Dona Torr, ed., vol. 1, ch. 26, 'The Secret of Primitive Accumulation'.

12. For this and the following paragraph I am indebted to A.V. Judges, ed., *The Elizabethan Underworld: A Collection of Tudor and Early Stuart Tracts and Ballads* (London, 1965) and its excellent introduction. Gamini Salgado, *The Elizabethan Underworld* (London, 1977), can be useful too.

13. A.L. Beier, 'Vagrants and the Social Order in Elizabethan England', *Past and Present*, no. 64 (1974).

14. Judges, *Elizabethan Underworld*, p. 507, and David Underdown, *Somerset in the Civil War and Interregnum* (London, 1973).

15. *Nova Britannia* (1609).

16. Abbot Emerson Smith, *Colonists in Bondage: White Servitude and Convict Labor in America 1607–1776* (New York, 1947).

17. James Horn, 'Servant Emigration to the Chesapeake in the Seventeenth Century', in Thad W. Tate and David L. Ammerman, eds., *The Chesapeake in the Seventeenth Century: Essays in Anglo-American Society* (New York, 1979).

18. Buchanan Sharp, *In Contempt of All Authority: Rural Artisans and Riot in the West of England, 1586–1660* (Berkeley, 1980), pp. 3, 158.

19. There are few words with as many meanings in the history of class description than the words 'labourer', 'skilled', 'unskilled' and 'middle rank'. This is not the place to puzzle through them. However, it should be noted that the most recent American discussion of the class experience of indentured servitude is characterized by its total failure to discuss the historical meanings of these terms or the tendentious quality of their ideological undertones. The failure to do this provides a late example of what C. Wright Mills called 'methodological inhibition'. Lying behind David Galenson's usages of the terms, for example, is a rigid model of 'human capital'. See 'British Servants and the Colonial

Indenture System in the Eighteenth Century', *Journal of Southern History*, no. 44 (1978).

20. Christopher Hill, *God's Englishman: Oliver Cromwell and the English Revolution* (London, 1970).

21. A.E. Smith, *Colonists in Bondage.*

22. Hilary McD. Beckles, 'Rebels and Reactionaries: The Political Response of White Labourers to Planter-Class Hegemony in Seventeenth Century Barbados', *Journal of Caribbean History*, no. 15 (1981); Christopher Hill, *The World Turned Upside Down.*

23. Joseph Douglas Deal III, 'Race and Class in Colonial Virginia: Indians, English-men and Africans on the Eastern Shore During the Seventeenth Century', unpublished PhD thesis, University of Rochester, 1981.

24. J.C. Jeaffreson, *A Young Squire of the Seventeenth Century* (1879), vol. II, p. 61.

25. Expuemelin, *The Buccaneers of America* (1678), Steve Gooch, *The Women Pirates, Ann Bonney and Mary Reed* (London, 1978), Marcus Rediker, '"Under the Banner of King Death"; The Social World of Anglo-American Pirates: 1716–1726', *William and Mary Quarterly*, 3rd Series, p. 38 (1981).

26. Christopher Hill, 'Robinson Crusoe', *History Workshop*, no. 10 (1980).

27. Public Record Office, 'Information of Clement Downing, 1724', High Court of Admiralty 1/55f. 79. Ranter Bay is again mentioned in the 'Information of Charles Collins', H.C.A. 1/55f. 77.

28. Thomas Edwards, *Gangraena* (1646), p. 41.

29. John Whiting, *Persecution Exposed, in some Memoirs Relating to the Sufferings of John Whiting, and Many others of the People called Quakers* (1714), pp. 426–7.

30. Many of the texts of the early Quaker opposition to slavery are reprinted in Roger Burns, *Am I Not a Man and a Brother: The Anti-Slavery Crusade of Revolutionary America 1688–1788* (New York, 1977).

31. Winstanley, *The Law of Freedom in a Platform* (1652).

32. K.G. Davies, *The Royal African Company* (London, 1957), ch. 2, and also the vivid documents collected in Michael Craton *et al.*, eds., *Slavery, Abolition and Emanci-pation: Black Slaves and the British Empire* (London, 1976).

33. Phillip Corrigan, 'Feudal Relics or Capitalist Monuments? Notes on the Sociology of Unfree Labour', *Sociology*, vol. 11 (1977).

34. Elmo Paul Hohman, *Seaman Ashore: A Study of the United Seaman's Service and of Merchant Seamen in Port* (New Haven, 1952), p. 224. Here, as elsewhere, I have been deeply stimulated by Marcus Rediker's studies of eighteenth-century sailoring.

35. Michael Cohn and Michael K.H. Platzer, *Black Men of the Sea* (New York, 1978).

36. British Library, 'Richard Simons Voyage to the Straits of Magellan & S. Seas in the Year 1689', Sloane MSS, 86, f. 57.

37. William Matthews, 'Sailor's Pronunciation in the Second Half of the Seventeenth Century', *Anglia: Zeitschrift für Englische Philologie*, vol. 59 (1935), pp. 193–251.

38. William Falconer, *An Universal Dictionary of the Marine* (1769).

39. J.L. Dillard, *All-American English* (New York, 1975), which develops the thesis of 'maritime languages' and their relation to the process of 'pidginization'. See also Francis Grose, *A Dictionary of the Vulgar Tongue* (1787).

40. Rediker, 'Under the Banner of King Death'.

41. James Walvin, *Black and White: The Negro and English Society, 1555–1945* (1973), pp. 15–52.

42. Jesse Lemisch, 'Jack Tar in the Streets: Merchant Seamen in the Politics of Revolu-tionary America', *William and Mary Quarterly*, no. 25 (1968), pp. 371–407.

43. Peter Linebaugh, 'Spose C.L.R. James had met E.P. Thompson in 1792', *Urgent Tasks: Journal of the Revolutionary Left*, no. 22 (1981).

44. Raymond Williams has criticized his own earlier work (*Culture and Society*) because it omitted discussion of the Civil War. In 1979 he wrote, 'I suspect that there are in fact very deep underground continuities from the period of defeat in the later 17th Century to the re-emergence of radicalism in the 1770s and 1780s.' See *Politics and Letters* (London, 1979), p. 131.

45. *The London Spy: The Vanities and Vices of the Town Exposed to View* (1927 edn), p. 54.

46. For a longer discussion of the relationship between famous criminals and the Levelling traditions, see Peter Linebaugh, *Crime and Labour in Eighteenth Century London* (forthcoming).

47. Tom Paine, *The Rights of Man.*

48. Alyce Barry, 'Thomas Paine, Privateersman', *Pennsylvania Magazine of History and Biography*, no. 101 (1977), p. 460.

49. The Ordinary of Newgate's *Account,* 19 July 1738.

50. *Letters of the Late Ignatius Sancho* (1782).

51. Cugoano's book is republished in Francis D. Adams and Barry Sanders, *Three Black Writers in Eighteenth Century England* (Belmont, Calif. 1971).

52. Contemporary descriptions of the surrender are contained in Henry Steele Commager and Richard S. Morris, *The Spirit of 'Seventy-Six: The Story of the American Revolution as Told by Participants* (New York, 1958), vol. II, pp. 1209–49, in which there is also some discussion of the song. J. Bruce Glasier, the poet and socialist, wrote a song called 'We'll Turn Things Upside Down' (1891).

53. Hill, *World Turned Upside Down*, p. 307.

54. John Fielding, *Penal Laws* (1768).

55. C.L.R. James, *The Black Jacobins: Toussaint L'Ouverture and the San Domingo Revolution* (New York, 1963).

56. On these revolutionists, see E.P. Thompson, *The Making of the English Working Class* (London, 1963), and Iorwerth Prothero, *Artisans and Politics in Early Nineteenth Century London: John Gast and His Times* (London, 1979).

57. Philip S. Foner, *The Life and Writings of Frederick Douglass*, vol. I, *The Early Years*, 1817–1849 (New York, 1950), pp. 22–3.

58. Immanuel Geiss, *The Pan-African Movement: A History of Pan-Africanism in Europe and Africa*, translated by Ann Keep (New York, 1974), pp. 335–6.

59. E.J. Hobsbawm, *Revolutionaries: Contemporary Essays* (New York, 1973), pp. 252–5, indicates the close relationship that was held between capitalist accumulation and progress against material scarcity. The same author's essay on 'The Historians' Group of the Communist Party', Maurice Cornforth, ed., *Rebels and Their Causes: Essays in Honour of A.L. Morton* (London, 1978), pp. 21–49, illustrates the depth of Communist Party sectarianism which neglected *The Black Jacobins* because of its 'author's known Trotskyism'.

60. 'William Blake Bicentenary Supplement', *The New Reasoner*, no. 1 (1957–8), pp. x–xi.

61. 'America', Geoffrey Keynes, ed., *Poetry and Prose of William Blake* (London, 1967), p. 203.

Good Hands, Stout Heart and Fast Feet: The History and Culture of Working People in Early America

Marcus Rediker

A band of indentured servants in Poplar Spring, Virginia, organized an insurrection in 1663. Some of these men had worn the red shirts of Cromwell's New Model Army; some had been Independents, Fifth Monarchy Men and Muggletonians. As 'Oliverian Soldiers' and radical sectaries they had struggled to turn England upside down, but with the restoration of the monarchy in 1660 came 'the experience of defeat': they and many others were 'sent to the colonies on long terms of indentured servitude'. But they were not yet defeated. They now aimed to capitalize on widespread labour discontent in Virginia and to 'overthrow [Governor] Berkeley and set up an independent commonwealth'. Wealth was already more common in Virginia than in England, but apparently not common enough to suit these rebels.[1]

A group of 'labourers' held a midnight meeting 'at Mr. Knights Little house in ye woods aboute a designe for their freedom'. They plotted to bring to the rising what 'Company, armes, and ammunicion' they could get, then to go to the residence of Colonel Francis Willis, a wealthy member of the governor's council, where they would 'seise upon his armes and drum'. The servants intended to appeal to others in bondage and to arm them 'to ye number of thirty'. They would then in a public parade 'march from house to house', visit the governor, demand their freedom, and 'be ye death of him' that resisted their solemnly sworn effort. Perhaps they should have 'been ye death' of a servant named Berkenhead, who later exposed the intended rising. Nine of the plotters were arrested; many others escaped. The planters of the province, relieved and grateful, rewarded their loyal informer with 5,000 pounds of tobacco and his freedom. Those planters who sat as Justices of the Peace tried and convicted the nine conspirators. Four men swung on the gallows for 'high treason'. To commemorate the discovery of the plot,

221

the day scheduled for the rising, 13 September, was to 'be annually kept holy'.[2] Planters and indentured servants probably kept the day holy in different ways.

This incident illustrates a transatlantic class conflict embedded in peculiarly American circumstances. English struggles, some epic and revolutionary, others prosaic but unrelenting, gave rise to a complex range of practices and ideas, many of which found their ways to American shores. There they survived and circulated among a diverse, internationally experienced body of labouring men and women, but only by adapting to the environment, circumstances and relations of production of a New World. Poplar Spring's rebels used their experience of the English Revolution to protest their exploitation, the uncommonly harsh treatment of their labour as a commodity, in the New World. Their ideas and activities as well as others that had emerged in England began to mingle with the rich traditions of working people from Africa, continental Europe, Ireland, Scotland, native America and numerous other spots around the rim of the Atlantic. From these many strands would emerge America's indigenous working-class traditions.

It is commonly acknowledged that the American working class had origins of staggering complexity. Yet these origins have been but rarely investigated: only a handful of scholars have studied the American working class before 1800. Worse yet, American historians, especially those looking back from the nineteenth and twentieth centuries, have tended to treat the working people whose lives pre-dated the factory system as pre-historic creatures, specimens of *genus pre-industrialus.* Surely these labouring men and women, like the movement and traditions they initiated, deserve a better fate.[3]

This essay – and it is just that, an initial and tentative effort in understanding – ranges far and wide across the circumstances and context, ideas, practices and experiences of early American labouring lives. It examines the structural and cultural dimensions of continuity and change in the diverse relations between capital and labour, outlining some of the processes within which early American working-class activities and ideas were formed. This broad, if speculative, survey – partly theoretical and partly empirical – presents arguments which, given the radically underdeveloped state of early American working-class history, must be understood as a set of questions and as a challenge to further research.

The history of working people in seventeenth- and eighteenth-century America was part of the protracted, essentially two-stage, world-wide transition from feudalism to capitalism. The second stage, featuring the ascent of modern industry, has received careful and learned study.

During the extended period of industrial revolution, dating from the late eighteenth century, vast amounts of labour were enclosed within factories, and labour processes were revolutionized by the introduction of machinery. Working people came face to face (or better, mind-and-hand to supervisor-and-machine) with the discipline of the factory.

Stage one was longer and less tidy; it was also absolutely essential to everything that followed. This stage, spanning the years between 1500 and 1800, was the era of 'primitive accumulation', the social and economic process by which labour was transformed into a commodity, primarily through rural dispossession, the centralization of agricultural production, and population growth. Great masses of men and women were, in the words of Karl Marx, 'suddenly and forcibly torn from their means of subsistence, and hurled onto the labour-market as free, unprotected, and rightless proletarians'. Forced to sell their labour power and to submit to the discipline of the wage contract, these workers faced the impersonal, often wrenching fluctuations of an expanding market economy. A sailor in 1709 summed up this proletarian condition in a pithy and poetic question: what, he wondered, was a man to expect when he had 'but a pair of good Hands and a Stout Heart to recommend him'?[4]

In the early modern period countless English tenants and labourers were loosed from the land. They had, in the words of E.P. Thompson, 'escaped from the social controls of the manorial village and were not yet subject to the discipline of factory labour'.[5] Betwixt and between the grips of lord and factory master, these masterless men and women roamed the countryside as free and independent economic actors, and they posed in unprecedented ways the problem of discipline. They were the 'seething mobility', tramping their collective way toward becoming the 'free-born' English working class of a later period, and, once transplanted, the 'free-born' Yankee worker of nineteenth-century America. The road, however, was not always straight and narrow. Indeed the grandparents or perhaps great-grandparents of the free-born Yank, those who crossed the Atlantic to the New World, often experienced a jarring detour into the world of unfree labour.[6]

The reasons for this detour lie in the peculiar circumstances of America. As C.L.R. James, Grace C. Lee and Pierre Chaulieu (Cornelius Castoriadis) observed of the sweep of capitalist development: 'Marx discerned in capital accumulation two laws, twin themes of the same movement, the law of the concentration and centralization of capital and the law of the socialization of labor.'[7] The process of primitive accumulation in England, Europe and even Africa divorced direct producers from the means of production, and in fact helped to make possible the settlement and cultivation of the New World. Many of the workers who remained in England were redeployed, and by the eighteenth century a swelling majority depended partially or fully on wages for their livelihoods. The concentration of capital and the collectivization of labour advanced with the organization of agriculture and manufacture. England's economy in the sixteenth and seventeenth centuries grew increasingly centralized, emerging as an interdependent, national whole.

Yet the experience of early America demonstrated that these sweeping movements in the history of capital and labour were reversible. The transfer of society and economy to the New World immediately helped to create a fragmented productive system, a simplified division of labour, decentralized relations of production, and an initial deconcentration of capital and labour. Working people often found themselves reattached to the means of production. The more fortunate acquired tools and land and became independent commodity producers in craft manufacture or freehold agriculture. The less fortunate did not acquire property but rather *became* property, as indentured servants and slaves, two kinds of dependent commodity producers. Once reattached to the means of production, the vast majority of these workers would experience primitive accumulation anew, though in radically different ways: by escape or emancipation from servitude or slavery, by dispossession of landed or craft property, or through sheer population growth, labouring men and women would once again be separated from the means of production. They would once again be 'free' to sell their labour power on an open market. In many ways they would replicate the experiences of their forefathers and mothers. The concentration of capital and labour advanced with eastern development and the availability of slave and free labour, deconcentration with westward migration and the availability of land. But even in the west the process of concentration resumed in earnest as settlers were linked to the expanding market economies of the east. Capitalist and non-capitalist economies existed side by side in early America.[8]

The imperial economy, organized by the policies of mercantilism, supplied the most immediate context for the development of working-class experience in early America. Since the colonies, as outposts of empire, were necessarily part of a transatlantic world, many working people in America from the beginning produced for a market, frequently an international market. The mercantile economic framework linked the colonies to markets around the world, primarily through London, the swirling vortex of the empire. Consequently the colonies developed neither a national centre of production nor any unifying economic or political organization. Colonial America became a complex social formation consisting of multiple regional economies, class structures and cultures.[9]

From the outset, production in North America was organized on a terrain fundamentally different from that of England. It was a landscape quickly littered with the dead bodies and broken cultures of a diverse native American civilization. English settlers employed microbes and misdeeds, firearms and firewater to secure their various footholds. They found – and further created – a New World unencumbered by a feudal past. They seized from Indians the choicest lands and transformed them into commodities, preserving for themselves as owners absolute use-rights in this prized new property.[10]

The guild system, so central to English feudalism, was never successfully transplanted to the colonies. Shipbuilding, colonial America's most vigorous manufacturing enterprise, developed little or no formal craft organization. The few guilds formed in the colonies were unable to maintain their cohesion against the pressures of incessant immigration, the relatively smooth transition from journeyman to master, and the high wages commanded by almost all types of labour.[11] Capital and labour could be moved to the New World, but specifically English relations of production could not. The equilibrium that had developed in England between a powerful gentry and the plebeian masses had to be recreated; new class and cultural relations had to be negotiated.[12] Many of the reciprocal obligations and duties that marked the historical experience of feudalism were never present in America, except perhaps in a limited psychological sense, and this along with other circumstances made possible the transplantation of some of the most advanced and aggressive aspects of European capitalism.[13]

Yet the early stages of capitalist expansion, as Immanuel Wallerstein and Philip Corrigan have shown, regularly generated unfree forms of labour. The scarcity of labour in the colonies ripped aside any illusion of a rough and 'natural' balance between labour supply and demand. The impersonal workings of the market and the wage contract did not, from the point of view of colonial employers, provide sufficient discipline in the New World setting: free wage labour was both too 'undependable' and too expensive.[14] Once it became clear that North American Indians were not to be transformed into a docile and pliant labour force, the colonists who wanted to turn their money into capital faced problems of labour supply and organization quite unprecedented in human history. What was a poor expectant capitalist to do?

Labour market entrepreneurs and employers, facing simultaneously a grave labour scarcity and a lucrative world market in commodities, began to calculate labour needs abstractly, to think of labour as a commodity divorced from social context. They anticipated in practice a central idea of political arithmetic and neo-classical economics: labour was merely a 'factor of production'. But this labour had to exist in a transportable form. And employers knew that scarce labour could not be permitted to circulate freely on a market like other commodities. As a result of these contradictory needs, they drew upon and ferociously exaggerated a practice that had developed in England as a means of disciplining the masterless men and women who rambled to and fro about the country. As Maurice Dobb put it, 'compulsion to labour [in early modern England] stood in the background of the labour market'.[15] In America compulsory labour leaped to the foreground. Most Africans and some American Indians were forced into lives of permanent unfree labour, and many European workers left behind a life of labour increasingly dominated by the wage contract to take up a life literally bound to an indenture, an unwaged contract. The machinery of labour transportation, the complex business network that scoured the world to supply the labour-hungry colonies, was a crucial mechanism in the treatment of labour as a commodity in early America. Indentured servitude – or as Hilary Beckles has called it, white 'proto-slavery' – and slavery itself resolved, at least temporarily, the problems faced by both the suppliers and the employers of labour: these forms of bound labour permitted general calculation of need and use, were fairly easily transported, and once in America did not circulate on an open market.[16] Servitude and slavery were the dominant transatlantic commodity forms of labour.

The Europeans – mostly English, Scottish, Irish, and German – who came to the colonies as servants acquired their indentures in various ways. Most merely sought a passage to the New World, and agreed to trade two to nine years of labour for the hope of a life of genuine freedom after working off their time. Others, quite simply, were kidnapped. Another 50,000 came as 'His Majesty's Seven Year Passengers' – a mocking euphemism for transported convicts – and yet others were political prisoners exiled to America. Rebellious Scots were shipped to the colonies in the 1640s, 1650s, 1670s and 1680s; Loyalists in the 1650s; Quakers and other dissenters in the 1660s; Monmouth Rebels after 1685; Jacobites after 1715; and even more Scottish insurgents after 1745.[17]

Those who arrived as indentured servants – mostly men, because women were believed to be too 'troublesome', meaning too hard to discipline, too likely to become pregnant, or too unsuited to the work – represented a broad cross-section of ordinary folk in their society of origin. The vast majority were between fifteen and twenty-four years of age; the younger the servant, the longer his or her indenture was likely to be.[18] A few came as apprentices to skilled workers.[19] Some servants came with property, more without; some with skills, more without; some with friends, more without. But for a letter of introduction from Ben Franklin and a settlement of £35 that he used to pay his passage, Tom Paine might well have arrived in America as an indentured servant. He would have been as penniless and as friendless as the multitude who walked off the ship and into a humiliating 'cattle-market', where their muscles were squeezed and their docility carefully judged by prospective employers, or where they were taken in gangs by 'soul drivers' to be peddled in the back-country.[20]

These basic forms of compulsory labour were only the beginning, for the various colonial ruling classes found countless other ways to demand toil from workers who had arrived free or who gained their freedom once in the colonies. Most residents of early America were forced to engage in public works. This 'class obligation', from which elites generously exempted themselves, exacted labour for agriculture, road construction, river-work and the building trades: the construction of forts, dams, bridges, jails and workhouses. Another form of compulsory labour was mandatory participation in the local militia. Colonists were also impressed into the armed forces, for conscription was universal in early America. Pressed labour provided an easy way for the Crown to hold down wages in building a fort, and of course the army and the navy had to be stocked with muscle enough to fight the wars of the eighteenth century, all of which had colonial dimensions.[21] Workmen protested compulsory military service in a variety of ways, from lopping off the fingers of a press-gang thug who tried to board a merchant ship, to organizing tumultuous seaport crowds to protest the navy's 'barbarous business' of body-snatching.[22]

Courts in early America acted the part of alchemists, transmuting the common – almost every conceivable type of offence – into the precious – labour services. Prosecutions for idleness led to forced labour; for debt, forced labour; for an enormous assortment of crimes, forced labour.[23] And of course any servant who committed a crime had his or her indenture extended by a substantial amount of time. Some colonial employers, backed by the courts, used systems of credit and debt to control workers who were technically free.[24]

In a recent review of historical work on the movement of labouring men and women to English America, Richard S. Dunn has concluded that 'about half of the whites who came to the colonies from Britain and continental Europe during the colonial period arrived as servants'. And virtually all Africans came as chattel slaves. Roughly four out of five men and women who came to the New World experienced a stint, if not a lifetime, of unfree labour.[25] African slaves found fewer and fewer openings to freedom, but what of those who completed their contracted terms as bond labourers? Like the slaves, many did not survive their condition: they died before completing their indentures. Only one in ten acquired land. The remainder perished, went back to Europe, or began to work for wages. Former servants found land much easier to acquire early in the colonial period, and in Virginia, Maryland and the Carolinas.[26]

Early American labour systems varied greatly by region. Each major area of British America, according to Dunn,

> evolved a distinctive labor system: in the Caribbean sugar colonies, a quick dependence on African slave labor; in the southern mainland colonies, a slow conversion from white servants to black slaves, with a heavy use also of white family labor; in the mid-Atlantic colonies, a mix of family and wage labor with immigrant servants, and slaves; and in New England a prime reliance upon native-born family and wage labor.[27]

The labour systems of the colonies were plural and diverse, and they functioned according to different time schedules and principles of change. Yet given the overall tendency toward the concentration and centralization of capital and the socialization of labour – whether on sugar or tobacco plantations, large farms employing tenants or wage labour, or urban manufactories – there were crucial similarities in the inner logic and process of change.

From the point of view of capital, seven distinct types of labour existed in the colonies: hunting, practised by Indians and many Europeans who lived on the frontier; craft labour or petty production, largely in urban areas, organized early in the colonial period by custom order, but increasingly oriented toward larger markets; domestic labour, performed in all areas by both servants and unwaged women workers; free wage labour, present in both cities and countryside, relatively unskilled and employed in casual and seasonal labour markets; and three types of agricultural labour: the free unwaged independent farmer; the temporarily unfree and unwaged indentured servant; and the permanently unfree and unwaged slave. Despite the relatively low social division of labour in the colonies, the structural divisions among working people ran extraordinarily deep.

Hunting was commonplace in early America, both as the source of a major industry, the fur trade, and as a means of subsistence that supplemented agricultural pursuits or underlay an entire way of life. Hunters of the latter sort were usually nomadic frontier dwellers who modelled their lives upon the practices of North American Indians. In early eighteenth-century Lousiana *voyageurs* or *coureurs des bois*, neither husbandmen nor herdsmen, 'led a simple, non-accumulative life, more Indian than French': they preferred drink and gambling to the 'steady, arduous labour of agricultural work'.[28] Such hunters, derisively called 'white Indians' and known as 'people who avoid work and prefer to wander around in the woods', were also prominent in the Southern piedmont region, including parts of Virginia, the Carolinas and Georgia. In the South Carolina upcountry, communities of such hunters coalesced into 'banditti' gangs – consisting of red, black, white, mulatto and 'half-breed' members – to contest the expansion of slave-based commercial agriculture into the South Carolina upcountry.[29] It is impossible to know how many early Americans depended upon hunting as a way of life and labour, but clearly hunting was available to many as a means of survival during hard times, and represented an alternative to the more traditional, sedentary worlds of agriculture work.

Most craft labourers lived in the Northern towns and cities, where crafts proliferated with the growth of commerce. Shipbuilders, riggers, mastmakers, blockmakers, caulkers, joiners, coopers and others practised their skills along the waterfront. Craftsmen also flourished with the growth of consumption among middling and especially upper classes, who regularly demanded the services of carpenters, cabinet-makers, blacksmiths, hatters, glass-makers, cordwainers, tailors and numerous others.[30] Colonial craftsmen toiled in the workshop, the basic productive unit, often located in or near the master's home. Although the ideal workshop contained the traditional triad of master, journeyman and apprentice, the poorer craftsmen rarely employed journeymen, while the wealthier ones often owned slaves. The typical workshop in America was small by European standards, containing only a handful of workers, ranging as high as twenty-five in the largest shipyards and ropewalks.[31] The division of craft labour steadily increased over time, especially after 1750, despite efforts by Britain to limit colonial capacity to produce craft goods. Craft workers with different specialities, such as those in the maritime trades, often co-operated to complete portions of a larger job. Both settled and tramping artisans practised the art and mystery of their crafts in rural areas.[32]

Craft labour was organized in fluid fashion for much of the colonial period, permitting considerable horizontal mobility from one craft to another, as well as substantial vertical movement from apprentice to journeyman to master.[33] Master–journeymen relations were generally less antagonistic than in England – which helps to explain the unity of the two groups in the anti-British protests of the 1760s and 1770s – but this relative harmony was shaken in the 1780s when journeymen undertook independent organization.[34] Given the relative absence of guilds, the chronic shortage of skilled labour and the desire to protect themselves from market fluctuations, colonial workmen often diversified, developing multiple skills and talents: 'The blacksmith was a toolmaker, the soap boiler a tallow chandler, and, despite restrictive legislation, the tanner often acted as currier and shoemaker.' Richard Morris in 1946 used the career of Paul Revere to illustrate both the co-operation within the craft division of labour and the progression – the 'really revolutionary way', in Karl Marx's words – from master crafts-man to industrialist:

> Paul Revere, the distinguished silversmith, who gained greater renown for carrying the messages of the Committees of Correspondence and the Sons of Liberty, was also a well known copperplate engraver, although not a very good one, a dentist who set false 'fore-teeth,' a manufacturer of clock faces for clockmakers, of branding irons for hatters, and of spatulas and probes for surgeons. After the Revolution, while continuing his workshop craft as a silversmith, he branched out into large-scale industry, setting up a foundry and later a mill for rolling copper into sheets; this has now become one of the greatest establishments of its kind in the country.[35]

Domestic labour was performed in all households, wealthy or poor, urban or rural, by indentured servants, waged servants, wives or chil-dren. Although the nature of domestic labour changed with the passage of time, its central components remained the reproduction and upkeep of the household: child-rearing, gardening and food preparation, and other activities such as sewing, weaving, spinning, quilting, preserving, and soap- and candle-making were crucial, often undertaken to help make the household self-sufficient. In addition to regular chores, domes-tic labour after 1750 often came to include the production of cloth, clothing, shoes, hats and other items for sale in regional markets. The broad transition in early America from household manufacture for personal self-sufficiency to domestic manufacture for a merchant, and eventually to full-scale factory production, continually redefined women's work through a pervasive process of de-skilling, and made women central to the formation of America's early industrial prole-tariat.[36]

Other forms of waged labour were most prominent in the seaport cities, where maritime, construction and transportation industries produced steadily expanding markets for seasonal and casual labour. Waged labour increased significantly after 1750, and was employed in merchant shipping, docks and warehousing, fishing, lumbering, forge and furnace industries, breweries, distilleries, paper and powder manu-factories, the military and at the lower end of many of the crafts, particularly in the shipyards and the ropewalks. Some journeymen toiled for their wages by piecework. They, along with apprentices, day labour-ers, and sailors, constituted the rowdiest and most radical part of the urban population, often coalescing into a crowd demanding popular justice.[37]

Recent work in the social history of early America has discovered a prominent and apparently permanent pool of tenants and free wage labourers in agricultural areas, both north and south. Jackson Turner Main in 1965 suggested that 10–40 per cent of the rural population was landless around the time of the Revolution, and more recent work has extended this picture back into the late seventeenth century. Farm labour centred on the household: farmers, their sons and perhaps a servant or two performed most rural work, but waged labour was employed in the fields at harvest time to clear land, remove stumps, build walls and fences, and split wood. Landless tenants who hired themselves out for specific tasks provided most of this labour. The number of tenants and wage workers in rural regions increased throughout the eighteenth century and especially after 1750, though most of them laboured for wages in order to supplement a living gained largely by the land.[38]

Alongside agricultural waged labourers stood the unwaged, the farmers who became small independent producers. 'In the main,' Richard Morris has observed, 'the ultimate economic objective of colonial workmen was security through agriculture rather than industry.' It is not clear how colonial workers weighed property in land against property in skill and tools in their quest for independence, but it is clear that a freehold always provided more security than working for wages.[39] Regrettably little is known about the ways of labour on family farms, but it is certain that many colonial workers sought to retire from the wage labour market to the land. As New Englander William Wood wrote in 1634, 'if any man doubt the goodness of the ground, let him comfort himself with the cheapness of it'.[40] Relatively high wages and cheap land were a matched pair until the late seventeenth century, providing at least some opportunity for the propertyless to acquire land, and with it a largely autonomous and independent social existence. Had not the Leveller Gerrard Winstanley insisted that land ownership was the birthright of every Englishman?[41] Moreover, as the latter-day leveller Karl Marx wryly commented, the 'transformation of wage-labourers into independent producers, who work for themselves instead of for capital, and enrich themselves instead of capitalist gentlemen, reacts in its turn very adversely on the conditions of the labour-market. Not only does the degree of exploitation remain indecently low, the wage labourer also loses, along with the relation of dependence, the feeling of dependence on the abstemious capitalist.'[42] The transition from wage labour to independent production not only lowered the level of the exploitation of labour, but changed its very character: no longer was the point of production the primary locus of exploitation, as it was on the ship, in the manufactory, or in the workshop.[43] The independent farmer gained full control over his own labour (and the labours of all in his household). But this control operated within limits. As regional, national and international market relations extended into the countryside, exploitation came to reside at the point of exchange, in the power relations established between the small farmer and the market. Such relations were usually mediated, depending on the region, by larger farmers, planters, merchants and colonial or metropolitan state officials. Rural self-sufficiency and autonomy were declining by the outbreak of the War for Independence.[44]

In the westward migration many settlers made the move from wage labourer to tenant farmer to freeholder, though the last third of that journey became increasingly arduous in the course of the eighteenth century. Some working people discriminated between different forms of dependency, choosing tenancy over wage labour. As Stephen Innes said of Springfield, Massachusetts, 'men without sufficient capital to purchase the land, provisions, and equipment required to start their own freehold, saw tenancy as an attractive alternative to the life of a wage laborer'.[45]

Large parts of the colonial economy, particularly the farms and plantations of Virginia, Maryland and the Carolinas where the most intensive commercial agriculture was practised, depended on slave labour. The grand plantation represented the greatest concentration of capital and labour in all of North America. Supervision and labour discipline were crucial to the plantation regimen, and were as easily applied to manufacturing as to agricultural efforts. Under the vigilant gaze of overseers, most slaves spent their lives tending export crops such as sugar, tobacco and rice. But slaves also undertook flax, cotton and wool spinning; salt, gunpowder and potash manufacturing; brewing, tanning, brick-making, cooperage and other types of labour. Virginian Robert Carter, owner of 300,000 acres and 350 slaves in the early eighteenth century, boasted an extraordinary division of labour on his plantation: in addition to his agricultural pursuits, he set slaves and white artisans to work in a blacksmith shop, a wool-spinning and weaving shop, a grain mill, a fulling mill and two bake ovens.[46] Most slaves, of course, lived on much smaller farms, in less collective communities of labour, particularly in the piedmont South.[47]

Having surveyed the setting and assembled the fundamental parts of the labour systems of early America, it is now time to set the contraption in motion, to see how the situation of labour changed over time. Early in the colonial period, Richard Morris has indicated, most 'productive enterprises were sufficiently small that they could be adequately financed by individuals or partnerships'. Not only was capital in short supply, but several other factors, some of them imposed by the mercantile

organization of the economy, inhibited the growth of larger productive units, especially in manufacture. Little money was available due
to the chronic scarcity of specie; interest rates ran high. Workers' refusal
of wage labour in favour of independent production lessened the
availability of labour and drove wages up. Finally, imperial policies
subordinated colonial to British manufactures.[48]

The 1760s and 1770s brought changes. The non-importation agreements stimulated domestic manufacturing and led to the 'establishment
of larger units of production employing more labour'. The War for
Independence spurred manufactures to meet military needs.[49] The
surplus of women's and children's labour in the eastern cities, coupled
with an increasing population of the dependent poor, facilitated the
growth of manufacture. Entrepreneurs such as William Molineaux
organized the poor in the 'Manufactory House', built by the Boston
Society for Encouraging Industry and Employing the Poor. The United
Company of Philadelphia for Promoting American Manufacture
arranged a similar incarceration of the needy.[50] American woollen and
worsted industries were boosted by the transatlantic transfer of working-
class skill: numerous British military prisoners and deserters personally
declared independence from the King by remaining in America after the
war. Other industries, such as shipping, ironworks and gristmills, were
also beginning to show a considerable concentration of both capital and
labour.[51] The social division of labour in early America grew rapidly
more complex in the second half of the eighteenth century, and larger
numbers of men, women and children entered new, more co-operative
labouring relationships. This process was not confined to northern urban
centres, but was equally visible in the South, where concentrated capital
and collectivized labour typified the slave plantation.

One of the greatest concentrations of labour during the colonial
period occurred in the military. Life in the army or the navy, whether for
the enlisted man or the soul unlucky or clumsy enough to be nabbed in a
hot press, produced a collective experience of extraordinary proportions. Little is known of the concrete nature of work in the military, and
equally little of the colonists' response to it. Yet there is evidence of
disciplined strike activity and mass desertions by New England soldiers
during the Seven Years' War.[52] The military also furnished vital experiences for colonial elites. Merchants and planters, for example, accumulated valuable logistical and supervisory experience during wartime.
George Washington, well prepared to be a general by his experience in
overseeing an army of slaves (who worked at cloth manufacture as well
as agriculture), probably learned lessons from the battlefield about the
deployment of human resources that furthered his own accumulation of
capital after the War for Independence.[53] War also posed for colonial

elites the problem of scarce labour power, pitting civilian and military economies against each other in ways that required extensive strategy and planning. For both rich and poor, war produced new and intensified experiences of class relations.[54]

Service in the colonial militias was equally important. The militia, as Steven Rosswurm's innovative work on Philadelphia has shown, served as an arena for the politicization and radicalization of lower artisans, journeymen and other free labourers, and as an institution capable of generating important democratic principles, understandings and beliefs. Certain radical sentiments were already circulating among Philadelphia's 'lower order', for, when the militia was formed in April 1775, the rank and file quickly 'objected to the uniforms which their officers had recommended. They instead proposed hunting shirts which not only would be cheaper, but also would "level all distinctions"'.[55] Richard Morris has noted that '[e]ven as late as the Revolution the New England militia was looked upon as a hotbed of democracy, with a great many officers in proportion to men and the pay of officers and men too nearly equal, although the practice of having the men choose their officers was by no means confined to New England'.[56] The election of officers, demanded by the Levellers in England's New Model Army, became a common and radical plebeian demand in the New World.[57] Both militia and military service were formative parts of working-class experience.

James Henretta has argued that colonial American society was 'militarized' after the Seven Years' War: 'There were more arms and ammunition now available in America than ever before and more men experienced in their use.'[58] Militarized perhaps, but also democratized: military experience was obviously crucial to the popular victory in the world's first war for colonial liberation. And arms and ammunition may also have made for other kinds of plebeian independence: as Edmund S. Morgan has observed of late seventeenth-century Virginia, 'Men with guns are not as easily exploited as men without them.' Indeed, firearms could be 'great Levelers'.[59]

The increasing concentration of labour in colonial production posed the problems of supervision and discipline in unprecedented ways. Increased productivity, output and profit, the driving impulses behind the aggregation of labour, all required careful co-ordination of the productive process. The supervisor of the Hibernia Iron Works reported in 1774: 'Gillis McPherson is so lazy and impertinent that I cant manage him without useing Violence which [I] would choose to avoid if possible.' Many employers began to realize the necessity of a 'capable vigilant manager' and the wisdom of sayings such as 'The diligent eye of the master will do more work than both his hands' and 'Not to oversee your workers is to leave them your purse open'.[60] Such were the imperatives if certain workers were to be 'managed'. The concentration of capital and labour brought forth new concerns for orderly accumulation as well as new resistance that was frequently denounced as 'disorder'.

Increases in the size of colonial productive units were part of a complex and interrelated cluster of changes within the labour systems of mid-eighteenth-century America, part of a transition that is only beginning to be understood. Indentured servitude began a broad decline after 1760, amid mounting criticism of the 'traffick of White People'.[61] Poverty increased dramatically, as did geographic mobility, and land grew increasingly scarce, especially in New England.[62] As population density increased, many people were forced to leave overcrowded family farms. Some farmers began to move toward more commercial production, and from extensive to intensive agricultural techniques, paving the way for the expansion of domestic manufacture.[63] The depletion or parcellization of land and an attendant underemployment, largely of women, encouraged family farms to channel labour into the production of shoes, cotton, woollens and linen for the market. The period from 1775 to 1815 became the 'heyday of domestic manufactures' in America.[64]

Free wage labourers began to appear in vastly larger numbers, particularly in urban settings, between 1750 and 1790. Philadelphia's taxable day labourers nearly tripled between 1756 and 1774, and even this increase probably understates the actual growth.[65] The urban casual labour market expanded, and the relatively easy mobility from journeyman to master, so prominent throughout the early part of the colonial period, began to diminish. The growing scarcity of land contributed to the growth of craft and class consciousness. After the War for Independence there was a near-simultaneous emergence of trade unions and masters' associations. Masters had of course organized themselves throughout the colonial period, but after the Revolution they created inter-craft trade associations to protect their larger social and economic interests. Labourers soon turned 'to the more permanent type of trade-union organization'. American workers seized the strike as a prime economic weapon. These changes accompanied the transition from custom to market production in the cities, increasing market production in the agricultural sector, a growing complexity in the division of labour and greater integration into a world economy. Even though 83 per cent of the American population in 1800 remained in agriculture, dynamic changes, most apparent in the cities, were well under way. The Seven Years' War and the period between 1750 and the War for Independence seem to have been crucial to the transition.[66]

The structural forms and dimensions of change in early America had co-ordinates in culture, in the formation of a popular culture of working people in the colonies. Did an equivalent of English plebeian culture develop in the colonies? Alfred F. Young has recently argued that some of the conditions for a 'massive carryover of popular culture from Britain to the colonies' did in fact exist: in particular, there was a constant transit and renewal of culture through successive waves of immigration; a similar oral tradition; and increasing social stratification that presented opportunities for the use of older cultural practices such as status reversal. Yet as Young notes, a 'custom out of its social context loses its meaning and withers'.[67]

Cultural transfer and retention were limited in several ways. First among them was the radically changed nature of the class relation between the gentry and plebeian elements of North American society. Paternalism, the defining feature of English gentry hegemony,[68] was diluted in the colonies by a huge array of conditions and circumstances: by the dispersion of population and the consequent limits on reciprocal social obligations, by the 'independence' of petty commodity producers in crafts and agriculture, by geographic mobility, by labour scarcity, high wages and competition among employers for labour, by extraordinary racial and ethnic diversity, by upward social mobility and by the unstable power and limited wealth of colonial elites, except perhaps in the South, until well into the eighteenth century. Further, colonial upper classes demonstrated relatively little cohesion, representing, as they did, different regional economies and class strutures, and lacking a national centre of political power and culture like London.

Yet by 1750 a plebeian culture was emerging in the cities, their surrounding countrysides, in large parts of New York, Pennsylvania and (with a difference) in many areas of the South. Urban upper and working classes took shape as the seaports of Boston, New York, Philadelphia, Baltimore and Charleston grew and became sub-metropolises for their surrounding regions. Plebeian culture formed from the common and co-operative experiences of craft, domestic, free waged, free agricultural and bound labourers. One of the keys to the cultural dimension of class formation was mobility, and here free wage labourers played a leading part.

The cultural world of free wage labour was essentially picaresque, brimming with those whom the upper classes never tired of calling rogues, rascals and tramps, and who swarmed with restless movement.[69] It featured journeymen, day labourers, landless agricultural workers, seamen, and escaped servants, slaves and apprentices. These men and women may have had more international experience than any other 'labour force' in history. Separated (often self-separated) from the means of production, they faced the discipline of the wage contract and the increasingly violent fluctuations of an increasingly international economy. Their culture developed within the class relations of their work, forming around the 'free' in free labour. Mobility had a special place and meaning in labour-scarce America.

Workers took to their feet, or threatened to take to their feet, in an effort to influence the conditions of their labour. They ran, individually and collectively, in 'confederacies' and after 'conspiracies', from city to countryside, or vice versa, in search of better work, from seaport to seaport looking for better maritime wages, or from one seasonal or casual labour market to another.[70] They were truly footloose, pushed or pulled according to the vagaries of the economy and their own spontaneous urges, and they used their mobility in an effort to maintain a continuity of income in an era when there was often little or no continuity of work.[71]

Their culture took shape within the class contest over the availability of labour, a struggle peculiarly intense in labour-scarce America, particularly between indentured servants, a major social source for an emergent culture of mobile labour, and their masters. As Richard Morris has explained, 'The absentee and the deserter posed a serious problem for the colonial producer. From earliest days bound laborers sought to terminate their contracts of employment unilaterally.' The 'loss of time from absenteeism and desertion laid a heavy tax upon the profits of colonial productive enterprise'. Further, 'the administrative and judicial machinery' of the colonies was helpless 'to restore fugitive servants to their masters and to keep them at work'.[72]

Not that the machinery was not well oiled and running at breakneck speed; quite the contrary. In every colony strict, even ruthless, punishments were administered to runaways, ranging from floggings and brandings ('R' for 'Rogue') to the imposition of as much as ten days' additional service for every day away. This last penalty varied significantly by region and tended to be most rigorously applied where indentured labour was central to the economy, as it was in Virginia and Maryland.[73] Penalties could be especially severe when white servants and black slaves found common cause and 'stole themselves' by stealing away. Legislators devised and implemented indentification systems that required working people to carry passes or certificates to attest to their freedom. Planters marked their wandering property by shaving the heads of previous runaways. Numerous laws were passed against those who 'harboured' fugitives, and against any 'straggling' free labourer – usually a seaman – who might set a bad example to servants and slaves. It is not clear who taught whom more about 'Laziness Idleness & wickedness', but elites clearly feared the contact between these different parts of the working class.[74] Workers' self-termination of contracts kept the colonial courts and legislatures steadily at work, even if the courts and legislatures were not always able to do the same to the colonial worker.

There is an intriguing possibility that this movement of labour was more orderly than it has appeared. In fact, it is distinctly possible that something like an early version of the underground railroad existed for escaped servants and other unfree labourers. Richard Morris has noted that '[f]ugitives were harbored by sympathetic folk', and that '[n]o servant was allowed to go on board ship without a pass, as this was a favorite means of escape'.[75] Seamen were apparently sympathetic folk. There is evidence of an underground trading network among servants that dealt, almost surely, in stolen goods. These concerns, along with restrictions on servants' uses of taverns and even horses, perhaps suggest the outline of a material reality that was instrumental to a culture of mobile labour.[76] Many runaways gravitated toward the frontier, particularly to Georgia, whereas others sought the anonymity of the city. Most significantly, as Abbott Emerson Smith has concluded in *Colonists in Bondage*, '[p]robably the great majority of runaways got successfully away'.[77] This mobility had significant effect upon the decline of indentured servitude in the colonies. Lawrence Towner strongly implies that the fleet evasions of bound labourers were central to the demise of servitude in New England. And Douglas Deal has made a similar, explicit, convincing and important case for colonial Virginia.[78]

Other labourers used their feet to good ends. Sailors were notorious for their willingness to leave ship and break a labour contract at the slightest grievance. As Morris points out, 'Legislation was enacted against deserting seamen similar in character to the statutes against fugitive servants.' Desertion from the merchant service and the Royal Navy was reckoned by many to be one of the most troublesome problems of the day. Sailors ran from port to port in search of a few shillings more a month, beer that did not stink, biscuit that did not move by itself, a less 'precise' master, or a safer ship.[79] Wives ran from their husbands, initiating what Alfred F. Young has called 'the poor woman's form of divorce.'[80] Domestic servants fled the houses of Philadelphia's nabobs in search of their families, freedom and fairer, less tyrannical masters. Journeymen and apprentices also kept on the move, prompting in 1767 an association of masters, the Cordwainers' Fire Company of Philadelphia, to create an insurance system 'against loss of their workmen'.[81] Other employers sought to limit the mobility of free labourers. In 1771 Henry Steigel, owner of a Pennsylvania glass manufactory, sought through legal means the return of one of these workers. The labourer responded, 'I am no servant', and 'I am not by the laws of nature, to drudge and spend my whole life and strength in performing my part of the articles [wage contract], and Mr. Steigel not paying me my wages.'[82] Some employers trapped free workers within a 'debt peonage' in an effort to circumscribe their mobility.[83]

In sum, running away was a vital part of the self-activity of the early American working class. While legislatures denounced the practice as a crime, and Cotton Mather denounced it as a sin,[84] the desertion of a job was a form of struggle that enjoyed wide circulation among working people. Such movement was well suited to class relations in America. The same factors that made full-scale revolt by either indentured servants or slaves nearly impossible – that is, the dispersion of population and the fragmentation of the productive system – served to encourage desertion and mobility. Working people used their feet to exploit competition among employers and to assert their own ends. Not for nothing did mercantilist writers call workers 'the Feet of the Body Politick'. What these writers did not quite understand was that workers acted the part of the Feet to get away from those who styled themselves the Head.[85]

Workers' mobility has traditionally been seen in a negative light, perhaps because of early trade-union efforts to make workers stay and fight their bosses in a particular location. But this earlier 'labour movement' had a positive side, helping to define and extend the community and culture of working people in early America. As Christopher Hill demonstrated in another context, a mobile worker, whether an itinerant craftsman, a soldier, a seaman or an escaped apprentice, not only carried information and ideas among different groups of labouring people, but also used the new experiences of movement to generate new ideas.[86] The culture of mobile labour was, in fact, the only cross-regional culture of working people in early America. Footloose workers were strategically situated in the social division of labour to be able to contact many other kinds of working people. This footloose group served as something of a medium for the exchange of experience and information within a more broadly defined plebeian culture. When the early eighteenth-century seaman wondered what the proletarian with only 'a pair of good Hands and a Stout Heart' was to expect, his mates might have answered that he could expect to use his Fast Feet.

Running away was only one means of resistance used by working people to assert their own interests. In both town and country working men and women protested their plight with actions that ranged from strikes and slow-downs to arson and the murder of their masters.[87] The 'redlegs' – mostly Scottish and Irish indentured servants – of the 'whole island' or Barbados 'conspired for the slaughter of their masters' in 1634. Failing that, in 1649 they selected a day 'to fall upon their

Masters, and cut their throats, and by that means, to make themselves not only freemen, but Masters of the Island'.[88] They failed that too, but not before they gave their ruling class a fright not soon or easily forgotten. Virginia's men of means trembled before similar tumults. In 1672 the Assembly passed a militia act which 'admitted into the armed services only those white servants whose terms had nearly expired, and who would therefore have little incentive to turn their weapon against their masters'.[89] Once freed, however, these former servants did not cease their troublesome ways. 'How miserable that man is,' wrote Governor Berkeley, 'that Governes a People wher six parts in seaven at least are Poore Endebted Discontented and Armed.'[90] Governor Berkeley's misery grew as he watched landless freemen, servants and slaves respond to the 'class rhetoric' of a leader to form a poor man's army in Bacon's Rebellion. In fact, Virginia's leaders constructed over time a 'bourgeois militia' explicitly designed to deal with those they called 'unruly home spirits'.[91]

Despite the diversity of regional productive systems and class structures in early America, certain activities and trends suggest a growing cultural coherence, often in subterranean fashion, over sizeable areas of the world of labour. After fifteen years of study devoted to crowds and popular protest in the colonies, it is clear that co-operation among different sorts of labourers was, at the most critical of moments, extensive.[92] Alfred F. Young has affirmed that the mob in America, like its counterpart in England, was a 'horizontal' sort of beast, full of concerted solidarity. More specific work is needed on the networks of communication and the bases for co-operation and collective action within the culture of working people. Important in this regard is T.H. Breen's work on the 'giddy multitude' in seventeenth-century Virginia, 'an amalgam of indentured servants and slaves, of poor whites and blacks, of landless freedmen and debtors'. Equally important – and closely related – is Edmund S. Morgan's discussion of the actions taken by the Virginia ruling class to criminalize the co-operation between white servants and black slaves.[93] Other intriguing instances of co-operation include a band of pirates – just a group of seamen who had crossed the line into illegal activity – who in 1717 captured a ship full of bound servants and immediately ripped up the indentures and set the servants free.[94] What were the sources and significance of the solidarity of slaves, servants and seamen who took to the streets in common protest in Philadelphia and Boston in the 1770s?[95] In addressing these issues and others, historians should follow the lead of Susan G. Davis, who has recently revealed some of the deeper significance of the street as a medium of political communication in her extraordinary work on folk drama in post-revolutionary Philadelphia.[96]

Other trends suggest a convergence toward general cultural patterns. The shared experience of primitive accumulation and of moving to the New World as *unfree labourers* could have had an impact upon the development of broadly held values, particularly in producing a driving aspiration among working people toward self-sufficiency and independence. The collective experience of unfree labour, labour scarcity and class struggle over mobility suggest that the activities and ideas of the 'War for Independence' had a special meaning for many working men and women. As Richard Morris has argued, 'the bulk of the settlers in this country had a greater respect for the dignity of hard labor, and the working class in turn was possessed of a greater spirit of independence'. Further, Morris adds, 'the high wages commanded by colonial workmen, the relative independence enjoyed by them, and the wide recognition of the importance of labor accounted in large part for the greater esteem accorded workmen, particularly skilled craftsmen, in the colonies than in the mother country'.[97] Morris has suggested that this powerful position blunted the growth of class consciousness in the colonies, when in fact it seems more likely that the very respect and self-esteem he describes were expressions of an advanced consciousness among American working people. In any case, his conclusion is certainly a measure of plebeian power in early America.

Other points of cultural convergence among diverse groups of working people were a rough egalitarianism with distinctly democratic tendencies, and an ethic of sustenance and security that tempered impulses toward acquisition and accumulation. The transatlantic antinomian Samuel Gorton spoke for more than himself – in his own time and after – when he asked a Massachusetts magistrate, 'Whose oxe or whose asse have I taken[?]'; 'Or when and where have I lived upon other men's labours and not wrought with mine owne hands for things honest in the sight of men[?]'[98] As we have seen, not only did some refuse to live on other men's labours, but they refused – by refusing waged and unfree labour – to let other men live on theirs. Many of those who peopled the colonies, Gary Nash reminds us, came from places 'where the Protestant ethic did not beat resoundingly in every breast'.[99] In fact a quite contrary pounding of the heart, perhaps first and most clearly heard in the bodies of the religious radicals in the English Revolution, came to beat to a distinctly American rhythm.

Class relations in early America developed within diverse productive systems, all of which were created beyond the constraints of a feudal past, but firmly within the constraints of a labour-scarce present and future. The social relations of power and reciprocity that had been worked out between ruler and ruled in England, Europe and Africa had to be established anew with the massive and momentous move across the Atlantic. Labouring men and women were in numerous ways reattached to the means of production. Compulsory labour was commonplace. Many among the working people of early America withstood deep and varied bondage and coercion. The experience of unfree labour lies coiled like a snake in the heart of early American working-class history.

These early experiences and this snake are intricately intertwined with America's sweeping history of ferocious, often violent conflict at the point of production. The snake has generations of wisdom and frequently says, 'Don't Tread on Me.'[100] If early American elites and employers, facing extraordinary labour scarcity and a diverse working class, gained unprecedented experience in dealing with labour as a commodity, then by the same logic and process, American working people accumulated equivalent experience in defining, limiting and resisting this treatment. Classes, as Marx said, develop *together*. The radical soldiers and sectaries who found themselves labouring in Poplar Spring, Virginia, took their places beside the other servants, the hunters, slaves, domestic workers, craftsmen, farmers and sailors who throughout the colonial period struggled so variously and valiantly against the processes by which their labours were transformed into, and exploited as, commodities. These labouring folk in early America learned that they needed Good Hands to get a living, a Stout Heart to endure grisly oppression, and Fast Feet to free themselves from exploitation and to assert autonomous values and interests.

Notes

This is a revised version of a paper presented at the Conference on the World Turned Upside Down, held by the Philadelphia Center for Early American Studies in November 1981, and published in *Labour/Le Travailleur* 10 (1982), pp. 123–44. I would like to thank Richard R. Beeman, Rhys Isaac, Walter M. Licht, Jack Michel, Gary Nash, Daniel Vickers, Bryan Palmer, Sunie Davis, Dan Schiller, Nancy Hewitt, Christopher Hill, Alfred F. Young, Amy Dru Stanley, Leslie Rowland and, especially, Peter Linebaugh and Wendy Goldman for their help and encouragement.

1. See Christopher Hill, *The Experience of Defeat: Milton and Some Contemporaries* (New York, 1984), and Richard E. Morris, *Government and Labor in Early America* (New York, 1946), pp. 173, 174.

2. Ibid. See also the statements of seven of the labourers in 'The Servants' Plot of 1663', *Virginia Magazine of History and Biography*, no. 15 (1908), pp. 38–43, from which several of the above quotations are taken. See also Robert Beverly, *The History and Present State of Virginia*, Louis B. Wright, ed. (original edn 1705; Chapel Hill, 1947), pp. 68–70. For an interesting study of related radical ideas in New England, see Philip F. Gura, *A Glimpse of Sion's Glory: Puritan Radicalism in New England, 1620–1660* (Middletown, Conn. 1984).

3. Morris, *Government and Labour*, is the most thorough and serious study to date. It is, in fact, a neglected classic. Originally written in 1946 and recently republished by

Northeastern University Press, this book assembles a colossal array of data, including some 20,000 court cases, to discuss a wide range of topics. The scholarship is skilled and scrupulous, and stands as the zenith of early American labour history. This essay is deeply indebted to it, and to a quickly developing, more recent secondary literature. See Gary B. Nash, *The Urban Crucible: Social Change, Political Consciousness, and the Origins of the American Revolution* (Cambridge, Mass., 1979); Sharon V. Salinger, 'Colonial Labor in Transition: The Decline of Indentured Servitude in late Eighteenth-Century Philadelphia', *Labor History*, vol. 22 (1981), pp. 165–91; Billy G. Smith, 'The Material Lives of Laboring Philadelphians, 1750–1800', *William and Mary Quarterly*, vol. 38 (1981), pp. 163–202 (hereafter *WMQ*); Eric Guest Nellis, 'Communities of Workers: Free Labor in Provincial Massachusetts, 1690–1765', PhD dissertation, University of British Columbia, 1979; Stephen J. Rosswurm, 'Arms, Class, and Culture: The Philadelphia Militia and the "Lower Orders" in the American Revolution, 1765–1783', PhD dissertation, Northern Illinois University, 1979; Daniel F. Vickers, 'Maritime Labor in Colonial Massachusetts: A Case Study of the Essex County Cod Fishery and the Whaling Industry of Nantucket, 1630–1775', PhD dissertation, Princeton University, 1981. For a biographical approach to working-class experience in early America, see the splendid article by Alfred F. Young, 'George Robert Twelves Hewes (1742–1840): A Boston Shoemaker and the Memory of the American Revolution', *WMQ*, vol. 38 (1981), pp. 561–623.

4. Karl Marx, *Capital: A Critique of Political Economy*, vol. 1 (New York, 1977), p. 876 and Part 8 generally, pp. 873–940. The second quotation is by Barnaby Slush, *The Navy Royal: or a Sea-Cook turn'd Projector* (London, 1709), p. 16.

5. E.P. Thompson, 'Patrician Society, Plebeian Culture', *Journal of Social History*, vol. 7 (1974), p. 386. For a recent survey of enclosure see J.R. Wordie, 'The Chronology of English Enclosure, 1500–1914', *Economic History Review*, 2nd series, vol. 36 (1983), pp. 483–505. I do not mean to imply that the move from manor to factory was unilinear. The remainder of this essay discusses the huge variety of productive relations that existed during the transition.

6. E.P. Thompson, *The Making of the English Working Class* (New York, 1963), pp. 77–101; Mike Davis, 'Why the US Working Class is Different', *New Left Review*, no. 123 (1980), p. 14. In this paragraph, as throughout the essay, I am deeply indebted to Christopher Hill, *The World Turned Upside Down: Radical Ideas in the English Revolution* (New York, 1972). See also *The Experience of Defeat*.

7. C.L.R. James, Grace C. Lee, Pierre Chaulieu, *Facing Reality* (Detroit, 1974 [1958]), p. 103.

8. For a fine discussion of the 'articulation' of capitalist and non-capitalist economies in the nineteenth-century American South, see Steven Hahn, *The Roots of Southern Populism: Yeomen Farmers and the Transformation of the Georgia Upcountry, 1850–1890* (New York, 1983).

9. For surveys of the English economy in the early modern period, see D.C. Coleman, *The Economy of England, 1450–1750* (London, 1977), and B.A. Holderness, *Pre-Industrial England: Economy and Society, 1500–1750* (London, 1976). For a longer perspective on international development, see Rodney Hilton, ed., *The Transition from Feudalism to Capitalism* (London, 1976), and Immanuel Wallerstein, *The Modern World-System: Capitalist Agriculture and the Origins of the European World-Economy in the Sixteenth Century* (New York, 1976), and *The Modern World-System*, vol. 2 *Mercantilism and the Consolidation of the European World-Economy, 1600–1750* (New York, 1980). See also Morris, *Government and Labor*, pp. 1–54.

10. See Neil Salisbury, *Manitou and Providence: Indians, Europeans, and the Making of New England, 1500–1643* (New York, 1982), for an important discussion of how Indian lands were integrated into a nascent capitalist economy. See also Stephen Innes, *Labor in a New Land: Economy and Society in Seventeenth-Century Springfield* (Princeton, 1983), ch. 3.

11. Morris, *Government and Labor*, p. 141; Joseph A. Goldenburg, *Shipbuilding in Colonial America* (Charlottesville, 1976), p. 14.

12. For an elaboration on this point, see Joyce Appleby, James Jacob and Margaret Jacob, 'Introduction', in Jacob and Jacob, eds., *The Origins of Anglo-American Radicalism*

(London, 1984), p. 11.

13. Eric Foner, *Tom Paine and Revolutionary America* (New York, 1976), pp. 39, 32; Davis, 'US Working Class', p. 10.

14. Wallerstein, *Modern World-System*, vol. 1, ch. 2; Philip Corrigan, 'Feudal Relics or Capitalist Monuments? Notes on the Sociology of Unfree Labour', *Sociology*, vol. 11 (1977), pp. 435–63; Abbott Emerson Smith, *Colonists in Bondage: White Servitude and Convict Labor in America, 1607–1776* (New York, 1947), p. 27.

15. Maurice Dobb, 'Growth of the Proletariat', in his *Studies in the Development of Capitalism* (New York, 1947), p. 233; Morris, *Government and Labor*, p. 3.

16. Morris, *Government and Labor*, p. 404. See also Hilary McD. Beckles, 'Plantation Production and White 'Proto-Slavery': White Indentured Servants and the Colonisation of the English West Indies, 1624–1645', *The Americas*, vol. 41 (1984–5), pp. 21–45. Smith, *Colonists in Bondage*, pp. 19–20: 'The invention and acceptance of this system [of trading in servants] made it possible to handle emigration as a business proposition, and to treat white labor as a commodity.'

17. Smith, *Colonists in Bondage*, chs. 1, 4–9; A. Roger Ekirch, 'Bound for America: A Profile of British Convicts Transported to the Colonies', *WMQ*, vol. 42 (1985), p. 188.

18. Salinger, 'Colonial Labor in Transition', p. 169; idem, "Send No More Women": Female Servants in Eighteenth-Century Philadelphia', *Pennsylvania Magazine of History and Biography* (hereafter *PMHB*), vol. 107 (1983), pp. 29–48; David W. Galenson, *White Servitude in Colonial America: An Economic Analysis* (Cambridge, 1981); idem, 'British Servants and the Colonial Indenture System in the Eighteenth Century', *Journal of Southern History*, vol. 44 (1978), pp. 41–66, and '"Middling People" or "Common Sort"?: The Social Origins of Some Early Americans Reexamined', *WMQ*, vol. 35 (1978), pp. 499–524; Mildred Campbell, 'Response', Ibid., p. 525–40; David W. Galenson, 'The Social Origins of Some Early Americans: Rejoinder', *WMQ*, vol. 36 (1979), pp. 264–77; Mildred Campbell, 'Reply', Ibid., pp. 277–86.

19. Morris, *Government and Labor*, p. 368; John Rule, *The Experience of Labour in Eighteenth-Century English Industry* (New York, 1981), pp. 113, 114.

20. Foner, *Tom Paine*, p. 16; Smith, *Colonists in Bondage*, p. 221; Kenneth Morgan, 'The Organization of the Convict Trade to Maryland: Stevenson, Randolph and Cheston, 1768–1775', *WMQ*, vol. 42 (1985), p. 217.

21. Morris, *Government and Labor*, pp. 7–10, 279, 295–6.

22. Ibid., pp. 281, 273; Christopher Lloyd, *The British Seaman, 1200–1860: A Social Survey* (Rutherford, 1970), p. 139.

23. Morris, *Government and Labor*, pp. 6, 356, 346–57. Occasionally fines were imposed, but anyone unable to pay 'was accordingly sold into service' (p. 347).

24. Daniel Vickers, 'The First Whalemen of Nantucket', *WMQ*, vol. 40 (1983), pp. 571–4, 579–83; Stephen Innes, 'Land Tenancy and Social Order in Springfield, Massachusetts, 1652 to 1702', *WMQ*, vol. 35 (1978), p. 53; idem, *Labour in a New Land*, pp. 64–71.

25. Richard S. Dunn, 'Servants and Slaves: The Recruitment and Employment of Labor in Colonial America', in Jack P. Greene and J.R. Pole, eds., *Colonial British America: Essays in the New History of the Early Modern Era* (Baltimore, 1984), pp. 159, 165. By Dunn's calculations, roughly 1.8 million slaves and servants were shipped to British America between 1600 and 1780. For other estimates, see Morris, *Government and Labor*, p. 315, and Smith, *Colonists in Bondage*, p. 336.

26. Smith, *Colonists in Bondage*, pp. 300, 297. Smith's conclusions need finer testing. Darrett B. Rutman and Anita H. Rutman, in *A Place in Time: Middlesex County, Virginia, 1650–1750* (New York, 1984), p. 130, argue that only a minority of indentured servants 'lived to the end of their service and joined the ranks of the free'. See also Russell R. Menard, 'From Servant to Freeholder: Status Mobility and Property Accumulation in Seventeenth-Century Maryland', *WMQ*, vol. 30 (1973), pp. 37–64, and 'From Servants to Slaves: The Transformation of the Chesapeake Labor System', *Southern Studies*, vol. 16 (1977), pp. 355–90. Paul Clemens in his *The Atlantic Economy and Colonial Maryland's Eastern Shore: From Tobacco to Grain* (Ithaca, 1980), p. 99, notes that prior to 1680 'it was not unusual for servitude to be followed by tenancy and tenancy by landownership'.

Yet his 'work with more than 200 post-1680 immigrant servants found virtually no evidence of freedmen acquiring land'.

27. Dunn, 'Servants and Slaves', p. 157.

28. James T. McGowan, 'Planters without Slaves: Origins of a New World Labor System', *Southern Studies*, vol. 16 (1977), p. 10.

29. Rachel N. Klein, 'Ordering the Backcountry: The South Carolina Regulation', *WMQ*, vol. 38 (1981), pp. 668, 672, 675. See Richard Slotkin, *Regeneration Through Violence: The Mythology of the American Frontier, 1600–1860* (Middletown, 1973), pp. 233, 156–7, p. 262, and James Axtell, 'The White Indians of Colonial America', *WMQ*, vol. 32 (1975), pp. 55–88, for discussions of how Europeans were 'Indianized' in America.

30. Carl Bridenbaugh, *The Colonial Craftsman* (Chicago, 1950).

31. Morris, *Government and Labor*, p. 42. A great deal of work remains to be done on workshops and the organization of craft labour in early America.

32. Ibid., p. 24; Foner, *Tom Paine*, p. 37. See also the excellent forthcoming study by David P. Jaffee, 'Artisan Entrepreneurs and the Transformation of Rural America, 1760–1860'.

33. Foner, *Tom Paine*, p. 32; Morris, *Government and Labor*, p. 49.

34. Morris, *Government and Labor*, pp. 188, 200; Sharon V. Salinger, 'Artisans, Journeymen, and the Transformation of Labor in Late Eighteenth-Century Philadelphia', *WMQ*, vol. 40 (1983), p. 64.

35. Ibid., pp. 34–5; Dodd, *Studies*, p. 123; Innes, *Labor in a New Land*, pp. xviii, 80.

36. See Alice Kessler-Harris, *Out to Work: A History of Wage-Earning Women in the United States* (New York, 1982), chs. 1, 2; Nancy F. Cott, *The Bonds of Womanhood: 'Women's Sphere' in New England, 1780–1835* (New Haven, 1977), ch. 1; Lyle Koehler, *A Search for Power: The 'Weaker Sex' in Seventeenth-Century New England* (Urbana, 1980), ch. 4; Nash, *Urban Crucible*, pp. 189–97.

37. Smith, 'Material Lives', p. 183. For a later period see David Montgomery, 'The Working Classes of the Pre-Industrial American City, 1780–1830', *Labor History*, vol. 9 (1968), pp. 3–22. See also Morris, *Government and Labor*, pp. 40–1; Foner, *Tom Paine*, pp. 45–56.

38. Jackson Turner Main, *The Social Structure of Revolutionary America* (Princeton, 1965), pp. 18, 46, 61, 62. Innes, in *Labor in a New Land* (p. xxi), argues that waged labour was commonplace in seventeenth-century Springfield, while available land was not. See also James A. Henretta, 'Families and Farms: Mentalité in Pre-Industrial America', *WMQ*, vol. 35 (1978), pp. 6, 7, 9; Darrett B. Rutman, *Husbandmen of Plymouth: Farms and Villages in the Old Colony, 1620–1692* (Boston, 1968), p. 42; Jack Michel, in 'Cottagers, Yeoman, and Gentlemen Capitalists: The Culture of Rural Pennsylvania, 1682–1735' (PhD dissertation in progress, University of Chicago), discusses the increase in landless tenants and labourers. For example, the 298 houses in Bradford Township, Chester County, Pennsylvania, in 1798 belonged to only thirty-one owners. See also Michael Merrill, 'Cash Is Good to Eat: Self-Sufficiency and Exchange in the Rural Economy of the United States', *Radical History Review*, vol. 4 (1977), pp. 42–71.

39. Morris, *Government and Labor*, p. 48. This important issue also awaits further study.

40. Quoted in Rutman, *Husbandmen of Plymouth*, p. 61.

41. Christopher Hill, 'Pottage for Freeborn Englishmen: Attitudes to Wage Labor', in his *Change and Continuity in Seventeenth-Century England* (Cambridge, Mass., 1979), pp. 228–9.

42. Marx, *Capital*, vol. I, p. 936. For a contrasting situation in which control was maintained by denying settlers property inland, see Gerald M. Sider, 'The Ties that Bind: Culture and Agriculture, Property and Propriety in the Newfoundland Village Fishery', *Social History*, vol. 5 (1980), pp. 1–39.

43. Marx, *Capital*, pp. 931–40.

44. Merrill, 'Cash Is Good to Eat', pp. 61–6; Christopher Clark, 'Household Economy, Market Exchange, and the Rise of Capitalism in the Connecticut Valley',

Journal of Social History, vol. 13 (1979), 169–89; Daniel Vickers, 'Fathers and Sons: Field Work in Essex County, Massachusetts, 1630–1675', in Stephen Innes, ed., *Work and Labor in Colonial America* (Chapel Hill, 1988), ch. 10.

45. Innes, 'Land Tenancy and Social Order', p. 144; Henretta, 'Families and Farms', p. 8.

46. Richard B. Morris, 'The Organization of Production During the Colonial Period', in Harold F. Williamson, ed., *The Growth of the American Economy* (New York, 1946); Morris, *Government and Labor*, pp. 38–9. On the increase in the size of the productive unit in the South, see Russell R. Menard, 'The Maryland Slave Population, 1658 to 1730: A Democratic Profile of Blacks in Four Counties', *WMQ*, vol. 32 (1975), p. 44, and Allan Kulikoff, 'The Origins of Afro-American Society in Tidewater Maryland and Virginia, 1700 to 1790', *WMQ*, vol. 35 (1978), p. 229.

47. Gloria L. Main, *Tobacco Colony: Life in Early Maryland, 1650–1720* (Princeton, 1982), pp. 128–39.

48. Morris, *Government and Labor*, pp. 38, 44; Morris, 'Organization of Production', p. 57; Salinger, 'Colonial Labor in Transition', p. 189; Foner, *Tom Paine*, p. 32; James F. Shepherd and Gary M. Walton, *Shipping, Maritime, Trade and the Economic Development of Colonial North America* (Cambridge, 1972), p. 25.

49. Morris, *Government and Labor*, pp. 44, 13; Morris, 'Organization of Production', pp. 64, 65.

50. Montgomery, 'Working Classes', p. 19. See also Nash, *Urban Crucible*, pp. 333–8.

51. Morris, *Government and Labor*, p. 305; Morris, 'Organization of Production', p. 60; Bernard Bailyn and Lotte Bailyn, *Massachusetts Shipping, 1697–1714: A Statistical Study* (Cambridge, Mass., 1959), pp. 46, 68.

52. F.C. Anderson, 'Why Did Colonial New Englanders Make Bad Soldiers? Contractual Principles and Military Conduct during the Seven Years' War', *WMQ*, vol. 38 (1981), pp. 395–417. See the same author's *A People's Army: Massachusetts Soldiers and Society in the Seven Years' War* (Chapel Hill, 1984).

53. James Henretta, *The Evolution of American Society, 1700–1815* (Lexington, 1973), p. 129; Morris, *Government and Labor*, p. 38.

54. Morris, *Government and Labor*, p. 528.

55. Rosswurm, 'Arms, Class, and Culture', p. 112. See the same author's '"As a Lyen Out of his Den": Philadelphia's Popular Movement, 1776–1780', in Jacob and Jacob, eds., *Origins of Anglo-American Radicalism*, pp. 300–323. See also Foner, *Tom Paine*, pp. 53–5.

56. Morris, *Government and Labor*, p. 506.

57. See Hill, *Experience of Defeat*, pp. 283–8; Innes, *Labor in a New Land*, pp. 159–64.

58. Henretta, *Evolution*, p. 128.

59. Edmund S. Morgan, *American Slavery, American Freedom: The Ordeal of Colonial Virginia* (New York, 1975), pp. 240, 379.

60. Morris, *Government and Labor*, pp. 462f., 39. On the importance of the manager, see the letter from Henry Drinker to Richard Blackledge, 4 October 1786, as produced in Thomas M. Doerflinger, 'How to Run an Ironworks', *PMHB*, vol. 108 (1984), p. 363. See also Paul F. Paskoff, *Industrial Evolution: Organization, Structure, and Growth in the Pennsylvania Iron Industry, 1750–1860* (Baltimore, 1983), pp. 14–16.

61. Morris, *Government and Labor* p. 322; Foner, *Tom Paine*, p. 44; Salinger, 'Colonial Labor in Transition', pp. 189–91.

62. Gary B. Nash, 'Poverty and Poor Relief in Pre-Revolutionary Philadelphia', *WMQ*, vol. 33 (1976), pp. 3–30, and *Urban Crucible*, pp. 253, 185; Douglas L. Jones, 'The Strolling Poor: Transiency in Eighteenth-Century Massachusetts', *Journal of Social History*, vol. 8 (1975), pp. 28–54, and 'Poverty and Vagabondage: The Process of Survival in Eighteenth-Century Massachusetts', *New England Historical and Genealogical Register*, vol. 133 (1979), pp. 243–54.

63. Henretta, *Evolution*, p. 19.

64. Morris, 'Organization of Production', pp. 58–9; Henretta, 'Families and Farms',

pp. 30–1.

65. Smith, 'Material Lives', p. 181; Salinger, 'Colonial Labor in Transition', p. 189; Foner, *Tom Paine*, p. 45.

66. Morris, 'Organization of Production', p. 55; Morris, *Government and Labor*, pp. 200 (quotation), 198–202, 523, 525; Nash, *Urban Crucible*, p. 321; Salinger, 'Colonial Labor in Transition', p. 190; Henretta, *Evolution*, p. 205; Salinger, 'Artisans, Journeymen, and the Transformation of Labor', pp. 64–70; Billy G. Smith, 'The Career Patterns of Laboring Philadelphians, 1756–1798', in Innes, ed., *Work and Labor*, ch. 6.

67. Alfred F. Young, 'English Plebeian Culture and Eighteenth-Century American Radicalism', in Jacob and Jacob, eds., *Origins of Anglo-American Radicalism*, pp. 186–187; Nash, *Urban Crucible*, p. 262.

68. Thompson, 'Patrician Society, Plebeian Culture', pp. 382–405; see also his 'Eighteenth-Century English Society: Class Struggle without Class?', *Social History*, vol. 3 (1978), pp. 133–65.

69. I follow Sidney W. Mintz and Richard Price, *An Anthropological Approach to the Afro-American Past: A Caribbean Perspective*, ISHI Occasional Paper in Social Change, No. 2 (Philadelphia, 1976), defining culture as a body of beliefs and values, socially acquired, patterned and articulated, that serve a group as guides of and for behaviour. For working people, a chronic tension is produced by the conflict between the demands of work and the desires to assert autonomous interests and values. Cultures, therefore, even when transferred from one continent to another, will always be formed and reformed within the class relations of work. Part of this formulation is adapted from Richard Johnson, 'Three Problematics: Elements of a Theory of Working-Class Culture', in John Clarke, Chas Critcher and Richard Johnson, eds., *Working Class Culture: Studies in History and Theory* (London, 1979), pp. 201–37. Cultures, like classes, 'always stand in relations of domination – and subordination – to each other, are always, in some sense, in struggle with one another'. See John Clarke, Stuart Hall, Tony Jefferson and Brian Roberts, 'Subcultures, Cultures and Class', in Stuart Hall and Tony Jefferson, eds., *Resistance Through Rituals: Youth Subcultures in Post-War Britain* (London, 1975), pp. 12, 9–74. I take the term, 'picaresque' from Thompson, 'Eighteenth Century English Society', p. 157.

70. Nash, *Urban Crucible*, p. 19; Smith, *Colonists in Bondage*, p. 297.

71. This theme, crucial for early American labour, is developed by M. Sonenscher, 'Work and Wages in Paris in the Eighteenth Century', in Maxine Berg, Pat Hudson and M. Sonenscher, eds., *Manufacture in Town and County Before the Factory* (Cambridge, 1983), pp. 147–72. See also Nash, *Urban Crucible*, p. 10.

72. Morris, *Government and Labor*, pp. 434, 435, 519.

73. Ibid., pp. 452, 457, 425–31; Douglas Deal, 'Race and Class in Colonial Virginia: Indians, Englishmen and Africans on the Eastern Shore During the Seventeenth Century', PhD dissertation, University of Rochester (1981), pp. 152–66.

74. Morris, *Government and Labor*, pp. 449, 416–17, 450; Smith, *Colonists in Bondage*, pp. 265–6, 269; Philip D. Morgan, 'Black Life in Eighteenth-Century Charleston', *Perspectives in American History* (New Series) 1 (1984), p. 206 (quotation); Peter H. Wood, *Black Majority: Negroes in Colonial South Carolina from 1670 through the Stono Rebellion* (New York, 1974), pp. 239–270; T.H. Breen and Stephen Innes, *'Myne Owne Ground': Race and Freedom on Virginia's Eastern Shore* (New York, 1980), pp. 27–31, 106–107; Rutman and Rutman, *A Place in Time*, p. 264; Deal, 'Masters and Slaves'. Gerald Mullin, *Flight and Rebellion: Slave Resistance in Eighteenth-Century Virginia* (New York, 1972), p. 114.

75. Ibid., Morris, *Government and Labor*, pp. 416, 455f, 435.

76. Ibid., pp. 455, 510–11; Morgan, 'Black Life', pp. 193, 198–9, 202, 215, presents interesting material on slave runaways and their networks in Charleston. See also Mullin, *Flight and Rebellion*, ch. 3.

77. Smith, *Colonists in Bondage*, pp. 269, 297; Morris, *Government and Labor*, pp. 439, 460.

78. Lawrence Towner, '"A Fondness for Freedom": Servant Protest in Puritan Society', *WMQ*, vol. 19 (1962), pp. 215, 217; Deal, 'Race and Class'.

79. Morris, *Government and Labor*, pp. 230 (quotation), 247; Marcus Rediker, *Between the Devil and the Deep Blue Sea: Merchant Seamen, Pirates, and the Anglo-American Maritime World, 1700–1750* (New York, 1987), ch. 2.

80. Alfred F. Young, personal communication, November 1985.

81. Morris, *Government and Labor*, p. 446; Salinger, 'Send No More Women', pp. 34, 38–40; and idem, 'Artisans, Journeymen, and the Transformation of Labor', pp. 72–4.

82. Morris, *Government and Labor*, p. 446. See also Doerflinger's comments on the industrialist Henry Drinker's worries about workers' mobility in the labour-scarce Delaware Valley in 'How to Run an Ironworks', pp. 359–60.

83. Vickers, 'Maritime Labor in Colonial Massachusetts', ch. 4.

84. Towner, 'Fondness for Freedom', p. 213.

85. Quoted in Galenson, 'Middling People or Common Sort', p. 522. See Hill, *Experience of Defeat*, p. 296, for his observation that radicals after the English Revolution 'raised flight to a moral principle'. For a similar argument about the relationship between the social division of labour and the circulation of radical ideas, see Carlo Ginzburg, *The Cheese and the Worms: The Cosmos of a Sixteenth-Century Miller* (New York, 1980).

86. Hill, *The World Turned Upside Down*, chs. 3, 4. See also Kulikoff, 'Origins of Afro-American Society', pp. 226–59, for a very useful study that approaches community through mobility.

87. Morris, *Government and Labor*, pp. 197, 467; Towner, 'Fondness for Freedom', p. 209. See the interesting comments and document presented in T.H. Breen, James H. Lewis and Keith Schlesinger, 'Motive for Murder: A Servant's Life in Virginia, 1678', *WMQ*, vol. 40 (1983), pp. 106–20.

88. Father Andrew White and Richard Ligon as quoted in Jill Sheppard, *The 'Redlegs' of Barbados: Their Origins and History* (Millwood, NY, 1977), pp. 15, 23.

89. Morris, *Government and Labor*, pp. 287–8.

90. Quoted in Dunn, 'Servants and Slaves', p. 167. See also Morgan, *American Slavery, American Freedom*, pp. 215–92; Wilcomb E. Washburn, *The Governor and the Rebel: A History of Bacon's Rebellion in Virginia* (New York, 1957).

91. T.H. Breen, 'A Changing Labor Force and Race Relations in Virginia, 1660–1710', in his *Puritans and Adventurers: Change and Persistence in Early America* (New York, 1980), p. 137. See also Morgan, *American Slavery, American Freedom*, pp. 215–70; William L. Shea, *The Virginia Militia in the Seventeenth Century* (Baton Rouge, 1983), pp. 130, 129, 114–15. Gary A. Puckrein, *Little England: Plantation Society and Anglo-Barbadian Politics, 1627–1700* (New York, 1984), pp. 119–120, 141, notes the radical ideas among indentured servants in seventeenth-century Barbados.

92. For examples, see Gordon Wood, 'A Note on Mobs During the American Revolution', *WMQ*, vol. 23 (1966), pp. 635–42; Pauline Maier, *From Resistance to Revolution: Colonial Radicals and the Development of American Opposition to Britain, 1765–76* (New York, 1972); Dirk Hoerder, 'Boston Leaders and Boston Crowds, 1765–1776', in Alfred F. Young, ed., *The American Revolution: Explorations in the History of American Radicalism* (DeKalb, 1976), pp. 235–71; John Lax and William Pencak, 'The Knowles Riot and the Crisis of the 1740's in Massachusetts', *Perspectives in American History*, vol. 10 (1976), pp. 163–214.

93. Breen, 'A Changing Labor Force', p. 128; Morgan, *American Slavery, American Freedom*, pp. 311, 312, 327–37.

94. Young, 'English Plebeian Culture and Anglo-American Radicalism', p. 41; Thompson, 'Patrician Society, Plebeian Culture', p. 397; Morris, *Government and Labor*, pp. 136, 273, 313.

95. Foner, *Tom Paine*, p. 54.

96. Susan G. Davis, 'The Career of Colonel Pluck: Folk Drama and Popular Protest in Early Nineteenth-Century Philadelphia', *PMHB*, vol. 109 (1985), pp. 179–202.

97. Morris, *Government and Labor*, vol. 52, pp. 50–51. On the importance of 'independence' and its relationship to petty commodity production, see Hahn, *Roots of Southern Populism*.

98. Quoted in Gura, *A Glimpse of Sion's Glory*, p. 301; on Gorton generally see

pp. 49–92, 276–303.

99. Gary B. Nash, 'Up from the Bottom in Franklin's Philadelphia', *Past and Present*, vol. 77 (1977), pp. 59, 68; Smith, 'Material Lives', p. 180; Henretta, 'Families and Farms', p. 19; Alfred F. Young, 'Afterword', in his *The American Revolution*, pp. 456–7.

100. See Ronald Hoffman, 'The "Disaffected" in the Revolutionary South', in Young, ed., *The American Revolution*, pp. 273–316.

'The Seed Plot of Sedition': The Struggle for the Waldo Patent Backlands, 1800–1801

Alan Taylor

During the last two decades Christopher Hill and several other British scholars have cast new light into those 'dark corners' of seventeenth and eighteenth-century England, the forest communities. Their work recasts the forests as centres of egalitarian ferment, as focal points of conflict with an encroaching society long characterized by hierarchy and newly committed to capitalism. Recently, several American historians have looked anew at their forests during the eighteenth century. In the several extensive episodes of rural insurgency from the Carolinas to Maine they discern a common pattern: the organized resistance of relatively poor and powerless rural folk to the local operation of laws seen to serve the hostile interests of wealthier, more powerful outsiders. This paper draws upon both bodies of work to examine a single episode of rural insurgency that occurred during the years 1800–1801 in the Sheepscot backcountry located in central Maine, then a part of the Commonwealth of Masschusetts. The essential similarity between the English and the American forest lies in the drive of common folk in both areas to escape economic dependence by obtaining direct access to land and its resources. The differences emerge from the greater abundance available in the vast American forests. This meant that, after the initial years of extreme hardship, the American settler could put far greater distance between himself and dependence than the English forester. Accumulating property could become more than a search for competency, it could become an end in itself: a never-ceasing cycle of investment, sale and reinvestment in pursuit of ever-mounting profits. In short, conditions encouraged many (but not all) to conclude that outstripping their neighbours in a competitive race for wealth and its power provided the only sure independence: the devil could take the hindmost.[1]

Early American historians debate when and how most rural folk

251

absorbed the capitalist ethos. Some see the conversion as voluntary and
occurring early in the colonial era; others regard the transition as
essentially involuntary and occurring in most locales quite late, after the
American Revolution. This paper does not attempt to characterize and
date the transition to capitalism in the colonies as a whole. Instead, it
examines an episode for the points of tension in rural Americans' minds
over how to use the American wilderness to underwrite a freedom from
dependence. This episode begins with a direct confrontation across class
lines: poor backcountry squatters obstruct the attempts of a wealthy
landed proprietor to expand his claim to include their homesteads. But
the proprietor – General Henry Knox, a distinguished veteran of the
Revolutionary War and of President George Washington's Cabinet –
triumphs by enlisting another set of common folk to his capitalist vision
of land use and social relations.[2]

As chief heir to the Waldo Patent, General Henry Knox claimed
thousands of wilderness acres in central Maine, then a part of the
Commonwealth of Massachusetts. He meant to add to his fortune by
retailing lots of 100–200 acres to actual settlers at $2–6 an acre. In the
spring of 1800 the general prepared a party of surveyors to venture into
his 'backlands' located north-west of the coastal towns along the western
shore of Penobscot Bay. He charged the surveyors with subdividing the
tract into four townships each containing over one hundred settlers' lots.
He named the projected townships Knox, Lincoln (now Thorndike),
Washington (now Brooks) and Jackson, to honour himself and his close
friends, Generals Benjamin Lincoln, George Washington and Henry
Jackson. By marking the survey lines before settlers arrived in the
'backlands' Knox hoped to avoid the problems with squatters endemic
to central Maine. The general meant to screen would-be settlers and
suffer only men 'of good character' on to his claim, men who would not
plunder the timber on unsold lots and who would not suffer squatters
into their midst. No one could settle without first posting both a note
and a mortgage as double security for payment in cash over the ensuing
three years. In May Knox announced his programme with printed
notices posted in the coastal towns at the edge of his backlands. These
proclaimed his intent to mandate 'orderly settlement' in contrast to the
'unauthorized intrusions' that were 'entirely subversive of the blessings
of the social compact'.[3]

But Henry Knox's surveyors were too late. In July 1800 they entered
the backlands and found about fifty families living in crude one-room
cabins beside small new clearings filled with stumps. Those scattered
settlers were the sons, daughters, brothers and sisters of several hundred
other families dwelling to the west on the Plymouth Patent, just beyond

the fringe of Knox's claim. The ill-defined boundary between the two patents bisected the hinterland between the Kennebeck River to the west and the Penobscot River and Bay to the east; this was the Sheepscot backcountry. Its inhabitants were squatters who regarded proprietary surveys as the advance guard of an encroaching enemy. On the morning of 18 July 1800 seven of Knox's surveyors led by Robert Houston of Belfast ran a line in Lincoln (now Thorndike), the north-westernmost of the four projected townships. A scouting party of armed squatters 'blacked and disguised like Indians' ambushed the surveyors wounding three with their volley. Knox's servants withdrew to Belfast on the coast and the general abandoned his efforts until the next spring. George Ulmer, one of Knox's land agents, observed, 'Our defeat occasioned exultation among the greater part of the people in the suspected regions on the Plymouth Company's lands.' In June 1801 Knox sent his survey-ors back into the backlands, but on the 22nd an ambush again sent them reeling back to Belfast, bearing a wounded man with them.[4]

Few of the suspected 'White Indians' dwelled on the backlands; most came from the adjoining Plymouth Patent or from Davistown, a settle-ment within the Twenty Associates' claim. After touring the Sheepscot backcountry in August 1801 two of Knox's agents, the Reverend Thurston Whiting and Major Benjamin Brackett, explained that settler solidarity extended across patent lines. 'The idea of making "a common cause" of the disputes between proprietors & settlers seems to have been a favorite & prevalent idea with the latter.' Knox's surveys threat-ened to pre-empt a district that otherwise would continue to be settled by the friends and relatives of the neighbouring squatters. This preemp-tion would diminish their allies in the backcountry, hindering their capacity to resist the Plymouth Company (or 'Kennebeck Proprietors') and Twenty Associates. Whiting and Brackett found that the back-country inhabitants

> considered the cause of the settlers on both patents as a common cause. That their enterprise was the nature of 'changing work,' that they expected the time would come when they would need the assistance of their brethren & neighbours on the Waldo Patent to drive off surveyors from the Plymouth Patent, that if the settlers of the W[aldo] patent were quieted they should have no ally nigh at hand to join them in their warfare with the Plymo[uth] Co[mpany].

Knox concluded that the squatters opposed 'the orderly settlement of the country' because they were 'desirous of having settlers on the Waldo Patent of the same description as themselves'.[5]

Never one to brook insubordination the general resented poor backcountry settlers who exploited their isolation from authority to resist his claims. In lurid tones he warned the governor that unless he sent in troops to impose order 'a collection will soon be made of the most audacious and blood thirsty villains that ever disgraced the surface of New England'. In a letter probably drafted by Knox, his agents assured the governor that the backcountry 'banditti' had formed 'a settlement of men in opposition to the rights of property and the utter subversion of all laws relative thereto'. Privately the general could not believe that anyone would oppose his plans: 'My object is to fill the country with industrious settlers and to make it flourish in all respects. A few wretches may from the darkness of ignorance oppose my views but they cannot be many.'[6]

This scene – a powerful gentleman offended by an independent people dwelling in a forest recess and exercising competing claims to 'his' property – is familiar to those who have read Christopher Hill's work. He and other scholars have described seventeenth-century England's forest recesses inhabited by squatters who prized their relative isolation. They abhorred dependence on wage labour or servitude as akin to chattel slavery. England's poor knew, without reading John Locke, that only men with property enjoyed any liberty. Determined to maintain their tenuous autonomy, the forest folk were extremely defensive of the paltry property that barely enabled them to obtain their own subsistence.[7]

In the seventeenth century, at the same moment that England's forest recesses virtually vanished as an alternative vision of society, many of England's poor found a vast new forest refuge across the Atlantic in North America. Professor Hill points out that the same pool of itinerant labourers and craftsmen who roamed the English countryside, squatted in forest recesses, served in armies and in ships' crews, or crowded into London's burgeoning slums, also spilled across the Atlantic to the new colonies. They were, he notes, 'prepared to run desperate risks in the hope of obtaining the secure freehold land (and with its status) to which they could never aspire in overcrowded England'. They brought with them an insistence that those in need had a just priority to seize the vacant lands and their resources. Consequently, during the eighteenth and early nineteenth centuries, virtually all observers of American frontier settlement contemptuously described the earliest settlers as desperately poor men profoundly disrespectful of authority and determined to live free from levies to support their 'betters'. Instead of the forest expanding to embrace the nation and wither away private property, as the Diggers had hoped, the nation conquered a vast new forest where for a few generations unprecedented numbers could obtain their own lots of land. By the close of the American colonial era unprecedented numbers of Englishmen owned land, mostly in the colonies where the vast new tracts compensated for the ongoing constriction of the yeomanry in the homeland.[8]

The sheer magnitude of the American forest meant that poor folk could obtain resources unprecedented and undreamed of in over-crowded England where thousands envied those few able to procure clear title to a mere handful of acres. American abundance meant new opportunities and new economic strategies in pursuit of the same goal: freedom from dependence. Faced with a far more constraining world of scarce resources and powerful and entrenched enemies, the Diggers had resorted to mutual support and collective work as a permanent model. By contrast, in the American world of seemingly endless forest, co-operative work was an occasional, festive affair: barn-raisings, wool-combings, log-rollings, corn-huskings and spinning-bees. These 'chang-ing works' brought settlers together to socialize and to perform tasks beyond the capacity of a single nuclear family. As such they supple-mented and sustained the private ownership of extensive (100 acres or more) homesteads by individual families. In America fathers could often obtain enough land to settle their sons nearby on substantial homesteads of their own. Application of English notions of the poor man's customary rights to commons land to America's vast wilderness created 'the homestead ethic', the idea that poor men should be able to lay unobstructed claim to as much land as they and their children could improve (but not more). In 1760 Benjamin Franklin explained that industrial wage labour would not soon develop in America because 'no man who can have a piece of land of his own, sufficient to subsist his family in plenty, is poor enough to be a manufacturer and work for a master'. American historian Jack P. Greene notes, 'Perhaps the most powerful drive in the British-American colonizing process from the seventeenth century through much of the nineteenth century, and from the eastern to the western coasts of North America, was the drive for *personal independence*.'[9]

But, as Henry Knox could attest, this new scale of opportunity did not mean an absence of conflict in the American backcountry. Indeed direct, free access to America's wilderness land rarely went unchal-lenged. The privileged few with superior political power meant to expand their fortunes by securing a share in the produce that the settlers' labour extracted from the soil. As judicial, executive and legislative officers they meant to finance their fees and salaries with taxes levied upon backcountry settlers. Often they exercised their political capital to procure colonial land grants amounting to thousands, and sometimes hundreds of thousands of acres. These 'great proprietors' meant to profit by obliging settlers present and future to purchase or rent their home-steads. By virtue of their politically acquired 'title' to the land these proprietors could resort to the judiciary for assistance against 'squatters', those who refused to buy or rent. In this light the titles sold by proprietors were amnesties from their prosecutions.[10]

Ideology reinforced self-interest in these efforts to impose payments on backcountry settlers. With characteristic optimism Franklin felt that the occupation of wild land by poor men wrought a double benefit: settlers became propertied and civilized by converting the wilderness into an agricultural landscape. But many other gentlemen distrusted the capacity of the poor to shift for themselves; they were certain that the poor abused unregulated access to the forest, degrading themselves as well as the land. America's gentlemen shared their English counterparts' deep concern over forest refuges that enabled clusters of poor folk to apparently live outside the national economy. They felt that whenever the poor folk could live in economic autonomy they lapsed into idle dissipation, declining to contribute their purposeful labour to national wealth and power. This was alarming enough in England where only a dwindling number of confined forests were at stake; but in America the abundant wilderness raised the chilling (to gentle folk) prospect that the poor would pre-empt the continent. They would establish a squatter barbarism that would squander the continent's resources to underwrite their drunken indolence. This would imperil America's potential as a disciplined, commercial society.[11]

Throughout British North America observers complained that no sooner had the Indians been dispossessed from the land but the allegedly idle poor took their place. In 1808 A.J. Dallas, a New York landlord's lawyer, wrote of backcountry squatters, 'The Indians have hardly with-drawn from the ground; and they are succeeded by a population almost as rude and as ferocious as themselves, coming from the most part from countries, where the poor know nothing of the blessings of property and care little about its rights.' In 1758 a Boston minister, the Reverend Thomas Barnard, lamented that abundant free land enabled too many frontier folk to support themselves 'by the spontaneous Products of Nature with Little Labour; Experience has shewn, that Habits of Idle-ness and Intemperance have been contracted, much to the public Damage'. Upon touring his backcountry land claims the Virginia gentry-man William Byrd lamented, 'Surely there is no place in the world where the inhabitants live with less labor than in North Carolina. It approaches nearest the description of lubberland than any other, by the great felicity of the climate, the easiness of raising provisions, and the slothfulness of the people.' With characteristic acerbity the Anglican Reverend Charles Woodmason ascribed the poverty of South Carolina's backcountry settlers to 'their extreme Indolence for they possess the finest country in America'.[12]

This perspective concluded that national development urged the displacement or re-education of the backcountry poor. This could be done by imposing incentives to additional labour beyond mere subsistence: taxes and land payments. These would impel people to what they would not do if left alone. They would either move on or adopt the disciplined labour and moral restraint necessary to meet their new responsibilities. The backcountry, its inhabitants and the nation would all benefit from this transformation. This was what Henry Knox meant by the 'orderly settlement' mandated by his surveys and land payments. This perspective promoted an insensitivity to backcountry complaints, an insensitivity that frequently brought settler resentments to the brink of rebellion.

Backcountry settlers preferred to ignore politics and concentrate on the hard work of developing their wilderness homesteads. Except in times of pressing danger from Indians or bandits they wanted government to leave them alone. But settlers could suddenly and explosively abandon their ordinary preoccupation with their private concerns whenever they concluded that their taxes or land payments had attained extortionate proportions. This conclusion pushed them to temporarily expand their concerns beyond the bounds of their particular farms. This conclusion obliged them to think about the public nature of their plight, of their common interests with other small farmers afflicted by the same pressures from the same foes: the furnishing merchant, the landlord and the county squire. In several backcountry districts this generated a succession of popular movements where settlers organized to violently resist execution of the laws. In each case the backcountry folk sought to protect the property that was their safeguard from dependence. Government was supposed to protect the property of 'the many' from the greed of 'the great'. Backcountry folk organized when, instead, government was seen as assisting 'the great' in their extortions. To defend their interests backcountry settlers insisted upon the right of local majorities to suspend the local operation of particular laws which they regarded as oppressive threats. By such local nullification they meant to oblige their rulers to reconsider and rescind the distasteful measures. Organizing their own militia units with elected captains, the backcountry insurgents acted to seal off their home regions from the operations of a legal establishment that they perceived as in the service of wealthy outsiders. To this end they obstructed surveyors, interrupted court sessions, prevented the service of legal writs in their locales, harassed potential witnesses against them, and forcibly liberated imprisoned compatriots.[13]

These insurgencies began in 1676 with Virginia's 'Bacon's Rebellion' over inadequate protection from Indians despite the mounting burden of taxes to support the colony's rulers in aristocratic style. In the 1740s and 1750s New Jersey settlers organized an extensive resistance against their proprietors. From 1753 to 1767 a succession of tenant and squatter uprisings threatened New York's manor-lords. In 1763 the 'Paxton Boys' of Pennsylvania's backcountry marched on Philadelphia to try to force the government to wage war on the Indians. In the late 1760s, when the politically dominant lowcountry refused to act against outlaws, South Carolina's backcountry 'Regulators' took up arms to establish their own vigilante court system and threatened to march on Charlestown. From 1768 to defeat at Alamance in 1771 North Carolina's backcountry 'Regulators' rebelled against their corrupt county cliques of merchants, lawyers, officers and speculators supported by the provincial government. In the 1770s Vermont's Yankee settlers threw off the control of land speculators by taking up arms to successfully secede from the state of New York.[14]

These backcountry insurgencies persisted after the American Revolution. In the 1780s Elyites and, subsequently, Shaysites in the backcountry of New Hampshire, Massachusetts, and parts of Connecticut and Vermont took up arms to escape burdensome taxes, heavy private debts and an expensive judicial system that collectively threatened to wrest away many of their farms. In the 1780s and 1790s Connecticut-born settlers in the upper Susquehanna Valley resisted Pennsylvania's authorities and land speculators. Rural pockets of armed resistance against some New York landlords persisted into the 1790s. In 1792 (the 'Whiskey Rebellion') and 1799 ('Fries Rebellion') parts of rural Pennsylvania took up arms against new federal taxes and land policies that favoured speculators over homesteaders. And, in the longest-simmering insurgency, beginning in the 1760s and persisting into the 1810s, central Maine's settlers resisted their great proprietors.[15]

In sum, Frederick Jackson Turner's notion of the frontier as a 'safety valve' – a source of abundant free land that drew off the discontented from the east, continuously diffusing class conflict – does not work very well when applied to the eighteenth century. The discontented may have pushed inland but instead of free land they found themselves pursued by the coastal 'great men' demanding distasteful taxes and land payments. During the eighteenth century the conflicting processes of frontier settlement and political fortune-building brought America's class tensions to a head in the backcountry. Frontier migration concentrated the most on discontented folk in backcountry districts. Possessing little else, the settlers clung with stubborn pride to the land that provided an independent subsistence if little more. Hunger for autonomy brought poor men to districts where local conditions demanded constant vigilance to preserve their independence. An outlaw raid, and Indian incursion, a plague of grasshoppers, a summer drought, a late spring, an early frost, the extortionate charges of county officials, a new tax, or the demands of a proprietor or landlord for payment, could imperil the settler's marginal surplus, plunging him into the dependence of debt, and perhaps ultimately deprive him of his land. So in times of stress settlers spoke with dread of losing their cherished freeholds and lapsing into the 'wooden shoes and uncombed hair' of 'peasants'.[16]

But the pressure upon the backcountry folk provides but half the answer to these episodes of insurgency. Rebellion is not an automatic response to a threshold of hardship. Many hard-pressed people have been unable to overtly rebel for lack of the proper circumstances – the necessary 'social room' to organize themselves and cultivate self-confidence in their struggle. In the words of George Rude and Eric Hobsbawm how people respond to perceived oppression 'depends on their situation among other human beings, on their environment, culture, tradition, and experience'. The same relative isolation that entailed marginality and a greater vulnerability to additional burdens also enabled backcountry settlers to think for themselves and organize to defend their autonomy. A backcountry rebellion began with some sense of pressing danger to their tenuous but jealously cherished autonomy. But none occurred unless the people in a given district could sustain a consensus that organized resistance was a moral imperative, that their foes were evil incarnate.

Rebellion did not occur where the rural poor had already lost their autonomy. In the eighteenth century eastern Maryland contained the colonies' largest proportion of landless whites; on the eve of the Revolution over half the colony's white population were tenants obliged to rent their homesteads. Gregory A. Stiverson's careful examination of their circumstances reconstructs a bleak picture: debt peonage, cramped, unfinished housing with dirt floors, and without window glass, or stone chimneys, men and the soil both exhausted by tobacco, a labour-intensive and land-eating crop. If rebellion emerged from deprivation alone, eastern Maryland should have been the most explosive district in British North America. In fact it experienced none of the rural unrest characteristic of most of the other colonies during the eighteenth century. The Maryland tenant lived amidst a confident and conspicuous planter elite that expected and received regular displays of deference. Long-standing economic ties for debt and rent to their 'betters' confirmed the tenantry to an acceptance of the status quo. Stiverson notes their susceptibility to 'the mental and motivational impairment that could result from abject poverty'. For some rural Americans rebellion was inconceivable. The pattern of tenant rebellion in New

York supports this point; the tenants in the older communities along the Hudson, amidst the landlords' 'seats', remained loyal; only the new settlements in the hills away from the river and the landlords participated in the anti-rent resistance. Similarly, Virginia escaped rural rebellion in the eighteenth century because the sons of its lowcountry elite moved into the backcountry as its settlement began.[18]

Relative isolation provided settlers with sufficient ideological autonomy to develop through discussion ideas relevant to protecting their interests. In colonial America wherever numerous men of wealth and standing resided they commanded sufficient dependence and deference to set the 'tone'. Their influence against 'licence' among their neighbours provided scant scope for men to conceive of challenging their authority. Migration to the frontier generally removed men to locales where no gentry resided to define the proper nature of order. Timothy Dwight conceived of the initial migration to a frontier district as a political process; referring to the first settlers he observed:

> After censuring the weakness and wickedness of their superiors ... in many an eloquent harangue, uttered by many a kitchen fire, in every blacksmith's shop, and in every corner of the streets, and finding all their efforts vain, they become at length discouraged; and, under the pressure of poverty, the fear of a jail, and the consciousness of public contempt leave their native places and betake themselves to the wilderness.

There they found like-minded men rather than reproving superiors.

> In established society, influence is chiefly the result of personal character, seen and known through the period in which the character is formed and the conduct by which it is displayed. In such a society ... a man of worth and wisdom will ... be almost always more respectfully regarded than persons destitute of these characteristics, and will have a superior efficacy on the affairs of those around him. But in a state of society recently begun, influence is chiefly gained by those who directly seek it; and these in almost all instances are the ardent and bustling. Such men ... clamor everywhere about liberty and rights, are patriots of course and jealous of the encroachments of those in power.[19]

Such a people 'jealous of the encroachments of those in power' and ready to 'clamour everywhere about liberty and rights' developed in the Sheepscot backcountry. Their ideas emerged from the interaction of their historical experiences with their geographic circumstances. Most spent their childhood or adolescence to the immediate south along central Maine's rugged Sagadahock coast, located between the Kennebeck and the St George's Rivers. Many descended from Scotch–Irish immigrants drawn there in 1730 by promises from Colonel David Dunbar of free Crown land grants. In 1731 under pressure from competing private proprietaries the Crown retreated from its claim to the region. This left the settlers without any legal title to defend themselves against proprietary ejectment suits. Those·proprietors generally failed to press these suits because successive Indian wars and the Revolution recurrently disrupted the region's courts during the next sixty years. Because so many of the proprietors remained loyal to Britain, the Revolution inspired the wishful belief that the Commonwealth of Massachusetts had confiscated the Sagadahock coast and its hinterland (the Sheepscot backcountry) for free settlement by those who most needed their own homestead. Harassed by British naval raids, and cut off from outside provisions, during the war hundreds of coastal inhabitants migrated up the Sheepscot and Damariscotta vallies to settle on the presumably free land in the hills. In the two decades after the war several thousand more men and women from throughout eastern New England followed the initial settlers into the Sheepscot backcountry. Most were war veterans or their relatives; they felt that no one deserved the Loyalists' lands more than the poorest of the victors. These settlers felt betrayed when in 1785 and 1788 the Massachusetts General Court reconfirmed the Waldo and Plymouth patents to the pre-war owners or their heirs. Pressured by renewed proprietary surveys, demands for payment and threats to sue, the settlers thought, read their Bibles and talked with one another. Particularly articulate, thoughtful and mystical men became popular local orators who helped to focus these explorations and rally conviction and consensus behind their conclusions. Wherever they gathered to consider the proprietors' demands for payment – at sawmills, firesides and taverns – settlers considered how and why they should take up arms to resist the law.[20]

In August 1801 Henry Knox sent Thurston Whiting and Benjamin Brackett into the region to investigate. They held extensive and remarkably frank discussions with individual settlers and mass meetings. Upon returning in early September they reported that the older settlements in the centre of the Sheespscot backcountry comprised 'the grand seed plot of sedition & insurrection'. They found

a striking similarity of temper & vein of talking among the inhabitants.... Their long & deep rooted repugnance to proprietors (whom they view as their natural enemies) & to every one that advocates their pretensions, the apprehension they must have of the precarious tenure by which they hold their lands & their habitual fear of being at some time or other disseized of them, has absolutely perverted their understanding & judgement & cankered & corrupted the best principles of the heart & withal induced a certain ferociousness in their countenances, gestures & language whenever *title of land* is the subject of conversation.

They described previously pacific settlers from the backcountry's periphery who visited the core settlements: 'their tempers appear to be soured & they discover systems of ill-nature & malevolence.'[21]

What was the content of their dangerous 'pretensions'? The settlers' imperilled autonomy enabled and pushed these backcountry people to rediscover ideas familiar to Gerrard Winstanley and his fellow Diggers. In August 1801 Thurston Whiting and Benjamin Brackett toured the Sheepscot backcountry and held extensive meetings and conversations with the insurgents. Knox's emissaries found that the squatters felt that the American Revolution was incomplete and ongoing. In their eyes Henry Knox and the other proprietors were 'Tories', betrayers of the poor veteran's trust, the equivalents of Oliver Cromwell and the Puritan magnates of the English Revolution. Whiting and Bracknett summarized what they heard.

> Instead of reasoning they resort to harangue. All old & young, husbands & wives, mothers & sons have gotten the same story by rote & two or three demagogues in & about Sheepscott Pond Settlement deliver it with a great deal of impassioned & boisterous eloquence. 'We fought for land & liberty & it is hard if we can't enjoy either. We once defended this land at the point of the bayonet & if drove to the necessity are now equally united, ready & zealous to defend it again in the same way. It is as good to die by the sword as by the famine & we shall prefer the [former]. Who can have a better right to the land than we who have fought for it, subdued it & made it valuable which if we had not done no proprietor would ever have enquired after it. God gave the earth to the children. We own no other proprietor. Wild land ought to be as free as common air. These lands once belonged to King George. He lost them by the American Revolution & they became the property of the people who defended & won them. The General Court did wrong & what they had no right to do when they granted them in such large quantities to certain companies & individuals & the bad acts of government are not binding on the subject.'[22]

The expressions that it is better to die by the sword than by famine and that God gave the earth for his children to share, and the idea that the King's land ought to go to the poor who bore the brunt of the revolutionary war are all commonplaces in Digger rhetoric. Maine's squatters certainly possessed neither well-thumbed copies of Winstanley's pamphlets nor even any sort of specific folk memory about the man. Nor did they mean to carry these ideas to his collectivist conclusion; at no time did they move away from their devotion to private property as socially liberating if equally available to all. Rather, I would suggest that Maine's squatters, like Diggers before them, operated from a militantly Protestant popular culture with the Bible as its rhetorical touchstone. Furthermore, Maine's squatters found themselves in an analogous position: poor veterans short-changed by their revolution when its leaders denied them the free land they sought. Drawing from their similar popular culture to help them deal with a similar situation. Maine's 'White Indians' came to speak a language of protest much like that of their Digger predecessors.[23]

These ideas, the work of years of fireside and woodlot meetings, took root in the settlers' minds, providing a strong line of defence against Whiting and Brackett's insistence that the settlers' notions were dangerously novel 'in the eyes of all virtuous, good citizens, in the eyes of government & of the world & if persisted in could not fail to bring down wretchedness & ruin on themselves & families'. In their report to Knox the emissaries reported, 'They appear to have contracted an inflexible perversity & obduracy of mind which renders them callous to all argument & persuasion. They are determined to prevent the survey of lands on your patent as well as that of the Plymo[uth] Company at the hazard of everything dear & valuable on earth.' Relative isolation enabled the settlers to nurse their ideas – ideas so different from what passed for the truth, the just, the necessary, the obvious in the more hierarchical world they had left – through the fragile initial stage of experimentation. The settlers had time to hone their notions into utter conviction and consensus. Without these the White Indians had no chance resisting Henry Knox, the Plymouth Company and the Commonwealth of Massachusetts.[24]

The ideas that stiffened the squatters' resolve were not innate to the common folk throughout America; they were the product of men and women under particular pressures who dwelled in circumstances that encouraged them to think anew about issues of property and authority. Henry Knox ultimately prevailed over them because he could hire many poor men from older towns outside the backcountry to do his bidding: men without the opportunity to fundamentally challenge the pre-eminence of the powerful, men not schooled by experience to trust in one another against gentlemen of wealth and standing, men who dared not directly occupy the wild lands they sought for cherished independence. Henry Knox could bank on their 'realism', their limited sense of the possible, their assurance that the proprietors and the state must prevail. Knox invited these common folk to conclude that their best opportunity lay in serving the certain victors; in that manner they could earn generous wages and relatively favourable terms for the lands they helped to wrest away.

At Knox's request, on the night of 25 June 1801 Captain Thomas Knowlton led a company of militia from the coastal towns of Northport and Belfast into the backcountry to arrest settlers suspected of attacking Knox's surveyors. The militia men were reluctant to turn out until Knowlton appealed to their poverty with a pledge 'that government would handsomely reward their services'. He turned out forty-five men, only six of whom came from Northport, which had a troubled history with Knox's ownership. Instead, the great majority came from Belfast, an adjoining commercial town with no absentee great proprietor but with more than its share of poor newcomers inexperienced with the land unrest but eager to earn a dollar. Need dictated the service of most. Thirty of the forty-five appeared on Belfast's 1801 tax list. Twenty-one of the thirty possessed no improved land and sixteen of them no land at all. Only six owned a horse (two of them were officers), a symbol of economic achievement. Only nine had any cattle and only ten possessed any oxen. Moreover, twelve possessed no ratable property at all, paying tax only on their poll. Transients were well represented among Knowlton's men; half (fifteen) were not recorded in the town's federal census return taken the year before and almost half (thirteen) were gone by the 1810 census. Marching overnight to Lincoln (Thorndike), Sandy Stream (part of Unity) and Smithtown (Freedom), Knowlton's men surprised and seized seven more suspects who they roughly dragged back to Belfast. After interrogation a justice of the peace released two and dispatched the remaining five across the bay to join three other suspects already gaoled in Castine.[25]

The arrest and brutal treatment accorded the suspects enraged their neighbours. Musket-armed men who were, in George Ulmer's words, 'dressed in the Indian stile & perfectly black' gathered on Belfast's outskirts. On the morning of the 26th they briefly seized Northport's blacksmith, John Clark, when he ventured out with a basket to collect coal from 'a cole pit'. After interrogating him about the prisoners' whereabouts and about their guards, the White Indians sent him back toward Belfast with their threat to burn that town to the ground for assisting the proprietary enemy. 'This place', Ulmer wrote from Belfast, 'is in constant alarm.' But the quick removal of the prisoners across Penobscot Bay and the continued presence of militia men under arms in the streets of Belfast convinced the White Indians to disperse to their backcountry homes.[26]

For lack of evidence the magistrates in Castine released all but three of the arrested suspects. Intent on liberating the remaining three, on 4 July 1801 hundreds of armed men mustered in the backcountry for a march on Castine. It was the twenty-fifth anniversary of American independence and the sixteenth anniversary for the General Court's confirmation of the Waldo Patent to Henry Knox and the other Waldo heirs. The largest body – from 200–300 men – massed at Reed's tavern in Davistown. A second body of about 150 men assembled at Smithtown. Another body of 100 men in Waldoborough, on the southern edge of the backcountry, and Captain Spencer's militia company at Sebasticook, on the northern end, held themselves in reserve, prepared to turn out if even greater numbers were needed. The main body at Reed's tavern elected officers, cast bullets, filled their canteens with rum, and prepared to march. At the last minute Davistown's Reverend William Pickles interceded, insisting that there was no need to proceed because the remaining prisoners had been, or would soon be, released on bail. The settlers agreed to wait a day before marching. When, the next day, one of the released prisoners arrived to confirm Pickles's information the White Indians dispersed to their homes. For lack of willing witnesses the court ultimately discharged the suspects.[27]

In late August the general prepared his third attempt to survey the backlands. Knox could not legally obtain what he called 'the strong arm of government to smite ye guilty' until a clear-cut act of 'insurrection' occurred involving a large body of men who were obviously beyond the capacity of the local authorities to control. So far the survey attacks had been by small patrols that did not quite cross the legal threshold of 'insurrection'. Recognizing the need to provoke an unambiguous confrontation involving large numbers of his opponents, Knox prepared a survey party composed of over twenty hired and armed men: only a large body of White Indians, not a small patrol, could stop such a survey. On 29 August 1801 George Ulmer led twenty-four armed surveyors into the backlands. For a week Ulmer's party pressed their survey without interruption, although they were frequently conscious of a White Indian patrol at their heels. Apparently lacking the numbers to confront Ulmer's party and awaiting reinforcements from their home settlements, the patrol instead struck at two nearby settlers who assisted the surveyors. On the night of 3 September the 'Jacobins of the wilderness', as Ulmer called them, secretly set fire to and destroyed the barns belonging to Joseph Jones of Lincoln (Thorndike) and Benjamin Bartlett of Sandy Stream (part of Unity).[28]

At last, on 9 September, four days after Ulmer's party finished their work, about seventy armed men from Sheepscot Great Pond, Davistown, Patricktown and Smithtown mustered in Smithtown. They sat down to cast bullets for the expected battle. Waterman Thomas found them there and conversed with one of their officers, Jonathan Bartlett of Sheepscot Great Pond, 'who informed me that they ware going a bare hunting'. Others were somewhat more forthright, saying, 'They ware going up the country to sittle as neighbours to Esqr. Ulmer who was a dam cross fellow and it was necessary to go armed as he was settled under a guard of armed men.' The next day the Liberty Men ventured into Lincoln and Jackson in search of the surveyors; finding none they systematically followed their lines, pulled up every stake, scattered the stone monuments at the corners, and cut out all the lot numbers inscribed on the corner trees. To intimidate Jackson's Cates family who had assisted the surveyors, the White Indians fired frequent vollies into the air and burned a three ton stack of hay.[29]

On 17 September, a week after the White Indians departed for home, another armed survey party – this time twenty-nine in number and led by John Gleason of Thomaston – marched into the backlands to re-survey what had been damaged. They finished the work a week later without incident despite repeated warnings of an impending attack 'determined to murder & massacre the whole of our party'.[30]

Knox had won. On his fourth try Knox had at last secured control over the valuable backland district that he claimed. With the western-most half of the backlands completely surveyed by Gleason's party, Knox secured 'a sort of barrier ... against the lawless' enabling him to safely survey the unsettled eastern half at a quarter of the expense with a handful of unarmed men. Recognizing Knox's triumph, his three leading opponents in the backlands, Samual Parkhurst, John Phinney and John Foot sued for peace, promising to pay his price for their lots.[31]

To the victor went the spoils. With the surveys finished, in the late autumn of 1801 Knox summoned all who had agreed for or wished to buy his backlands lots to come to 'Montpelier', his mansion in coastal Thomaston. They trooped to Thomaston by the dozen to post their notes and mortgages in exchange for the general's bonds to deliver a warrantee deed for a specified lot in a specified township in three years when the payments were to be complete. One hundred and thirty-six men agreed to pay a total of $72,267.63 for a combined 24,460 acres, or an average of $2.95 per acre and $531.38 per purchase. Two-thirds of the purchasers (89 of 136) bought 200 acres. Almost all the rest (39 of 47) bought 100 acres. Twenty-five of the purchasers had served in Knowlton's posse, or in the armed surveys, some in both. The leading dissidents – Parkhurst, Phinney and Foot – collectively pledged to pay $872 for their lots; by itself this sum probably covered the entire cost of Knox's eighteen-month campaign to secure the backlands. And because the sales made in 1801 represented only a third of the lots available in the backlands, Knox stood to make even more money in ensuing years selling the remaining lots at prices in excess of $5 an acre.[32]

In a letter to his wife Lucy in Boston the general trumpeted his victory, 'as it confirms my judgement of the measures I have pursued. This you will call vanity. I own it and rejoice therein. But when the lowest acre will command obligations for 5 dollars with the good will of the people, and when hope points to no distant period *at ten* and higher, the heart that has been compelled to endure anguish for deficiency has a well founded claim to dance a little. But this [is] between ourselves.' For Knox, his settlers' participation in the speculative mindset that could accept paying $3 an acre in anticipation of a sustained rise in land values to $5 and $10 an acre was as important as the immediate notes and mortgages.[33]

In mid September an informant, Nathaniel Robinson of Sheepscot Great Pond, explained why his neighbours failed to respond to Gleason's armed survey, 'I heard today that they had given up the idea of resistance on K[nox]'s patten for this – because those on it were so fond of buying.' Knox's sustained pressure with hired surveyors first wore down the resolve of the dispersed, vulnerable backlanders. Indeed several backlanders broke with the majority to actively assist the surveyors. They seem to have concluded that the insurgents could not long hold out against the persistent application of Henry Knox's wealth; they meant to obtain favourable terms by assisting in the general's success. Most of the backlanders seem to have lapsed into a watchful neutrality, hopeful that their Plymouth patent neighbours would repel Knox's surveys, but no longer daring to take an open stand with them. With a critical corn harvest to get in, the Sheepscot backcountry's settlers no longer had the time or the patience to help those who would not do much to help themselves.[34]

Given the previous degree of settler anger the Sheepscotters' sudden withdrawal from the contest for the backlands is very striking. But this pattern of suddenly unleashed resentments, momentarily intense intellectual creativity, and an equally sudden relapse into accommodation recurs in all populist movements throughout American history. In his search for personal independence the farmer felt pulled by both a fascination with a collective assertion of egalitarian hope and by the suspicion that he could do no better than through the private pursuit of individual advantage. At his most quiescent he sustained 'a deep, if in ordinary times usually sublimated, yearning for fraternity and communal dependence'. At his most rebellious, he retained fears about the probability of success and about the personal consequences of neglecting his private interests. Given the chronic and intensive demands of this private homestead for his labour the American farmer could not long give himself over to mass meetings and military musters. When militant action did not yield quick results against the entrenched foe he could quickly abandon his public commitment, leaving his neighbours to look after themselves.[35]

Knox could not have prevailed without men to do his bidding. Two lists in his papers reveal the names of forty-seven men who, at various times, served in the backlands surveys. Except the leaders – John Gleason, Robert Houston, Philip Ulmer, George Ulmer, Bradstreet Wiggins and Jonathan Wilson – the survey workers were chiefly young men new to the region. Excluding the six leaders, only four of the fifty-one workers appeared on the 1800 federal census for Hancock county. Belfast, a coastal town committed to mercantile enterprise and lacking any legacy of warfare against proprietors, supplied the largest contingent; nineteen of the fifty-one appeared on the 1801 tax list for that town. As the principal market town for the western shore of Penobscot Bay, Belfast attracted a steady stream of poor newcomers, mostly young, seeking wages immediately while looking out for a piece of land to eventually settle on in the interior. In Belfast they could find work by the day or by the month as farmhands, dockworkers, land-clearers and journeymen artisans while they familiarized themselves with the local opportunities to obtain land. This meant that Belfast had a large body of men who owned neither land nor their own house. In 1801 a third of the resident taxpayers (57 of 174) owned no real estate. That was twice the percentage of landless taxpayers in the same year in the adjoining town of Northport (17 of 108, or 16 per cent), a much poorer town with little commerce and, consequently, little opportunity for wage labour. Similarly, in 1801 only 14 per cent (40 of 279) of the taxpayers in Balltown – the principal settlement in the Sheepscot backcountry and the home of many of the White Indians – possessed no land of their own.[36]

Knox's servants recruited his survey assistants, just as they had recruited Knowlton's posse, from the newly arrived labouring poor in Belfast. Fifteen of the nineteen to be found on the 1801 Belfast tax list possessed no real estate; no doubt most of the eighteen others who can be linked to no other town in the area were landless men who arrived in Belfast after the town's assessors took the valuation.[37]

As new arrivals these men possessed no prior experience with the land conflict that had prepared the Sheepscot backcountry squatters to take up arms against the proprietors. Where the squatter was already in possession of land and regarded the proprietor as an unwanted interloper who sought to extort deserved payment from him, the Belfast newcomer was landless and arrived in 1800 or 1801 after Knox had secured hegemony over the nearby coastal lands. If direct access to wild lands in the remote interior allowed the settlers to develop their own independent notions and rules about property, Belfast's newcomers had never had the opportunity or time to think such thoughts. In contrast to the backcountry settlers who passed through the Sagadahock coastal communities with a tradition reaching back to Colonel Dunbar of hostility to proprietors, most of Belfast's newcomers came from older communities in western Maine, communities that lacked such a tradition. As younger men who had not served in the Revolution they lacked the mixed sense of grievance and determination that fuelled the backcountry resistance. These newcomers migrated from towns where land could only be acquired by purchase; they sought land at a time when the coastal inhabitants in the adjoining towns had come to accept Knox's control, and at a time of escalating local land prices that seemed to promise early purchasers a certain profit. Naturally, obtaining a piece of Henry Knox's land before the price went up was their principal concern. The chainmen and guards in Knox's surveys earned unusually high wages – a dollar a day – at least twice the going rate for day labour at that time. In addition, they learned the conditions and opportunities available in the backlands and got first pick of the lots.[38]

Knox shrewdly designed his land sales programme to develop his purchasers' acquisitive commitment to economic individualism. In this way he meant to link their interest with his own. Men who signed for his lands in 1801 could obtain 200 acres apiece at $2–3 per acre. Knox pledged that subsequent arrivals would have to pay at least $5 an acre. Because 100 acres was sufficient for a farm the first settlers could develop half their 200-acre 'double lots' for profitable future sale to latecomers while retaining the other half as a homestead. In this manner Knox held out the lure that ever increasing land values would ultimately enable the first settlers to obtain 100 acres without cost. As fellow capitalists they would share with their proprietor in the land market's anticipated boom. Latecomers would foot the bill. Knox hoped to develop among the earliest arrivals – who would exercise considerable influence over their maturing children and subsequent arrivals – an 'interest' that supported his claim and his efforts to steadily increase the price of land.[39]

A September 1801 exchange in a Belfast blacksmith shop reveals the yawning gap that separated backcountry settlers with their notion of common struggle rooted in the Revolution from younger newcomers who saw no way to get a landed foothold except by individual effort within the prevailing context of property and power. In August 1800 Waterman Thomas of Waldoborough returned from a tour of the backcountry with a renewed appreciation of those for whom the American Revolution was still alive. *En route* home he struck up a conversation with the working men gathered at a Belfast blacksmith's shop. He insisted that no settler should have to pay more than one dollar per acre to a proprietor. He then pointedly asked, 'Who would go on surveying land for General Knox and raising the price to 5 dollars p[er] acre?' A newcomer named William Stewart replied that 'he would for one and why should he not have five dollars p[er] acre if the settlers were willing to give it?' Thomas spoke for the moral economy of the Sheepscot backcountry and asked who could undercut the claims of fellow labouring men. Stewart saw it as a simple matter of supply and demand: Henry Knox deserved whatever the market would bear and the Belfast labourer ought to make the best of any artificially inflated wage. The devil could take the backcountry settlers; Stewart would follow Henry Knox in driving the hardest bargain he could. Such matter-of-fact acceptance of the market and of Henry Knox's title among the swelling number of newcomers entering the frontier through Belfast represented the tide turning against the White Indians.[40]

The newcomers' pursuit of individual advantage came at the expense of the backcountry settlers; those who lived in the backlands had to pay several hundred dollars to secure their homesteads from an ejectment suit, those who lived on the adjoining Plymouth Patent lost allies and a stock of vacant lands to provide homesteads for their children. Ironically, the survey assistants owed their good wages to the White Indians; were it not for their resistance, Henry Knox would not have had to hire so many men at such an expensive rate. But the general knew that the generous wage he paid to his survey guards and assistants was in fact a pittance compared to the returns their work guaranteed him from the settlers, present and future. The most expensive of Knox's several backlands' surveys, Gleason's triumphant survey in September 1801, cost the general $142.53: this was less than what he subsequently received for a single 100-acre lot in that tract, and the surveys sliced the backlands into over 400 lots. It is unlikely that Knox's total expenses for the entire year and a half struggle to conquer the backlands exceeded $800, an amount he recouped by selling three double lots.[41]

Loss of the backlands staggered the settlers in the balance of the Sheepscot backcountry, inducing about half of them to come to terms in 1803–4 when the Plymouth Company and the Commonwealth established a special commission that awarded title to most applicants for between one and two dollars an acre. A second wave of agreements in 1808–10 brought most of the rest to pay between two and four dollars an acre. A few pockets of violent resistance persisted until about 1820.[42]

Notes

I am grateful to Samuel Kline Cohn, Jr, Robert A. Gross, James P.P. Horn and Marvin Meyers for their helpful criticism of this essay.
    1. For the British literature see Alan Everitt, 'Farm Labourers', Ch. 7 of Joan Thirsk, ed., *The Agrarian History of England and Wales*, vol. 4, *1500–1640* (Cambridge, 1967), pp. 396–465; Joan Thirsk, *Economic Policy and Projects: The Development of a*

Consumer Society in Early Modern England (Oxford, 1978); Douglas Hay, 'Poaching and the Game Laws on Cannock Chase', in Hay *et al.*, eds., *Albion's Fatal Tree: Crime and Society in Eighteenth-Century England* (New York, 1975), pp. 189–253; E.P. Thompson, *Whigs and Hunters: The Origin of the Black Act* (London, 1975); E.P. Thompson, 'The Grid of Inheritance: A Comment', in Jack Goody *et al.*, eds., *Family and Inheritance: Rural Society in Western Europe, 1200–1800* (New York, 1976), pp. 329–40; Christopher Hill, 'Puritans and "The Dark Corners of the Land"', in Christopher Hill, *Change and Continuity in Seventeenth-Century England* (Cambridge, 1975), pp. 3–47; and Christopher Hill, *The World Turned Upside Down: Radical Ideas During the English Revolution* (New York, 1972), pp. 32–44. On America see Richard Maxwell Brown, 'Back Country Rebellions and the Homestead Ethic in America, 1740–1799', in Richard Maxwell Brown and Don E. Fehrenbacher, eds., *Tradition, Conflict, and Modernization: Perspectives on the American Revolution* (New York, 1977), pp. 73–96; Barbara Karsky, 'Agrarian Radicalism in the Late Revolutionary Period, 1780–1795', in Erich Angermann *et al.*, eds., *New Wine in Old Skins: A Comparative View of Socio-Political Structures and Values Affecting the American Revolution* (Stuttgart, 1976), pp. 88–108; Edward Countryman, 'Out of the Bounds of the Law: Northern Land Rioters in the Eighteenth Century', in Alfred F. Young, ed., *The American Revolution: Explorations in the History of American Radicalism* (DeKalb, Ill., 1976), pp. 39–61; and Elisha P. Douglass, 'A Three-Fold American Revolution', in John Parker and Carol Urness, eds., *The American Revolution: A Heritage of Change* (Minneapolis, Minn., 1975), pp. 69–83. On British North America's abundant wilderness land allowing homesteads impossible in the cramped forests of England see the 1774 commentary of the anonymous British visitor to the colonies in Harry J. Carmen, ed., *American Husbandry* (New York, 1939), pp. 178–80.

2. The literature on this question is voluminous. For the early and voluntary perspective see Charles S. Grant, *Democracy in the Connecticut Frontier Town of Kent* (New York, 1961); James Lemon, *The Best Poor Man's Country: A Geographical Study of Early Southeastern Pennsylvania* (Baltimore, 1972); and Winifred B. Rothenberg, 'The Market and Massachusetts Farmers, 1750–1855', *Journal of Economic History*, vol. 61 (1981), pp. 283–314. For the late and involuntary perspective see Christopher Clark, 'The Household Economy: Market Exchange and the Rise of Capitalism in the Connecticut Valley, 1800–1860', Journal of Social History, vol. 13 (1979), pp. 169–83; James A. Henretta, 'Families and Farms: Mentalité in Pre-Industrial America', *William and Mary Quarterly*, 3rd series, vol. 35 (1978), pp. 3–32; and Michael Merrill, 'Cash Is Good to Eat: Self-Sufficiency and Exchange in the Rural Economy of the United States', *Radical History Review* (Winter 1977), pp. 42–71.

3. Indenture of Henry Knox with George Ulmer and Benjamin Smith, 22 May 1800, and Smith and Ulmer to Knox, 25 May 1800, Land Record Book, Henry Knox Papers (HKP hereafter), Maine Historical Society, Portland, Maine (MeHS hereafter). George Ulmer to Henry Knox, 8 September 1800, Knox to Ulmer, 5 June 1801, and Henry Knox's notice, 26 May 1800, HKP 43:99, 44:1 and 52:79, Massachusetts Historical Society, Boston, Massachusetts (MHS hereafter).

4. George Ulmer to Henry Knox, 14 August 1800, Land Records Book HKP, MeHs; Knox to Ulmer, 22 July 1801, HKP 44:34, MHS; Thurston Whiting and Benjamin Brackett to Henry Knox, 7 September 1801, HKP 52:87, MH5. Robert Houston's deposition, 14 August 1800, Bradstreet Wiggins's deposition, 15 August 1800, and George Ulmer to Henry Knox, 23 July 1800, Related Papers filed under Resolve of 15 November 1800, Massachusetts State Archives, Boston, Massachusetts (MA hereafter); Ulmer to Knox, 10 August 1800, HKP 43:78, MHS; and Ulmer to Knox, 6 November 1801. HKP 44:121, MHS. George Ulmer to Henry Knox, 18 March 1801, Knox to Ulmer, 28 May and 5 June 1801, Ulmer to Knox, 20 June 1801 and Robert Houston to Knox, 26 June 1801, HKP 43:153, 174, 44:1, 8 and 13, MHS; George Ulmer *et al.*, deposition, 31 October 1801, Box 6 HKP, MeHS.

5. Thurston Whiting and Benjamin Brackett to Henry Knox, 7 September 1801, HKP 52:87, MHS; and Henry Knox memo, n.d., c.1801, HKP 52:89, MHS. On roaming crowds to discipline Tories and the phenomenon of neighbouring communities 'changing works' in these affairs see Dirk Hoerder, *Crowd Action In Revolutionary Massachusetts, 1765–1780*

(New York, 1977), pp. 335–50; and Gregory H. Nobles, *Divisions Throughout the Whole: Politics and Society in Hampshire County, Massachusetts, 1740–1775* (New York, 1983), pp. 162–85.

6. Henry Knox to Governor Caleb Strong, 15 August 1800, and Robert Houston and George Ulmer to Strong, 12 August 1800, Related Papers filed under Resolve of 15 November 1800, MA; and Knox to Ulmer, 11 July 1801, HKP 44:25, MHS.

7. Hill, 'Puritans and "The Dark Corners of the Land"', pp. 3–47; and Hill, *The World Turned Upside Down*, pp. 32–44. On the extreme defensiveness of the newly independent poor in the American backcountry see Jack P. Greene, 'Independence, Improvement, and Authority: Toward a Framework for Understanding the Histories of the Southern Backcountry during the Era of the American Revolution', in Ronald Hoffman, Thad W. Tate and Peter J. Albert, *An Uncivil War: The Southern Backcountry During the American Revolution* (Charlottesville, Va., 1985), pp. 13–14. See also Robert W. Malcolmson, '"A Set of Ungovernable People": The Kingswood Colliers in the Eighteenth Century', in John Brewer and John Styles, eds., *An Ungovernable People: The English and Their Law in the Seventeenth and Eighteenth Centuries* (New Brunswick, NJ, 1980), p. 85; Hill, *The World Turned Upside Down*, pp. 32, 36–7, 40–42, 59, 62–5; Hill, *Change and Continuity*, pp. 220, 224, 232–3; Everitt, 'Farm Labourers', pp. 409–12, 418, 439; and Brian Manning, *The English People and the English Revolution, 1640–1649* (London, 1976), pp. 112–37.

8. The quote is from Hill, *The World Turned Upside Down*, p. 39; see also Hill, *Change and Continuity*, p. 220. For observations on the frontier poor see Timothy Dwight, *Travels in New England and New York* (Cambridge, Mass., 1969, reprint of 1821), vol. II, pp. 321–4; Rachel N. Klein, 'Ordering the Backcountry: The South Carolina Regulation', *William and Mary Quarterly*, 3rd series, vol. 38 (October 1981), p. 671; A. Roger Ekirch, '"A New Government of Liberty": Hermon Husband's Vision of Backcountry North Carolina, 1755', *William and Mary Quarterly*, 3rd series, vol. 34 (October 1977), p. 639; A. Roger Ekirch, *'Poor Caroline': Politics and Society in Colonial North Carolina, 1729–1776* (Chapel Hill, NC, (1981), p. 179; J.E. Crowley, *This Sheba Self: The Conceptualization of Economic Life in Eighteenth-Century America* (Baltimore, 1974), p. 83; and Drew R. McCoy, *The Elusive Republic: Political Economy in Jeffersonian America* (Chapel Hill, NC. 1980), p. 105.

9. On the superior abundance available in America see Carmen, ed., *American Husbandry*, p. 50; Benjamin Franklin is quoted in McCoy, *The Elusive Republic*, p. 51. A similar view of Maine is expressed in Benjamin Lincoln to William Bingham, 26 February 1793, in Frederick Allis, Jr. ed., *William Bingham's Maine Lands, 1790–1820*, vol. 36 and 37 of *Publications of the Colonial Society of Massachusetts* (Boston, 1954), vol. 36, p. 259. On the homestead ethic see Brown, 'Back Country Rebellions', pp. 73–96. Jack P. Greene's words appear in 'Independence, Improvement and Authority', p. 12. He detects a second drive in the same backcountry settlers, a drive 'for improvement'. This allegedly led the great majority to seek a replication of the commercial and hierarchical society that prevailed in the lowcountry. Surely Professor Greene is correct to find both drives in the backcountry, but he slights the fact that most backcountry folk had their hands full preserving their tenuous independence, their modest 'competency'. Few could nourish any dreams of achieving equality with the coastal gentry. Consequently, he underestimates the potential for the majority to feel that encroachment by the hierarchical society of the lowcountry threatened their personal independence. At those moments the backcountry minority with a complete commitment to 'improvement' felt their neighbours' rage. For an example of backcountry distaste for the hierarchical social order of the lowcountry see Ekirch. 'A New Government of Liberty', pp. 632–46.

10. Edmund S. Morgan, *American Slavery, American Freedom: The Ordeal of Colonial Virginia* (New York, 1975); and Brown, 'Back Country Rebellions', pp. 73–98. For a more benign reading of frontier landlords see Sung Bok Kim, *Landlord and Tenant in Colonial New York: Manorial Society, 1664–1775* (Chapel Hill, NC, 1978), pp. 3–43, 129–61.

11. On the belief in England that the poor could not be entrusted with economic autonomy see E.P. Thompson, 'Patrician Society, Plebeian Culture', *Journal of Social*

History, vol. 7 (1974), pp. 383–7.

12. Dallas quoted in Albert T. Volwiler, 'George Croghan and the Development of Central New York, 1763–1800', New York State Historical Association, *Quarterly Journal* (now *New York History*), vol. 4 (January 1923), p. 40 n. 47; Byrd is quoted in Richard R. Beeman, 'The Political Response to Social Conflict in the Southern Backcountry: A Comparative View of Virginia and the Carolinas during the Revolution', in Ronald Hoffman, Thad W. Tate and Peter J. Albert, eds., *An Uncivil War: The Southern Backcountry During the American Revolution* (Charlottesville, Va., 1985), p. 221; Barnard quoted in Henry Nash Smith, *Virgin Land: The American West as Symbol and Myth* (New York, 1950), p. 252; Woodmason is quoted in Crowley, *This Sheba Self*, p. 83. See also Peter B. Porter quoted in Sidney Ratner, *et al.*, *The Evolution of the American Economy: Growth, Welfare and Decision-Making* (New York, 1979), p. 107; John Adams, *Diary and Autobiography of John Adams*, L.H. Butterfield, ed., vol. 3 (Cambridge, Mass., 1961), p. 224; and William Douglass, *Summary, Historical and Political, of the First Planting, Progressive Improvement, and Present State of the British Settlements in North America*, two vols. (Boston, 1750, 1751), vol. II, p. 7n.

13. In general see Brown, 'Back Country Rebellions', pp. 73–98; Karsky, 'Agrarian Radicalism', pp. 87–114; and Countryman, 'Out of the Bounds of the Law', pp. 39–61. On backcountry privatism see Greene, 'Independence, Improvements, and Authority', pp. 3–36.

14. On Bacon's Rebellion see Morgan, *American Slavery, American Freedom*, pp. 192–290. On New Jersey see Gary S. Horowitz, 'New Jersey Land Riots, 1745–1755', PhD dissertation, Ohio State University, 1966; and Thomas L. Purvis, 'Origins and Patterns of Agrarian Unrest in New Jersey, 1735–1754', *William and Mary Quarterly*, 3rd series, vol. 39 (October 1982), pp. 600–627. On New York See Irving Mark, *Agrarian Conflicts in Colonial New York, 1711–1775* (New York, 1940; Staughton Lynd, *Anti-Federalism in Dutchess County, New York* (Chicago, 1962); Edward Countryman, *A People in Revolution: The American Revolution and Political Society in New York, 1760–1790* (Baltimore, 1981); Kim, *Landlord and Tenant*, pp. 281–415; and Sung Bok Kim, 'Impact of Class Relations and Warfare in the American Revolution: The New York Experience', *Journal of American History*, vol. 69 (1982), pp. 326–46. On Paxton see George William Franz, 'Paxton: A Study of Community Structure and Mobility in the Colonial Pennsylvania Backcountry', PhD dissertation, Rutgers University, 1974. On South Carolina see Klein, 'Ordering the Backcountry', pp. 661–80; and Richard Maxwell Brown, *The South Carolina Regulators* (Cambridge, Mass., 1963). On North Carolina see Marvin L. Michael Kay, 'The North Carolina Regulation, 1766–1776: A Class Conflict', in Young, *American Revolution*, pp. 73–106; James P. Whittenberg, 'Planters, Merchants, and Lawyers: Social Change and the Origins of the North Carolina Regulation', *William and Mary Quarterly*, 3rd series, vol. 34 (March 1977), pp. 215–38; and Ekirch, *Poor Caroline*, pp. 161–210. On Vermont see Countryman, 'Out of the Bounds of the Law', pp. 39–61.

15. On Ely's Rebellion see Robert E. Moody, 'Samuel Ely: Forerunner of Daniel Shays', *New England Quarterly*, vol. 5 (1932), pp. 105–34. On Shaysism see David P. Szatmary, *Shays' Rebellion: The Making of an Agrarian Insurrection* (Amherst, Mass., 1980). On Susquehanna see Gerald H. Clarfield, *Timothy Pickering and American Diplomacy, 1795–1800* (Columbia, Mo., 1969), pp. 12–14. On the continued troubles in New York see David Maldwyn Ellis, *Landlords and Farmers in the Hudson-Mohawk Region, 1790–1850* (Ithaca, NY, 1946), pp. 34–5; and Alfred F. Young, *The Democratic Republicans of New York: The Origins, 1736–1797* (Chapel Hill, NC, 1967), pp. 203–6, 534–5. On the Pennsylvania unrest see Karsky, 'Agrarian Radicalism', pp. 87–114. On Maine see Gordon E. Kershaw, *The Kennebeck Proprietors, 1749–1775* (Portland, Me.: Maine Historical Society, 1975), pp. 150–81; Moody, 'Samuel Ely', pp. 105–34; Robert H. Gardiner, 'History of the Kennebeck Purchase', Maine Historical Society, *Collections*, 1st series, vol. 2 (Portland, 1847), pp. 269–94; and Thomas A. Jeffrey, 'The Malta War', MA thesis, University of Maine, Orono, 1976.

16. Frederick Jackson Turner, *Frontier and Section: Selected Essays of Frederick Jackson Turner*, Ray Allen Billington, ed. (Englewood Cliffs, NJ, 1961), pp. 56–62;

Jackson Turner Maine, *The Social Structure of Revolutionary America* (Princeton, NJ, 1965), pp. 9–27; and McCoy, *The Elusive Republic*, pp. 78–122. On the fear of lapse into peasantry see Ekirch, *Poor Caroline*, p. 190. On rural debt see Hector St John de Crevecoeur, *Sketches of Eighteenth Century America: More 'Letters from an American Farmer'*, Henri L. Bourdin *et al.*, eds, (New Haven, Ct., 1925), pp. 89–90.

17. Eric J. Hobsbawm and George Rude, *Captain Swing* (London, 1969), p. 56. On the fiercely moralistic content of eighteenth-century protest see Gordon S. Wood, 'Rhetoric and Reality in the American Revolution', *William and Mary Quarterly*, 3rd series, vol. 23 (1966), pp. 3–32; and E.P. Thompson, 'The Moral Economy of the English Crowd in the Eighteenth Century', *Past and Present*, vol. 50 (February 1971), pp. 76–136.

18. Gregory A. Stiverson, 'Landless Husbandmen: Proprietary Tenants in Maryland in the Late Colonial Period', in Aubrey C. Land *et al.*, eds., *Law, Society, and Politics in Early Maryland* (Baltimore, 1977), pp. 197–202; Kim, *Landlord and Tenant*, pp. 281–415; on Virginia see Beeman, 'The Political Response to Social Conflict', pp. 222–3. To account for the social peace that reigned in the Virginia backcountry Beeman prefers to stress the greater responsiveness to backcountry interests by the Virginia assembly rather than deference.

19. Gordon S. Wood, 'Evangelical America and Early Mormonism', *New York History*, vol. 61 (October 1980), pp. 365–6; and Dwight, *Travels*, vol. 2, pp. 322, 329–30.

20. Robert E. Moody, 'The Proposed Province of Georgia in New England, 1713–1733', *Colonial Society of Massachusetts Publications*, vol. 34, pp. 255–73; Robert E. Moody, 'The Maine Frontier, 1607–1763', PhD dissertation, Yale University, 1933; Kershaw, *Kennebeck Proprietors*, pp. 150–90, 285ff; Oscar Handlin and Mary Handlin, *Commonwealth: A Study of Government in the American Economy; Massachusetts, 1774–1861* (Cambridge, Mass., 1969), pp. 9–12; Robert Hallowell Gardiner, 'History of the Kennebeck Purchase', Maine Historical Society, *Collections*, 1st series, vol. 2 (Portland, Me., 1847), pp. 269–94; and Jasper Jacob Stahl, *History of Old Broad Bay and Waldoboro* (Portland, Me., 1956), vol. 1, pp. 528–36. On the work of one settler ideologist see Alan Taylor, '"Stopping the Progress of Rogues and Deceivers": A White Indian Recruiting Notice of 1808', *William and Mary Quarterly*, 3rd series, vol. 42 (January 1985), pp. 90–103.

21. Thurston Whiting and Benjamin Brackett to Henry Knox, 7 September 1801, HKP 52:87, MHS; and Thurston Whiting and Benjamin Brackett, 'Journal', 30 August 1801, HKP 44:54, MHS.

22. Thurston Whiting and Benjamin Brackett to Henry Knox, 7 September 1801, HKP 52:87, MHS.

23. Hill, *The World Turned Upside Down*, p. 100; and Gerrard Winstanley, 'Declaration from Wellingborough', in George H. Sabine, ed., *The Works of Gerrard Winstanley* (New York, 1965), p. 650.

24. Thurston Whiting and Benjamin Brackett to Henry Knox, 7 September 1801, HKP 52:87, MHS.

25. George Ulmer to Henry Knox, 26 June 1801, Box 6 HKP, MeHS wrote, 'I am extremely sorry to add that there was great difficulty in procuring the men and that they are very badly equipped.' The quote is from Captain Thomas Knowlton and Lieutenant Jonathan Wilson to Governor Caleb Strong, 25 January 1802, in Related Papers filed with the Resolve of 4 March 1802, MA; Robert Houston to Knox, 26 June 1801, HKP 44:13, MHS; Belfast Valuation, 1801, Box 397, Massachusetts State Library, Boston, Massachusetts (MSL hereafter); Belfast Federal Census Returns for 1800 and 1810, Federal Record Center, Waltham, MA; Knowlton's men are listed in resolve CXI, 4 March 1802, *General Court Resolves, 1802* (Boston, Mass., 1802, Shaw-Shoemaker no. 2626), 58. The six men from Northport, in addition to Thomas Knowlton were Sergeant John Clark and Privates William Adams, John Harvey, Stephen Knowlton, Samuel Brown and Jonathan Hodgdon. See also George Ulmer to Henry Knox, 28 June 1801, HKP 44:14, MHS.

26. Thurston Whiting and Benjamin Brackett, 'Journal', 26, 27 and 31 August 1801 entries and Whiting and Brackett to Henry Knox, 7 September 1801, HKP 44:54 and 52:87; and George Ulmer to Knox, 28 June 1801, HKP 44:14, MHS. On 'blacking' in an

English forest see Thompson, *Whigs and Hunters*, pp. 55–79.

27. Abraham Welch to George Ulmer, 11 July 1801, HKP 44:24, MHS; Simon Towle to Captain Hunter, 16 September 1801, HKP 44:82, MHS; John Scobey to George Ulmer, 9 July 1801 (misdated 9 June 1801), HKP 44:3, MHS; Ulmer to Henry Knox, 11 July 1801 and Knox to Ulmer, 22 July 1801, HKP 44:27 and 44:34, MHS; Ulmer *et al.*, deposition, 31 October 1801, Box 6 HKP, MeHS; recognizances of Joshua Smith, James Smith and Jonathan Spaulding, 3 July 1801, Box 167 Hancock County SJC files, MeSA; *Castine Journal* (Castine, Me.), 10 July 1801.

28. George Ulmer to Henry Knox, 9 and 11 July 1801, Knox to Ulmer, 11 and 22 July Ulmer to Knox, 12 September 1801, and Knox to Ulmer 19 and 22 September 1801, HKP 44:22, 26, 27, 34, 77, 83 and 86; Knox to Henry Jackson and Benjamin Lincoln, 30 August 1801, HKP 44:65, MHS; Knox to George Ulmer and Robert Houston, 23 August 1801, HKP 52:86, MHS. George Ulmer to Henry Knox, 28 August 1801, HKP 44:62, MHS; Ulmer to Thurston Whiting and Benjamin Brackett, 3 September 1801, HKP 44:68, MHS; Ulmer to Whiting and Brackett, 30 August 1801, Box 6 HKP, MeHS; George Ulmer *et al.*, deposition, 31 October 1801, Box 6 HKP, MeHS; Thurston Whiting and Benjamin Brackett, 'Journal', 2 and 3 September 1801 entries, HKP 44:54, MHS; Whiting and Brackett to Henry Knox, 7 September 1801, HKP 52:87, MHS; Ulmer to Knox, 5 September 1801, HKP 44:71, MHS; Knox to Joseph Jones, 13 September 1801, Box 6 HKP, MeHS.

29. Simon Towle to Captain Hunter, 16 September 1801, HKP 44:82, MHS; Waterman Thomas to Henry Knox, 22 September 1801, HKP 44:87 MHS; George Ulmer *et al.* deposition, 31 October 1801, Box 6 HKP, MeHS; Henry Knox memo, n.d. c. September 1801, HKP 52:89, MHS; deposition of John, Benjamin and James Cates, 31 October 1801, HKP 44:117, MHS; John Gleason to Henry Knox, 24 September 1801, HKP 44:89, MHS.

30. John Gleason to Henry Knox, 24 September 1801, HKP 44:89; MHS.

31. Henry Knox to Philip Ulmer, 12 September 1801 and George Ulmer to Henry Knox, 29 October 1801, Box 6 HKP, MeHS.

32. The totals are derived by adding up the acres sold and prices recorded for the land sales in Washington, Knox, Lincoln, and Jackson recorded on Henry Knox's list of settlers who received his bonds and gave mortgage and note security in 1801, HKP 44:168, MHS. On Phinney, Parkhurst, and Foot see George Ulmer to Henry Knox, 29 October 1801, Box 6 HKP, MeHS.

33. Henry Knox to Lucy Knox, 13 December 1801, HKP 44:169; MHS.

34. Henry Knox to George Ulmer, 13 September 1801, HKP 44:78, MHS; Nathaniel Robinson to Henry Knox, n.d. c. September 1801, Box 6 HKP, MeHS.

35. On the volatility of backcountry mobilization see especially Greene, 'Independence, Improvement, and Authority', p. 31.

36. For lists of those employed in the surveys see the surveying account, 26 September 1801, Box 6 HKP, MeHS; and 'List of Persons Employed in Surveying Business in July 1800 and May and June 1801', Box 6 HKP, MeHS. The 1801 valuation lists for Balltown, Belfast and Northport are on microfilm. Boxes 397–8. Massachusetts State Library, Boston.

37. Belfast valuation, 1801, Box 397, Massachusetts State Library, Boston.

38. On the south-western Maine origins of most of these men see 8 September 1801 list, Land Records Book HKP, MeHS, Limington, Standish, Gorham and North Yarmouth supplied the greatest numbers. Because the Cates family and their connections who composed the nucleus of Jackson's first settlers came from Gorham that settlement was often known as 'New Gorham' prior to its incorporation. On the Gorham connection see also the 1 November 1799 and October 1800 entries, Land Records Book, HKP, MeHS. For Knox's wage rate see the surveying account dated 26 September 1801, Box 6 HKP, MeHS.

39. Indenture of Henry Knox with George Ulmer and Benjamin Smith, 22 May 1800 and Smith and Ulmer to Knox, 25 May 1800, both in Henry Knox's 'Land Record Book', HKP, MeHS.

40. Captain John Hunter to Henry Knox, 7 October 1801, HKP 44:101, MHS

recorded the conversation. The blacksmith shop may have belonged to George Carr who lived in Belfast and had participated in Knox's surveys. Hunter, who recorded and sympathized with Stewart's sentiments, had been one of Knox's survey assistants.

41. For survey costs see the 26 September 1801 surveying account, Box 6, HKP, MeHS.

42. For a more detailed look at the White Indians see 'Liberty-Men and White Indians: Frontier Migration, Popular Protest, and the Pursuit of Property in the Wake of the American Revolution', PhD dissertation, Brandeis University, 1985.

=PART IV=

Christopher Hill and the Future of the English Revolution

So where are we? Can we arrive at any conclusion, however interim? I believe that the makings of a new synthesis are appearing.... Let us deal less on the revisionists' errors of over-enthusiasm than on their new insights. But let us relate these insights ... to the findings of post-revisionists.... Then we may see a way forwards.

Christopher Hill, *Past and Present*,
no. 92 (August 1981), p.118.

The Bourgeois Revolution of Seventeenth-Century England Revisited

Lawrence Stone

Nearly one hundred and fifty years ago Guizot, Marx and Engels were the first to suggest that the English Civil War of the seventeenth century marked a stage in the shift from feudalism to capitalism. There were three semi-independent parts to the argument. The first was that the opposing forces represented two different attitudes towards labour and property. The second was that the parliamentarians consciously willed the resulting destruction of feudalism. And the third was that the outcome was a distinctively bourgeois society characterized by the ideal of possessive individualism. The first of these three arguments was certainly put forward by Guizot and Engels, the former declaring that 'even in the days of Elizabeth, the House of Commons had laboured with ardour to destroy the forces of feudalism'.[1] Nearly fifty years ago Christopher Hill and R.H. Tawney took much the same line. Tawney used it in his famous article on 'The Rise of the Gentry' in 1941. In 1940 Hill argued that in the sixteenth century the Crown held 'the balance between the bourgeoisie, and progressive gentry on the one hand, and the feudal lords on the other'. By the seventeenth century 'the new class of progressive landlords was there, thrusting its way forward, hampered by feudal survivals without whose abolition it could not develop freely; in the revolution, it took over the state, creating conditions without which further expansion was impossible'.[2] Although half a century old – and now abandoned by Hill – this first part of the argument is so deep-seated and long-enduring a part of the Marxist paradigm, that it is still worth while to see what truth there is to it.

The evidence for this idea about the composition of the parliamentary forces has never been as secure as its proponents could wish. It certainly seems that the lesser bourgeoisie and shopkeepers in the towns tended to side with Parliament, and that those peers and baronets who did take sides aligned themselves with the King by a ratio of two to one. But except for London the core of the leadership of both parties came not from townsmen or noblemen but from gentry. Engels got around this difficulty by assuming that the gentry who sided with Parliament were 'bourgeois' modernizers determined to maximize their profit margins, regardless of the social costs, while those who sided with the King were 'feudal' traditionalists more interested in preserving ties of personal service than in increasing income. Tawney observed that 'Landowners living on profits and rents of commercial agriculture, and the merchant and banker who was also a landowner, represented not two classes but one. Patrician and Parvenu both owed their ascent to causes of the same order. Judged by the source of their income, both were equally bourgeois.' Marx had long before commented that 'the English gentry became a bourgeoisie of its own particular kind'.[3] By this neat taxonomic reclassification, a section of the gentry were made honorary bourgeois. 'It is still the same old bourgeois revolution,' concluded Judith Schklar, 'but at least it has been ruralized.'[4]

But how is one to prove that a connection between the bourgeoisie and political radicalism in fact existed? As far as the urban patriciate is concerned, Valerie Pearl and Robert Brenner have shown conclusively that in London the ruling elite were predominantly royalist in their sympathies, and had to be ejected from power by a revolution from below before the political allegiance of the city could be shifted to Parliament.[5] The same appears to be true of Newcastle and York, while the citizens and patriciates of Bristol and other cities were mostly neutral, anxious above all to save their homes and shops from the horrors of military occupation by disorderly troops, siege or sack. The available evidence suggests that such links as existed between the economic attitudes and activities of the urban bourgeoisie and their political opinions have to be sought in differences in commercial interests and control of political power rather than in a natural elective affinity to Puritanism or parliamentarianism. All this is hardly surprising when it is realized that these patrician elites depended for their political power and economic prosperity on royal charters and monopolies rather than on talent and entrepreneurial initiative. The dissidents and parliamentarians were those excluded from this charmed circle of privilege and those driven by religious zeal. This is a split which more or less conforms with Marx's division between parasitic and innovative merchant groups.[6]

For the 'rural bourgeoisie', the entrepreneurial gentry and squirearchy, the evidence at present is virtually non-existent. Hill has argued that there is significance in the fact that the 'parliamentary areas were the South and East, both economically advanced, while the strength of the Royalists lay in the still half-feudal North and West'. At first sight this seems very persuasive. Hardly anyone would deny that the south and east were indeed economically more advanced areas than the north and west, even if most of the extractive industries, the mining of coal, iron, tin and lead, were concentrated in the latter area. And it is certainly true that for most of the war the south and east were under the control of the parliamentary forces, and the north and west were under the control of the royalist forces. But there are two reasons why the admitted premise does not necessarily lead to the alleged conclusion. The first is that the argument is exposed to the well-known ecological fallacy. It is not enough to show that broad geographical configurations correspond to certain political behaviour patterns. It must also be proved that it was a certain type of person living in the area who displayed these behaviour characteristics. In other words, it must also be proved that it was the more feudal rather than the more entrepreneurial landlords in the admittedly more feudal and unprogressive north and west who supported the King; and that it was the more entrepreneurial rather than the more feudal landlords in the admittedly more entre-preneurial and progressive south and east who supported Parliament. No such proof has yet been discovered.

Secondly, the geographical location of the power bases of the two parties during the Civil War might equally well be ascribed to relative distance from London, or to the degree of Puritan feeling in the areas, or to the existence of the two universities in the south and east, or to mere chance which determined which activist minority moved fastest to seize power in the first few weeks of the war. What we do know is that on either side of the front line there were very numerous dissidents who, given a chance, would have thrown in their lot with the other side. This is exactly what one might expect, and is a situation that has occurred in most civil wars, for example the Spanish Civil War in the 1930s. In Kent, for example, apparently a solidly parliamentarian county, there was in fact a large number of closet royalists, and the same goes for Suffolk.[8] The distribution of royalist baronets points to the same conclusion. Geographical argument is therefore suggestive, but hardly decisive.

Failing this, what other evidence is available? Hill has endorsed D.H. Pennington's tentative suggestion that a 'study of how the estates of landed members [of Parliament] were managed might reveal an econ-omic line of cleavage corresponding to a political one'. No such study has been made, however, and indeed the evidence for one is almost certainly lacking. There do not survive enough estate accounts and correspondence to reconstruct the business habits of more than a small minority of members of the Long Parliament.[9] Three very careful studies of local gentry in Kent, Sussex and Yorkshire, using all the available evidence, have been unable to find any significant correlation between attitudes to landlord–tenant relationships and political opinion.[10] In Lancashire, on the other hand, all the oppressive and exploitative landlords we know about were royalist, as were most of those who had developed coal-mines on their estates.[11]

Contemporary comments on this matter are particularly confusing. Clarendon certainly subscribed to the view that the parliamentarians were men of low social standing, or *nouveaux riches*, envious and anxious to displace their social superiors. But he could see no distinction in political attitudes between entrepreneurial and conservative landlords. On the contrary, he noted, regretfully, that 'the revenues of two many of the Court consisted principally in enclosures and improvements of that nature'.[12] If this is true, it would drive a coach and horses through the Marxist theory of the class basis of the English Civil War, since it would mean that substantial numbers of 'capitalist' landlords were fighting on the allegedly 'feudal' side.

Testing Clarendon's hypothesis is not easy, and in any case the issue itself is fraught with psychological ambiguities. Some early seventeenth-century magnates, like the Earls of Shrewsbury, combined a feudal, semi-medieval life-style with vast entrepreneurial enterprises in mining, metallurgy and wood production.[13] Shrewsbury was an entrepreneurial 'feudalist', and no doubt there were others. An examination of the parliamentary peers certainly reveals an unusually high proportion of men with some stake or other in overseas trade, colonial development, mining, metallurgy and estate improvement. Of the thirty parliamentarians, ten were directors or investors in the Providence Island Company, and ten (some of them the same persons) had other colonizing interests. Five were involved in large-scale fen drainage, and at least four were actively engaged in mining and metallurgy. At least five were enclosers, while Salisbury and Bedford were the two largest urban developers in London.[14]

On the other hand, a majority of the parliamentary peers have left no record of such enterprise, while plenty of royalists were also involved in all these same activities. A few, like Carlisle and Arundel, were even colonial investors or developers. The only entrepreneurial characteristic of the parliamentarians that stands out as exceptional is interest in the Providence Island Company and in the settling of Puritan emigrants on the shores of New England. But the motivation for the former was as much geo-political and religious as commercial, a desire to harass the Catholic Spanish in the Caribbean, while the second was primarily religious. None of this evidence, therefore, offers more than very inconclusive support for the hypothesis that the parliamentarians were more entrepreneurial than the royalists, although it certainly does not disprove it. A more reliable test of this hypothesis has to come from some other angle.

The acid test of an entrepreneurial or a paternalist and feudal attitude towards land and tenants is the degree to which landlords refrained from, or indulged in, the most cold-blooded, profit-oriented kind of activity, namely the enclosing of land in a manner which involved the eviction of the tenants and the depopulation of the countryside. Since the key element of traditionalism was the mutual personal bond of service and protection between lord and man, depopulating enclosure was the most overtly and ruthlessly 'modern' act a landlord could perform. It is the epitome of possessive individualism, the concept that a man has a right to do what he likes with his own, regardless of the social and economic effects upon others.

It is true that examples of landlord oppression and profit maximization may be found at all periods of English history from the thirteenth century onwards. On the other hand, it is the Marxists themselves, including Tawney and Hill, who – very reasonably – have stressed the significance of depopulating enclosure as marking a shift of attitudes from feudalism to capitalism. If this test is rejected, it is hard to see what could be substituted for it. Secondly, in terms of ultimate motivation, ruthless depopulating enclosure may be proof not of true entrepreneurial zeal but rather of economic desperation. Some of the most traditionalist of noblemen were eventually forced by the mounting burden of debt to resort to this anti-social action.[15] These debts as often as not turn out to have been caused by conservative estate management over the years, combined with a traditional style of life involving lavish hospitality in the country seat, the maintenance of large numbers of servants and retainers, and extravagant building. The link between action and motivation is thus not a secure one, for 'modern' action to maximize income may be the direct result of 'traditional' patterns of expenditure in the very recent past and indeed the present. If this argument is carried to its logical conclusion, it means that the Marxist theory cannot be proved one way or the other, since 'bourgeois' deeds – which are all we can ever hope to document – do not necessarily spring from 'bourgeois' attitudes. But this is to take too gloomy a view of the situation, and it is reasonable to suppose that among the gentry, if not the court aristocracy, a substantial proportion – certainly a majority – of ruthless expropriators and depopulators were efficient modernizers rather than bankrupt traditionalists desperate for a quick fix. If so, it would be very revealing to discover the political attitudes of depopulators during the Civil War.

In his seminal article on the 'Rise of the Gentry' Tawney mentioned a list of landlords who in the years shortly before the Civil War had been obliged to compound with the Crown by a fine for having carried out illegal depopulating enclosures on their estates.[16] This was one of those many once-and-for-all fiscal devices resorted to by the Crown during the eleven years of non-parliamentary rule from 1629 to 1640. Like the Distraint of Knighthood, or Forest Fines, or the composition for illegal building in London, it was a means of raising ready cash by exacting a fine by way of pardon for the commission of an illegal act at some time in the past. Not much is known about this particular device, but it raised £44,000 for the Crown between 1637 and 1639, and was sufficiently important a grievance to appear in the Grand Remonstrance of 1641.[17] Tawney found that in the five counties inhabited by the great majority of those fined – Lincolnshire, Leicestershire, Nottinghamshire, Northamptonshire and Huntingdonshire – one in every two members of Parliament had, in their own persons or those of relatives, been victims of this fiscal weapon. He concluded that this demonstrated the resentment aroused in entrepreneurial circles by 'antique restrictions' on the freedom of economic action, and explained why petitions to the Long Parliament against enclosure met with such a stony reception. But he does not state what side in the Civil War was taken by the Members of Parliament in question, although it certainly seems to be implicit in his argument that they in fact became parliamentarians. But did they? They certainly had two powerful incentives: resentment of the regime which maintained these 'antique restrictions', so inimical to their economic interests; and desire for revenge upon a regime which had treated them so patently unfairly by inflicting heavy fines upon them.

The political affiliations of all the MPs in the five counties have been compared with the list of those convicted of depopulation.[18] Of the thirty-five MPs from the five counties only nine were fined for depopulation, if one includes members of their nuclear families but excludes more distant relatives. These nine divided six to three for Parliament against the King. At first sight this might seem quite impressive, but its significance vanishes when it is discovered that the full thirty-five MPs in these counties divided twenty-five to ten for Parliament, a rather higher ratio than among the depopulators alone. The hypothetical relationship between estate entrepreneurship and political affiliation among this small group of the political elite thus crumbles to dust between one's fingers.

The next step is clearly to widen the sample. To examine the political sympathies of all the six hundred or so men on the list of depopulators is not possible, since many of them were very obscure persons, but something can be done to test the sympathies of those who were socially prominent and those who, from the size of the fines, must have been enclosing on a large scale. For this purpose all those with the status of knight and above and all those fined £200 or above have been taken into the sample. Since what we are looking for is evidence of strong political affiliation, the only tests applied are whether or not these men appear as royalist compounders ten years later, being fined by the parliamentarians for their active support for the King during the Civil War; or whether they served in Parliament at Westminster during the war or were nominated as members of the many county committees which ran the local administration for the parliamentarian authorities.[19]

Those fined for depopulation from the five counties can be divided into four groups, on the basis of declining social status. The first consists of the fourteen peers, who paid no less than 10 per cent of all the fines. One of them died in 1640 leaving heirs too young for political participation in the war. Of the remaining thirteen, ten were royalist compounders, and one a passive royalist sympathizer, while only two sat on parliamentary committees (see Table 1). Five to one is a higher proportion of active royalists to active parliamentarians than the average for the peerage as a whole, which was more like two to one. At this level, therefore, the depopulators were if anything biased in a royalist direction.

The depopulating baronets also sided disproportionately strongly for the King against Parliament – in a ratio of twelve to one (see Table 1). The depopulating knights who were politically active were evenly divided, while a majority stayed out of the conflict altogether. Only the handful of squires fined £200 or more clearly threw in their lot with Parliament, by a ratio of seven to two, and two neutral. Their animosity

Table 1 Political affiliations in 1642 of those fined for depopulation*

	Peers	Baronets	Knights	Squires fined £200+
Active royalists	11†	12	10	2
Active parliamentarians	2	1	9	7
Neutral or unknown	—	4	25	2
Totals	13	17	44	11

Notes
* In the five counties of Huntingdonshire, Leicestershire, Lincolnshire, Northamptonshire and Nottinghamshire.
† One was only a Royalist sympathizer.

towards the King can reasonably be explained by a justified resentment at the severity of their fines. These figures, though suggestive, do not mean very much unless they can be compared with those from the same area who were not fined for depopulation. The only group for whom a reasonably accurate list can be compiled is the baronets, the political affiliations of whom are set out in Table 2.[20] The numbers are admittedly small – seventeen depopulators and twenty-one non-depopulators – but the results are very striking. The depopulators lined up twelve to one for the King, while the non-depopulators sided eleven to eight for Parliament, the remainder staying neutral. The contrast is very stark, and it suggests that the entrepreneurial depopulating enclosers were in fact far more likely to be royalist than were those who avoided being fined for such activities. One is forced to conclude that this evidence not only does not support, but tends directly to contradict the theory that bourgeois attitudes towards land management led to support of Parliament. At the highest social level of peers and baronets in the Midlands, there is actually an inverse correlation between being fined for depopulating enclosure and displaying clear parliamentary sympathies; only with heavily fined esquires does a strong positive correlation appear. Thus the only documents we have which throw any clear light on the validity of the hypothesis have provided a negative answer to the suggestion that the political split among the gentry in the Civil War was between those holding 'feudal' or 'traditional' and those holding 'bourgeois' or 'modern' attitudes to land ownership. Correlations do exist, other than personal whim or local factionalism, but they have to be sought in such things as religious attitudes, age, and the degree of family newness or antiquity in each particular status-group.[21]

Table 2   Political affiliations in 1642 of baronets*

	Depopulating baronets	Non-depopulating baronets
Active royalists	12	8
Active parliamentarians	1	11
Neutral, dead or unknown	4	2
Totals	17	21

Note
   * In the five counties of Huntingdonshire, Leicestershire, Lincolnshire, Northamptonshire and Nottinghamshire.

It should be stressed that these negative conclusions in no way effect the more recent argument put forward by Hill, namely that the English Revolution resulted in a significant psychological and political shift towards free enterprise and possessive individualism.[22] These characteristics were certainly far more pronounced in the second half of the century than in the first, although there were signs of them before the war. There is little doubt that Charles I and Laud had dreams of erecting a continental-style baroque absolute monarchy, resting on the three pillars of arbitrary taxation, unquestioned acceptance of the Divine Right of Kings and an intimate union of Church and Crown. If they had succeeded, the fragile pre-war developments of ideas about possessive individualism would certainly have come to a grinding halt.

Hill and I are thus now in agreement that the English Revolution was not caused by a clear conflict between feudal and bourgeois ideologies and classes; that the alignment of forces among the rural elites did not correlate with attitudes towards ruthless enclosure; that the parliamentarian gentry had no conscious intention of destroying feudalism; but that the end result, first of the royal defeat and second of the consolidation of that defeat in the Glorious Revolution forty years later, was decisive. Together they made possible the seizure of political power by landed, mercantile and banking elites, which in turn opened the way to England's advance into the age of the Bank of England, the stock-market, aggressive economic liberalism, economic and affective individualism, and an agricultural entrepreneurship among the landed elite to whose unique characteristics Brenner has recently drawn attention.[23] But, as I have argued elsewhere, even the bustling world of Daniel Defoe can hardly be described as a bourgeois society, because of the continued dominance of an admittedly entrepreneurial landed elite.[24]

Notes

1. M. Guizot, *The Causes of the Success of the English Revolution, 1640–1688* (London, 1850), p. 10. For Engels, see L. Stone, *Social Change and Revolution in England, 1540–1640* (London, 1965), pp. 3–5.

2. R.H. Tawney, 'The Rise of the Gentry', *Economic History Review*, vol. 11, (1941); C. Hill, *The English Revolution of 1640* (London, 1940), pp. 27, 29.

3. Tawney, 'Rise of the Gentry', p. 18; Marx, quoted in C. Hill, 'A Bourgeois Revolution?', in J.G.A. Pocock, ed., *Three British Revolutions* (Princeton, 1980), p. 130.

4. Stone, *Social Change and Revolution*, p. 104.

5. V. Pearl, *London and the Outbreak of the Puritan Revolution* (Oxford, 1961), ch. 4.

6. R. Brenner, 'The Civil War Politics of London's Merchant Community', *Past and Present*, no. 58 (February 1973); R. Howell, 'The Structure of Urban Politics in the Civil War', *Albion*, vol. 11 (1979). While making a valuable advance, this article perhaps over-stresses local factors at the expense of national ideology.

7. Stone, *Social Change and Revolution*, p. 61.

8. A. Everitt, *The Community of Kent and the Great Rebellion, 1640–60* (Leicester, 1966), pp. 118–19; *Suffolk and the Great Rebellion*, A. Everitt, ed. (Suffolk Rec. Society, vol. 3, Ipswich, 1960), pp. 13–14.

9. Stone, *Social Change and Revolution*, p. 89; M.F. Keeler, *The Long Parliament, 1640–41* (Philadelphia, 1954).

10. Everitt, *Community of Kent and the Great Rebellion*; A. Fletcher, *A County Community in Peace and War* (London, 1975), pp. 276–90; J.T. Cliffe, *The Yorkshire Gentry from the Reformation to the Civil War* (London, 1969), pp. 354–6.

11. B.G. Blackwood, *The Lancashire Gentry and the Great Rebellion, 1640–60* (Chetham Soc., 3rd series, vol. 25, Manchester, 1978), p. 61; B.G. Blackwood, 'The Lancashire Cavaliers and Their Tenants', *Transactions of the Lancashire and Chesire Historical Society*, vol. 117 (1965), p. 31.

12. Edward Hyde, Earl of Clarendon, *The History of the Rebellion and Civil Wars in England*, W.D. Macray, ed., 6 vols. (Oxford, 1888), vol. 2, p. 296; vol. 1, p. 431.

13. L. Stone, *The Crisis of the Aristocracy, 1558–1641* (Oxford, 1965), p. 375.

14. W.H. Schumacher, 'The Peers and the Parliamentary Party', unpublished seminar research paper, Princeton, 1971. I am indebted to Dr Schumacher for permission to quote from his paper.

15. Stone, *Crisis of the Aristocracy*, pp. 329–30.

16. Tawney, 'Rise of the Gentry', p. 12; F.C. Dietz, *Receipts and Issues of the Exchequer during the Reigns of James I and Charles I* (Smith College Studies in History, Northampton, Mass., 1928).

17. F.C. Dietz, *English Public Finance* (London, 1932), p. 283.

18. Public Record Office, London C212/20; D. Brunton and D.H. Pennington, *Members of the Long Parliament* (London, 1954), appendices 5–6.

19. *Calendar of the Proceedings of the Committee for Compounding, 1643–60*, M.A.E. Green, ed., 5 vols. (London, 1888–92); *Acts and Ordinances of the Interregnum, 1642–60*, C.H. Firth and R.S. Rait, eds., 3 vols. (London, 1911).

20. PRO, SP 16/405, gives a list of JPs in 1638 which is helpful, but excludes many baronets already active in opposition politics. Firth and Rait publish several lists of parliamentary committee-men. A full list of all baronets and their native seats is provided by C.J. Parry, *Index of Baronetage Creations* (Institute of Heraldic and Genealogical Studies, Canterbury, 1967).

21. For a perceptive, but over-simplified, examination of the religious factor, see J. Morrill, 'The Religious Context of the English Civil War', *Trans. Roy. Hist. Soc.*, 5th series, vol. 34 (1984). I am preparing a detailed study of the sociological correlations of the landed elite with their political affiliations in the Civil War, which will offer some positive findings to offset the purely negative conclusions of this article.

22. Hill, 'A Bourgeois Revolution?'

23. R. Brenner, 'Agrarian Class Structure and Economic Development in Pre-Industrial England', *Past and Present*, no. 70 (February 1976).

24. L. and J.C.F. Stone, *An Open Elite? England, 1540–1880* (Oxford, 1984), chs. 7, 12.

The Counties and the Country: Some Thoughts on Seventeenth-Century Historiography

Cynthia Herrup

In the historiography of seventeenth-century England, the Crisis of the Aristocracy and the Crisis of Parliaments have been followed close on by the crisis of historians.[1] A proliferation of county studies in the last two decades has altered our awareness of the importance of the world beyond Westminster and Whitehall, but this needed expansion of our horizons has also confounded our understanding of the causes of the English Civil War and the English Revolution.[2] The difficulties of incorporating evidence drawn from local rather than from central sources and focused on economic and social rather than strictly political changes has heightened disharmony among students of a field long famous for its controversies. Any brief characterization of the disagreements between 'revisionist' and 'non-revisionist' historians risks caricature, but most of the conflicts concentrate on one or more of three questions: (a) Was the outbreak of war in 1642 a natural continuation of a disillusionment that can be traced back at least to the 1620s, or was the fighting born of more limited and fortuitous circumstances? (b) Did allegiances in the war and later turn upon ideological principles, or upon local necessities and opportunism? (c) Did the heart of governance rest in Parliament, or can the Civil War best be comprehended by studying politics outside Westminster and by including the political lives of men other than the shire gentry?[3] The intensity of the debate that has sprung up around these issues suggests not that any set of positions must eventually prevail, but rather that we ought to re-evaluate the analytical tools brought to these endeavours. Perhaps the arguments have been so heated because our methods have not been adequate to the demands made upon them.

This essay cannot slice through the Gordian knot of Civil War historiography, but it will sharpen the methodological knife. The study

of the English Civil War and the English Revolution will always generate different interpretations wrought of different political approaches,
but we have a single problem; the problem of explaining events in
England as a whole, not simply in the capital or the localities or among
any one segment of the population. The search for new approaches is
necessarily long and collective, but I would like to argue the value of a
shift in perspective away from the study of centralized institutions and
'county communities' and towards the study of more inclusive and more
dynamic situations. The suggestions offered here are deliberately
provocative and speculative rather than definitive and certain. They
come at the beginning of my own interest in certain problems and, as
such, they are aimed at stimulating the discussion of issues rather than at
the defence of set conclusions.

Effective government in England depended upon the willingness of male
citizens to act as agents of central institutions. In some cases, for
example with justices of the peace, this meant operating as the government in particular times and places. In other cases, such as with grand
jurors, it meant co-operating with representatives of the government
sent from Westminster. Neither role was well defined nor was it exclusive. In the absence of a large salaried bureaucracy, both sorts of participation set strict limits on the capabilities of the central administration.
Ruling was a repeated exercise in compromise, co-operation, co-
optation and resistance.[4] We need to look closely at the mechanisms of
interaction between Westminster and the localities where aristocrats,
gentry and men of lesser property routinely worked together to execute
numerous tasks defined in the capital. These 'participatory situations'
allow the scholar a valuable opportunity to study the system of governance in motion. Such occasions have been studied as barometers of
administrative efficiency, but they are most rewarding when examined as
mechanisms of a fluid functional partnership between various interests
in society.[5] The routineness of these exchanges, the importance of their
unimportance, provides a comprehensive perspective missing from the
analysis of more critical or exceptional occurrences.
    The administration of law in the shires illustrates easily both types of
participatory situation. For two or three days twice a year, each county
hosted the Assizes, a temporary tribunal presided over by two professional judges on circuit from Westminster.[6] The influence of the judges,
however, depended upon the assistance provided to them by local
citizens. To be effective, the Assizes needed the active help of local
property holders (husbandmen, yeomen and gentlemen of all ranks)
participating as justices of the peace, sheriffs, undersheriffs, bailiffs,
coroners, grand jurors and trial jurors. A typical meeting of the court in

Sussex, for example, involved the sheriff, usually fifteen to twenty members of the peace commission, about forty lesser gentry and yeomen who filled the posts of undersheriff, bailiffs, coroners and grand jurors and twenty-four additional freeholders who became trial jurors. To this must be added the citizens summoned but excused from jury duty, and those present as special duty jurors, criminal victims, testifying witnesses and recognizance sureties. This list includes only those with some official role in a criminal proceeding, and in a more populous or more criminal conscious county it would certainly be longer. The government complained repeatedly about the low proportion of officers who regularly attended the Assizes, but since full attendance would at least double the above roster, it is hard to imagine how everyone could have been accommodated if they had appeared. The government wanted attendance not simply for symbolic reasons. Judges relied upon local information to make their decisions in both criminal and administrative matters, and without local co-operation they could not assure that their commands would be enforced once the tribunal had adjourned. The relationship between the shire's legal officers and Westminster's was symbiotic as well as hierarchical.

In addition to emphasizing the interdependence of national and local governors in their pursuit of justice, the Assizes offered an important channel for general communication between the King and his countrymen. News passed both away from and towards the central government. Assize judges acted as royal propagandists and royal agents. Their formal speeches often focused on the current concerns of the King. For example, in 1606, Sir Edward Coke's address at the Norwich Assizes rehearsed for his listeners the history of recusancy in England, King James's title to the throne and the recently concluded peace with Spain.[7] The judges acted as the 'eyes' of the King; they supervised justices of the peace, advised privy councillors on the best choices for local office and reported on the general state of the realm. In return for listening to judicial speeches and enduring judicial surveillance, local men used the judges as the seventeenth-century equivalent of ombudsmen. In private conversations, public petitions and formal presentments, they offered the judges their opinions on royal policies and they expected their grievances to be reported to someone in the King's immediate administration. As Sir Francis Bacon explained, the judges rode on circuit not only for judicial reasons, but 'to feel the pulse of the subject and to cure his disease'.[8]

The quarter sessions courts, held roughly every three months and presided over by resident justices of the peace, encompassed the government's need for both co-operation and delegated authority. The presiding officers filled most of the roles played by the judges at the Assizes.

Local justices supervised lesser officials, represented governmental policies, delivered orations on the importance of order, and acted as a conduit for information between specific areas and Westminster. Although Privy Councillors were routinely a part of most shire peace commissions, the men who regularly officiated at the quarter sessions were major local landholders. The same magistrates who were expected to attend the Assizes to learn from professional judges were the judges in the quarterly tribunals, and the vitality of these courts owed as much to the familiarity of the landlord as to the formality of a national connection. For the men of minor property whose assistance and opinions were required at the sessions, the court was both local and national. From either angle, the demands on small freeholders for co-operation were essentially the same. For the greater gentry who were magistrates, however, the quarter sessions was an opportunity not simply to co-operate in government, but also to embody it.

Both courts and both sorts of participation served various integrative functions. First, these occasions united the shire's gentry and men of modest property as active participants in government. Participation affirmed some level of agreement on the ideals of justice and local quiet. Second, the courts supported the central government because participation implicated those involved by linking them to the administration of policy. The result was to legitimate national power by adding the sanction of community authority. Third, the tribunals provided a chance to air disagreements of both national and local significance. Their agendas had a place not only for a prosecution of thefts, but also for complaints against the collection of ship money. This flexibility absorbed discontent as well as aired it. The local courts, moreover, were only one of several situations that cut across the divisions of social status and local boundaries. These participatory situations exemplify the conflict and the cohesion within English government. Parliamentary contests, subsidy collections, militia musters, churchwarden presentments and overseas adventures through chartered trading companies are just a handful of similar occasions. The breadth of flexibility of such occurrences as well as their constantly changing cast of participants make them an important addition to the study of conventional institutions.

Moreover, historians need to change not only what we study, but also whom we study. We must give more direct attention to the men who literally governed the English shires. The gentlemen of England were terribly important, but the notion that they actually ruled through Parliament and county institutions is, at best, problematic. Despite the responsibilities of the gentry as Members of Parliament, justices of the peace and captains of the local militia, the weight of power fell not upon them but upon men of less exalted social standing. In law enforcement, for example, almost nothing was accomplished on the authority of any single individual or even with the endorsement of a single level of the official hierarchy. Most defendants who appeared in the Assizes or the quarter sessions from East Sussex did so with the concurrence of not only an alleged victim, but also at least two witnesses, two constables, two sureties of good behaviour (or in more serious cases, two prison escorts), and one or more justices of the peace. At least twelve grand jurymen had to agree before a suspect was indicted and conviction necessitated unanimity among twelve more men acting as trial jurors. Each party had some part in framing accusations and in determining what punishments best suited what convictions. Judges and justices, the only members of this group traditionally defined as of the ruling class, had a major influence, but judges and justices stood at the end, not at the beginning, of a long string of choices made outside of the courtroom or the manor house.

A similarly amorphous collection of minor gentry, yeomen and husbandmen, not the major gentry, controlled all the offices of the parish, the hundred, and the larger subdivisions of the counties. They were the churchwardens held responsible for each parish's moral discipline and ecclesiastical conformity. They were the assessors and collectors charged with the translation of subsidies into income. They were the freeholders wooed in any electoral contest. The county community picture of local government must be replaced by one that recognizes that there was not a single ruling class in England, but that within the ranks of propertied men there were several distinct ruling classes.[9] To try and explain the English Civil War and the English Revolution without including these men is an enterprise doomed to inadequacy.

Marxist historians have long recognized the importance of men of modest property in the conflicts of the mid century.[10] Recently, this appreciation has begun to extend to the contribution of 'middling' men in the more mundane tasks of governing England in times of peace.[11] However, it has proven easier to acknowledge the collective presence of the middling sort than it has to study them in action. There are no visitations of arms for such men and they are difficult to trace from group activities such as public protests or petitions. Keith Wrightson and David Levine in their analysis of Terling, Essex, have offered the most in depth example of the responsibilities, alliances and ideologies of individual office holders at the parish level. Although they do not focus on the immediate linkages between parish life and national politics, their approach to parish governors can be fruitfully extended to the study of the men who took part in participatory situations. These office holders can be a legitimate, albeit not necessarily a typical, sample that can help us learn more about the middling sort. Local offices were numerous and held usually for brief tenures, so the number of middling men who can be identified in participatory situations is far greater than the comparable number of known officials from the upper classes. Developing a sample from the records of official responsibility, moreover, in many cases provides the added advantage of documents that identify an individual by his home residence as well as by his name. The study of active local officers can help us to understand how such persons organized their world and their exercise of authority.

Any full comprehension of the middling sort also demands a re-evaluation of the gentry. The fact that the gentlemen of the shire could not govern on their own reveals nothing about what they wanted to do and nothing about what they might have independently accomplished. The seventeenth century has been characterized as a time when gradations of status among men of property grew less important than the gulf between these men and the unpropertied masses.[12] However, it is unclear if all propertied men shared a single vision of good government, or, if they did, whether these principles bore the stamp of warmed over hegemony. In the treatment of thefts in East Sussex, it was the middling men, not gentlemen or nobles, who prosecuted criminals most regularly and most vehemently. Since the elite undoubtedly could discipline miscreants more informally, the distinction itself is not too surprising.[13] However, we need to seek out such differences and to understand how they corresponded to divergent views on the proper use of governmental institutions. The advantage of the study of participatory situations is that their inclusiveness can provide the raw material for such comparisons.

Once we have identified participatory situations and examined their active members, we must consider what meaningful change in such forums would look like. Even situations such as the Assizes, which brought national representatives from Westminster to the shires rather than making residents into national representatives, relied heavily on local assistance. Many of these participants interacted repeatedly in a variety of circumstances. Among such men, a steady stream of conflicts is natural; discontent will not always be readily recognizable. It is perhaps not accidental that community historians have generally stressed the neutrality of most of England in the upheavals of mid century, while national historians have generally perceived both deeper and earlier divisions in the political centre. The integration of historical research on individual counties and on events in the capital has been stymied by the assumption that political polarization can be identified by universally applicable measures of unrest. We have expected change in the shires and change in Parliament or the Privy Council to mirror one another, and our loyalty to this concept has rested the study of both the countryside and national institutions on shaky foundations. Participatory situations combine evidence of the communal stability shown in investigations of the provinces with the elements of change apparent from the study of central government. Because of this mixture, participatory situations rarely break down even in near revolutionary circumstances, but they can show signs of strain overtly and through subtle changes in matters such as personnel, agendas or scheduling.

The study of participatory situations, then, can help historians break some of the constraints implicit in current methodologies because by definition these situations are unique and routine, national and local, aristocratic, genteel and middling. This methodological focus is in many ways an extension of some of the best recent scholarship on the early seventeenth century. However, even the authors most willing to reject the standard categories for study have done so usually to recast our understanding of conventional political units. This concern underlies not only the work of Wrightson and Levine, but also that of Conrad Russell, Clive Holmes and Ann Hughes. As important as such scholarship is, it has not gone far enough. The particular interest of each author, be it parish, Parliament or shire, has limited the reach of the final product. Participatory situations have their own limitations, but they transcend the limits of locality and rank in a way that will prove a needed supplement to current scholarship. This potential can be easily illustrated by returning once more to the example of the Assizes and the quarter sessions and by analysing criminal court business from East Sussex.

A study of court agendas from the Assizes shows that between 1634 and 1640 the number of criminal indictments considered by the court declined sharply (see Figure 1) at the same time that comparable business in the court of the quarter sessions, where local gentlemen rather than lawyers from Westminster presided, was increasing. The local magistrates offered justice more frequently, more conveniently and more informally than did the judges at Assizes. Quarter sessions prosecutions were also cheaper and conducted in a more familiar setting than that of the semi-annual court. The Assizes met on the northern border of the county, while the quarter sessions normally convened in the major market centres of each division in the shire. Because East Sussex and West Sussex normally held separate quarter sessions, the magistrates, jurors and other personnel at each meeting were drawn from a geographical area about half the size used to choose officials for the unified Assizes.[14] Although Assize judges had greater authority and greater discretionary powers than quarter sessions justices did, practical considerations traditionally affected what business was channelled into which type of court. In the late 1630s, however, the quarter sessions in

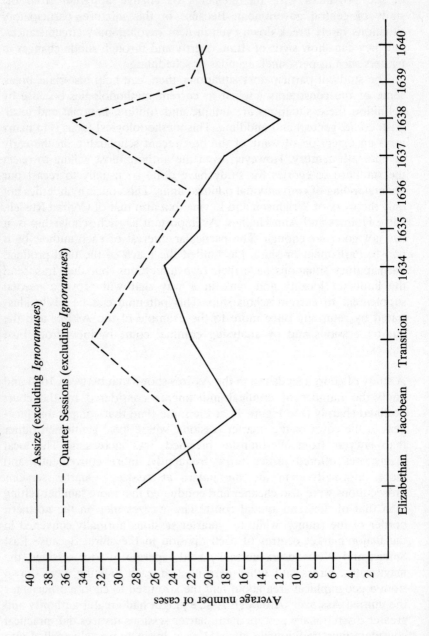

Figure 1: Assize and quarter sessions yearly business

Assize (excluding *Ignoramuses*)
Quarter Sessions (excluding *Ignoramuses*)

Average number of cases

Elizabethan   Jacobean   Transition   1634   1635   1636   1637   1638   1639   1640

East Sussex oversaw a disproportionate number of criminal prosecutions.

This shift is best seen from a long temporal perspective. The government had campaigned since at least the last decade of the sixteenth century to limit the jurisdiction of justices of the peace at quarter sessions to minor crimes and administrative matters. By the 1630s, the Assizes in Sussex monopolized the prosecution of felonies apart from larcenies, and the court steadily established itself as the favoured tribunal to avenge the costliest thefts as well. The most commonly reported capital offences, however, remained larcenies of goods valued at less than £5, and the Assizes never established full control over the handling of these infractions. Between 1636 and 1640, moreover, the quarter sessions dealt with a larger proportion of felonious thefts, punished more criminals found guilty of such felonies, and administered more grants of benefit of clergy to mitigate capital convictions than it had done either in the 1590s or in the earlier years of Charles's reign. This picture of encroachment by the quarter sessions is strengthened by the evidence of cases referred from that court to the Assizes for prosecution. The justices were supposed to transfer all serious felonies and any case about which there was 'ambiguity and doubt' to their more professional brethren at the Assizes. Between 1636 and 1640 they sent only seven cases to the semi-annual court, less than half the number that they found to be outside their purview during the two-year period for which records have survived from the 1590s (1594 and 1595). Considered as a percentage of criminal indictments, the decline is even more striking, from 7 per cent of the cases in the Elizabethan sample to only 1 per cent of Caroline case business.

To facilitate communication and exchange, the quarter sessions of East Sussex and West Sussex met together during the summer months and this meeting directly preceded the Assizes. Both courts met in the same town and the quarter sessions devoted itself primarily to administrative business that affected the entire county. The summer sessions were a regular reminder of the unity of the shire and of its connection to Westminster. The summer meetings were held separately for only two known extended periods between 1594 and 1640: 1627–9 and 1638–9. Both were times of war and political uncertainty, and in these years a single quarter sessions convened in the East Sussex town of Lewes, leaving the Assizes to meet in a different week at the traditional site of East Grinstead. When the summer quarter sessions sat at Lewes, the division of business between East Sussex and West Sussex as well as between Assizes and quarter sessions was affected. In 1636 and 1637 together, the summer quarter sessions, meeting in conjunction with the Assizes, tried only four criminal cases, three of them petty larcenies. In contrast, the quarter sessions of the summers 1638 and 1639 handled ten trials, of which nine were grand larcenies. Criminal business at the Assizes dropped accordingly. In the late 1620s, when the shire was relatively united in its unhappiness over war and billeting, citizens from West Sussex were willing to travel east for the summer meeting. The list of attending magistrates, jurors and persons with business before the court included citizens from across the shire. In the late 1630s, however, the governors of East Sussex and West Sussex were often religiously and politically at odds with one another. Correspondingly, the participants in the summer quarter sessions in 1638 and 1639, whether they brought business to the court or acted as officers of the court, came almost exclusively from the eastern half of the county.[15]

In the same years that the Assizes lost business to the quarter sessions and ceased to meet concurrently with that court, internal Assize procedures also seem to have been in flux. As a group, English freeholders were never famous for their enthusiasm in accepting the obligation to serve as grand jurors, trial jurors or constables, but the Assize courts held between 1634 and 1640 contain more repetition of personnel than the extant rosters from earlier decades.[16] More strikingly, between 1623 and 1640, one man, Thomas Jefferay of Chiddingly, dominated the job of grand jury foreman. He chaired the jury twenty-one times, serving at least once in every year except 1632. In addition to this changing pattern of participation, some of the decisions rendered by the Assizes from 1634 to 1640 suggest a new divergence between decision-making groups over the definition of guilt and punishment.[17] In at least thirteen cases between 1592 and 1640 grand jurors took it upon themselves to reduce accusations rather than simply to indict a suspect or dismiss him; ten of these thirteen cases were heard in courts during the reign of Charles I. Between 1592 and 1640 trial jurors returned partial verdicts in at least thirty-six cases that altered decisively the punishment of a convicted criminal; 39 per cent of these occurred after 1634. In the same period, judges at the Assizes stiffened their approach to punishment in at least two ways. They became increasingly strict in testing pleas for benefit of clergy and increasingly sceptical about other non-capital penalties as well. Between 1634 and 1640 almost one in every five attempts at the Assizes to plead clerical exemption from the gallows failed.[18] In contrast, the quarter sessions in these years in East Sussex was more willing than it had been earlier to hear and grant such pleas. Judges also began to add disciplinary penalties to non-capital sentences almost routinely and even to modify some acquittals in this way. For example, at the Assizes in the winter of 1636 the judges supplemented ten out of fourteen verdicts; in winter 1640 they altered eight out of fifteen cases. Whether they were responding to what they saw as softheartedness by jurors, or whether jurors felt themselves fighting a holding action against a judicial crack-down, the dissatisfaction on both sides is apparent.

It is not necessary to posit a deliberate or conscious opposition to realize that the administration of law in the 1630s in East Sussex functioned less smoothly than it had once done. The absence of Parliaments in this decade gave the non-judicial functions of the Assizes a new importance. The court was undoubtedly more and more identified with the steadily, if not perceptibly, sinking royal ship of state.[19] The concurrence of this tightening identification of court with King and the signs of growing tensions in the court's judicial process is probably not accidental.

The growing gap between the Assizes and the quarter sessions indicates a local dissatisfaction with Westminster's view of justice if not with the government *per se*. The loss at the Assizes does not correspond to any major short-term political, economic or demographic crises either at the national or the local level. The redistribution of business was probably the result of the convergence of numerous grievances against the central government. The dominant magistrates of East Sussex were Puritan enough and active enough that other justices complained angrily that the 'godly' controlled the local peace commission and imposed their own particular brand of justice. The government repeatedly tried to purge the commission of zealots or at least to balance it with moderates and Arminians, but such campaigns were never quite successful.[20] The contracting pool of jury members in the Assizes may have resulted from a parallel set of tensions to those between the government and the justices of the peace. Either a desire for men more sympathetic to Charles's views or a desire for men more inclined to godliness could explain the small number of freeholders who appeared for jury duty.[21] Without more extensive prosopographical studies of such men it would be foolish to argue either way; however, it is worth noting that Thomas Jefferay, the dedicated jury foreman, was one of the shire's leading Puritans. Keith Wrightson and David Levine found that in Terling the middling sort quickly recognized the power of parish offices as a weapon in the war for moral governance and Brian Manning discovered a similar deliberateness among Puritans in London. Such behaviour was certainly a logical extension of the zeal of a godly magistrate, and it may underlie many of the changing practices apparent in East Sussex.[22]

The slow growth of tension in the Sussex Assizes was not unique. In the 1630s many participatory situations that had flourished earlier were either restricted or entirely eliminated. The membership of local peace commissions was scrutinized and in some places manipulated with new vigour. The expansion of magisterial duties that followed from the promulgation of the new Book of Orders was accompanied by an equal expansion of administrative scrutiny by the Assizes. After at least a decade of expanding interest, opportunity and participation in parliamentary contests, no elections were held between 1628 and 1640. In numerous boroughs, charters were reissued with terms that set new limitations on the governmental involvement of the local population. Similar restrictive changes were instituted in several important guilds and in many overseas trading companies. The government tried to end discussions about religious appointments and to extend its control over chartered companies that engaged in overseas expansion. Men of modest property found themselves scrutinized as churchwardens by agents of Archbishop Laud, bypassed as tax assessors by royal appointees, and disciplined as militia members by professional soldiers. The reduction of these opportunities to participate freely in governance affected middling men more than their social superiors, because petty gentry, yeomen and husbandmen had fewer alternative occasions for common participation. The vast social network that linked the great families with one another probably had no extensive counterpart among those with less money and less leisure than the shire gentry. Many men undoubtedly welcomed fewer obligations and less national involvement, but, for the minority who took their public duties most seriously, the declining number of occasions for participation may explain the frustration and tension obvious in the remaining opportunities such as the Assizes, and the strength of more local participatory situations such as the quarter sessions. In the simplest sense, the disintegration of many *ad hoc* forums for involvement may have led to the alienation that made possible the Civil War and the Revolution.

This explanation, of course, begs two larger questions. What prompted the elimination of these meetings in the first place? And why were some individuals willing to take up arms against their King? Definitive answers to these questions have eluded scholars for centuries and may always do so, but we can learn much by looking at a variety of participatory situations over time, and preferably looking at them in a region small enough to allow a comparison of the persons involved in different forums. An analysis just concerned with elections, or with Assizes or with Church discipline, in other words, will not suffice. The material presented above from a single example is suggestive, but without broader study, the explanations given here are merely plausible. Moreover, we need to know more about the details of decision making in participatory situations and we need to study the importance attached to participation as an idea as well as a reality.

We may discover that participatory situations suffered in the 1630s as a direct result of their earlier success as participatory outlets. Charles's government approached the long-standing structural weaknesses of the monarchy quite differently from the governments of his predecessors; he stood apart from earlier monarchs in nothing so much as in his determination to govern. No scenario of creeping absolutism is necessary to recognize that the Caroline vision of good governance was too tidy to suit the diffuse, decentralized and often disorganized system of shared authority that existed in the shires. It seems likely that in his effort to rationalize governance Charles (probably unwittingly) limited the effectiveness of many participatory situations and eliminated others; what he gained in improved administration was lost in terms of communal involvement. By the 1640s Charles and a goodly proportion of his propertied subjects had lost all normal avenues of communication and were mired in a swamp of mutual distrust. It is not the anger of the 1630s that needs explaining, but rather the growth of royalism in the early 1640s. What distinguished those who were mollified by Charles's minimal resurrection of participatory situations in 1640 and those who were not? Quite possibly religion was a crucial factor here. In the areas later identified as parliamentarian and Puritan, an analysis of participatory situations may well reveal not only increased tensions in the 1630s, but also new patterns of participation. If any group shared Charles's vision of tidiness and consistency – despite grave differences in both the nature of their confidence and the definition of their beliefs – it was the English Puritans. Their world-view was every bit as 'thorough' as that of Charles and his advisers. It is likely that in Puritan areas distrust of Charles was accompanied by a determination to gain control of the remaining participatory situations and to use them to shape governance with a Puritan mentality. We may find that Charles and those who later became 'the opposition' came to blows not only because of their differences, but also and equally because of their similarities.

What I have suggested here is a means of tracing conflict within a governing structure based upon community. The initial crisis in seventeenth-century England was one of the governing structures and of the willingness and confidence of men of property to trust in those structures. The close investigation of participatory situations will allow us to draw together much of the current work on both national and county institutions, to test generalizations about the governing experiences of propertied Englishmen ranked far below the level of the gentry, and to trace change within generally stable communities. The fact that the middling men of England participated in government, that they acted as jurymen, voters or churchwardens, does not mean that this was primarily a society of consensus. It means rather that for participants the satisfactions of participation outweighed standing differences. When we understand the alteration of that balance among the yeomen and husbandmen as well as among the gentlemen of England, we will be much closer to a deep understanding of not only the English Civil War and Revolution, but also the nature of national and local life in pre-industrial England.

Notes

An earlier version of this essay was presented to my colleagues in the history department of the University of Michigan in March 1982. I would like to thank them collectively for their perceptive criticisms, and I particularly thank Geoff Eley for encouraging me to pursue the subject further. Since that time, Judith Bennett, Christopher Hill, Donald Reid, Conrad Russell, Keith Wrightson and the editors of *Social History* have read this essay. I have benefited greatly from their advice.

1. This refers respectively to the seminal works by Lawrence Stone (Oxford, 1965) and Conrad Russell (London, 1971).

2. The most influential local studies in this context include Alan Everitt, *The Community of Kent and the Great Rebellion* (Leicester, 1966); Everitt, *Change in the Provinces* (Leicester, 1969); J.S. Morrill, *Cheshire 1630-1660: County Community and Society During the English Revolution* (Oxford, 1974); Morrill, *The Revolt of the Provinces: Conservatives and Radicals in the English Civil War 1630-1650*; David Underdown, *Somerset in the Civil War and Interregnum* (Newton Abbott, 1973); Anthony Fletcher, *A County Community in Peace and War: Sussex 1600-1660* (London, 1975). For examples of how the perspective of such work has altered our understanding of traditional subjects such as Parliament, see Kevin Sharpe, ed., *Faction and Parliament: Essays on Early Stuart History* (Oxford, 1978); Conrad Russell, *Parliaments and English Politics 1621-1629* (Oxford, 1979); and Anthony Fletcher, *The Outbreak of the English Civil War* (London, 1981).

3. Contributions to the imbroglio appear almost monthly. The works cited above provide a good introduction to revisionism. The most perceptive direct criticisms include the articles by J.H. Hexter and Derek Hirst in the *Journal of Modern History*, vol. 50 (1978); Stephen D. White, 'Observations of Early Stuart Parliamentary History', *Journal of British Studies*, vol. 18 (1979), pp. 160-71; Clive Holmes, 'The County Community in Stuart Historiography', *Journal of British Studies*, vol. 19 (1980), pp. 54-73; David Underdown, 'Community and Class: Theories of Local Politics in the English Revolution', in *After the Reformation: Essays in Honor of J.H. Hexter*, Barbara Malamant, ed. (Philadelphia, 1980), pp. 147-66; John Morrill, *Seventeenth Century Britain 1603-1714* (Folkestone, 1980), pp. 124-6; Christopher Hill, 'Parliament and People in Seventeenth Century England', *Past and Present*, no. 92 (1981), pp. 100-124; Mary Fulbrook, 'The English Revolution and the Revisionist Revolt', *Social History*, vol. 7 (1982), pp. 249-64. Recent scholarship that rejects many of the implications of revisionism includes Clive Holmes, *Seventeenth Century Lincolnshire* (Lincoln, 1980); Ann Hughes, 'Militancy and Localism: Warwickshire Politics and Westminster Politics, 1643-1647', *Transactions of the Royal Historical Society*, 5th series, vol. 31 (1981), pp. 51-68; Theodore K. Rabb and Derek Hirst, 'Revisionism Revised: Two Perspectives on Early Stuart Parliamentary History', *Past and Present*, no. 92 (1981), pp. 55-99; Perez Zagorin, *Rebels and Rulers, 1500-1660* (Cambridge, 1982).

4. See, for example, Derek Hirst, 'The Privy Council and Problems of Enforcement in the 1620s', *Journal of British Studies*, vol. 18 (1978), pp. 46-66 and Peter Lake, 'The Collection of Ship Money in Cheshire', *Northern History*, vol. 27 (1981), pp. 44-70.

5. In addition to the works cited in note 2, see W.B. Willcox, *Gloucestershire: A Study in Local Government 1590-1640* (New Haven, 1940); Wallace MacCaffrey, *Exeter 1540-1640: The Growth of an English County Town* (Cambridge, Mass., 1958); Thomas

G. Barnes, *Somerset 1625-1640: A County's Government During the Personal Rule* (Cambridge, Mass., 1961); Brian Quintrell, 'The Government of the County of Essex 1603-1642', unpublished dissertation, University of London, 1965; Peter Clark, *English Provincial Society from the Reformation to the Revolution: Religion, Politics and Society in Kent 1500-1640* (London, 1977).

6. Except as noted general information on the Assizes relies on J.S. Cockburn, *A History of English Assizes 1558-1714* (Cambridge, 1972). The history of the court in East Sussex is based upon a sample of forty-two meetings of the Assizes between 1592 and 1640; material on the quarter sessions is based on a forty-five-court sample covering the same time period. See Cynthia Herrup, 'The Common Peace: Legal Structure and Legal Substance in East Sussex 1594-1640', unpublished dissertation, Northwestern University, 1982, pp. 42-88.

7. *The Lord Coke, His Speech and Charge* (London, 1607).

8. Cited in *The Letters and the Life of Francis Bacon*, compiled by James Spedding (London, 1872), vol. 6, p. 306.

9. The works of Clive Holmes, David Underdown, Christopher Hill and John Morrill cited in note 3 emphasize the need to study more than the greater gentry in order to understand local government.

10. This, of course, has been a repeated theme throughout the work of Christopher Hill. The most in-depth study of the middling sort in the seventeenth-century crisis is Brian Manning, *The English People and the English Revolution 1640-1649* (London, 1976). See also Buchanan Sharp, *In Contempt of All Authority: Rural Artisans and Riot in the West of England 1586-1660* (Berkeley, 1980).

11. Derek Hirst, *The Representative of the People? Voters and Voting in England Under the Early Stuarts* (Cambridge, 1975); Keith Wrightson and David Levine, *Poverty and Piety in an English Village: Terling, 1525-1700* (New York, 1979); Keith Wrightson, *English Society 1580-1680* (London, 1982); John Morrill, *The Cheshire Grand Jury 1625-1649: A Social and Administrative Study* (Leicester, 1976); Herrup, 'The Common Peace'. An earlier generation of studies with similar interests have still not been surpassed in their comprehensiveness; see Sidney and Beatrice Webb, *English Local Government: The Parish and the County* (London, 1906); Eleanor Trotter, *Seventeenth Century Life in the Country Parish* (Cambridge, 1919); Mildred Campbell, *The English Yeoman Under Elizabeth and the Early Stuarts* (New Haven, 1942). On methodology, see Alan Macfarlane in collaboration with Sarah Harrison and Charles Jardine, *Reconstructing Historical Communities* (Cambridge, 1977).

12. Most recently in Wrightson, *English Society*.

13. See Douglas Hay, 'Property, Authority and the Criminal Law', in *Albion's Fatal Tree*, Douglas Hay, Peter Linebaugh, John G. Rule, Edward P. Thompson and Cal Winslow, eds. (New York, 1975), pp. 17-64; Herrup, 'The Common Peace'.

14. The separate quarter sessions suited the distinctive economic, social and religious structures of the county as well as its exceptional length. See Fletcher, *A County Community*, pp. 3-60; Herrup, 'The Common Peace', pp. 23-41. Except as noted, references below concern only business from East Sussex.

15. For the political history of Sussex, see Fletcher, *A County Community*.

16. In a study of 155 sample careers of Assize grand jurors, 69 per cent of those called between 1592 and 1603 were sworn to five or less grand juries; under James I, the proportion of jurors who appeared on five or less juror listings rose to 77 per cent; under Charles I, only 48 per cent of the sampled jurors appear so infrequently. See Herrup, 'The Common Peace', pp. 139-48, 192-211, appendices 3, 6,7.

17. Herrup, 'The Common Peace', pp. 149-91, 212-50.

18. J.S. Cockburn, 'Trial by the Book? Fact and Theory in the Criminal Process 1558-1625', in *Legal Records and the Historian*, J.H. Baker, ed. (London, 1978), pp. 77-8 dates this practice from the 1590s. Although he is correct from the vantage point of the entire Home Circuit, only a handful of earlier pleas in East Sussex were rejected.

19. Cockburn, *Assizes*.

20. Fletcher, *A County Community*, pp. 92-3, 127-34, 239-43.

21. It is interesting to note that the later 1630s was, with the brief exception of 1566-

72, the first time since the thirteenth century that Sussex did not share a sheriff with Surrey.

22. Wrightson and Levine, *Poverty and Piety*, pp. 103–86; Manning, *English People and English Revolution*, p. 62.

Spectral Origins of the English Revolution: Legitimation Crisis in Early Stuart England

William Hunt

One source of the continuing power of Christopher Hill's work is that it 'settles' nothing; it remains endlessly provocative. In the preface to the second edition of *Society and Puritanism* he concludes a survey of recent scholarship, much of it critical of his own conclusions, by observing, with evident gusto, that 'the debate goes on'! And in the introduction to the book whose title I have parodied in my own, *Intellectual Origins of the English Revolution*, which is perhaps the most contestable of his mature books, he declares that 'my object was not to write a definitive work, but with luck to start a discussion'.[1] That statement could serve as epigraph for Hill's entire corpus. He would, I believe, accept it as high praise that he is a historian eminently worth quarrelling with. There is a fruitful research project to be extracted from virtually every page of his mature books. The many bones one wishes to pick with him are, for the most part, rich in intellectual nutrients.

Even Hill's inconsistencies, ambiguities and rhetorical slippages – his notoriously labile social categories, for example, and the elasticity of his notion of Puritanism – would repay close analysis. They mark the vestigial boundaries of a rather archaic Marxist episteme, a paradigm of historical structure and causality which Hill has massively amended and qualified but never replaced or fully restructured. I suspect that an honest and competent 'deconstructive' reading of Hill, conducted in good faith and grounded in a recognition that slippage and inconsistency are ineradicable traits of all discursive practice, would enhance rather than diminish the fertility of Hill's major texts.

I shall attempt no such analysis here, however. What follows is rather an extended gloss on pages 213–19 of *Intellectual Origins*, in which Hill first drew the attention of modern historians to the importance of James I's son Henry, Prince of Wales (1594–1612) and his circle. Hill showed that Henry's court formed a link between the Protestant imperialist faction of Leicester, Walsingham and Sidney under Elizabeth, and the 'political Puritan' opposition under James and Charles. The death of the young prince in 1612, Hill implied, was the real watershed between the Elizabethan and Stuart era, in literature as well as politics. (Hill's identification of this 'Henrician moment' is generously acknowledged by Sir Roy Strong in his fine recent biography of Henry, a book to which this paper also owes much.)[2]

My discussion of Puritanism on pages 322–4 also derives from Hill, specifically from the introductory chapter of *Society and Puritanism* on 'The Definition of a Puritan'. I have tried to tie up some loose ends left flapping by that stimulating but frustrating text, wherein Hill brilliantly displays the contemporary polysemy of the word 'Puritanism', without finally locating a stable core of reference.

This article is a report on work in progress. I am engaged on a study of the crisis in political culture which I believe to have occurred in England between roughly 1612 and 1629. For reasons of space I have been unable in this paper to treat a number of themes essential to the overall argument. I have said little about the socio-economic pressures of the early modern period, which constitute the material context of the cultural crisis – demographic growth, the commercialization of agriculture, the emergence of a rural proletariat, the erosion of guild organization by the 'proto-industrial' putting-out system and the expansion of foreign trade. I have barely alluded to the complex influence of militant Protestantism and humanist education upon the English aristocracy's sense of identity and purpose, particularly in relation to the evolving state apparatus. I have said something, but too little, about the sanctification afforded by Protestant theology to the authority of provincial and parochial officials.[3]

My focus here is upon the fate of a legitimating ideology, and with the frustrated potential of that ideology to articulate a coalition of class fractions and interest groups, linked to and buttressing the state apparatus. In a sense I am dealing with the abortion of a Gramscian hegemonic block.[4] Accordingly, I have been led to stress the relative autonomy of cultural representations. I do not mean to imply that ideology, and that particular form I have termed national myth, is ethereally independent of social practice. I am seeking rather to establish a plane of cultural analysis capable of integrating the social, economic and political dimensions, without positing an ultimate determinant or a 'last analysis'. *Pace* Engels, there is no 'last analysis' in history, only widening circles of interpretation, multiplying levels of reciprocal determination and dwindling reserves of analytic energy. I have tried to adopt as my framework a notion of culture sufficiently broad to permit free play to contingency and alternative possibility, without forfeiting legible pattern.

Stating the Obvious: Notes Toward a Theory of Frustration

In the middle of the seventeenth century, England, like many contemporaneous states, went through a Time of Troubles. These troubles comprised provincial rebellion, religious warfare, aristocratic resistance to the erosion of traditional liberties, and a good deal of confused and highly mediated social conflict. As elsewhere, the result was a considerable growth of state power: a rebellion provoked in part by the centralizing efforts of the monarchy produced a decisive extension of the fiscal and military apparatus. On the Continent such crises generally led to absolutism and to the scrapping or crippling of representative assemblies.[5] The difference in the English case is that Parliament, so far from disappearing, was confirmed as a central element of the political system. The Crown was restored, with its fiscal resources substantially enhanced, but it was restored by a Parliament that retained ultimate control of those resources, when its members chose to exercise it. Parliament remained the arena for the public definition of national purposes by representatives of the political nation. Parliament could, when it so chose, set the broad parameters within which policy could be effectively conducted. Those limits might in normal times be invisible, but they were also, as James II learned to his cost, inviolable.

Britain's Time of Troubles left Parliament securely anchored at the heart of the political culture. Government in defiance of its will, when that will was clearly expressed, was intolerable to the political nation and therefore impossible for the Crown. This process deserves, I believe, the name of the English Revolution. It effected a fundamental alteration in the relationship between the state and civil society, with lasting consequences for Britain and the world. Moreover the Revolution resolved the paralysis of the early Stuart state in ways which would have been highly improbable without the (temporary) overthrow of the monarchy.

The causes of the downfall of the Stuart monarchy in the mid seventeenth century have been the subject of controversy ever since the event itself. Let us start with basics, by determining what we have first to explain. In 1640 England was invaded by a Scots army. The Scots had been fellow subjects since 1603, but for a very long time before that they had been traditional enemies. Normally in such crises people rally to their government, however they may disagree with this or that aspect of governmental policy. In 1940 the vast majority of Labour Party supporters rallied behind Churchill. A year later, millions of non-communist

Russians rallied behind Stalin. In 1640, the English did not rally behind Charles. Instead, they used the emergency to extort concessions from him. Nor did they rally to the Crown the following year when faced with an even more detested enemy, the rebellious Catholic Irish. At a moment of great national peril the English refused to fight for their King. There is nothing like it in English history, apart from the Glorious Revolution of 1688.

It was this crucial moment of collective disobedience, this massive vote of no confidence in the Caroline regime that opened the way for all that followed: for the religious and constitutional reforms of the Long Parliament, the unwilled but irresistible slide toward civil war, the execution of Charles and the transient experiment in republican government. Whatever further causes we may uncover, the proximate cause of the English Revolution was the refusal of the political nation to defend the regime from attack. In other words, Charles's government had suffered a total loss of legitimacy. The legitimacy of a regime comes down finally to the readiness of people to fight for it when its very survival is at stake. In understanding the English Revolution, therefore, the clearest starting point is this simple, massive fact that the Crown had lost legitimacy in the eyes of its English and Scottish subjects.

If we take the problem of legitimacy as our starting point, as I suggest we should, then we have committed ourselves to an explanation in terms of culture – culture in its broad anthropological sense as the ensemble of patterned beliefs and behaviours that hold a social group together over time.

I would argue (following Gramsci in a loose, haphazard way) that regimes are legitimate when they are perceived as the vectors of an effective national myth, one which is generally, though never universally, endorsed by the dominant social strata, and at least passively acknowledged by the subordinate. By national myth I understand a complex of shared premises, values and purposes which maintains social solidarity and which justifies or sacralizes social domination.

When a regime comes into conflict with a strong national myth by disregarding or contravening its central integrative premises, then it is heading for trouble, though the nature and timing of that trouble will vary according to circumstance. This is what happened to the Stuart monarchy, not once but twice. The fall of Charles I, like that of his son in 1688, resulted from a crisis of national myth: more precisely from the perceived apostasy of the Crown from a concept of national *vocation* that was fervently espoused by a large and powerful fraction of the political nation, and that commanded considerable support among subordinate elites and the population at large.

The English would not fight for their King because they believed that his regime – not only its immediate policies, but its personal and governing ethos – 'stank in the nostrils of the Almighty', or, less colourfully, that it was fundamentally at odds with the ultimate purposes of the universe. J.S. Morrill has recently reminded us that the issues which drove men to take up arms in 1642 were primarily religious rather than narrowly constitutional.[6] What was at stake, in the minds of many contemporaries, was something more basic than mere politics, more basic even than the 'fundamental laws of England'. At stake was the very *telos* of the English polity, in relation to the author and ground of Being.

When we deal with culture and with collective mythologies, we are dealing with expectations. Now it is the property of expectations in this sublunary world to be quite frequently disappointed. I want to insist here on an obvious but critical point. Human consciousness is proleptic and projective. We feel, think and act with reference to an envisioned future, which gives meaning to our behaviour. To 'understand' a human act is, among other things, to grasp the envisioned future which that act implies. But all envisioned futures are, to some degree, deceptive. The expected proves unrecognizable. We all learn this fact of life quite early on, and most of us take adequate account of it in our daily affairs. Historians, however, too often neglect it. They forget that historical actors necessarily imagined a future different from what we think we see in retrospect. History is a tale of frustrated expectation. But frustrated expectation can itself become a historical force of terrific potency. Disappointed hopes and unrealized fears do not simply evaporate; they continue to suffuse the flow of experience; they inform subsequent decisions. The envisioned futures that never happen shape the future that does.

I want to suggest that historians of the English Revolution have been too narrowly concerned with explaining, in Ranke's admirable dictum, 'how it really happened'. We must pay more heed to how people hoped and believed it *would* happen, and how the falsification of those expectations affected their subsequent choices. I wish to suggest that the explanations of the English Revolution advanced so far – the most persuasive of which are still those put forward by Christopher Hill and Lawrence Stone – have taken too little account of the enormous potency of frustrated expectations. I will further suggest that our understanding has suffered from too exclusive a concern with living human beings. We have therefore overlooked one of the main characters, who happened to be a ghost.

The Death of Prince Henry

Henry Stuart was born in 1594, the eldest son of James VI of Scotland, later James I of England.[7] In 1610 he was invested with great ceremony as Prince of Wales. On 17 November, 1612 the Venetian ambassador to England, Foscarini, wrote to the Doge and Senate, 'The Prince died two hours after midnight. He has fallen when at the very flower of his high hopes.... This death will certainly cause great changes in the course of the world. The foes of this kingdom are freed of a grave apprehension, the friends are deprived of a high hope.' The Prince, said Foscarini had been the equal of Henry IV of France, in 'greatness, magnanimity, valour'. Like the French King he had been a loyal friend to the Venetian Republic in its desperate resistance to Hapsburg power. Foscarini would follow the princely bier 'with useless tears, with temporal mourning in my breast and sempiternal dolour in my heart'.[8]

Foscarini's grief was shared by all British Protestants, who had imagined themselves the future subjects of King Henry IX. Many years later Sir Simonds D'Ewes, the antiquary and parliamentary historian, recalled that the death of Prince Henry was 'the first public grief that I was sensible of'.[9] It was the universal experience of his generation. No Englishman before Nelson was more extravagantly mourned than Henry Stuart, Prince of Wales. At least fifty volumes of commemorative verse appeared, many of them anthologies by numerous hands.[10] (Only a modest trickle, by contrast, marked the passing of Queen Elizabeth. Her subjects had had more than enough of her by 1603.)

Great deeds were prophesied of Prince Henry from the moment of his birth. He was baptized lying on a tapestry which depicted the labours of Hercules – the prototype in Renaissance iconography of self-mastery and active virtue. Hercules had demonstrated his heroic precocity by strangling serpents in the cradle. Prince Henry too was destined to destroy monsters and vermin, or so the more militant Protestants of Scotland and England believed.[11] He would do battle with the great Beast itself, the Antichrist of Rome.

Henry began his public career shortly before his sixteenth birthday, with a series of magnificent festivals that culminated in his investiture in June 1610 as Prince of Wales. In the words of the Venetian ambassador, Henry was 'athirst for glory as ever any prince was.... His whole talk was of arms and war.' This was unfair to Henry. Athirst for glory he most certainly was, and he had 'few equals in the handling of arms ... on horse or foot'. But Henry had other interests besides the systematic killing of men.[12] He supported artists, scientists, preachers and architects, and he energetically promoted colonial ventures.[13]

His court drew together the most brilliant, ambitious and bellicose young aristocrats of the realm. As Sir Henry Wotton described it, Henry's household was 'as it were an academy of young nobles, submitted to the severest discipline and entirely devoted to the pursuit of glory, so that the noblest deeds were confidently expected of them'.[14]

The ethos of this court was not new. The prince and his followers were resurrecting the values and policies of the Elizabethan war party. This was the faction of Leicester, Walsingham and Philip Sidney, which the Earl of Essex inherited after their deaths, and which eventually led to disaster.

This 'Protestant Chivalry', as Roy Strong aptly terms it, was shattered by the catastrophe of Essex's rebellion in 1601. Essex had claimed to be acting in defence of the rights of King James of Scotland, whose succession to the English throne he believed to be endangered by the pro-Spanish faction at Elizabeth's court. James regarded Essex as a loyal, if misguided, adherent. James released the Earl of Southampton, Essex's close friend and reluctant partner in rebellion, from prison, and restored many of the surviving members of the faction to royal favour.[15] Essex's son and heir was invested with his father's title and installed in Henry's court as a personal companion to the Prince. The hour of the Protestant chivalry had sounded at last. King Henry IX would lead the Protestant crusade of which Leicester and Sidney had dreamed.

During the brief time granted him Henry made an impressive start. He helped arrange the marriage of his beloved sister Elizabeth to Frederick V, Elector Palatine of the Rhine. The Palatine was the leading Calvinist state in Germany. Heidelberg, its capital, had succeeded Geneva as the political and intellectual nerve-centre of militant continental Protestantism.[16] The dynastic link with the Palatinate would therefore commit the English Crown to the defence of Protestant, and especially Calvinist interests in Europe. (Or such, at least, was the intention of Henry and his followers: his father saw the world differently.) The Palatine connection, moreover, afforded scope for Henry's personal ambitions. According to Foscarini, Henry aspired to lead the confederation of German Protestant princes. Henry also maintained close contacts with the aristocratic leaders of the French Huguenots. English kings, let us remember, still styled themselves kings of France.

Before the onset of his fatal illness, Henry was making plans to escort his sister and her husband into Germany, accompanied by 'an almost infinite number of young nobles'. But the Venetian ambassador surmised that 'higher aims moved him, which he kept to himself and a very few of his confidants'. On his death-bed Henry ordered all his papers and correspondence burned. Unfortunately for later historians, Henry's dying wishes were obeyed. It is likely that those papers would have confirmed Foscarini's suspicions.[17]

Henry's reign promised to be an age of Protestant imperialism. England would advance the cause of Reformation on the Continent and despoil Spain of its American empire. But the Prince aroused hopes that transcended the sphere of ordinary secular politics. Religious conflict had infused the politics of that fevered age with an eschatological flavour. The vision of Protestant empire took on overtones that were literally apocalyptic: the English victories expected against Hapsburg power would fulfil the prophecies in the Book of Revelation. Some of the predictions centering on the Prince concerned not only 'great changes in the course of the world', but the end of the world itself. Thus John Donne, not normally classed as a wild millenarian, wrote in his elegy:[18]

> Was it not well believed, that he would make
> This general peace th'eternall overtake?
> And that his times might have stretched out so far
> As to touch those of which they emblems are?
> For to confirm this just belief, that now
> The last days came, we saw that heaven did allow
> That but from his aspect and exercise
> In peaceful times, rumors of wars should rise?

These lines have never, to my knowledge, received adequate notice; they deserve unpacking. Donne is saying many people believed that Henry's rule would establish universal peace throughout Christendom, and that this peace would precipitate the Second Coming and Last Judgement. The empire of King Henry IX would both prefigure and initiate the kingdom of God.

How seriously Donne took his own rhetorical trope is anybody's guess. The question of authorial sincerity in conventional, public poetic forms is largely irrelevant anyway. Even by Donne's standards, this elegy is laboured and artificial. Donne later claimed that he had sought to rival in obscurity the elegy written by his friend Sir Henry Wotton, and he brilliantly succeeded. But the passage is of interest as exemplifying the conventions that Donne found it profitable on this occasion to milk. Even if Donne intended them as mere hyberbole, these lines exploit ideas which many of his contemporaries took very seriously indeed, especially at moments of high political tension. (Similar apocalyptic prophecies had been made about Elizabeth, on the floor of the House of Commons.)

Christopher Hill and others have taught us that in the sixteenth and seventeenth centuries, sane, even sensible, men could envision the imminent end of the word without losing their competence in temporal affairs.[19] Eschatological dreams were quite compatible with worldly prudence, although they inevitably shaped the objects of worldly policy. We must also keep in mind the irresistible fascination of analogy for the early modern mind. Note Donne's statement that the anticipated Henrician peace was an *emblem* of the eternal peace, to which it *might* extend. The point here is the ease with which the Jacobean mind could shuttle between literal and analogical frames. The same imagery was appropriate to both type and archetype. Thus apocalyptic rhetoric could be meaningfully applied to Henry, even if his reign were only analogically related to the Eternal Sabbath.

Whether the reign of Henry IX was expected to inaugurate the Kingdom of God, or merely to prefigure it, the myth of the monarchy acquired thereby an eschatological dimension, entailing tremendous prerogatives and obligations. The apocalyptic analogy was an ideological resource of enormous potency, but also, as we shall see, of great potential danger to the Crown itself.

The Protestant Vocation

The cult of Prince Henry sprang from a distinctive sense of collective identity that I shall call the Protestant vocation. This was a mode of national consciousness that was fully and articulately espoused by a highly influential minority of Englishmen, and tacitly or partially accepted by many more. I prefer the term vocation to 'identity', which may connote a merely passive self-concept; vocation better conveys the necessary implication of divinely mandated mission. The particular form of national consciousness I wish to discuss was based on the belief that the English nation had been called by God to play a pivotal role in the advancing of his kingdom, and that God would reward or punish the English according to their fidelity to this mission. This Protestant vocation was articulated by zealously anti-Catholic preachers, patronized and, when necessary, protected from episcopal harassment by militantly Protestant aristocrats. It comprised a dual engagement: to imperialism abroad and reformation at home.

The theology upon which the Protestant vocation was based can most conveniently be termed Anglo-Calvinism. It acknowledged a great debt to the Genevan master, but by 1600 it had evolved into a distinctively English tradition, owing much to Bullinger of Zurich and the theologians of Heidelberg, as well as to English divines such as William Whitaker and William Perkins.[20] Anglo-Calvinists proclaimed the Pope to be the Antichrist foretold in Revelation, and based their reading of contemporary history upon this identification. They asserted the fundamental unity of the Reformed Church, based on common doctrine, despite diversity of ceremony and governance. This unity mandated solidarity among the various national churches in the conflict with the papal Antichrist and its secular allies, like the House of Hapsburg.

Anglo-Calvinists believed that England had been endowed with a national vocation to advance the cause of the Reformed faith both at home and abroad. This vocation had been conferred by the many 'mercies' that God had bestowed upon the English people. The special custodians of this vocation were those few believers whom God had predestined to eternal salvation. There has lately been some confusion on this point among historians. Those who accepted the Protestant vocation sometimes spoke of England as the 'Elect Nation' of God. But they never believed that all, or even most, Englishmen would be saved. England was elect in the sense that the elect minority of the English had a special obligation to proclaim God's will, and to impose it, so far as possible, upon their unregenerate countrymen.[21]

Unlike Calvin himself, who taught that God's decrees were unknowable by mortal men, Anglo-Calvinists maintained that believers should seek, and could achieve in this life, full 'assurance' of their election to life everlasting.

In future I shall, for convenience, describe adherents of this tradition 'Protestant', with a capital 'P', to distinguish them from other members of the Church of England who rejected some of the main tenets of Anglo-Calvinism, but who deserve to be considered, at the very least, protestants in the lower case. Laud and his followers, for example – the so-called Arminians – rejected the Anglo-Calvinist position on predestination and denied the substantial unity of all Protestant Churches. Despite the accusations of their Protestant enemies, however, they continued to reject papal supremacy and communion with the Church of Rome. They remained protestants.

Anglo-Calvinists believed their doctrine to be the orthodoxy of the Church of England. This was the position of George Abbot, Archbishop of Canterbury from 1610 to 1633. It was also the position of Prince Henry and most of his closest friends.[22] (As we shall see, there were dissident views on the matter.) Anglo-Calvinism saw the world as a theatre of cosmic warfare betweem the forces of Christ and Antichrist, a war in which there were no neutrals, and which would lead, within historical time, to the destruction of popery. As Peter Lake has shown, this obsessive eschatological vision must be distinguished from the conventional and less demanding belief that the papacy was merely in some loose sense 'antichristian'.[23]

In this cosmic war, England had a special responsibility. God had already conferred innumerable 'mercies' upon England. In the time of Wyckliffe God had revealed the light of the reformed gospel 'first to his

Englishmen', as Milton later put it. These mercies had continued down to the present. Preachers regularly cited, as evidence of God's special blessing, the Reformation under Henry VIII and Edward VI, the deliverance of England from popish tyranny through the death of Mary Tudor and the accession of Elizabeth, the defeat of the Spanish Armada, the frustration of the Gunpowder Plot, and so on. Such mercies conferred corresponding obligations. The English Church was an integral part of the true Reformed Church throughout the world, a church whose essential integrity lay in common doctrine rather than uniformity of outward practice. 'The Religion', as the Protestant faith was called, thus embraced Scottish Presbyterians, French Huguenots and German Calvinists along with the episcopally governed Church of England. Diversity of ecclesiastical ceremony and polity did not violate the fundamental unity based on the principles of faith. Hence true English Protestants were obliged to defend their co-religionists abroad in their life and death struggle with the forces of popery.

The battle with Antichrist, however, was not merely external; it involved more than alliance with other Protestant powers against Catholic aggression. The papacy might be Antichrist's supreme incarnation, but his legions included not only Catholics, but all of unredeemed (and unredeemable) humanity: drunkards, fornicators and blasphemers, as well as Jesuit conspirators. Hence the Protestant vocation required moral and cultural reform at home as well as international solidarity with the Protestant cause.

We have learned from the work of Keith Wrightson and David Underdown – developing and modifying Hill's pioneering insights – to distinguish two cultures in Elizabethan and early Stuart England, two contrasting and often conflicting sets of values.[24] In many areas, notably in the manufacturing towns and the rural–industrial regions, local authorities were pursuing what contemporaries called the 'reformation of manners'. Magistrates, vestrymen and ministers were trying to close alehouses, suppress fornication and enforce observance of the Sabbath by banning maypole-dancing and parish revels. These reforming campaigns were often bitterly divisive. The reformers were opposed not only by their obvious adversaries – drunkards, fornicators, fiddlers and the like – but also by cultural conservatives of all classes who valued neighbourliness more than moral rigour. Against the reformers' pursuit of cultural *discipline*, they defended a culture of *fellowship*, sustained by ritual, festivity and paternalism.

Leadership in the campaign for the reformation of manners was very often supplied by earnestly Protestant magistrates and local officials, in alliance with an energetic minister of similar persuasion. These were the people who referred to themselves as 'the godly', or simply as 'professors' (of the Gospel). Their enemies called them 'Puritans'. I shall have more to say about the contemporary usage of that vexatious word. But whatever we choose to call them, the godly formed a recognizable community in early Stuart England, and one that was in fact recognized, by friends and foes alike. 'Godliness' in this special, advanced Protestant sense of the word established ties of spiritual solidarity between people of widely divergent rank and deportment: between, for instance, an aristocratic 'professor' like Lord Saye and Sele, and a pious London wood-turner like Nehemiah Wallington, whose mental world has been wonderfully illuminated by Paul Seaver's fine new book.[25]

Objections have recently been raised (notably by Margaret Spufford) against this connection of Puritanism with cultural reform.[26] It has been correctly pointed out that 'Puritans' had no monopoly of concern with the problems of bastardy and drunkenness. But while it is perfectly true that one did not need to be a Puritan to desire social discipline, it is equally true, and more pertinent, that reforming zeal was an essential and conspicuous aspect of Puritanism. Both friends and foes agreed that 'the godly' were the most ardent proponents of cultural reform. Conversely, anyone trying to suppress Sunday amusements, especially if he cited biblical authority for doing so, was likely to be called a Puritan.

Under the influence of William Perkins, and later John Preston, Anglo-Calvinist preachers urged their followers to seek inner *assurance* of their divine election.[27] Now, 'Zeal for God's glory', as manifested in the struggle against alehouses and in defence of the sabbath, was considered to be among the most reliable tokens of election. Thus the quest for certainty about the next life fostered activism in this one. It encouraged the censorious meddling that Ben Jonson ridiculed in 'Zeal-of-the-Land Busy', the Puritan preacher of *Bartholomew Fair*.

Calvinist theology thus intensified and envenomed the cultural conflict. But the secular motivations for that campaign – rising population, spreading poverty, widening social and cultural differentiation – enlarged the audience for the Protestant discourse. That audience came to include many local worthies who were 'respectable' rather than strictly 'godly'; who were not necessarily attracted by Puritan piety, or interested in the details of Reformed theology, but who admired the vigour of the godly in combating popular vice, and were prepared to support them against attack from profligates and reactionaries, and to accept, within limits, godly leadership in the reform of their own parishes.

Such, briefly, was the national vocation which Henry seemed destined to fulfil. His enthusiasm for war, his obvious desire to place himself at the head of the Protestant cause in Europe, and his zeal for colonialization and maritime plunder all displayed his commitment to Protestant imperialism. His personal piety, and the decorum which he established in his household, where even casual oaths were punished by fines, implied sympathy for the domestic reformation of manners: so did his predilection for militant Protestant divines, from Archbishop Abbot down to younger chaplains like Lionel Sharpe and Henry Burton.

Henry Revived?

Two thousand mourners marched in Henry's funeral procession. At the burial site in the chancel of Westminster Abbey, the officers of Prince Henry's household broke their staffs and cast them into his grave.[28] The regime of Henry IX was interred, symbolically, along with the Prince's corpse. In China under the Shang dynasty, the ministers of a deceased ruler were sacrificed and entombed with their master, to keep him company in the after-life, a practice which no doubt made for tidier transitions from one regime to the next. Not so in Jacobean England. The servants of Prince Henry, and the vast numbers of young men who aspired to serve him according to their station, lived on into the confusions of the mid seventeenth century – religious war on the Continent and constitutional crisis at home. Bereft now of leadership, they had shared a brief vision of power and glory, the vision of the Protestant empire they would win with their prince. This vision would haunt them all their days, shaping their response to the baffling events through which they lived.

By the end of the century, as it turned out, this vision had been largely realized, although some (only some) of its eschatological foliage had by that time been pruned away. After 1688 a vastly strengthened English state proved capable of preserving the European balance of power while creating the overseas empire of which Henry and his followers had dreamed. But by the time this came to pass, the Stuart dynasty had been twice overthrown. Why?

As the cult of Prince Henry demonstrated, Anglo-Calvinism was by no means inimical to strong monarchy. The Protestant vocation, with its apocalyptic imagery and implications, could be used to justify a massive augmentation of royal power, commensurate with the magnitude of the Crown's divine mandate. Anglo-Calvinists constantly invoked the figure of the godly magistrate, enforcing God's commands upon the mass of unregenerate mankind. The supreme manifestation of this figure was the Godly Emperor historically typified by Constantine. (Nor was it lost on Anglo-Calvinists that the original Constantine had been British-born.)[29]

The Protestant vocation, then, afforded the Stuarts a potent legitimating myth. But that myth was, so to speak, booby-trapped. It imposed a dangerously ambitious policy upon the Crown, and it justified criticism and even, in extreme cases, 'loyal opposition' should the Crown fall away from its divine calling. Implicit in the notion of vocation was the possibility of apostasy, and the duty of loyal subjects to denounce and oppose it. For the doctrine of assurance applied not only to parochial vestrymen but to Members of Parliament and Privy Councillors as well, who were charged with providing the sovereign with fearlessly honest counsel, even in the teeth of royal displeasure. The same 'zeal for God's glory' that impelled vestrymen to close alehouses and tear down maypoles drove godly MPs to denounce Elizabeth's projects to marry a Catholic prince, and inspired some at least of Essex's followers to take up arms against the Queen.

James, like Elizabeth before him, had ample reason to distrust this Protestant vocation with which the militant Protestants were so eager to invest him. James loathed the very idea of religious war, entertained no imperial ambitions in either the Old World or the New. When he was not feeling immediately threatened by Jesuit assassins he was disinclined to intensify the persecution of English Roman Catholics. In principle, he welcomed the effort to improve public morals. He approved the suppression of disorderly alehouses. But he had no appetite for the thorough-going cultural reformation demanded by godly zealots. He was deeply suspicious that such reformers, despite their outward allegiance to the Church of England, nursed a secret preference for Presbyterianism, which had so tormented him in Scotland. He was inclined, therefore, to credit the clerical conservatives who warned him that the sabbatarian movement, which aimed to replace traditional games and dances with afternoon sermons, catechizing and household prayer, was really a covert Presbyterian plot. And he realized, quite rightly, that a full-blown 'reformation of manners', conducted by militant Calvinists, would violently disrupt social life at the parish level, antagonize conservatives and thwart his hopes for the gradual assimilation of Catholic recusants into the Anglican fold.[30]

As might be expected, James found the cult of his son something of an embarrassment, and even a threat. James intended to balance the Protestant marriage of his daughter with a Catholic match for Prince Henry, thereby establishing a European peace through dynastic union. Henry, in contrast, was said to have sworn that two religions should never lie in his bed. By 1612 the Prince and his circle had become the reversionary interest, the magnet for everyone distressed by James's lack of Protestant zeal. We need not doubt that as a father James was stricken by Henry's death, but as a king he must have felt some relief.[31]

If so, that relief was premature. Not only did Prince Henry's myth survive him; so did the consequences of Henry's major political accomplishment – the marriage that he had promoted between Elizabeth and Frederick. It was called the marriage of the Thames and the Rhine, an image that captured the geo-political import of the match. The remainder of James's reign, down to his death in 1625, can be read in terms of the conflict between James's own policy – dynastic alliance with Spain in return for Spanish financial assistance – and the Protestant imperialism associated with his dead son.

In 1619, Frederick accepted the Bohemian Crown from the rebellious Bohemian estates, thereby producing a Protestant majority in the imperial electoral college.[32] James was appalled by his son-in-law's irresponsibility; Protestant imperialists were exultant. Archbishop Abbot, who had attended Henry during his last agony and preached for two hours at his funeral, hailed the Bohemian revolution as an act of divine providence. Frederick and his court had for over a decade envisioned the possibility of his succession to the Bohemian throne, and Henry had very likely promised him support in any such enterprise. When Frederick and Elizabeth journeyed to Prague to be crowned as King and Queen of Bohemia, Henry's followers must have felt that their prince was on the verge of posthumous victory. Already in 1613 the son born to Elizabeth and Frederick had been hailed by the poet Henry Peacham as 'Prince Henry Revived'.[33]

The euphoria was short-lived. Frederick lost Bohemia to the Hapsburgs at the Battle of White Mountain, and shortly thereafter he and Elizabeth were driven from the Palatinate as well. The Protestant party in England clamoured for war with Spain to recover at least the Palatinate, if not the Bohemian Crown, for the dispossessed couple, whom their supporters persisted in styling, to James's intense displeasure, the King and Queen of Bohemia.

Elizabeth in particular became the object of intense chivalric devotion. The cult of Elizabeth Stuart, known as the Winter Queen from her brief tenure of the Bohemian Crown, deserves more attention than it has received. She was a romantic enough figure in her own right, as charming, courageous and unfortunate women always are. Her very name evoked associations with Elizabeth Tudor, increasingly idealized, as James's reign wore on, by partisans of the Protestant cause. She was the sister of Prince Henry; and now mother of 'Henry Redivivus'. In addition to her own personal magnetism, Elizabeth thus subsumed the myth of Henry and eroticized it, fusing it with the myth of Gloriana and the Faery Queen. One suspects that the title of Winter Queen added yet another poignant mythic overtone: Elizabeth as the enchanted, and imprisoned (and icily inaccessible) sleeping beauty whom the young, and not-so-young knights of the Protestant chivalry longed to rescue and vicariously possess.

If this sounds unnecessarily exotic, consider the astounding demonstration on Elizabeth's behalf during the Parliament of 1621. An insignificant lawyer of papist sympathies named Fludd or Floyd had been heard to make disparaging remarks about the Queen of Bohemia and her progeny. When word of his indiscretion reached the House it produced an outburst of rage unparalleled in parliamentary history. The Mother of Parliaments was transformed for several hours into a lynch mob, as members vied with each other in sadistic ingenuity to prescribe penalties for Fludd.[34]

What kind of behaviour is this, on the part of grown men – English gentlemen and statesmen to boot? It is, I suggest, the behaviour of men bent on avenging a sister's honour. Many of these MPs would have been among the 'infinite number of nobles' who intended to escort Elizabeth and Frederick into Germany under Prince Henry; others would have longed to do so. Older men, who had been young when the cult of Gloriana was at its zenith, found their youthful ardour rekindled by the young Queen. In piling savage punishments upon the miserable Mr Fludd, these excited gentlemen, no longer hot-blooded youths but aflame with outraged chivalry, were assuming the role of Elizabeth's dead brother.

Elizabeth, of course, had a living brother as well, not to mention a father. Neither was of much use to her in 1621, however, nor in the years to follow. One of the most urgent issues of the English politics of the 1620s was the fate of Elizabeth and her less interesting husband, and, more broadly, the role England should play in the renewed religious wars on the Continent. The failure of the Crown to engage itself effectively on the side of 'the Religion', at a time when continental Protestantism seemed threatened with extinction, was perhaps the greatest single cause of its disastrous loss of prestige between 1618 and 1629. This haemorrhage of legitimacy helped render the nation vulnerable to civil war a decade later.

There were, to be sure, other sources of friction between Crown and Parliament during the reign of King James – disputes over finance, parliamentary privileges, episcopal power in the Church, and so on. But it may be doubted whether any of these issues was fundamentally unresolvable. If a broad consensus had been preserved about national purposes, Crown and Parliament might well have reached compromise agreements on most of these issues, while the mere passage of time would have obscured or obliterated the rest. Such a result would have greatly enhanced the prospects for English absolutism.

It must be understood that the chief parliamentary leaders of the 1620s, and indeed of the Long Parliament of the 1640s, were seeking not so much to *reduce* royal power, as to recall the Crown to its

Protestant vocation. In fact the most responsible and influential of these leaders – Warwick, Saye and Manchester in the House of Lords; Pym, Rudyerd, Digges and Rich in the Commons – realized that the crown had to be endowed with resources adequate to its tasks. They wished to induce a *strengthened* Crown to pursue the policies once expected of King Henry IX.

But these were not the policies of King James. After the death of Henry, James became increasingly convinced that Anglo-Calvinism was subversive of his royal authority, and of the stable, comprehensive and deferential culture he wished to establish. He dissociated himself from the reformation of manners in its integral 'Puritan' form, by issuing the Book of Sports in 1618. Villagers were not to be hindered in their traditional Sunday afternoon provided these did not interfere with the morning service.

This attack upon strict Sabbatarianism placed the monarchy on the side of the traditionalists in the countryside, the champions of 'good fellowship', and against the divisive partisans of godly discipline. This alliance would be deepened and elaborated by Charles and the Laudians in the 1630s. But already in 1622 James's Directions for Preachers severely restrained preachers from expounding to popular audiences the central Anglo-Calvinist doctrines of predestination and assurance. It was another blow to reformation, since the preaching of sound pre-destinarian doctrine was the best way to arouse would-be saints to show 'zeal for God's glory' in the crusade against public sin. Thus a cultural counter-reformation had already begun during the latter years of James. The King wished to elude the dangerous powers and obligations conferred by the Protestant vocation.

This reaction was dramatically interrupted, however, in the mid 1620s, by a sudden reversal of policy on the part of Henry's younger brother. Charles's character was unusual: he was both stupid and fairly complex. Charles had admired and envied his brother; he was devoted to his unfortunate sister. It was to regain the Palatinate for Elizabeth and her children that in 1622 Charles undertook with Buckingham his lunatic expedition to Madrid to court the Spanish Infanta. The logic, if that is not too strong a word, of this *demarche* was to obtain the restitution of the Palatinate as a provision of the marriage treaty. The expedition was of course a fiasco, and once back in England Charles and Buckingham threw in with the Protestant party demanding war with Spain.

Charles and Buckingham had at last accepted the Protestant vocation. The ghost was abroad once again: in 1624 the London Lord Mayor's pageant, written by John Webster, included a gigantic effigy of the late Prince Henry, entitled 'A Monument of Gratitude'.[35] Charles himself had assumed the role of Henry Redivivus. Or so it seemed.

There is no space here to describe in detail how that expectation was frustrated. Suffice it to say that from 1624 to 1628 Charles and Buckingham attempted to exploit the Protestant myth without realizing what that myth entailed, and without allaying the suspicions of the Protestants on whose support they had perforce to rely. The attempt in 1625 to sack Cadiz and sieze the Spanish silver fleet was a disastrously inept application of the strategy advocated by Henry and his circle in 1610–12. The expedition in relief of the Huguenots of La Rochelle was Buckingham's attempt to play the Protestant hero in the mould of Sidney and Essex. It was a desperate gamble to win fame and popular support by acting as Henry might have done.[36]

But Buckingham and Charles sabotaged their own strategy: Buckingham by his sheer incompetence, and Charles by marriage with the Catholic Henrietta Maria and by the promotion of the anti-Calvinist clergymen around William Laud.[37] The result was to arouse first the suspicion and then the disgust of those staunch Protestants who should have been the Crown's most enthusiastic supporters.

Baffled and enraged by the parliamentary resistance of the later 1620s, Charles abandoned his fruitless attempt at a 'Henrician' policy after the assassination of Buckingham. Indeed he turned decisively against the whole Protestant tradition, which he permitted the now dominant Laudian party to brand as 'Puritan'. Here we need to pause to consider the meaning, in historical practice, of that highly controversial and multivalent word.

The Name of Puritan

Historians, who have long tied themselves and each other into knots over what Puritanism 'really was', should stop seeking some essential definition and concentrate instead on who called whom 'Puritan', and why. Judging from the remarks of contemporaries like Joseph Mede, Henry Parker, Thomas Fuller and others, there were at least four distinct, but interrelated, ways in which the term was commonly applied before the accession of Charles I. Or better, there were three modes of use and one of polemical abuse.[38]

In 1623, Mede distinguished three kinds of Puritan: the ecclesiastical, the moral and the political. These three species, he believed, had appeared in historical succession. First there were the ecclesiastical Puritans, who objected to various features of the ritual and governance of the established Church of England: these, clearly enough, were the Elizabethan Presbyterians. Next came the moral Puritans, characterized by 'singularity of living' and, as Mede uncharitably put it, 'hypocrisy both civil and religious'. These we can identify with the religiously motivated partisans of the reformation of manners. Most recently there had appeared the political Puritans, who were the defenders of parliamentary liberties and the advocates of a forward Protestant foreign policy. Three semantically distinct categories, then. How were they related?

The 'Name of Puritan' was a weapon. Giles Widdowes in 1631 called it 'ambiguous, and so fallacious', but it was precisely this ambiguity that made the word polemically powerful, since each meaning could convey overtones of the others. The Elizabethan Presbyterian movement had been crushed by the state. James, like his predecessor, was known to regard Nonconformity in general and Presbyterianism in particular as intrinsically subversive. In this context, to call someone a Puritan was thus to insinuate that he was at least inwardly disloyal to the Crown. So the word lent itself to malicious extensions. In 1613, the fifth Earl of Huntington claimed that the word was generally used 'either by Papists, that do hate all ministers except those of their own sect, or atheists, or men extremely vicious [who] think every man that will not be drunk, swear, lie, or whore is a Puritan'.

During the controversy over the Spanish match, it was (correctly) alleged that Spanish agents, open and secret, used the word to defame loyal Protestants. In 1624, the year in which Prince Henry's effigy appeared in the streets of London, Protestant propagandist Thomas Scott – who may have been in the pay of Frederick and Elizabeth – claimed that it was 'made an infallible note, of a Puritan, and so of an ill subject' to demand intervention in Germany.

Words are known by the company they keep. The reputation of 'Puritan' suffering greatly, among respectable Protestants, from its use as a ploy by papists, Hispanophiles and 'men extremely vicious'. Those who used it therefore risked incurring, as well inflicting, guilt by association: the 'Puritan' ploy could be hazardous to its operator. This was due to the paranoid fear of Catholicism from which so many English Protestants suffered. Catholics, as Thomas Fuller put it, loved to work *in cunniculis* – the threat was insidious and invisible. It was vital therefore to identify the symptoms of *covert* popery, and to spot them in time. The malicious use of the word 'Puritan' might thus be interpreted as a telltale mark of the Beast.

After 1625, according to Fuller, the word underwent a drastic enlargement of reference. The High Church, anti-Calvinist Arminians applied it to doctrinal Calvinists in general, however submissive to the ceremonies and episcopal structure of the English Church. In this they were following the established practice of Hispanophiles and Catholics both foreign and domestic, a practice detested by many Protestants who were neither 'ecclesiastical' nor 'moral' Puritans. By branding as schismatic and subversive a tradition hitherto regarded as within the mainstream of Anglican orthodoxy, the Arminians did more than antagonize the minority who were egregiously godly. They identified themselves as secret papists, in the minds of ordinary Protestants.

Pleasure Reconciled to Virtue

Charles's strategy was ultimately suicidal, but it had a logic which we must reconstruct.[39] Its unifying principle was anti-Puritanism: rejection of both Protestant imperialism and of domestic reformation. Charles abandoned his futile attempt to imitate his dead brother; he opted out of the whole Protestant chivalric mythos. He reverted to his father's conception of kingship, with more decorum and a finer aesthetic sensibility, but a good deal less common sense.

The Caroline cultural programme was coherent. The sanguine view of human nature expressed in the court masques of Jonson and his successors had affinities with the partial rehabilitation of the human will in Arminian theology. By contrast with the Pauline gloom of Calvinism, Caroline culture was nearly Pelagian in its marriage of matter and spirit. The Laudian ideal of the 'beauty of holiness' found its secular counterpart in the title of Jonson's masque, *Pleasure Reconciled to Virtue.* Incidentally, that very title implied a rejection of the topos of Hercules, which had been associated with the infant Prince Henry. For Renaissance topology, the heart of the Hercules myth lay in the hero's resolute decision for Virtue *as opposed to* Pleasure.[40]

This Caroline ethos, conveyed to the court through the masques of Jonson and Davenant, was transmitted to the village by the Book of Sports, which Charles and Laud reissued in 1633. The local emissaries of this counter-reformation were the Laudian clergy, who encouraged, in alliance with local conservatives, the resurrection of good fellowship. Maypole-dancing and church ales revived, much to the grief and fury of godly reformers.[41]

This paternalist exploitation of popular culture was not without success. The important recent work of David Underdown suggests that in the West Country popular royalism was strongest in the open-field regions, where traditional festivity was most vital. At the Restoration, of course, the maypole became the symbol of the restored monarchy. Anti-Puritanism no doubt had considerable popular appeal, in more conservative areas. But far too many Englishmen, especially in the towns, clothing villages and forest-pasture regions, regarded the whole Caroline enterprise as apostasy, which would bring disaster upon the realm.[42]

God's Three Arrows

The Anglo-Calvinist doctrine of Providence asserted that God inter-
vened directly in temporal affairs. Protestant preachers told their
congregations that England, by the receipt of so many divine mercies,
had entered into covenant with the Almighty. Fidelity to that covenant –
which meant solidarity with the Protestant cause and the repression of at
least flagrant public sin at home – would bring, as a general rule,
prosperity. Negligence or backsliding, failure to honour the divine
national debt, as it were, would infallibly bring disaster. Michael
McGiffert has coined the useful term 'Hosead' for the genre of sermon
in which these warnings were conveyed, since the book of Hosea was
especially packed with relevant texts.[43] *God's Three Arrows*, preached in
1631 by William Gouge, is a representative example.[44] The three arrows
were pestilence, famine and war. At the time of Gouge's sermon,
England had recently suffered the first two; Gouge warned that war
would soon follow if the English failed to repent.

The belief that God would inflict temporal punishment for national
sins was widespread among English Protestants. It was not a 'Puritan'
monopoly: hence its political importance. The providentialist reading of
history, discerning the direct hand of God in current events, was
especially cogent in times of anxiety or disaster. There was plenty of
both during the reign of Charles. As early as 1625 Members of Parliament were complaining about the relaxation of the recusancy laws,
muttering that

> all goes backward since connivance [that is, *de facto* toleration of Catholics]
> came in, both in our wealth, honor, valor, and reputation.... God blesses
> nothing that we take in hand. Whereas, in Queen Elizabeth's time, who stood
> firm in God's cause, all things did flourish.[45]

The 1620s were a decade of disaster – military defeats, plague, a
crippling depression in the cloth trade, several bad harvests. Real
wages remained at or near their lowest point in recorded history. The
1630s were only relatively more prosperous. The nation was at peace for
most of the decade, but there was dearth in 1631, plague and renewed
depression in 1636, and rebellion in Scotland from 1638. There was
plenty of evidence here for God's anger with England, plenty of material
for Hoseads calling on the nation to turn from its sins. And what sins
were more flagrant than the profanation of the Sabbath by royal decree,
and the intrusion of idolatrous ceremonies into the Church of England?

Given more favourable circumstances, Charles might have found in
the defence of traditional good fellowship a source of popular support

for the Crown independent of nationalistic Protestantism. But the association, in the public mind, of Arminianism with popery proved fatal. Many might have welcomed the Book of Sports had it not been accompanied by altar rails.[46] Many ordinary Englishmen must have found both Puritans and Laudians equally repugnant. But protestantism, however conventional and unreflective, was by now an integral part of most Englishmen's sense of collective identity. And Arminians were widely perceived not simply as conservative or even reactionary high churchmen, but as disguised papists, as the covert agents of Antichrist.

In trying to strengthen the Crown by exalting the ecclesiastical hierarchy, Charles was also flying in the face of deep-rooted Protestant assumptions about the very nature of sacerdotal power. He was committing, so to speak, a cultural oxymoron. Mainstream Protestantism was overwhelmingly supportive of secular authority. Protestant publicists insisted that it was not they but the papists, and more particularly the Jesuits, who justified rebellion and regicide. They pointed to the assassinations of William of Orange and Henry IV, the many attempts on the life of Elizabeth, and the Gunpowder Plot. It was axiomatic to Protestant historians, especially the greatest of them, John Foxe, that sacerdotal power unless strictly controlled by the sovereign was inherently destructive of legitimate secular authority. The main theme of Foxe's massive Church history is the struggle of emperors and kings against papal aggression. Foxe is consistently on the side of the lay ruler.[47]

By acknowledging the divine right of episcopal authority, and generally elevating clerical prestige, Charles appeared to many Protestants to be engaging in self-sabotage. Whatever his intentions, Charles was subverting his own sovereignty by encouraging the insatiable pretensions of the Arminian prelates and their followers. The danger was not so much that the Arminians would make Charles 'absolute'. An 'Arminian absolutism' would have seemed to Protestants almost a contradiction in terms. The fear was rather that Charles in his folly would wreck the monarchy altogether and the nation with it, surrendering England back into popish servitude, as in the days of Bloody Mary. From this perception it was but a short step, easily taken, to the belief that the King was no longer in his right wits, that his will was not truly his own. It was not disloyal, in such a case, to restrain the King from self-destruction, and to free him, by force of arms if need be, from the traitors who had seduced him.

Prince Henry's Ghost

Whatever else it may mean, revolution signifies that a regime has lost legitimacy. The government is no longer the centripetal focus of the social order, no longer the symbolic centre of the integrating collective myth. I should like to introduce here the concept of 'mythic capital' to denote the reservoir of legitimacy available to a regime. I would suggest that revolution is history's foreclosure upon a mythically bankrupt regime. A government that is mythically solvent, for whatever reasons, can endure appalling disasters (witness Russia in the Second World War), whereas a mythically depleted one may succumb to relatively trivial disorders (witness the France of Louis XVI).

Charles in the 1630s looked much stronger than he really was. John Morrill has argued that England during the Personal Rule possessed a strong monarchy but a weak king.[48] I would put it differently. I would suggest that the monarchy was fiscally solvent (barely) but mythically in the red. A mythically bankrupt regime can carry on for some time in the absence of external threats, just as a severely indebted firm can stay afloat in economically buoyant times. But the patient, to shift metaphors, may be in far worse shape than the outward symptoms indicate. Good luck cannot last for ever: debts come due, anaemic bodies fall ill. Prosperity may mask the underlying vulnerability of a regime for a considerable period of time, thereby making the eventual, highly probable, catastrophe seem more abrupt and 'accidental' than it really is. Later historians may then be misled into ignoring long-term causality, on the ground that the disaster was not 'inevitable'. In my view this has lately happened with regard to the English Revolution.

Just at the moment when Charles began to rule without Parliament, the role of Protestant champion that he had abandoned was taken up by the King of Sweden, Gustavus Adolphus. In 1630–2, as the Swedish armies swept through northern Germany, the old apocalyptic hopes once associated with Prince Henry revived among English Protestants. When Gustavus fell at Lutzen, John Bradshaw called it the greatest blow sustained by true-hearted English Protestants since the death of Prince Henry.[49] The unstated but clear implication was that true-hearted English Protestants would have little cause to lament the loss of their present king. In 1649 John Bradshaw presided over the trial that sentenced King Charles to death, in the name of the English people.

Charles's worst enemy, after himself, was his brother's ghost; he was overthrown by Henry's shadow regime. The men who first thwarted Charles in Parliament, provoking him to a disastrous experiment in absolutism, and then overthrew him in civil war, were the very men who should have been, and would much rather have been, Henry's loyal councillors and commanders.

Let us look briefly at a few main characters. The third Earl of Essex, son of Elizabeth's reckless favourite and of Sir Philip Sidney's widow, was among Henry's most intimate companions, introduced to his household as a part of James's plan to enlist the Protestant chivalry – the survivors and ideological descendents of the Leicester–Sidney–Essex faction – in support of the new dynasty. Throughout the 1620s the younger Essex was a leader of the war party in the House of Lords. He commanded troops on the Continent in defence of the Protestant cause.

Robert Rich, second Earl of Warwick, was first cousin to the younger Essex. His mother Penelope Devereux was the sister of the rebel earl, and the mistress of Philip Sidney, the Stella of his famous sonnet sequence. Warwick had been Prince Henry's partner in the Virginia Company. (In his youth, Warwick was also, like the Prince, a glamorous chivalric courtier in the Sidneyan mould, famed for his prowess in the tiltyard.) During the 1620s and 1630s he was the leading patron of the New England colonies and a founder of the Providence Island Company. Whenever he could secure royal licence, he sent out privateers against Spanish shipping. In 1627 he commanded a squadron of private vessels in a vain pursuit of the American treasure fleet. Warwick was also the leading aristocratic patron of the militant Protestant preachers Prince Henry had revered.

Essex and Warwick were thorough 'Henricians'. They remained committed all their lives to the Prince's policies. Could they have chosen their destiny Essex and Warwick would have served as Henry's commanders on land and sea. When the Civil War broke out, Essex assumed command of Parliament's army, Warwick of Parliament's fleet.[50]

Biographical connections between Henry's court and the Great Rebellion could be multiplied. The Puritan 'martyr' Henry Burton was a member of the princely household; so were Sir Robert Phelips, a leading parliamentary critic of royal policy during the 1620s, and Sir John Holles, the father of Denzil. But more important than these personal links is the deeper ideological continuity. Like Prince Henry and the Leicester–Sidney circle before him, the leaders of the Long Parliament were committed to the Protestant vocation of imperialism and reform.

There was continuity as well in the coalition of social interests woven together by this shared vocation. It included Protestant gentlemen hungry for martial glory, predatory capitalists eager to plunder the Spanish empire, colonial entrepreneurs, godly magistrates and parish officers, and the militant preachers whose Anglo-Calvinist theology held the whole constellation together. These were the social groups, supported by the more earnestly Protestant elements among the wider populace, that defeated Charles in the Civil War. They had also been Henry's most avid admirers. Had Charles been able to win their allegiance, as he seemed about to do in 1624, they might have enabled him to construct the only sort of absolutism that had any real chance of success in seventeenth-century England: a Protestant absolutism justified by imperial conquest.

The English political culture was in fact quite vulnerable to such an absolutism. There is nothing, I would submit, in the economic and social trends of the sixteenth and seventeenth centuries that *necessarily* inhibited the growth of royal power. The expansion of the lower aristocracy, for example – the celebrated 'rise of the gentry' – could well have produced a service nobility, dependent like the French *noblesse de robe* upon the expansion of the royal bureaucracy. So too with the crisis of the peerage described by Lawrence Stone. Comparison with other early modern states, from France to Russia, would lead one to predict that this crisis should have strengthened the monarchy rather than undermining it. More generally, I would argue that most of the social processes which have been – quite rightly – identified as 'the causes of the English Revolution', might equally well have become 'the causes of English absolutism', had the Stuart monarchy known how to exploit them.

Early Stuart Englishmen imagined the threat to their liberties as coming, by one route or another, from Rome, through the clerical usurpation of secular authority. The men who took up arms against Charles I believed they were resisting a popish conspiracy. They assumed that their liberties would be secure once that conspiracy had been smashed. But they had no ready defence against a *Protestant* absolutism. Given this blind spot, one wonders what might have been achieved by a really competent and aggressive Protestant monarch, capable of fully exploiting the mythology of Protestant imperialism, and enlisting the powerful ideological support of the firebrand Protestant preachers. A Calvinist absolutism is perfectly conceivable, after all: the Great Elector created one in Prussia.[51]

The death of Prince Henry and the ineptitude of Charles spared England that possibility. The one seventeenth-century English monarch who had the personal qualities to pull it off was William III. But William's victories came too late. Two revolutions, and the creation of a national bank under parliamentary charter, had confirmed the constitutional position of Parliament and ensured the permanent financial subordination of the Crown to the representatives of the political nation. Something very like Henry's imperial vision was indeed achieved – but under Parliament, rather than a Godly Emperor. Prince Henry's ghost was finally laid to rest, in the vaults of the Bank of England.

Notes

1. Christopher Hill, *Intellectual Origins of the English Revolution* (Oxford, 1965), p. viii.
2. Roy Strong, *Henry Prince of Wales and England's Lost Renaissance* (London, 1986), p. 212.
3. The most stimulating introductions to the social and political crisis of early Stuart England remain Christopher Hill, *The Century of Revolution*, 2nd edn (New York, 1980), and Lawrence Stone, *The Causes of the English Revolution* (New York, 1972). Derek Hirst provides a sensible synthesis of recent scholarship in *Authority and Conflict: England, 1603–1658* (Cambridge, Mass., 1985). For economic and demographic history, see also C.G.A. Clay, *Economic Expansion and Social Change: England, 1500–1700*, 2 vols. (Cambridge, 1984). The peculiarities, real and alleged, of the English aristocracy are discussed in M.L. Bush, *The English Aristocracy: A Comparative Synthesis* (Manchester, 1984). A fuller guide to current controversies is provided in the references to Geoff Eley's introduction to this volume.
4. It would be pretentious to attempt here more than the briefest bibliographical initiation to Antonio Gramsci and his influence, especially since I have not tried to apply Gramscian categories with any rigour. See Geoff Eley, 'Reading Gramsci in English: Observations on the Reception of Antonio Gramsci in the English-Speaking World', *European History Quarterly*, vol. 14 (1984), pp. 441–77. A penetrating although sympathetic critique is provided by Perry Anderson, 'The Antinomies of Antonio Gramsci', *New Left Review*, no. 100 (November 1976–January 1977). Eugene Genovese, *Roll, Jordan, Roll* (New York, 1974), has done much to render the concept of hegemony respectable among non-Marxist historians.
5. The points of departure for comparative study of the early modern state remain Barrington Moore, *Social Origins of Dictatorship and Democracy* (New York, 1967), and Perry Anderson, *Lineages of the Absolute State* (London, 1974).
6. J.S. Morrill, 'The Religious Context of the English Civil War', *Transactions of the Royal Historical Society*, 5th series, vol. 34 (1984), pp. 155–78.
7. The definitive biography is now Strong, *Henry Prince of Wales*. Also useful, although frequently pretentious and sometimes perverse, is J.W. Williamson, *The Myth of the Conqueror: Prince Henry Stuart, a Study in 17th Century Personation* (New York, 1978). The basic documentary sources are collected in Thomas Birch, *The Life of Henry, Prince of Wales* (London, 1760). E.C. Wilson, *Prince Henry and English Literature* (Ithaca, 1946), remains valuable for the elegaic outpouring occasioned by Henry's death.
8. *Calendar of State Papers Venetian* [hereafter, *CSPVen.*], *1610–13*, p. 448.
9. Simonds D'Ewes, *Autobiography and Correspondence*, J.O. Halliwell, ed. (London, 1845), vol. I, p. 46.
10. This material is thoroughly analysed by Wilson, *Prince Henry*, passim, and Williamson, *Myth*, pp. 171–95.
11. Williamson, *Myth*, pp. 2–4.
12. *CSPVen., 1610–13*, p. 450.
13. Strong, *Henry Prince of Wales*, pp. 86–137.
14. *CSPVen, 1610–13*, p. 463–4.
15. Vernon Snow, *Essex the Rebel* (Lincoln, Nebraska, 1970), chs. 1–2.
16. On the religious and political importance of the Palatinate, see Claus-Peter Clasen, *The Palatinate in European History 1555–1618* (Oxford, 1963), and Menna Prestwich, ed., *International Calvinism, 1541–1715* (Oxford, 1985).
17. *CSPVen, 1610–13*, p. 450.
18. *The Complete Poetry of John Donne*, John T. Shawcross, ed. (New York, 1967), p. 258.
19. For an introduction to the voluminous and expanding literature on apocalyptic thought in early modern England, see C.A. Patrides and Joseph Wittreich, eds., *The Apocalypse in English Renaissance Thought and Literature* (Ithaca, 1984). Christopher Hill, *Antichrist in Seventeenth-Century England* (Oxford, 1971), illustrates the variety of

political uses to which apocalpytic doctrine might be put.

20. The clearest account of this tradition is that by R.T. Kendall, *Calvin and English Calvinism* (Oxford, 1979). See also Peter Lake, 'The Significance of the Elizabethan Identification of the Pope as Antichrist', *Journal of Ecclesiastical History*, vol. 31, no. 2 (April 1980), pp. 161–78.

21. On this subject, see William Haller, *The Elect Nation: The Meaning and Relevance of Foxe's Book of Martyrs* (New York, 1963), a pioneering study which remains valuable despite Haller's apparent misinterpretation of Foxe's eschatology. For the necessary revisions, see Katherine R. Firth, *The Apocalyptic Tradition in Reformation Britain, 1530–1645* (Oxford, 1979), and Florence Sandler, '*The Faerie Queene*: an Elizabethan Apocalypse', in Patrides and Wittreich, eds., *Apocalypse*, pp. 148–74.

22. The standard life of Abbot is by Paul A. Welsby, *George Abbot: The Unwanted Archbishop, 1562–1633* (London, 1962). Henry's religious views are discussed in Strong, *Henry Prince of Wales*, pp. 52–4.

23. Lake, 'Significance'.

24. Keith Wrightson, *English Society 1580–1680* (Oxford, 1984); David Underdown, *Revel, Riot, and Rebellion* (Oxford, 1986). See also William Hunt, *The Puritan Moment* (Cambridge, Mass., 1983).

25. Paul Seaver, *Wallington's World* (Stanford, 1985).

26. Margaret Spufford, 'Puritanism and Social Control?', in Anthony Fletcher and John Stevenson, eds., *Order and Disorder in Early Modern England* (Cambridge, 1985), pp. 41–57.

27. The development of this doctrine is discussed in detail by Kendall, in *Calvin and English Calvinism*.

28. Strong, *Henry Prince of Wales*, p. 7.

29. Haller's treatment of this theme in *The Elect Nation* is undamaged by recent criticisms of his view of Foxe's eschatology.

30. In recent years the reputation of James I has enjoyed a dramatic – and in my view, exaggerated – rehabilitation. The largely negative assessment of D.H. Willson, *King James VI and I* (New York, 1967), must be balanced against the upward revisionism of Jenny Wormald, 'Two Kings or One?', *History* (1983) and Maurice Lee, *Government by Pen* (Urbana, Ill., 1980). A full-length study of James and his court is forthcoming from Professor Lee. I remain unconvinced that Willson did James any serious injustice.

31. But J.W. Williamson's insinuation (*Myth*, p. 168) that James may have murdered Henry is surely absurd.

32. For an up-to-date account of these events, see Geoffrey Parker, *The Thirty Years War*, revised edn (London, 1987), pp. 48–61.

33. Henry Peacham, *Prince Henry Revived* (London, 1615).

34. *Commons Debates 1621*, Wallace Notestein, Frances Helen Relf and Hartley Simpson, eds. (New Haven, 1935), vol. 3, pp. 122–7, vol. 4, pp. 286–7, vol. 5, pp. 128–30, 359–61.

35. John Webster, *The Complete Works*, F.L. Lucas, ed. (London, 1927), vol. 3, pp. 327 ff.

36. Roger Lockyer in *Buckingham* (London, 1981) provides a comprehensive and sympathetic account of Buckingham's policy during these years, but fails to recognize the 'Henrician' origins of Buckingham's hybristic designs. This failure weakens his attempt to defend, or indeed to render comprehensible, Buckingham's statesmanship.

37. The essential work on the Laudian party is now the long-awaited book by Nicholas Tyacke, *Anti-Calvinism: The Rise of English Arminianism* (Oxford, 1987). Revisionist sniping at Tyacke's thesis had begun even before the book appeared: see Peter White, 'The Rise of Arminianism Reconsidered', *Past and Present*, no. 101 (November 1983), and the riposte by Peter Lake, 'Calvinism and the English Church 1570–1635', *Past and Present*, no. 114 (February 1987). Suggestive analogies between anti-Calvinism and anti-communism are drawn by William Lamont in his review of Tyacke, *New Statesman* (16 October 1987).

38. As noted in the introduction, the following section depends heavily on Christopher Hill, *Society and Puritanism* (New York, 1967) ch. I, 'The Definition of a Puritan',

especially pp. 13–24, from which these examples of variant contemporary usage are drawn.

39. The following paragraphs are based on R. Malcolm Smuts, *Court Culture and the Origins of a Royalist Tradition in Early Stuart England* (Philadelphia, 1987).

40. In addition to Smuts, see Nicholas Tyacke, 'Puritanism, Arminianism, and Counter-Revolution', in Conrad Russell, ed., *The Origins of the English Civil War* (London, 1973), pp. 119–43.

41. Underdown, *Revel, Riot, and Rebellion*, pp. 63–72.

42. For this reaction in the county of Essex, see Hunt, *Puritan Moment*, pp. 274–8.

43. Michael McGiffert, 'God's Controversy with Jacobean England', *American Historical Review* (December 1983), pp. 1151–74.

44. William Gouge, *God's Three Arrows* (London, 1631).

45. Thomas Birch, ed., *The Court and Times of Charles I* (London, 1848), vol. 1, p. 36.

46. For the enduring popularity of what one might call 'mere Anglicanism' during the Interregnum, see J.S. Morrill, 'The Church in England, 1642–92', in Morrill, ed., *Reactions to the English Civil War 1642–1629* (London, 1982), pp. 89–114.

47. On this subject see, in addition to Haller, *Elect Nation*, William Lamont, *Godly Rule: Politics and Religion 1603–1660* (London, 1969).

48. Morrill, 'The Attack on the Church of England', p. 105.

49. Christopher Hill, *Puritanism and Revolution* (New York, 1964), p. 129.

50. For Essex and Warwick, see, respectively, Vernon Snow, *Essex the Rebel*, and Hunt, *Puritan Moment*, passim.

51. For a comparison of the political effects of militant Protestantism in England and Germany, see Mary Fulbrook, *Piety and Politics: Religion and the Rise of Absolutism in England, Württemberg and Prussia* (Cambridge, 1983).

Puritanism, Revolution and Christopher Hill

David Underdown

To attempt a brief assessment of the work of an historian as prolific and as influential as Christopher Hill is a daunting task. He has already written ten major books on seventeenth-century England, five volumes of essays, countless other articles, editions and miscellaneous pieces: both their sheer bulk and the weight of scholarship that invariably informs them may seem intimidating to lesser mortals – and the pace shows no sign of slackening.[1] Still, as one of those lesser mortals who has so often been enlightened, sometimes provoked to disagreement, always challenged and stimulated by his work, I think I can identify some of the issues that must immediately occur to anyone who has read even a part of this formidable output.

The first point is an obvious one: Christopher Hill has become above all else an historian of ideas in their social and political contexts – not just the ideas of the elite, of people inhabiting the world of high culture, but also the ideas of the hitherto often neglected middling and common sorts of people. He has written brilliantly and provocatively about literature – about Milton, Defoe, Richardson, Marvell and numerous other major authors.[2] He has produced two powerfully coherent syntheses of English history in the early modern period, has elsewhere written extensively on political, social and economic history, and in the books on Cromwell and Milton has made a couple of excursions into biography.[3] But it is what goes on in people's minds, and how these mental processes affect their actions, that really interests him. Whether he is talking about groups like Diggers, Ranters and Quakers, or off-beat individuals like Samuel Fisher or Arise Evans, we always encounter in his work the dynamic relationship of ideas to political and social context.[4] And in these discussions we nearly always find him exploring, circling around, turning over and over, the two great and interrelated themes of Puritanism and Revolution.

Puritanism, as we all know, is a tricky and treacherous subject. Hill is well aware of the difficulties of definition, as anyone who has read the first chapter of *Society and Puritanism* will well remember.[5] But he has resisted the temptation to define Puritanism out of existence, to dismiss it, as Charles George tried to do in a brilliant essay, as a mere 'analytical concept' that obscures historical reality, or to expand its meaning so far that it encompasses all 'the hotter sort of Protestants'.[6] Puritans, for Hill, were not simply Calvinists who wished to carry the reformation of the Church to lengths beyond those allowed by the lay and ecclesiastical establishments, but people who wished to transform the whole of society – by implementing their vision of godliness, certainly, but also by rebuilding the paternalist, deferential, vertically organized communities in which they lived into more self-disciplined, individualistic, even capitalistic ones. Before 1640, he accepts, Puritanism appealed to people of a wide variety of social conditions – peers and gentry not least among them – but it was always most firmly rooted in the culture of the 'middling' and 'industrious' sorts.[7]

In advancing this argument, as he showed explicitly in his essay 'Protestantism and the Rise of Capitalism', and implicitly in many other places, Hill is of course presenting a modification and restatement of R.H. Tawney's familiar thesis about the relationship between these two great historical forces. 'Men did not become capitalists because they were protestants, nor protestants because they were capitalists,' Hill says. But 'in a society already becoming capitalist, protestantism facilitated the triumph of the new values', by enabling 'artisans and small merchants ... to trust the dictates of their own hearts as their standard of conduct'.[8] The Calvinist doctrines of election, the calling, and respect for the Sabbath, could thus be translated into doctrines of personal and social control, with the objective of creating a more disciplined and orderly society. The association of Calvinism and capitalist values, he accepts, was not a total one, and was most conspicuously present in the 'mainstream' Puritans – the Presbyterians and Congregationalists. Some of the more radical offshoots of Puritanism in the Interregnum sects were, however, as he shows in *The World Turned Upside Down*, inclined to push Protestant individualism to extremes that rejected order, discipline, and even private property and sin itself.[9]

Hill has sometimes been accused of making a reductionist equation of religion with class interest, through a selective use of sources.[10] It may well be that Hill, like many other historians, has sometimes been selective on points of detail, but anyone who reads his work carefully and as a whole can scarcely doubt that in fact he well understands the passionate moral and spiritual convictions that lay at the heart of Puritanism. He is

therefore not vulnerable to the charge recently made by Margaret
Spufford that historians who concentrate on the 'social control' aspects
of Puritanism miss its central meaning.[11] Still, there are some difficulties
in this identification of Puritanism, however defined, with the middling
and industrious sorts of people. It seems to work fairly well in London,
in towns like Norwich, Banbury and Dorchester, and in some rural
areas, particularly those which were centres of the cloth industry. But it
does not work as well in other rural areas – regions of arable farming
outside Puritan East Anglia, but also many pasture regions too, and the
towns within them. In these places yeomen, craftsmen and small traders
were just as market-oriented as those elsewhere, yet were more likely to
resist than to welcome the austerities of Puritan reformation.[12] And even
in London, where Puritan congregations flourished, many of the
middling sort seem to have devoured ballads and low-life literature of
the kind churned out by the 'water poet', John Taylor, and other Grub
Street writers before the Civil War, and 'gutter' newspapers like the
royalist *Man in the Moon* in the years immediately afterwards.[13] Puritans, as Hill often reminds us, saw themselves as a 'small remnant', a
beleaguered minority of the elect in an otherwise reprobate society. The
implications of this make it more difficult than he sometimes allows to
accept an across-the-board association of Puritanism with the middling
and industrious sort of people.

Hill's conception of Puritanism is of course far more subtle and
sophisticated that I am able, in this brief discussion, to indicate. So too is
his conception of the English Revolution of 1640–60. In his early
writings he presented a fairly straightforward class analysis of a bourgeois revolution,[14] but with each successive book and article an increasingly complex picture has emerged, with 1640–60 now playing a part,
though a decisively important one, in a whole 'Century of Revolution'.
The mid-century revolution is seen in its totality as one affecting, he tells
us, 'literature and the arts as well as economics, politics, law and
society'.[15] This eclectic approach is a refreshing corrective to the
common tendency of historians to compartmentalize, to see only their
own little corner of the canvas, and to downplay the relatively minor
changes they may observe there by resorting to limited, particularist
modes of explanation. Among other things, Hill's wider field of vision
enables him to resist the currently fashionable belief that the English
Civil War (not to be dignified with the title 'revolution', we have been
told) was an unfortunate historical accident – proved to be such because
nobody planned it, or because the parliamentary leaders constantly
protested their loyalty to the Crown and the ancient constitution.[16] Like
the rest of us, Hill has learned a lot from colleagues who have rightly
pointed out that there was no 'opposition' in early Stuart Parliaments,

and that criticism of the court did not come from people hell-bent on taking the country down a 'high road to civil war'. But by encouraging us to widen our focus to include the rich, teeming world of ideas outside the narrow arena of faction in court and Parliament, to decode the polite conventions of accepted political discourse, to allow for the effects of censorship, and to read the literature (and sub-literature) of the period as historians, not just as textual critics, he enables us to grasp the Revolution as the shattering historical event that it surely was.[17]

In the end, though, Hill leaves us with a modified version of the bourgeois revolution thesis, restated in his 1980 essay with that title (which has a query attached).[18] But this is a revolution neither made nor consciously willed by the bourgeoisie, the class in question turns out to be remarkably broadly defined so as to include many of the gentry, and they are not burdened with anything so anachronistic as class consciousness. When a concept is extended in this way it leads to a somewhat circular argument – a bourgeoisie revolution is one whose supporters are by definition members of the bourgeoisie, even though they have no consciousness of this and may not actually be pursuing bourgeois objectives. The doubts that I am expressing do not mean that I reject the argument that economic changes (in Hill's words, stresses created by 'the rise of capitalist modes of production') were among the most important contributory causes of the Revolution. And I also agree that the eventual consequences of the Revolution included a marked shift of English society in a bourgeois direction.

Hill's summary of these consequences reads something like this: it confirmed the already developing social and cultural polarization between people of property (middling-sort parish notables as well as gentry) and the poor; it completed the transition to absolute property rights for the gentry, by abolishing feudal tenures and turning land 'into a commodity like any other', but did not give copyholders similar security of tenure; it thus stimulated capitalist agriculture, and also removed restraints (notably monopolies) on commercial and industrial growth; it set the stage for Britain's subsequent expansion as a maritime, colonizing, imperial state; it confirmed the political authority of the landed elite, and in a negative way (out of fear of renewed anarchy and disorder) led the middling sort to acquiesce in their leadership; and it eventually made it impossible, whatever High Anglicans might think, to re-establish a monolithic state religion, or whatever Tories might think, to restore a divine right monarchy with all its prerogative institutions.[19] Hill does not always make clear how far the events of 1640–60 were the decisive stages of some of these transformations, and how far what happened later – in 1688 and afterwards – can be held responsible. But unless we think of the seventeenth century as part of a tranquil 'World

We Have Lost' in which nothing of real significance ever changed,[20] they sound like a convincing roll-call of the major developments that, for many historians, make the period worth studying. Whether we attach the term 'bourgeois revolution' to them is largely a matter of labelling, and thus of secondary importance.

Puritanism and Revolution: for Hill, as indeed for many people in the seventeenth century, the two things are inextricably connected. Puritanism provides a large part – though not the whole – of the answer to the question he posed in the introduction to *Intellectual Origins of the English Revolution.*

> For as long as history recorded [he reminded us] there had been kings, lords, and bishops in England. The thinking of all Englishmen had been dominated by the established Church. Yet, within less than a decade, successful war was levied against the King; bishops and the House of Lords were abolished; and Charles I was executed in the name of his people. How did men get the nerve to do such un-heard of things?[21]

Puritanism was not the main subject of that book, which dealt with a revolution in other aspects of thought – in science and medicine, in philosophy, history and the law. But if we take the whole of Hill's work together it is clear that he regards Puritanism as being at the heart of the matter. Puritans, he suggests, were people with a vision of society which could not be accommodated within the political assumptions of Stuart kingship and Laudian episcopacy. The Puritan moral crusade, blocked by the Crown, combined with other grievances to give Parliament the manpower to win the Civil War, and subsequently, to the distress of most of Parliament's original leaders, released forces that temporarily turned a large part of their world upside down.

Hill has thus given us a persuasive explanation of why the English Revolution happened, and of some of its most significant and far-reaching consequences. In the end, though, he has not given us a total understanding of that revolution – what single historian could be expected to? His work tends to relegate to relative obscurity some of the things that might explain why, in spite of the momentous events of 1640–60, so much of the old order survived. In *The World Turned Upside Down* he recognizes (implicitly but not explicitly) that both the radicals who made the Revolution and those who wished to carry it further were a small minority of the total population, as indeed revolutionaries usually are.[22] But he has always seemed less interested in the mental world of the less-than-radical majority. This may in part be because he has always worked mainly from printed sources, of which his mastery is overwhelming. Lower-class people who resorted to print tended to be radical activists; the more traditional outlook of the majority can only be explored in manuscript sources such as local court records. The result is that Hill gives the impression that lower-class royalists, for example, were simply people trapped in the bonds of deference and dependence, the reluctant, or at best apathetic pawns of their landlords and superiors.[23] At the level of the common people only the radicals, it appears, are effectively politicized.

Some years ago I published a book on my home county, Somerset, in the Civil War,[24] and was greatly looking forward to Christopher Hill's review. He would not be much interested in the military history, I supposed, but he would surely have some comments on the chapters dealing with the risings of the Clubmen, the great popular eruptions of 1645 against the oppressions of both sides in the war, which I had found the most exciting parts of the book to write. Here were men living their own history, plebeians who could not be written off as the obedient pawns of the elite, because they were in fact revolting against the authority of the leading gentry of their shires: just the subject for Christopher Hill, I thought. Alas, the review, although gratifying in other ways, did not mention the Clubmen, who, like the middling and lower-class people who made up the rank and file of the King's army (and who were by no means all recruited under compulsion), are difficult to fit into Hill's general conception of the Revolution.[25] For him, Puritanism and the Parliament were the causes of the middling and industrious sorts, and when we find great masses of people from these groups espousing a different ideology – of conservative localism – they create a problem. What can he make of a popular leader like Humphrey Willis, spokesman for the Somerset Clubmen, who supported Parliament but used the 'world turned upside down' image only to deplore the fact that it had happened?[26]

So, while Hill's work casts plenty of light on the social and intellectual formations promoting change in seventeenth-century England, that light leaves the conforming majority still largely in the shadows. Yet we need to understand these people if we are to realize the limits as well as the achievements of the English Revolution, the reasons for its failure (to the extent that it failed), and why it was possible for so much of the old society to survive the years of upheaval. Now I am not trying to suggest, as has recently been argued, that England remained a 'confessional state' right down to the nineteenth century.[27] But even if we reject such absurdities, the popular acquiescence in, and even temporary enthusiasm for, the Restoration cannot be dismissed as simply a matter of elite manipulation. Traditional beliefs in the patriarchal family and the ordered, unified local community had still retained a powerful appeal, even at the height of the Revolution, which is one reason why sectaries like the Quakers, who split families and communities and were perceived as threatening male authority, were unpopular in so many places.[28] And the continuing survival of these beliefs explains why aristocratic and Anglican hegemony remained so strong – admittedly in modified forms and subject to much lower-class opposition – throughout the eighteenth century.

I have raised some questions about the balance between the forces of continuity and change in Christopher Hill's interpretation of seventeenth-century England. In a sense, however, they are irrelevant questions, because for him to strike the balance in a different way would require him to be a different kind of historian. Like Tawney, whose mantle he has been said to have inherited, Hill is also a moralist, someone who has wanted to write history in large part to encourage us to become better, more complete human beings. 'All knowledge of the past should help to humanize us,' he wrote in the conclusion to *Change and Continuity*, and he has regularly invited us, most notably in *The World Turned Upside Down*, to enter imaginatively into 'the struggles of men and women trying to make their world a better place'.[29] Now if you have no sympathy for people trying to make the world a better place, or perhaps believe that our society either needs no improvement or that it is pointless to struggle to improve it, then you are presumably immune to argument and unlikely to be convinced of the value of Hill's contribution. The rest of us, if we read him critically – as we should – may regret his inability to enter the minds of the conservative majority of the population of Stuart England and suspect that his 'bourgeois revolution' formula is based on a circular argument. But if we read him with an open mind – as we also should – we must surely be grateful for his insights into the mentalities of the human beings who changed, or tried to change, their worlds. Both the scholarship and the moral purpose ensure that his works will endure and remain supremely worth reading. Without them, we should be a lot further from an understanding of many other matters even more important than Puritanism and Revolution.

Notes

This essay is a revised version of a paper delivered at the American Historical Association meeting in Chicago, 29 December 1986. It is also to be published in *The History Teacher* (1988).

1. For a bibliography of Hill's major publications through 1977, compiled by M.F. Roberts, see Donald Pennington and Keith Thomas, eds., *Puritans and Revolutionaries: Essays in Seventeenth-Century History presented to Christopher Hill* (Oxford, 1978), pp. 382–402. Hill's most important publications since 1977 are *The Experience of Defeat*:

Milton and Some Contemporaries (New York, 1984) and three volumes of his *Collected Essays* (Brighton, 1985–6).

2. *Milton and the English Revolution* (New York, 1977); 'Daniel Defoe (1660–1731) and *Robinson Crusoe*', in *Collected Essays*, vol. 1, pp. 105–30 (see also part 3 of this volume for other essays on literature); 'Society and Andrew Marvell', and 'Clarissa Harlowe and Her Times', in *Puritanism and Revolution: Studies in Interpretation of the English Revolution of the 17th Century* (London, 1958), pp. 337–94.

3. *The Century of Revolution 1603–1714*, 2nd edn (New York, 1980); *Reformation to Industrial Revolution: The Making of Modern English Society, 1530–1780* (New York, 1968); *God's Englishman: Oliver Cromwell and the English Revolution* (New York, 1970). For Milton see above, note 2.

4. See especially *The World Turned Upside Down: Radical Ideas During the English Revolution* (New York, 1972).

5. *Society and Puritanism in Pre-Revolutionary England*, 2nd edn (New York, 1967), pp. 13–29.

6. C.H. George, 'Puritanism as History and Historiography', *Past and Present*, no. 41 (December 1968), pp. 77–104. Patrick Collinson, *The Religion of Protestants: The Church in English Society 1559–1625* (Oxford, 1982).

7. Hill has developed this argument most extensively in *Society and Puritanism*.

8. 'Protestantism and the Rise of Capitalism', in *Change and Continuity in Seventeenth-Century England* (London, 1974), especially pp. 99, 91. Tawney's modified version of Max Weber's original formulation of the connection was made in his *Religion and the Rise of Capitalism* (New York, 1926).

9. *The World Turned Upside Down*, chs. 7–15.

10. This tendency, grossly exaggerated by the reviewer, was the basis of J.H. Hexter's notorious review of *Change and Continuity*, in *The Times Literary Supplement*, 24 October 1975, p. 1252.

11. M. Spufford, 'Puritanism and Social Control?', in Anthony Fletcher and John Stevenson, eds., *Order and Disorder in Early Modern England* (Cambridge, 1985), pp. 41–57.

12. I have developed this argument at length in my *Revel Riot, and Rebellion: Popular Politics and Culture in England 1603–1660* (Oxford, 1985).

13. For popular literature and its readership, see Margaret Spufford, *Small Books and Pleasant Histories: Popular Fiction and Its Readership in Seventeenth-Century England* (Cambridge, 1985).

14. The best example is his essay in *The English Revolution, 1640: Three Essays* (London, 1940), published separately as *The English Revolution 1640* (London, 1955). See also his edition (with Edmund Dell) of *The Good Old Cause* (London, 1949), a collection of extracts from original sources.

15. 'The Pre-Revolutionary Decades', in *Collected Essays*, vol. 1, p. 4.

16. Hill summarizes, and answers, many of the revisionists' arguments in 'Parliament and People in 17th-Century England', in *Historical Essays*, vol. 3, pp. 21–67.

17. 'The Pre-Revolutionary Decades', and 'Censorship and English Literature', in *Historical Essays*, vol. 1, pp. 3–71.

18. 'A Bourgeois Revolution?', in *Historical Essays*, vol. 3, pp. 94–124.

19. In addition to the summary of Hill's views in 'A Bourgeois Revolution?', see also *Century of Revolution*, pp. 161–4, 263–6.

20. As argued by Peter Laslett, *The World We Have Lost*, 2nd edn (New York, 1971).

21. *Intellectual Origins of the English Revolution* (Oxford, 1965), p. 5.

22. *The World Turned Upside Down*, pp. 91, 288, 303. Hill later conceded that he may have exaggerated the numerical strength of the radicals: *Experience of Defeat*, pp. 15–16.

23. See, for example, *Century of Revolution*, pp. 104–5, 121–2.

24. David Underdown, *Somerset in the Civil War and Interregnum* (Newton Abbot, 1973).

25. *New Statesman*, 2 August 1974, pp. 159–60.

26. Underdown, *Somerset*, pp. 118, 133–6. For the Clubmen, see also John S, Morrill,

The Revolt of the Provinces: Conservatives and Radicals in the English Civil War, 2nd edn (London, 1980), pp. 98–114, 196–200; and David Underdown, 'The Chalk and the Cheese: Contrasts among the English Clubmen', *Past and Present*, no. 85 (November 1979), pp. 25–48, reprinted in Paul Slack, ed., *Rebellion, Popular Protest and the Social Order in Early Modern England* (Cambridge, 1984), pp. 162–85.

27. J.C.D. Clark, *England Society 1688–1832: Ideology, Social Structure, and Political Practice During the Ancien Regime* (New York, 1985).

28. Underdown, *Revel, Riot, and Rebellion*, pp. 251–6.

29. *Change and Continuity*, p. 283. For Hill's attitude to Tawney, see R.C. Richardson, *The Debate on the English Revolution* (London, 1977), p. 97.

Talking with Christopher Hill:
Part II

Tim Harris and Christopher Husbands

Perhaps we might discuss the direction you think seventeenth-century studies should take.

Hill: Well, there was this broadening out which reached its peak in the 1950s with the Tawney–Trevor-Roper–Stone debate, which took place on a broad canvas,[1] and the consequence of all those broad generalizations about the gentry was that a lot of historians started to do detailed research on the gentry. This admirable research produced the 'county community' school of historians, and the tendency to isolate the county community, meaning the gentry; and you get the situation which John Morrill rather charmingly recognized when he quoted one of his friends saying that Morrill had conclusively proved there wasn't a civil war in 1642, and Morrill accepted the validity of the criticism! This is true as a tendency. The county community historians, looking just at the ruling group inside the county, find that they didn't want a civil war. Perfectly true – no one *wanted* a civil war. There were no revolutionary parties trying to seize power. I think you can only explain the civil war line-up in Brian Manning's way, as a reaction of the gentry to pressure from the lower orders. But that's a different story.[2]

There's a strong trend now that you can't study politics in isolation.

Hill: But there's a growing reverse trend – with the Conrad Russell school of historians of Parliament. Russell himself is a very good historian. But some of his epigones isolate the House of Commons and the Lords from the rest of the population. They read what the MPs said, which of course contains very great respect for the monarchy, and they say that these people can't be putting the political screws on. This is reverting to a narrow sort of politico-constitutional history from which I hoped we'd escaped. Interestingly, Russell himself is reacting against this, and is talking in terms of a socio-economic interpretation of the English Revolution again.

But don't these counter-trend historians assume the wider themes?

Hill: Yes, but a lot of people who adopt this very narrow discussion are inclined to use it to rule out the more fundamental socio-economic shifts. This tendency to see the House of Commons as stooges of the Lords, which makes disputes in the Commons a reflection of disputes in the Privy Council, or between peers who are 'out' and those who are 'in' – I'm caricaturing and exaggerating – I'm rather against. I think this work cuts off the Commons. It ignores, for instance, the work of Derek Hirst, who very much established the growing importance of the electorate in the early seventeenth century.[3] He is, I think, absolutely right. MPs aren't just stooges of the peers.

I think that a point has now been reached where there has to be a reaction against a narrow looking at the county community, just as there has to be a reaction against only looking at Parliament. It's a very good sign in John Morrill and Conrad Russell that they are becoming aware of this, so I would hope that we might move to a new synthesis between the overall and the detailed which will be – one has to use these awful clichés – a synthesis at a higher level. So it will have to include the Morrill stuff and the Russell stuff in a new socio-economic interpretation.[4] One book I found interesting is Wrightson and Levine's – the rather detailed book about an Essex village,[5] but what emerges is that the local elite which was strengthening in consequence of the economic crisis of the late sixteenth and early seventeenth centuries is beginning to co-operate with the gentry in administration of the poor law, the harrying of cottagers and preserving law and order. What Wrightson and Levine hint at – I don't know if they actually state it – is that this sort of elite found the ideology of Puritanism very convenient and suitable for the imposition of labour discipline, and they had very good reasons for disliking the Laudian regime, both because of the tendencies of central government to interfere with the control of parishes by local elites, and because its ideology seemed to be undermining the Puritan work ethic. This gave me a new slant on Laudianism. One always thinks of the seventeenth century as a period when the local oligarchy is starting to form at the beginning of the century and is firmly in control at the end, but if the Laudian decade is seen as an attempt to reverse that, the collapse of the church courts was an important breakthrough. This seems to me to put Laudianism and Puritanism in a new light. Along this line, combining detailed research with, particularly, the Joan Thirsk–

Alan Everitt stuff about champain country and pasture and woodland areas[6] will be a more complicated synthesis.

Of course, the Cambridge Group for the History of Population and Family Structure and your own work, and that of Joan Thirsk on agrarian history, have all remained separate.

Hill: But they could be brought together. And Conrad Russell, surprisingly, seems to be showing the way. I've always thought of Russell as a bit of a 'no-sayer', picking holes in any general theories. But he is now saying that if there is to be a new socio-economic synthesis of what happened in the seventeenth century (and he is scholarly cautious about whether there should be, but he doesn't exclude the possibility), then it would have to be based on the rise of the yeomanry rather than the rise of the gentry. And he has a very interesting passage about how artisans are stratifying, some getting richer and some poorer.[7] This conception of the stratification of elites might provide the basis of a new synthesis.

Notes

This interview is reprinted from *University History: A Forum for Student Historians*, no. 1 (1980), pp. 5–15.

   1. R.H. Tawney, 'The Rise of the Gentry', *Economic History Review*, vol. 11 (1941); L. Stone, *The Crisis of the Aristocracy* (Oxford, 1965); H.R. Trevor-Roper, *The Gentry, 1540–1640, Economic History Review Supplement* (1953). A useful guide to the debate, with a full bibliography is R.C. Richardson, *The Debate on the English Revolution* (London, 1979).

   2. B.S. Manning, *The English People and the English Revolution* (Harmondsworth, 1978).

   3. D. Hirst, *The Representative of the People? Voters and Voting in England Under the Early Stuarts* (Cambridge, 1975).

   4. J.S. Morrill, *The Revolt of the Provinces: Conservatives and Radicals in the English Civil War* (London, 1976); C. Russell, *The Crisis of Parliaments 1509–1660* (Oxford, 1971).

   5. K. Wrightson and D. Levine, *Poverty and Piety in an English Village: Terling, 1525–1700* (New York, 1979).

   6. Joan Thirsk, 'Seventeenth Century Agriculture and Social Change'; A. Everitt, 'Dissent and Woodland Communities'; both in Joan Thirsk, ed., *Land, Church, and People, Essays presented to H.P.R. Finberg, Agricultural History Review*, Supplement 1 (1970).

   7. C. Russell, *Parliaments and English Politics, 1621–9* (Oxford, 1979), p. 430ff.

Notes on Contributors

PETER BURKE teaches at Emmanuel College, Cambridge, and is the author of several books on the social and cultural history of early modern Europe, including *Venice and Amsterdam: A Study of Seventeenth-Century Elites* (London, 1974); *Popular Culture in Early Modern Europe* (London, 1978); and *The Historical Anthropology of Early Modern Italy* (London, 1987).

GEOFF ELEY is Professor of History at the University of Michigan, and the author of *Reshaping the German Right* (New Haven and London, 1980); *The Peculiarities of German History* (Oxford, 1984) (with David Blackbourn); and *From Unification to Nazism. Reinterpreting the German Past* (London, 1986). He is writing a book on nationalism and has a general interest in the comparative study of revolutions and political development.

MARY FULBROOK is a lecturer in German History at University College, London. She is the author of *Piety and Politics: Religion and the Rise of Absolutism in England, Württemberg and Prussia* (Cambridge, 1983), and a number of articles on social theory and English and German history. Her current work is on politics and society in East and West Germany since 1945, and she is also writing a social and political history of Germany since 1918.

C.H. GEORGE is Professor of History at Northern Illinois University in Dekalb, Illinois. He has written on cultural and social subjects drawn from English and European history in the early modern period. He is completing a monograph on a Gloucestershire gentleman and a general history of the agrarian origins of English capitalism.

348   *Reviving the English Revolution*

TIM HARRIS is Assistant Professor of History at Brown University and the author of *London Crowds in the Reign of Charles II* (Cambridge, 1987). He is now working on popular political discourse under the Protectorate.

MARGOT HEINEMANN taught at Goldsmith's College, London, and New Hall, Cambridge. Her books include *The Adventurers* (London, 1960), a novel about coalmining; *Britain in the Nineteen Thirties* (London, 1971) (with Noreen Branson); and *Puritanism and Theatre: Thomas Middleton and Opposition Drama under the Early Stuarts* (Cambridge, 1980).

CYNTHIA HERRUP is Associate Professor of History at Duke University and is interested in the social and cultural history of early modern England. She is the author of *The Common Peace. Participation and the Criminal Law in Seventeenth-Century England* (Cambridge, 1987).

WILLIAM HUNT is Associate Professor of History at St. Lawrence University in Canton, New York. He is the author of *The Puritan Moment* (Cambridge, Mass., 1983), and is currently engaged on a study of cultural conflict in early Stuart England.

CHRISTOPHER HUSBANDS recently finished his PhD at Cambridge University in early modern English agrarian history, and has published a number of articles dealing with seventeenth-century economic history.

VICTOR KIERNAN is Emeritus Professor of History at Edinburgh University, and has written on a wide variety of subjects, including books on Marxism, imperialism, and nineteenth-century Spain. He has published articles on Tennyson, Shakespeare, and Wordsworth, and translations of Urdu poetry. A first volume of his collected essays has been published as *History, Classes and Nation-States* (London, 1988).

PETER LINEBAUGH is Director of the Law and Justice Programme, University of Massachusetts (Boston). He was an editor and contributor of *Albion's Fatal Tree* (Harmondsworth, 1975). He is working on a book about the London hanged in the eighteenth century, which stresses the thanatocratic powers of the state as they were used to create wage relationships.

PHYLLIS MACK is Associate Professor of History at Rutgers University. She is the author of *Calvinist Preaching and Iconoclasm in the Netherlands 1544–1569* (Cambridge, 1978), and is currently engaged in a study of women visionaries in seventeenth-century England.

BARRY REAY teaches at the University of Auckland, New Zealand. He is the author of *The Quakers and the English Revolution* (New York, 1985); and co-author of *The World of the Muggletonians* (London, 1983), with Christopher Hill and William Lamont. He has edited volumes on radical religion and popular culture in the seventeenth century and has published widely on the same subjects.

MARCUS REDIKER teaches American history at Georgetown University. He is the author of *Between the Devil and the Deep Blue Sea. Merchant Seamen, Pirates, and the Anglo-American Maritime World 1700–1750* (Cambridge, 1987), and is working on the social history of Colonial America.

BUCHANAN SHARP is Professor of History at the University of California, Santa Cruz. He is the author of *In Contempt of All Authority: Rural Artisans and Riot in the West of England, 1586–1660* (Berkeley, 1980). He is currently working on a study of early English food riots, 1347–1547.

LAURENCE STONE is Professor of History at Princeton University. He is the author of several books of early modern English history, most recently of *An Open Elite? England 1540–1880* (Oxford, 1986), with Jeanne C. Fawtier Stone. He has published widely on matters of historiography and social history.

ALAN TAYLOR is Assistant Professor of History at the College of William and Mary. He is revising for publication his 1985 Brandeis dissertation, 'Liberty-Men and White Indians: Frontier Migration, Popular Protest, and the Pursuit of Property in the Wake of the American Revolution', and has published a number of articles arising from this research.

EDWARD THOMPSON is a freelance writer, historian, and peace activist. He is the author of several books, including *The Making of the English Working Class* (London, 1963); and *Whigs and Hunters* (Harmondsworth, 1975). His historical and political essays have been collected in a number of volumes, including *The Poverty of Theory*

(London, 1978); *Writing by Candlelight* (London, 1980); and *The Heavy Dancers* (London, 1985). He has a longstanding interest in dissenting traditions, secular and religious.

DAVID UNDERDOWN is Professor of History at Yale University and Director of the Yale Centre for Parliamentary History. He has published widely on the seventeenth-century English Revolution, most recently *Revel, Riot and Rebellion: Popular Politics and Culture in England 1603–1660* (Oxford, 1985).

Index

DATE DUE

HIGHSMITH   #LO-45220